The Essential Guide to Flex 3

Charles E. Brown

friendsof

DESIGNER TO DESIGNER™

an Apress® company

The Essential Guide to Flex 3

Credits

Lead Editor
Ben Renow-Clarke

Technical Reviewer
David Powers

Editorial Board
Clay Andres, Steve Anglin,
Ewan Buckingham, Tony Campbell,
Gary Cornell, Jonathan Gennick,
Kevin Goff, Matthew Moodie,
Joseph Ottinger, Jeffrey Pepper,
Frank Pohlmann, Ben Renow-Clarke,
Dominic Shakeshaft, Matt Wade, Tom Welsh

Project Manager
Sofia Marchant

Copy Editor
Ami Knox

Associate Production Director
Kari Brooks-Copony

Production Editor
Ellie Fountain

Compositor
Dina Quan

Proofreader
Nancy Sixsmith

Indexer
Broccoli Information Management

Interior and Cover Designer
Kurt Krames

Manufacturing Director
Tom Debolski

CONTENTS AT A GLANCE

CONTENTS

ABOUT THE AUTHOR

Charles E. Brown is one of the most noted authors and teachers in the computer industry today. His first two books, *Beginning Dreamweaver MX* and *Fireworks MX Zero to Hero*, have received critical acclaim and were consistent bestsellers. In early 2004, Charles coauthored a book on VBA for Microsoft Access—*VBA Access Programming*.

In addition to his busy writing schedule, Charles conducts frequent seminars as an Adobe Certified Trainer. His topics include Flex, Flash, Dreamweaver, ActionScript programming, and After Effects. He also does seminars about Java and web design, and he is frequently called in as a consultant for major websites.

Charles is a noted classical organist, pianist, and guitarist, and studied with such notables as Vladimir Horowitz, Virgil Fox, and Igor Stravinsky. It was because of his association with Stravinsky that he got to meet, and develop a friendship with, famed twentieth-century artist Pablo Picasso.

Charles can be contacted through his website, a continuous work in progress, at www. charlesbrown.com.

ABOUT THE TECHNICAL REVIEWER

David Powers is the author of a series of highly popular books on PHP, ActionScript, and Dreamweaver, including *Foundation PHP 5 for Flash* (friends of ED, 2005) and *The Essential Guide to Dreamweaver CS3 with CSS, Ajax, and PHP* (friends of ED, 2007). His most recent book, *PHP Object-Oriented Solutions*, also a friends of ED title, is due to be published in mid-2008. He is an Adobe Community Expert for Dreamweaver and teaches Dreamweaver professionally in London, UK.

David turned his hand to writing and teaching about web technologies after a successful career spanning nearly 30 years in BBC radio and television as a reporter, producer, and editor. He lived in Japan for nine years, first on loan from the BBC to the Japan Broadcasting Corporation (NHK) as an advisor on English-language broadcasting, and later as BBC correspondent in Tokyo reporting on the rise and collapse of the bubble economy. In 1991–92, he was President of the Foreign Correspondents' Club of Japan.

When not pounding the keyboard writing books or dreaming of new ways of using PHP and other programming languages, David enjoys nothing better than visiting his favorite sushi restaurant. He has also translated several plays from Japanese.

ACKNOWLEDGMENTS

I couldn't have done this book without the help of a lot of people.

Every time I thought I wrote the perfect chapter, David Powers, my incredible technical editor, brought me back to reality. His wisdom and guidance took this book in some slightly different directions from the first edition. I also want to thank him for his contributions regarding the use of the PHP technology.

I have to thank my project manager, Sofia Marchant, for developing more than a few gray hairs with an ever-changing production schedule. Working in a beta testing environment is not the easiest of things to do, and she was great about keeping everything moving smoothly.

I want to thank all of my many friends and co-developers (including some students at my training classes) for their invaluable suggestions and insights.

Finally, I want to thank the many kind readers who wrote words of encouragement on Amazon.com as well as other services (including e-mailing me). Their many words gave me some great ideas for this book.

INTRODUCTION

I can't believe that we have now reached the second generation of Flex. It seemed like I had just finished the first edition and, within a few weeks, we were in a long and ever-changing series of betas for Flex 3. In the course of that period, many of the chapters you read in this book were rewritten three or four times.

Let me begin by thanking the many readers who took the time to write kind reviews for Amazon.com and other places. I read nearly every suggestion and incorporated them into this edition. I cut down a bit on the technical ActionScript explanations and focused on the features of Flex itself.

After years of doing technical training, where I have only a couple of days to cover large topics, I have learned to substitute shorter, and more pointed, explanations that clarify a concept in place of larger, more technical (and often confusing) explanations. In other words, I often like to get right to the heart of the matter, without taking circuitous routes.

Please keep a few things in mind when reading this book. First, you will find that the techniques I show you are techniques that reflect my style of programming and design. Certainly, there are many alternative ways of arriving at the same point. It is impossible for any one book to cover all possible variations, especially with topics as large as I cover here. If you find a different way of doing something, by all means use it if it works for you.

Second, I very purposely kept my examples simple in order to illustrate a point. I do not want you, the reader, to get caught up in just following recipe-like instructions that do little more than test your ability to read and follow instructions. While I have a case study in the book, each chapter will stand on its own, without reliance on exercises done in previous chapters. For that reason, you can open to nearly any chapter and just work on the subject of that chapter.

Third, I am assuming that you already have at least a cursory knowledge of object-oriented programming concepts. While I do intersperse many of these concepts throughout the chapters, it is only a very basic introduction. OOP is a very large subject in which huge volumes have been written.

OK, enough of the warning and disclaimers.

What I hope this book does is give you enough of a taste of Flex and the ActionScript 3.0 environment that you will be able to solve the unique problems your own situations will require. I spend a great deal of time discussing how to find help by using the ActionScript 3.0 Language Reference.

I had to make a decision as to what server technology to show the dynamic side of Flex in. Since I use ColdFusion in my own work, I decided to use that technology. My wonderful technical editor, David Powers, is a world-leading authority on PHP, and he has written many books on the subject. He was kind enough to write an example of using PHP in Flex to show as an alternative to ColdFusion, and for that I thank him profusely.

I hope you will walk away from this book with the same sense of excitement that I have about Flex 3. I really encourage you to take the many examples in this book and experiment with them. Look upon this book as the beginning, not the end.

Let's get started learning.

Layout conventions

To keep this book as clear and easy to follow as possible, the following text conventions are used throughout.

Important words or concepts are normally highlighted on the first appearance in **bold type**.

Code is presented in `fixed-width` font.

New or changed code is normally presented in **`bold fixed-width font`**.

Menu commands are written in the form Menu ➤ Submenu ➤ Submenu.

Where I want to draw your attention to something, I've highlighted it like this:

> *Ahem, don't say I didn't warn you.*

Sometimes code won't fit on a single line in a book. Where this happens, I use an arrow like this: ➥.

```
This is a very, very long section of code that should be written all ➥
on the same line without a break.
```

1   FLEX BASICS

ADOBE® FLEX™ BUILDER™ 3

Built on Eclipse™

Welcome to Flex

Learn about how Flex provides unparalleled con experiences for both the web and desktop with t introductory video.

Let's begin with a couple of assumptions:

Your knowledge of Internet design doesn't go past HTML pages.

You haven't got the foggiest idea what Flex is.

Using this paradigm, we can start right at the very beginning. In this chapter, we are going to look at where Flex fits into the evolution of the Internet. From there, we will examine what exactly Flex is and how it is different from traditional web technologies.

Finally, before you can roll up your sleeves and get to work, you need to install Flex and its related technologies. I will walk you through that process.

The Internet, then and now

Before you can appreciate the benefits of Flex, you need a general understanding of the history of the Internet up to this point. I say historical because the various technologies we see today came about at various points in the timeline of the Internet's evolution. As I just stated in the short introduction to this chapter, it is important to understand this evolution in order to see where Flex fits.

HTML and dynamics

The earliest websites were just conveyors of text data. Frequently, they would have hyperlinks to other pages. Because of very slow Internet connection speeds (anyone remember 28K connection speeds?), graphics were kept to a minimum. You can still find some examples if you look, such as the contact page for the publisher of this book:

    www.friendsofed.com/contact.html

Figure 1-1 shows this contact page.

This is the traditional HTML (Hypertext Markup Language) site. Notice that there are just a few simple graphics (earlier websites had even simpler graphics) with the rest being text and hyperlinks. Also notice the file extension of .html. This web page will never change unless someone physically goes in and changes it.

HTML pages, such as this one, are referred to as **static** or unchanging pages. Unchanging is perhaps an unfair word. More specifically, it only changes when someone goes into the XHTML code and makes changes manually.

A word is in order to demonstrate how static pages are called.

Figure 1-1. The friendsofED site contact page

When you type www.friendsofed.com into your browser, the request is sent out over a series of routers on the World Wide Web until it arrives at the host web server. The web server searches its root for the requested HTML page, packages the HTML page up, stamps a return address on it, and sends it back to your browser. Your browser then reads the HTML code and displays the page as you see it here. A popular misconception, which I still hear in my training seminars, is that web pages are being viewed "over the Internet." The web pages are downloaded to your computer and viewed in your computer. Once the web server sends you the HTML page, its job is completed. More specifically, we say that you are viewing the pages on the **client** machine. You, being the consumer or viewer of the web page, are the client.

Of course, this discussion is really simplified. A detailed discussion of building and distributing HTML pages is out of the focus of this book. There are any number of books that discuss these details. I recommend *The Essential Guide to CSS and HTML Web Design* by Craig Grannell (friends of ED, 2007).

Let's evolve this to the next level.

Go to the following website:

```
www.adobe.com/cfusion/webforums/forum/index.cfm?forumid=60
```

This web address takes you to the Adobe Flex Support Forums, shown in Figure 1-2.

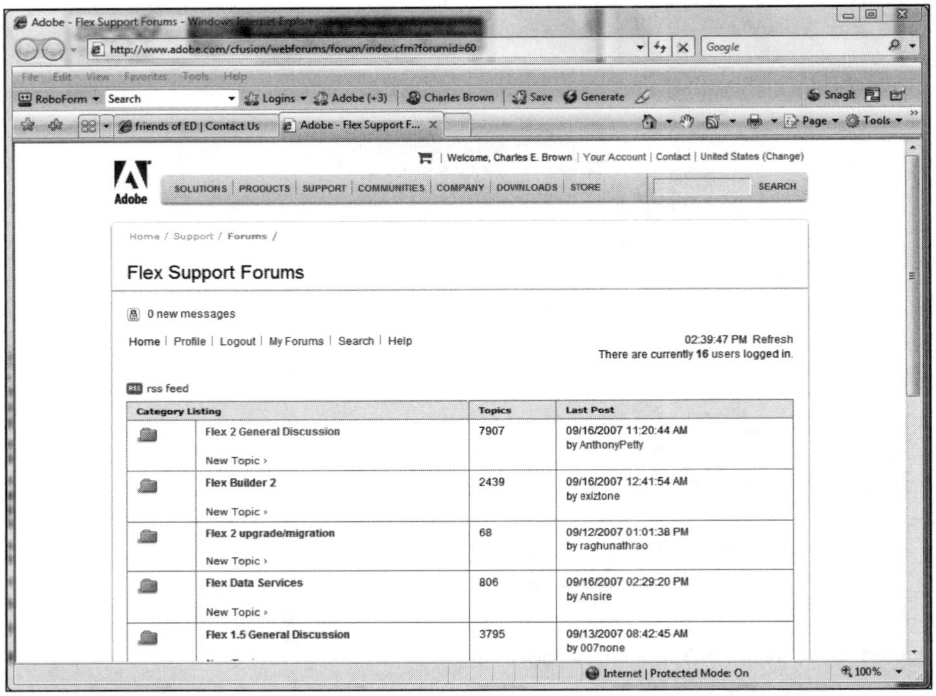

Figure 1-2. The Adobe Flex Support Forums

This is an example of what has been traditionally called a **dynamic website**. Let's discuss the mechanics here. They add a couple of additional steps to the preceding scenario for static pages.

Once you type the URL (web address) into your browser, it once again goes over a series of routers over the World Wide Web until it finds the Adobe web server. Here is where things change a bit.

Notice the letters cfm in the address. These letters tell the web server to send the request to another piece of software called an **application server**. There are five types of application servers that handle dynamic technology (actually, there are several more, but these are the most popular):

- **CFM**: ColdFusion
- **ASP**: Classic Microsoft Active Server Pages
- **ASPX**: Microsoft .NET Active Server Pages
- **JSP**: Java Server Pages
- **PHP**: A scripting language whose letters stand for nothing

My technical editor, David Powers, took an exception to my saying PHP stands for nothing. However, several websites call PHP a recursive acronym—PHP: Hypertext Preprocessor. It still begs the question what PHP stands for.

All five of these technologies ostensibly do the same thing with various degrees of ease and complexity. They receive the request from the web server and then reach out to a **database server** using SQL code in the request.

*If you are not familiar with the terminology, SQL stands for **Structured Query Language** and is a standardized way of ask a database a question. We will be touching on it only lightly in the course of this book while discussing Flex and data.*

When the database returns the requested information, the application server actually writes a brand-new XHTML page based on a template. The page contains the latest version of the data. From there, the application server returns the newly created XHTML page to the web server which, in turn, sends it back to your browser as before.

The only difference between the first and second examples is when the XHTML page is being written. In the first case, it was written by a developer and it doesn't change until that developer, or someone else, makes the changes. In the second case, it is written on the fly and reflects the latest data in the database.

In both cases, every time new data is requested, the entire process has to start over again. Since this all happens in a fraction of a second, and works most of the time, it may not seem like much to you. However, in the background, this requires a tremendous amount of server time and tremendous use of resources on the various servers and your own client computer. All the graphics need to be downloaded separately and held in your computer's memory, and all of the downloaded pages get stored in a folder in your computer.

Let's move forward again. Go to the following Adobe website:

    http://examples.adobe.com/flex2/inproduct/sdk/flexstore/flexstore.html

You need to have Flash Player, version 9 or later, plugged into your web browser to display this page, shown in Figure 1-3. If you don't, you will be prompted to download it. This should only take a few seconds.

As you look at the site, the differences from the earlier two pages should be quite obvious. Notice that when you click the tabs, you move from page to page smoothly without the reloading process you saw in the previous examples. Also, in the Products tab, if you change the price range of the cell phones, you will see the cell phones animate while re-arranging themselves.

Figure 1-3. A Flex site prototype

This is the prototype of a Flex site, and the mechanics will be, of course, the subject of this book. However, in its simplest form, all you really loaded was one file, a Flash SWF (pronounced "swif") file. From there, when the information needs to change, what you refresh is what gets changed instead of the entire page. This means fewer potential errors, faster data display, and a much nicer user experience. Also, as you will see as you progress through this book, it will take fewer resources and be ideal for today's emerging portable Internet devices.

How exactly is this technology different?

Flex and RIA

In order for you to fully understand what is going on with the last example, you might need to change your thinking a bit.

As you saw in the first two examples, a traditional web page goes from page to page by sending another request back to the server and going through the process just discussed. In the case of a dynamic page, the web server takes the request and sends it out to one of the five application servers discussed, which in turn sends it out to the database server. The data is then assembled by the application server, and a new HTML page is written, sent back to the web server, and, finally, sent back to your web browser for display. If you go to five different pages on a site, like Amazon.com, you end up going through that entire process five times. I think most would agree that, in retrospect, this isn't a terribly efficient way of doing things.

What's more, I think most people can easily distinguish between an Internet application, like the first two examples shown, and a desktop application like Microsoft Word. The whole look and feel is different.

Wouldn't it be nice if the whole process ran much more efficiently? And wouldn't it be even nicer if desktop and web applications had more or less the same look and feel?

Did the Flex prototype in the last example feel like an Internet application? Or did it feel closer to a desktop application?

To address these questions, Macromedia (now Adobe), with the introduction of Flash MX, introduced a new term: **rich Internet application** (**RIA**). This Flash-based technology overcomes many of the limitations of traditional HTML in that it is nearly indistinguishable from a desktop application.

RIA applications, as you have seen in the last example shown, do not need to be rebuilt completely. Only the requested data is returned and plugged in where needed. As I stated in the last section, this means decreased demands on the server and much smaller file sizes (which lends itself nicely to emerging mobile Internet technologies).

Also, in a traditional HTML environment, user interactivity is limited to forms and just a few buttons. Desktop functions, like menus and smooth transitions from section to section, often perform poorly and could add significantly to file sizes. Also, while developers use JavaScript for this functionality, browser security programs often prevent JavaScript from functioning. As a result, even more functionality is often lost.

Flash MX addressed these issues by giving the web developer a whole new set of programming tools that allowed for greater interactivity without the issues that HTML/JavaScript presented. Suddenly, in an RIA environment, users could have the same interactive experience as in a desktop application environment. As a bonus, this additional interactivity could be added without dramatically increasing the file size.

The release of Flash MX also saw the arrival of the first Flash server: **Flash Remoting MX**. This new server gave RIA environments a greater ability to interact quickly and smoothly with data transfer technologies such as XML files and web services. In addition, it could interact with the popular Java and .NET environments. This meant that Flash could now work as a presentation tool over a variety of programming environments. Many developers started to find this as a welcome alternative to the less-than-ideal Java and .NET presentation containers.

Flash MX, however, presented a few new and unique problems.

After the release of Flash MX, Macromedia introduced ActionScript 2.0 as an update. ActionScript 1.0 had been a rather primitive procedural language to assist Flash in creating animations. To address the newer needs of RIA, ActionScript 2.0 was a semi–object-oriented programming (OOP) language.

> *If you are a complete beginner to Flex or programming environments, you may not be familiar with the terms "OOP," "ActionScript," or "procedural languages." If not, don't worry. This is just a historical discussion. I will be carefully defining these terms as you progress through this book.*

While it followed some of the rules of OOP syntax, it also had to support the previous non-OOP ActionScript 1.0. The results were not always favorable, and many complained that the debugging tools were all but nonexistent.

Many developers also complained that to develop an RIA, they needed knowledge of many of the complexities of the Flash environment (timelines, scenes, and so on).

To address these many issues, Macromedia introduced Flex in 2004. This gave the developer a more traditional programming environment without many of the design complexities of Flash. It even had its own Dreamweaver-like development tool called Flex Builder. However, it never had the popularity hoped for due to the limitations of ActionScript 2.0.

It was clear a major overhaul was needed.

Flex, Flex Builder, and ActionScript 3.0

Flex 2 was introduced in the summer of 2006. It was not just an update from the original Flex, but a complete top-to-bottom overhaul. Central to the change was the introduction of ActionScript 3.0.

As you will be seeing as you progress through this book, ActionScript 3.0 is a full-fledged, open-source programming language similar to C++ and Java. While you may still associate ActionScript with Flash, its relationship is now only incidental. In other words, if you wanted to, you could build a complete application with just ActionScript alone without going near Flash.

If you were forced to describe what Flex is in just a couple of words, you could easily say that it is a **presentation server**. Chapter 2 examines this concept in detail. However, at the moment, you just need to know that in its simplest form, it sits over any of the application servers discussed earlier and takes the place of XHTML/JavaScript in presenting your data. Thus, rather than presenting your data as XHTML, it can be presented using the dynamic abilities of a Flash (SWF) file.

To accommodate this powerful new set of development tools, Adobe decided to not upgrade the Dreamweaver-like Flex Builder 1. Instead, Adobe turned to a development environment familiar to many programmers: **Eclipse**.

Eclipse and Flex Builder 3

Eclipse is a free programming development environment (we use the term **IDE** or **integrated development environment**) used extensively by many programmers, especially Java developers. It allows a developer to work in multiple programming environments simultaneously. You can find Eclipse at

www.eclipse.org

While Eclipse is heavily used by Java developers, its real power is the ability to accommodate **plug-ins** for a variety of programming languages. For instance, there are plug-ins for C++, PHP, and even an increasingly popular free plug-in for doing ColdFusion development. We will be using that plug-in a little later on in this book when we integrate Flex with ColdFusion.

While many of the plug-ins for Eclipse are free, Flex Builder 2 was not. However, Flex Builder 2 allowed developers to work in a traditional IDE with many of its powerful programming and debugging tools.

Flex Builder 3 presents even more powerful tools that, as you will see throughout this book, allow the developer to harness the power of Adobe's other powerful design and development tools. Among those improvements are

- An enhanced Design View to take advantage of the powerful Adobe CS3 design tools. This can improve workflow between designers and developers.
- Easier ways to connect with data sources and servers with new and enhanced data components.
- The ability to construct and deploy the new **Adobe Integrated Runtime** (**AIR**) tools within the Flex Builder IDE.

> *As of this writing, Adobe announced that it was making Flex fully open source. This means that other developers could create competing IDEs for Flex development. For the purposes of this book, however, we will be using Flex Builder 3.*

We will examine Flex Builder 3 with greater detail in Chapter 2. For now, however, we have to start installing this technology before we can use it. If you are ready to get it installed, let's move on to the next section.

Installing Flex Builder 3

Flex Builder consists of three separate components:

- **The Flex Software Development Kit**: This is the collection of ActionScript classes (we will be discussing class files in Chapter 3) necessary to build, run, and deploy Flex applications.
- **The Eclipse plug-in integrated development environment**: This plug-in assists in building the applications.
- **Flash Player 9**: Flex applications will only run with Flash Player 9 or later.

Flex can be installed in one of two ways:

If you are an existing Eclipse user, you can install the plug-in version. As you are installing, you will be prompted to enter the location of Eclipse, and the installer will know what to do from there.

If you are not an existing Eclipse user, you can install the stand-alone version. This is Flex Builder and Eclipse packaged together.

Both versions will get you to the same place in the end. However, there is a slight difference. Eclipse uses a technique called **Perspectives**. We will be looking at this a bit more in Chapter 2. However, for now just know that a Perspective is an arrangement of tools and windows needed to develop in a particular programming language. The Perspective for Java programming would be different from that for C++, and Flex would require yet a different Perspective. If you install Eclipse from its site, the default Perspective is for Java development. However, if you install the stand-alone version of Flex Builder, the default Perspective is Flex. Also, I found that other plug-ins, such as the ones for ColdFusion (www.cfeclipse.org), were easier to install and use through the plug-in version of Flex Builder 3. For that reason, I strongly recommend that you use the plug-in version of Flex Builder 3.

In this section of the book, I will be showing you how to install the plug-in version. Once we get past a certain point, the installation will be exactly the same. For that reason, I divide the installation into two sections.

The following install instructions are valid as of the writing of this book. Some of the steps and screens shown could change as Adobe makes adjustments.

As of the writing of this book, there is an emerging bug regarding installation of the Flash Player ActiveX control: any existing players are not being fully uninstalled. This may be fixed by the time you read this section. However, to play it safe, it would be a good idea to go to

    http://kb.adobe.com/selfservice/viewContent.do?externalId=tn_19254

and download the Flash Player uninstall tool to completely remove any instances of Flash Player you have installed. Flex will reinstall them properly.

Installing Flex Builder as an Eclipse plug-in

Before you can install the Flex Builder plug-in, you must first install Eclipse, so let's start there:

1. Go to www.eclipse.org and click the Download Eclipse button. You will be presented with a screen similar to Figure 1-4.

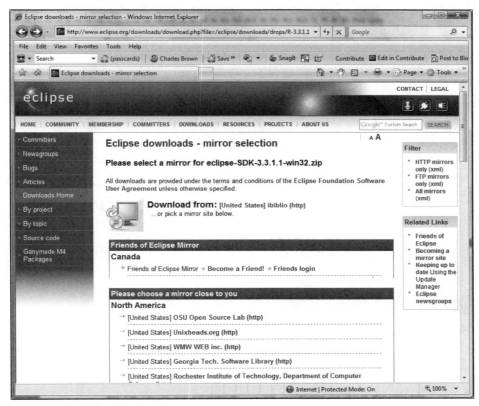

Figure 1-4. The Eclipse download screen

2. As you can see, the free Eclipse IDE is available for a variety of platforms. Click the link for the version you want.

3. Once it is fully downloaded, unzip the file to the directory of your choice. Because Eclipse is platform independent, there is no traditional install process.

4. If you installed in Windows, you will want to go into File Explorer, navigate to the folder that you installed Eclipse in, and right-click the EXE file associated with Eclipse. Select Send to ➤ Desktop as shown in Figure 1-5.

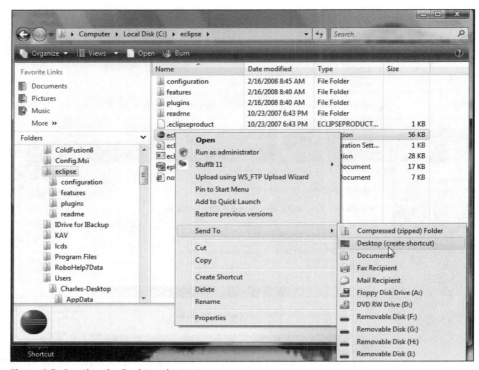

Figure 1-5. Creating the Desktop shortcut

That is all that is involved with installing Eclipse. From here on in, the install process is very similar no matter which version of the program you are installing.

Installing Flex Builder 3

As of this writing, Adobe will sell Flex Builder 3 either on disk or as a download. The download is about 345MB in size. Within those two choices, you can install it (as I have stated several times) either as a stand-alone version or as an Eclipse plug-in. The differences for installing the versions are very minor.

1. Depending on the operating system you are installing for, start the install process. A program called InstallAnywhere should start. It may take a couple of minutes before the first screen appears.

2. The first screen will prompt you as to the language you are installing in. Choose the language and click OK.

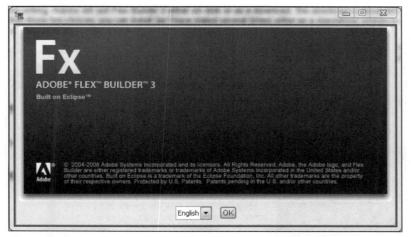

Figure 1-6. The opening install screen

3. It is a good idea to close all running programs and windows, especially browsers. This is because Flex Builder will install its own version of Flash Player 9. The next screen will prompt you for that. Once done, click Next.

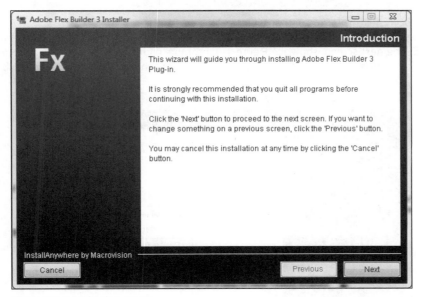

Figure 1-7. Introduction screen

4. This next screen, shown in Figure 1-8, is the licensing screen. Just accept the license agreement and click Next.

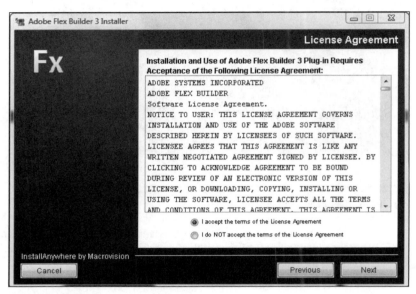

Figure 1-8. The License Agreement screen

5. The next screen, shown in Figure 1-9, prompts you for the default location. Unless you have a good reason to change it, just accept the location by clicking Next.

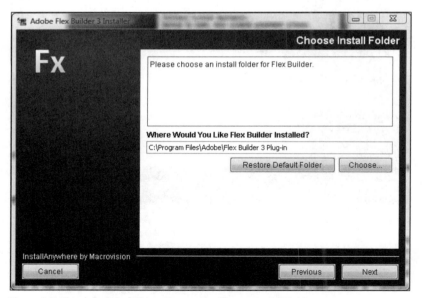

Figure 1-9. The default install location on the Choose Install Folder screen

6. The next screen, shown in Figure 1-10, will appear only if you are installing the plug-in version of Flex Builder 3. It will ask you for the location of the Eclipse installation (if you installed it earlier). You need to select Choose and navigate to the folder (in this example, my install directory was C:\Eclipse). Click Next when selected.

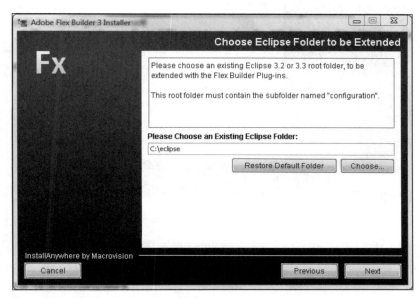

Figure 1-10. Selecting the location of Eclipse

7. The following screen, shown in Figure 1-11, is quite important. It prompts to install Flash Player in each of the installed browsers on your computer. This version of Flash Player, however, is not the one most end users download. This player has the ability to debug the SWF files you create in Flex, and it will play an important role as you progress through this book; you will have your first look at it in Chapter 2.

Earlier in the chapter, I mentioned an emerging bug with installing Flash Player 9. I strongly recommend reviewing that and uninstalling any existing versions of Flash Player. The installation shown here will reinstall everything properly. Once you do that, reinstall Flash Player for all browsers you have installed.

You are also prompted about installing additional Eclipse plug-ins if you want to do additional ColdFusion and JavaScript programming later on. Even if you don't have ColdFusion installed now, I strongly recommend that you select both of these options, if you plan on using either of these technologies later on.

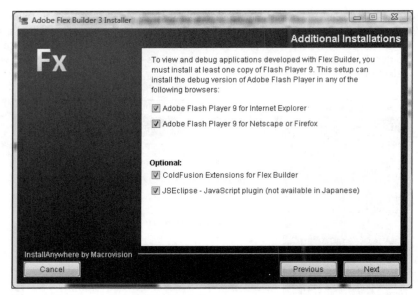

Figure 1-11. The installation of the Flash Players

8. The final screen before installation allows you to review the installation parameters of the program folder and the Debugging Flash Player (see Figure 1-12).

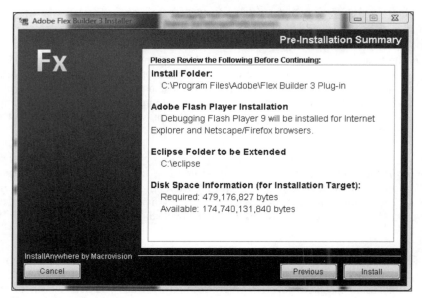

Figure 1-12. A final review

9. Assuming all is well, go ahead and click the Install button.

You will see a progress screen similar to Figure 1-13.

Figure 1-13. Install progress screen

10. A final screen should appear as shown in Figure 1-14, letting you know all installed properly. Click Done.

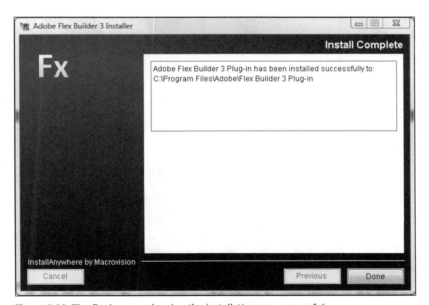

Figure 1-14. The final screen showing the installation was successful

If you installed in the Windows Vista environment, you will be returned to File Explorer and the Eclipse install directory, because the first time you open Flex Builder, Vista requires you to open it as an Administrator.

11. Go ahead and close this window. I am going to show you a slightly different technique for Windows Vista.

> *Since Flex Builder will run in Windows XP, Windows Vista, Mac OS X, and Linux, it would be difficult to discuss the details of each of these operating systems. Past this initial stage, the differences between running Flex Builder in these various operating systems are negligible.*

12. If you are using Windows Vista, select Start ➤ All Programs.

13. Select the Adobe folder.

14. Right-click the Adobe Flex Builder 3 Eclipse Launch **link and select** Run as administrator (see Figure 1-15).

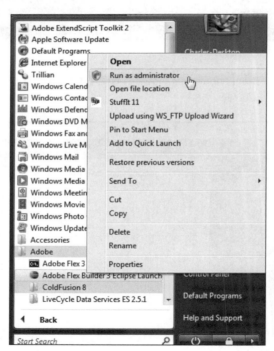

Figure 1-15. The Run as administrator menu command

You only need to do this the first time you run Flex Builder.

15. You will be first prompted about the default workspace, as shown in Figure 1-16. In Eclipse, the workspace is where your project files will be saved. This screen is just asking you if you want to use the default workspace. If you are a beginning Flex programmer, there is little reason to change this. Click OK.

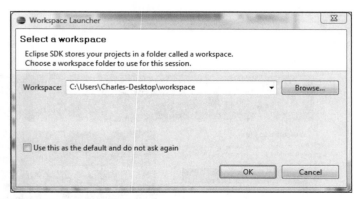

Figure 1-16. The default workspace screen

Depending on the operating system and which version of Flex Builder you decided to install, the following screen, shown in Figure 1-17, may look a little different on your system. Don't worry, you will fix that shortly.

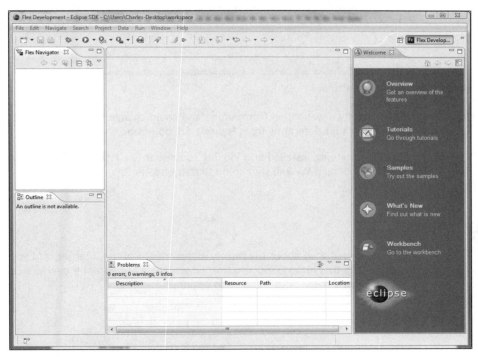

Figure 1-17. The Flex Builder opening screen

The Welcome panel shown on the right is for Eclipse, not for Flex Builder 3.

16. Close the Welcome panel by clicking the X located on the right side of the tab.

17. Click Help ➤ Flex Start Page. Your screen should look similar to Figure 1-18.

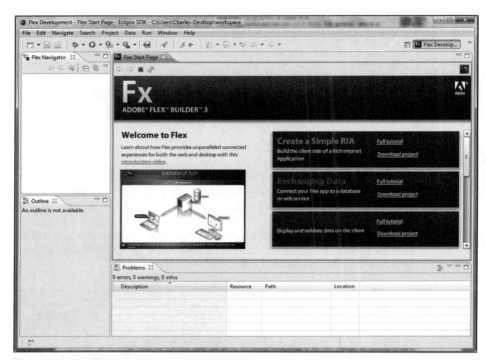

Figure 1-18. The Flex Start Page

This screen is dynamically downloaded from Adobe and could change from time to time. So, if your screen looks a bit differently from Figure 1-18, do not be concerned.

Assuming you have everything installed and looking somewhat like Figure 1-18, it is now time to start discussing details. We will start to do that in Chapter 2.

Summary

In this chapter, you learned a bit about the history and workings of the Internet, and you learned how Flex fits into that history. You also learned what Flex brings that is new to web design. Finally, you learned the various installation options.

Now that you have installed the Flex Builder IDE, with the bundled ActionScript SDK (as a matter of fact, as you will see in the next chapter, you installed two versions of the ActionScript SDK), you are now ready to start building applications. In the next chapter, you will do just that by taking a closer look at the Flex environment and the Flex Builder IDE.

1

2 FLEX AND FLEX BUILDER 3

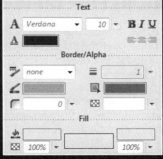
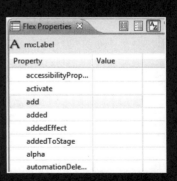

When I started doing Java programming, a typical workflow would have me typing code in a very low-level text editor, such as Notepad, and then switching to the command prompt (then called the DOS prompt) where I would have to enter a cryptic string of compiler commands. Finally, if all went well, I would then need to enter another command to run the program. However, if there was a mistake in the code somewhere, the compiler would return an error message that defied understanding by deities.

Happily, with the growth of integrated development environments, those inefficiencies are no longer necessary. Code errors are usually flagged as you type them, and compiler commands can be accessed with the click of a button. Also, most of today's IDEs offer a plethora of tools to help us turn around bug-free code quickly.

In many ways, this book is about two subjects: Flex and Flex Builder 3.

As I stated in Chapter 1, you don't need Flex Builder 3 to program in Flex. You could easily return to the scenario I spoke about earlier. But is that really a cost efficient way of doing things?

> *As of this writing, Adobe was making the source code for Flex available and opening the possibility of third-party IDEs. However, this book will be using Flex Builder 3 throughout.*

In this chapter, we are going to take a quick tour of the parts of Flex Builder 3 as well as explore some of the terminology it uses. We are also going to build a couple of simple Flex applications. Finally, we are going to examine the relationship of the Flex design language, MXML, and ActionScript 3.0. While doing that, I will discuss how to understand ActionScript documentation.

Let's start by getting Flex Builder 3 running.

Starting out in Flex Builder 3

Flex Builder 3 is the "official" IDE for creating Flex applications. As I stated in Chapter 1, Flex Builder 3 is built over the Eclipse IDE. This is a multilanguage IDE familiar to most programmers, particularly Java developers. Later in this book, we will be using this environment for ColdFusion coding.

In Chapter 1, I pointed out one small anomaly you should be aware of: if you are running Flex Builder 3 in the Microsoft Vista environment and are starting it for the first time, you must right-click the shortcut and open it as an Administrator. If you don't do that, you will receive an error message. Subsequent uses do not require this.

Assuming you got Flex Builder 3 going, and you followed the steps in Chapter 1, you should be presented with the View shown in Figure 2-1.

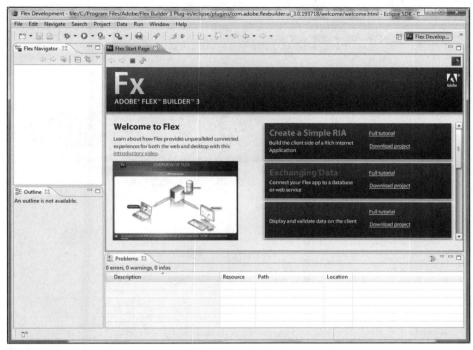

Figure 2-1. The Flex Start Page

The page that comes up by default is called the Flex Start Page, which consists simply of tutorials and sample applications. It is worth spending some time going through its contents. There is, in my opinion, a wealth of potential learning tools here.

> *If you installed Flex Builder 3 as a plug-in for Eclipse, you may not be able to see this page initially. Don't worry, you can get to the Flex Start Page at any time by selecting* Help ➤ Flex Start Page.

Of particular interest is the introductory video located on the left side of the Welcome to Flex screen. If you click it, you will see something like Figure 2-2 in a new window.

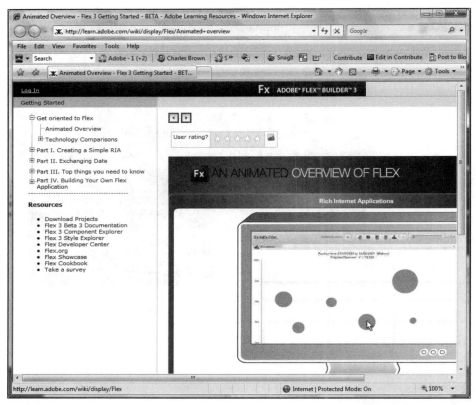

Figure 2-2. Flex Support Center

It is worth spending a few moments reviewing it as well as the other tutorials.

These screens and tutorials will be updated from time to time. So if your screen looks a little different from Figure 2-2, don't be concerned about that. Just use the latest version of the tutorial.

Now that you know how to use the Flex Start Page, let's take a quick look around Flex Builder/Eclipse. Please refer to Figure 2-1 if you don't have Flex Builder open.

Notice you have some additional windows open around the Flex Start Page. They are called the Flex Navigator, Outline, and Problems. We will discuss the function of these in a moment, when we create our first project.

In Eclipse, these additional windows are referred to as **Views**. We would say we are looking at the Flex Navigator, Outline, and Problems Views.

As I stated in Chapter 1, Eclipse is a multilanguage environment. Each language has its own requirement as to what tools and Views might be needed. Eclipse will automatically set up the tools and Views necessary for whatever language is used. This automatic arrangement is called a **Perspective**.

If you downloaded Eclipse on its own and later added the Flex Builder 3 plug-in, as discussed in Chapter 1, the default Perspective is for Java. However, if you downloaded the Eclipse/Flex Builder 3 bundle, the default Perspective is for Flex. That is why what you see may differ a little from some of the screenshots shown in this book.

We will be using Views and Perspectives in just a moment, as well as through most of this book. But before we can make that happen, we need to create our first **Flex project**.

Creating a Flex project

Eclipse, like most IDEs, requires that a project be defined before an application can be developed. A Flex project, like any project, is a managed environment that contains all of the files necessary to build, test, and deploy your application.

Let's build our first application. Like most beginning programming books, it will be a simple "Hello World" application.

1. Select File ➤ New to bring up the options shown in Figure 2-3.

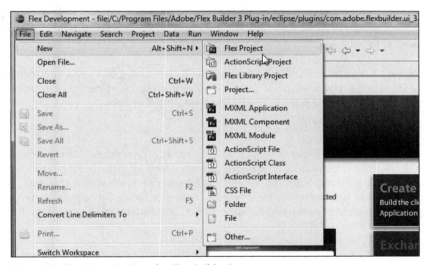

Figure 2-3. The New selections for Flex Builder 3

2. Select Flex Project. This brings up the dialog box shown in Figure 2-4.

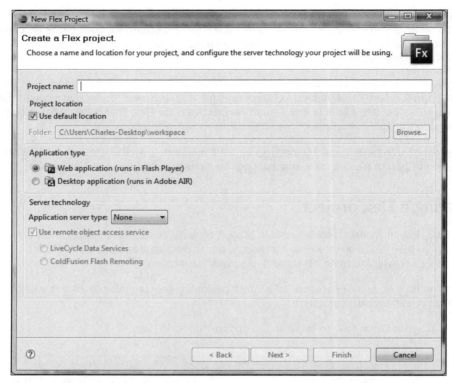

Figure 2-4. The New Flex Project dialog box

If you were a user of Flex Builder 2, this New Flex Project dialog box looks completely different. The first thing you will need to do is give your project a name. You can supply any name you want because it is used for identification purposes only.

3. In the Project name field, enter Welcome as the project name.

Under the Project name field, you should see a Project location section. There is a check box for using the default location to house your project, which we discussed a bit in Chapter 1. When Flex Builder installs, it sets up a folder called workspace. We will be discussing workspaces later on in the book, but for now just know this folder contains important tools needed by Flex in order to run and compile, as well as information where project files are located.

> *Flex Builder 2 set up a directory under the* Documents *folder called* Flex Builder 2. *Flex Builder 3 is a bit different. The working directory will vary depending on your operating system and installation type. For example, as you can see in Figure 2-5, the default directory is* workspace.

Figure 2-5. The default location

You will rarely, if ever, need to physically go into these folders, especially if you are a new user. So don't be too concerned about them now.

If you look under the check box for the default location, you should see the workspace directory with the name of the project after it. Since you are using the default location, it will be grayed out, as shown in Figure 2-5.

New to Flex Builder 3 is the selection of Application type. The Web application (runs in Flash Player) selection allows you to create SWF files that run over the Internet in a web browser. This is the traditional way of running SWF files and the way we will be concentrating on initially in this book.

Desktop application (runs in Adobe AIR) refers to a brand new technology that Adobe just released. The acronym **AIR** stands for **Adobe Integrated Runtime**. We will be discussing this much later on in this book. However, for now, understand that it allows the web application to run outside of the browser as a desktop icon. This goes back to the discussion at the beginning of Chapter 1, in which I mentioned it will become increasingly difficult to distinguish between web and desktop applications.

> *If you would like to see a demonstration of this new technology, go to*
>
>   http://desktop.ebay.com
>
> *You will be able to browse and shop on eBay using it.*

4. For now, make sure that Web application (runs in Flash Player) is selected.

As discussed in Chapter 1, Flex sits above any of the major server technologies such as .NET, PHP, Java, and ColdFusion. Flex will present the data that is outputted by one of these technologies.

The section Server technology allows you to select which server you will be running over. We will be talking about this a bit later on in this book.

5. Leave the Server technology set to None for the time being.

6. Click Next.

7. The next dialog box, shown in Figure 2-6, specifies where the finished files necessary to deploy your project will be located. The default is bin-debug. There is little reason to change that, so click Next.

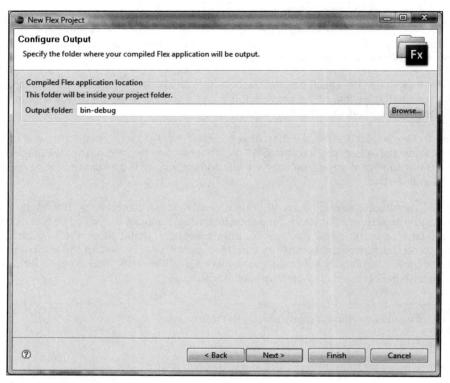

Figure 2-6. The default output folder

The next dialog box, shown in Figure 2-7, allows you to specify the name of the folder within the project that will house the **source files** for your project. The source files are the files you create, as well as any additional files, before they are converted to SWF files. By default, Flex Builder sets up a folder called src. There is very little reason to change this.

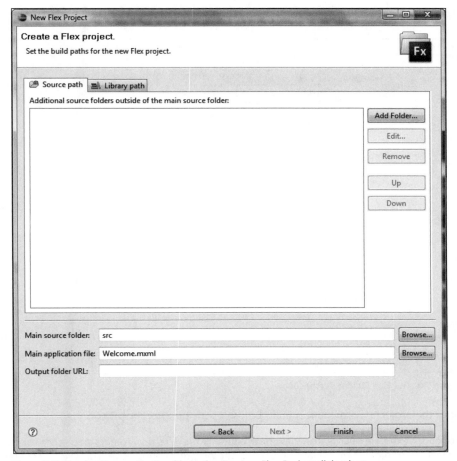

Figure 2-7. Naming the application file in the Create a Flex Project dialog box

If you have worked in Flash, you know that the working file has a file extension of `.fla`. In Flex, the working file has a file extension of `.mxml`. All Flex projects consist of one MXML file called the **application file** and several additional MXML files called **components**. Don't worry too much about this now. We will be discussing this in greater detail as we progress.

By default, Flex Builder gives the application MXML file the same name as the project. You can change this if you want, but there is no reason to do so now.

8. Click Finish.

Flex Builder will do a bit of housework and then open as shown in Figure 2-8.

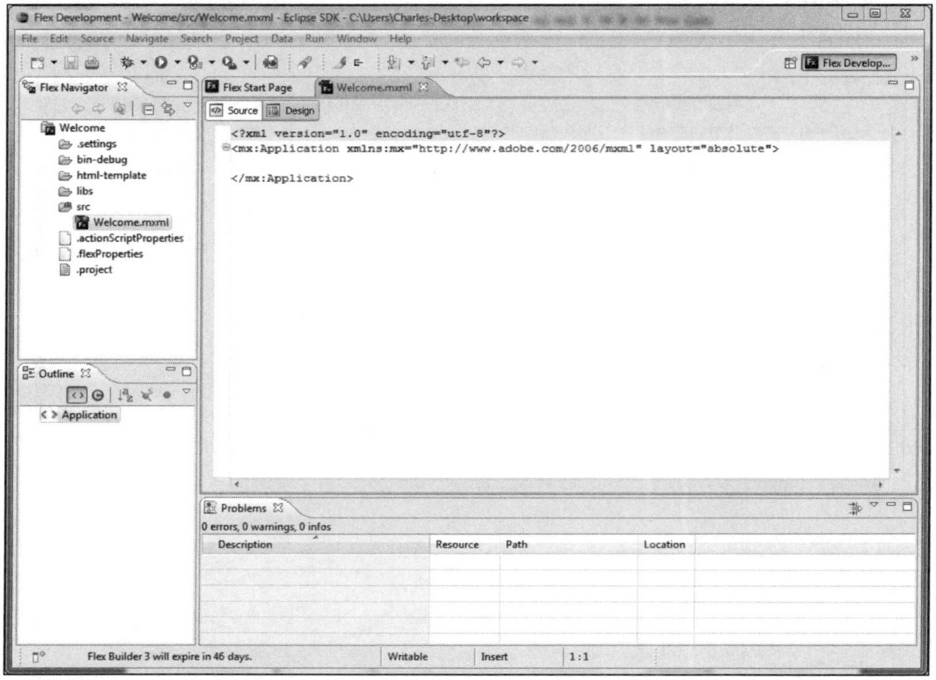

Figure 2-8. The Flex Builder Perspective

Once the project environment is built, Eclipse opens the Flex Perspective.

Notice that the Flex Navigator View now contains the files and folders necessary for this project. One folder, bin-debug, will contain the output of your code. The src folder contains the main application: Welcome.mxml. Throughout this book, we will be spending the bulk of our time in the src folder.

The Outline View will show us the structure of our application. We will be using that a bit later on in this chapter.

The main area, where the code is located, is the **Editor View**. This will be where we actually do our coding and design work.

Within the Flex Perspective, we have other sub-Perspectives. For instance, when you are seeing code in the Editor View, you are in the **Source Perspective**. But if you look in the upper left-hand corner, you will see two buttons: Source and Design. The Design button will put you in the **Design Perspective**.

9. Click the Design button to bring up the Design Perspective. It will look like Figure 2-9.

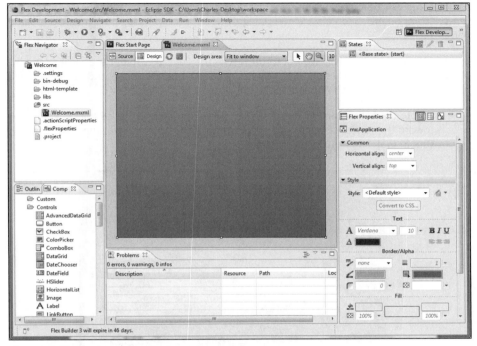

Figure 2-9. The Design Perspective

Notice that in the Design Perspective you see some Views that you didn't see in the Source Perspective. For example, you see the **Components View**, **States View**, and **Flex Properties View**.

In this Perspective, we can create our application visually in much the same way as Microsoft's popular Visual Studio program or Adobe's Dreamweaver.

It is in this Perspective that we will create our simple application.

Creating a Flex application

We will create a simple application here to help you get your feet wet using Flex and Flex Builder. For the time being, I will keep to a rather superficial discussion of the details. As we progress, we will dig much deeper.

Notice the Components View. Within that View, you have a number of folders, including Controls, Layout, Navigators, and Charts. These folders contain **components** that we need to build a Flex application.

A small word about components is in order here. A **component** is an additional ActionScript class file that is available only in Flex. In other words, even through Flash CS3 uses ActionScript 3.0, these very robust components can only be accessed in the Flex environment. As you progress through this chapter and the rest of this book, these components will be discussed in great detail. Also, when we discuss them, I will use the words "component" and "class" interchangeably. As you will see, they mean the same thing.

If necessary, click the small + symbol to the left of the Controls folder to reveal a long list of **controls**. Controls are simply components needed to receive or send data. As you will be learning, all of these components relate back to ActionScript files.

1. Locate the Label control and drag it into the Editor View. Notice that as you move toward the center of the design area, a vertical line appears indicating the center. It should look like Figure 2-10.

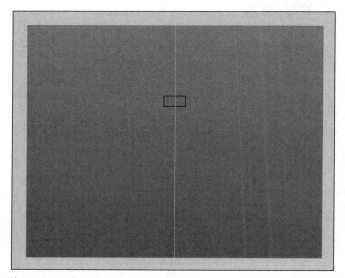

Figure 2-10. The Label control

Notice that the Label control has some default text in it called Label.

2. Double-click this default text and type Welcome to Flex Programming!.
3. Press the Enter key.

You can save your work by pressing Ctrl/Cmd+S or clicking the Save icon in the toolbar, as shown in Figure 2-11.

Figure 2-11.
Saving the application

We are now ready to give our masterpiece application a test.

Figure 2-12.
The Run Application
button

4. Click the Run Application button located just a bit to the right of the Save button you just used (see Figure 2-12).

The default browser should open displaying the application, as shown in Figure 2-13.

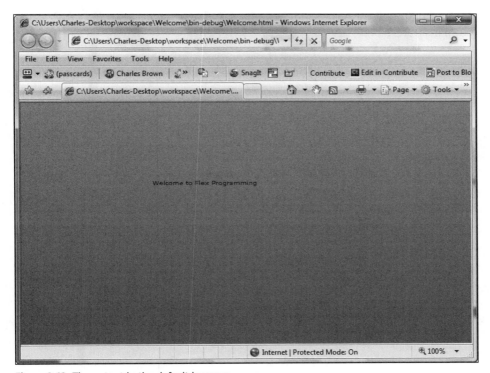

Figure 2-13. The output in the default browser

> *If you installed Flex Builder as a plug-in, you may get an interim screen asking you what type of application this is. Should you get this, just select* Flex Application *and click* OK.

Congratulations! You just created and ran your first Flex application!

5. Close the browser and return to Flex Builder.

Let's look at another way of changing the text of the Label control.

Changing the properties

When you added the text of your label, or more precisely changed the default text, you changed a **property** of the Label control. In this case, you changed the **text property**.

Flex Builder allows us to change the properties of many of the components we work with either programmatically or visually. Let's take a brief look at the visual aspect here.

Click the Label on the stage and look at the Flex Properties View on the right side, as shown in Figure 2-14.

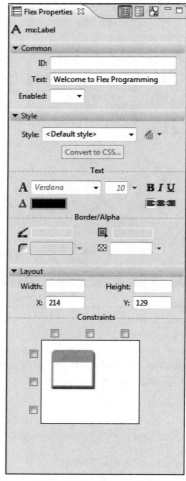

Figure 2-14. The Flex Properties View

This panel is context sensitive and will change depending on the component you are working with. For instance, if you are working with a Button component, the options will be different.

This panel, as you see it, shows only the most commonly used properties. However, there is an option to see all of the properties available.

At the top of the panel, to the right of the tab, you should see several buttons. The first button is **Standard View**, which is what you are looking at now. The second button is **Category View**, which displays as shown in Figure 2-15.

Figure 2-15. The Category View of properties

With this View, you can see the various properties that are available for the component you are working with. What makes this especially handy is that it is broken down by category. As you progress through this book, you will be encountering many of these properties. However, there is one other way you can look at these properties.

If you click the third button, it arranges the properties not by category, but in one long alphabetical list, as you can see in Figure 2-16.

Figure 2-16. The Alphabetical View of properties

You can use the three buttons to switch between Standard, Category, and Alphabetical Views.

> *The word "property" is rather broadly defined in Flex Builder. As you will soon see, things called event handlers are classified as properties.*

Now that we have crossed that hurdle, let's dig a little deeper into anatomy and mechanics of what we just created.

Anatomy of a Flex application

Switch back to the Source Perspective and look at the code generated. It should resemble what you see in Figure 2-17.

```
Fx Flex Start Page    Fx Welcome.mxml ⊠
</> Source   Design
    <?xml version="1.0" encoding="utf-8"?>
⊖ <mx:Application xmlns:mx="http://www.adobe.com/2006/mxml" layout="absolute">
        <mx:Label x="214" y="129" text="Welcome to Flex Programming"/>
    </mx:Application>
```

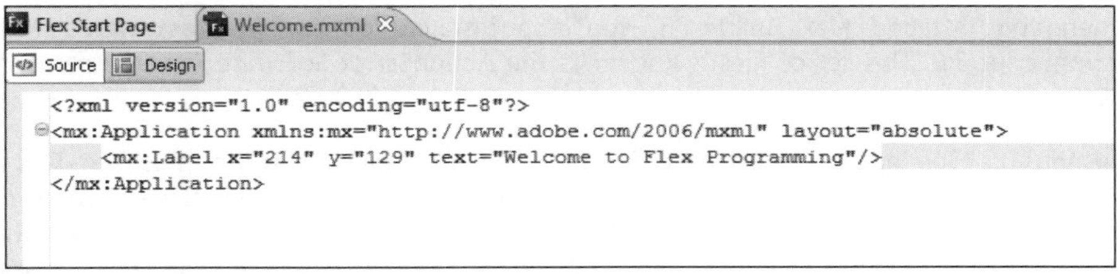

Figure 2-17. The code in Source Perspective

Let's take a closer look at the language of this code.

MXML

You create Flex applications by using two languages: MXML and ActionScript 3.0. Or do you?

What you see in Figure 2-17 is an example of **MXML**. MXML is an XML library-based language in that it has a library of specific tags and follows strictly the rules of XML. However, here is the interesting part: MXML is considered a **convenience language**. If you have never heard that term, it goes back to ColdFusion.

ColdFusion uses an HTML-based language called **ColdFusion Meta-Language** (**CFML**). It uses a relatively simple, tag-based language to write a more complex language in the background. In the case of CFML, Java is being written in the background. In the case of MXML, ActionScript is being written in the background. So, whether you create your application in MXML or code directly with ActionScript, everything will ultimately end up as ActionScript. I will prove that point shortly. Let's take a look at the anatomy of the code generated in our simple application. The first line of code is

```
<?xml version="1.0" encoding="utf-8"?>
```

All MXML documents begin with a **Document Type Declaration** (**DTD**) of XML. This means that the document will be checked to make sure it conforms to the rules of XML structure.

The next line is where the action begins:

```
<mx:Application xmlns:mx="http://www.adobe.com/2006/mxml"
layout="absolute">
```

The main application file, and ONLY the main application file, must begin with the Application tag. There is a lot to talk about here.

As you will shortly see, every MXML tag has a corresponding ActionScript class file in the background. If you are new to programming and don't know what a class file is, don't worry; we will be discussing that in Chapter 3. For now, you just need to know that by programming tradition, a class file begins with a capital letter. So the corresponding tag name also begins with a capital letter. But what is with the mx: before the tag name?

When you installed Flex Builder 3, you also installed all the files associated with ActionScript 3.0. This set of files is known as the ActionScript **Software Development Kit** (**SDK**).

The Application tag has a property called xmlns, which stands for XML namespace. This is a **namespace** property. What it does is enable you to substitute a small name in place of typing a whole path—in this case, the path where the ActionScript SDK is located. We will be using this a lot more when we start creating components. However, the Application tag uses a default namespace, called mx, as a substitute for the SDK path. So far it is quite clear. But now things get a little strange.

It defines the path of the SDK as being

        http://www.adobe.com/2006/mxml

Huh? Does that mean the SDK is located on the Adobe website? No!

While this may look like a URL, it is actually an internal command that tells the compiler where to find the SDK. If that namespace is not defined, exactly as it is shown, in the Application tag, your Flex application will not work. So, bottom line, don't change it!

Just to review, mx tells the tag where to find the SDK, and the name of the tag, in this case Application, is the name of the class it needs once it gets there. Beginning to see the connection of MXML to ActionScript?

There is another property called layout which is set, in this case, to absolute. I am going to ask you to just ignore that for a bit. We will get back to it shortly.

When you design in Flex, it is important to start thinking in terms of **containers**. As an example, the Application tag serves as the main container containing the rest of the application. The Label tag that follows it is a child of the Application container. This is important for understanding MXML syntax.

Notice that the Application tag, or container, closes a couple of lines down.

```
<mx:Application xmlns:mx="http://www.adobe.com/2006/mxml" ➦
layout="absolute">
    ...
</mx:Application>
```

When a container has children, you must have a closing tag after the last child. Note that the full tag name including the mx: must be included. But now let's look at the Label tag.

```
<mx:Label x="350" y="42" text="Welcome To Flex Programming!"/>
```

> *If you have different x and y properties, don't worry about that for now.*

Since the Label tag will not contain any children, we can use a shorthand way of closing the tag: />

I will be pointing this out a great deal as we move along.

Notice that in this example, the Label tag, based on the Label ActionScript class file, is using three properties: x to define the x-position, y to define the y-position, and text, which defines the content of the Label.

To get a better feel as to how all of this works, let's add a second Label tag to our application. Only this time, we will do it right here in the code.

1. Click after the close, />, of the Label tag and press the Enter key to create a new blank line.

2. Type the less than symbol (<) to start the tag.

As soon as you open the tag, Flex Builder gives you a list of the class files available in the mx namespace, as you can see in Figure 2-18.

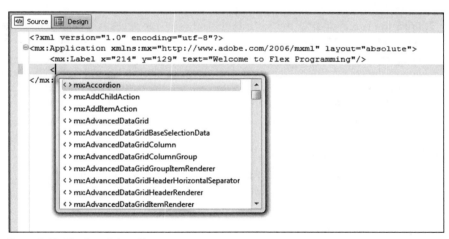

Figure 2-18. The list of class files

3. Type L to jump to the class files that begin with "L." If Label is selected, just press the Enter key, and your tag is started.

4. Now press the spacebar. Flex Builder displays a list of the properties associated with the Label class, as shown in Figure 2-19. You can tell they are properties because they begin with a lowercase letter.

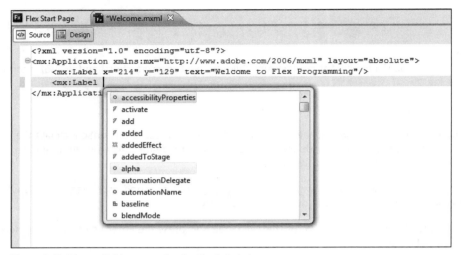

Figure 2-19. The available properties for the Label class

5. Type x and press Enter.

6. Notice that Flex Builder sets up the syntax, x = " ", so that all you need to do is fill in the value. Use 350.

7. Press the spacebar after the x attribute, and press the spacebar again; you will get the same list of properties. This time, select the y property and give it a value of 65.

8. Once again, bring up the list of properties and type t. Notice that it doesn't bring you to the text property right away. Just continue by typing e and it gets you there. Alternatively, once the menu is open, you can use the cursor keys to browse up and down through the properties, pressing Enter when you reach the desired one.

9. Press Enter to accept the text property and give it a value of "It is fun to work with!".

10. Close the Label tag with />.

11. Adjust the x and y properties of the previous Label to x="350" and y="42".

Your code should look as follows:

```
<?xml version="1.0" encoding="utf-8"?>
<mx:Application xmlns:mx="http://www.adobe.com/2006/mxml" ➥
layout="absolute">
    <mx:Label x="350" y="42" text="Welcome To Flex Programming!"/>
    <mx:Label x="350" y="65" text="It is fun to work with!"/>
</mx:Application>
```

12. Save the application and click the Run Application button like you did earlier. Your screen should resemble Figure 2-20.

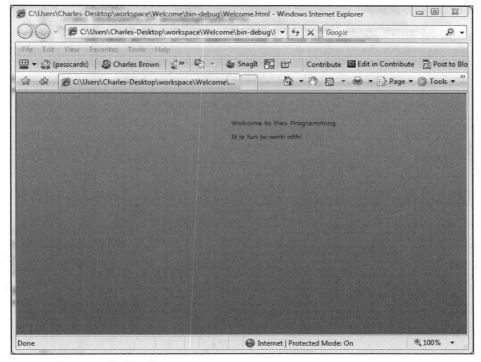

Figure 2-20. The modified application

13. Close the browser and return to Flex Builder.

To give you a graphic representation of the container-child relationship, look at the Outline View located on the lower-left side, as shown in Figure 2-21.

Here you can clearly see that the Application tag is the top-most container, with the two Label tags serving as children of the Application tag.

I am sure by now you are starting to get the idea. But how do you know which properties are available for all of the many class files you have to work with?

Getting help

At the heart of any programming language is the documentation. As a matter of fact, the Java programming environment contains nearly 150,000 class files. Without adequate documentation, the program would be all but useless to work with.

Figure 2-21.
The Outline View

Let's take a look at the Flex documentation.

1. Click the word "Label" inside of either of the Label tags, and press the F1 key on your computer.

Notice that a new View opens up called Help, as shown in Figure 2-22.

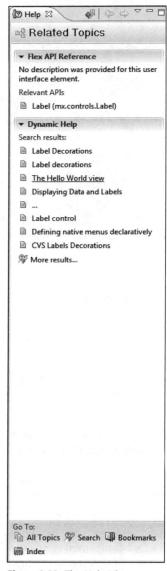

Figure 2-22. The Help View

If this is the first time you are using the Help View, it may take several minutes for the Help files to index and appear.

One of the great things about Eclipse is that you can double-click the tab of a View, and the View window will maximize. You may want to do that there.

Notice near the top it says Relevant APIs. You will learn that programmers have their own language. **Application programming interface (API)** is a very fancy term for documentation. Each class file has its own document. Where the class file is located, within the SDK, is called the **package**. It tells you that the Label class is part of the mx.controls package.

The location is actually a directory structure. This really says that class Label is located in a directory called controls, which is a subdirectory of mx. Each period in a package name designates another level of directory.

Since this is just a quick tour, we won't be getting into great detail here. But let's take a quick look.

2. Click the link Label (mx.controls.Label).

A new View opens up that displays the documentation for the Label class (see Figure 2-23).

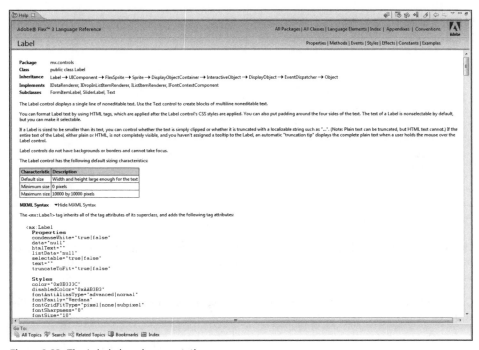

Figure 2-23. The Label class documentation

We will be examining the details of these documents as we progress through the book.

As you can see, it starts off with a brief description of the class. In this case, it is telling us that a Label control displays a single line of noneditable text. It also tells you that if you want to have multiple lines of text, you need to use the Text control. It then goes on to describe the various parts of the class.

Just to give you a little taste, scroll down to the section marked Public Properties.

If you scroll down a bit farther, within this section, you should see the text property that we just used (see Figure 2-24).

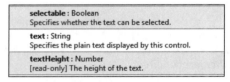

selectable : Boolean	
Specifies whether the text can be selected.	
text : String	
Specifies the plain text displayed by this control.	
textHeight : Number	
[read-only] The height of the text.	

Figure 2-24. The text property

Likewise, if you scroll down a bit further, you will see the x and y properties we used.

If you scroll down to the end of the class, an example is shown using the Label control (see Figure 2-25).

```
Examples How to use examples
LabelExample.mxml

        <?xml version="1.0" encoding="utf-8"?>
        <mx:Application xmlns:mx="http://www.adobe.com/2006/mxml">
        <!-- Simple example to demonstrate the Label control -->

            <mx:Script>
                <![CDATA[

                    private var htmlData:String="<br>This label displays <b>bold</b> and <i>italic</i> HTML-formatted text.";

                    // Event handler function to change the image size.
                    private function displayHTML():void {
                        simpleLabel.htmlText= htmlData;
                    }

                    // Event handler function to change the image size.
                    private function displayText():void {
                        simpleLabel.text="This Label displays plain text.";
                    }
                ]]>
            </mx:Script>

            <mx:Panel title="Label Control Example" height="75%" width="75%"
                paddingTop="10" paddingLeft="10">

                <mx:Label id="simpleLabel" text="This Label displays plain text."/>
                <mx:Button id="Display" label="Click to display HTML Text" click="displayHTML();"/>
                <mx:Button id="Clear" label="Click to display plain text" click="displayText();"/>

            </mx:Panel>
        </mx:Application>
```

Figure 2-25. A code example using Label

The key to understanding how to use Flex will be understanding how to use this documentation. Trust me, we will be spending a lot of time here as we progress through this book.

Go ahead and close the Help Views. We are going to now take a little peek behind the scenes.

Going behind the scenes

Now that you have some idea of the workings of Flex, let's take a look at what is going on in the background.

You are probably assuming that all of the real work of checking, compiling, and running your application happens when click the Run Application button.

Nope!

On the menu bar at the top of Flex Builder, select the Project menu item and make sure that Build Automatically is checked, as shown in Figure 2-26.

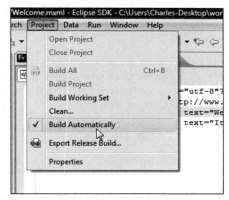

Figure 2-26. The Build Automatically option

By checking this option, all the work is done when you save the application and not when you run it. This could have enormous benefits for our workflow. Let's take a look at how.

Go to one of your Label tags and delete the closing /> as if you had forgotten it by accident. Then save your application.

As soon as you save, look at the Problems View at the bottom of Flex Builder (see Figure 2-27).

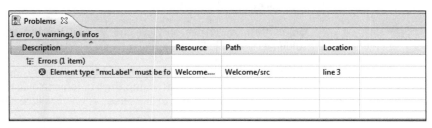

Figure 2-27. An error in Problems View

As soon as you saved, Flex Builder automatically compiled the code into a SWF file and, in the process of doing that, checked for any potential errors. If it found any, they are reported to you in the Problems View and again with a small red x on the problem line.

If you correct the mistake and resave, the error automatically clears. This means that you can catch errors earlier in the process, which makes for easier debugging.

> In Chapter 3, we will discuss the various types of problems that can turn up in the Problems View.

Let's take a look at exactly what happens when you do save.

Deploying the files

Flex applications, like those of its earlier predecessor Flash, run in a SWF file. Depending on who you talk to, SWF stands for either **small web format** or **Shockwave format**. This file is a **binary file** and is created from the ActionScript class files. If you could look inside of it, it would be nothing more than a collection of 0s and 1s.

The only thing that can read this binary file is Flash Player, located as a plug-in in the recipient's (the client's) browser.

As I just said, during the compilation process, the ActionScript class files are compiled into a binary SWF file. But here is where things get a little tricky. Just sending that SWF file up to the server is not enough. The client needs to call an XHTML file. Once that XHTML file gets to the client's browser, it in turn calls Flash Player and sends it the parameters needed to then make a call to the correct SWF file. The SWF file then downloads to the client, Flash Player reads it, and then it plays the file's contents.

Right now you are probably asking what you got yourself into. Do you now need to create XHTML files?

Flex Builder helps us out here.

Go to the Flex Navigator View and expand the bin-debug folder, as shown in Figure 2-28.

Figure 2-28.
The bin-debug folder

When you save your application, all of the necessary files to run that application are placed into the bin folder. You can literally just send that folder to the server, and you will be ready to run.

The files include the XHTML and SWF files for your application, a SWF file to check for the proper version of Flash Player, history files needed to run the browser history features, and all the necessary JavaScript files to interact properly with the browser. Flex Builder handles all that automatically for you. And, if you have not received any errors, they are fully debugged.

> Technically, you do not need to send the two files identified with "debug" to the server. However, if you did, it wouldn't hurt anything.

We will be delving into those files in greater detail as you progress through this book.

Let's wrap up this chapter with an even deeper look behind the scenes.

Looking at generated ActionScript code

As I have been stating all through this chapter, everything gets converted to ActionScript code. It is possible to see the generated code, and, if you are sufficiently knowledgeable, you can make any necessary adjustments.

A bit of a disclaimer here: while I will show you how to generate the code, I strongly suggest that you DO NOT make any changes unless you really know what you are doing. A seemingly minor alteration could cause serious problems later on.

1. From the menu, select Project ➤ Properties to bring up the window shown in Figure 2-29.

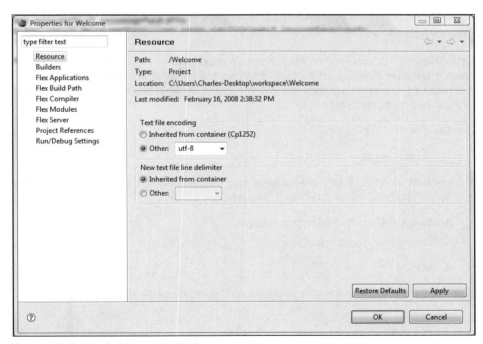

Figure 2-29. The Project Properties window

2. Select the Flex Compiler option located along the left side of the window (see Figure 2-30).

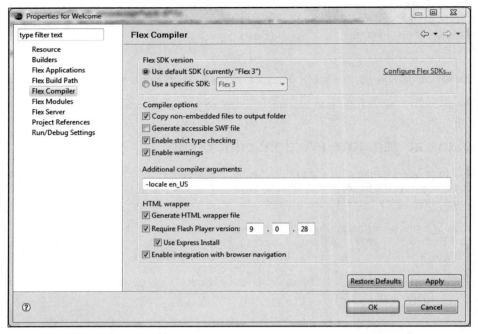

Figure 2-30. The compiler properties

Notice the line Additional compiler arguments. In programming parlance, this is sometimes called a **compiler directive**. Its purpose is to give the compiler any additional commands that might be needed to generate the SWF file. In the normal course of events, you should rarely, if ever, need to change this.

The directive

        -locale en_US

is the default directive. It tells the compiler that the code is in US English. Of course, this may vary if you installed for a different language.

3. Change the directive exactly as follows:

        -keep-generated-actionscript

4. Click OK.

Under the src folder, there is a new folder called generated (see Figure 2-31).

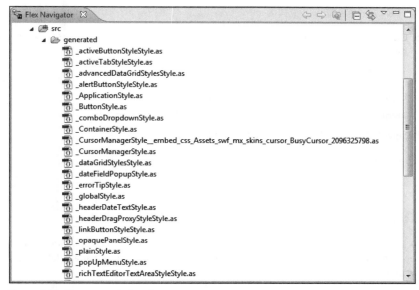

Figure 2-31. The generated code

As you can see, our simple application generated nearly 30 ActionScript files to handle the various tasks that need to be carried out.

If you double-click any one of them, you will see something like what is shown in Figure 2-32.

```
 1 package {
 2 import flash.utils.*;
 3 import mx.core.IFlexModuleFactory;
 4 import flash.system.*
 5 import mx.effects.EffectManager;
 6 import mx.core.mx_internal;
 7
 8 [Mixin]
 9 public class _Welcome_FlexInit
10 {
11    public function _Welcome_FlexInit()
12    {
13        super();
14    }
15    public static function init(fbs:IFlexModuleFactory):void
16    {
17        EffectManager.mx_internal::registerEffectTrigger("addedEffect", "added");
18        EffectManager.mx_internal::registerEffectTrigger("creationCompleteEffect", "creationComplete");
19        EffectManager.mx_internal::registerEffectTrigger("focusInEffect", "focusIn");
20        EffectManager.mx_internal::registerEffectTrigger("focusOutEffect", "focusOut");
21        EffectManager.mx_internal::registerEffectTrigger("hideEffect", "hide");
22        EffectManager.mx_internal::registerEffectTrigger("mouseDownEffect", "mouseDown");
23        EffectManager.mx_internal::registerEffectTrigger("mouseUpEffect", "mouseUp");
24        EffectManager.mx_internal::registerEffectTrigger("moveEffect", "move");
25        EffectManager.mx_internal::registerEffectTrigger("removedEffect", "removed");
26        EffectManager.mx_internal::registerEffectTrigger("resizeEffect", "resize");
27        EffectManager.mx_internal::registerEffectTrigger("rollOutEffect", "rollOut");
28        EffectManager.mx_internal::registerEffectTrigger("rollOverEffect", "rollOver");
29        EffectManager.mx_internal::registerEffectTrigger("showEffect", "show");
30        var styleNames:Array = ["fontWeight", "modalTransparencyBlur", "textRollOverColor", "backgroundDisabledColor",
31
32        import mx.styles.StyleManager;
33
34        for (var i:int = 0; i < styleNames.length; i++)
35        {
36            StyleManager.registerInheritingStyle(styleNames[i]);
37        }
38    }
39 } // FlexInit
40 } // package
```

Figure 2-32. The generated ActionScript code

Anyone care to code this by hand?

5. Go back to the compiler directive, using Project ➤ Properties, and set the compiler back to

   `-locale en_US.`

6. Close any AS files you might have opened.

7. Right/Ctrl-click the generated folder in the Flex Navigator View.

8. Select Delete. You will not need those files any longer.

Your application should work as before.

Summary

Well, you have now had the dime tour (alright, $10 with inflation) of Flex and Flex Builder. You got to build a simple application using some of the tools you have available. You even got a look behind the scenes a little bit.

Now that you hopefully understand the environment, we need to turn our attention to the heart of Flex: ActionScript. As I have stated repeatedly, that is where everything ends up at.

Time to understand how it works.

3 ACTIONSCRIPT

Top Level

See also

Data type descriptions
Type conversions
Regular expression syntax

trace() function
public function trace(... argum

Displays expressions, or writes to log
arguments. If any argument in a trace
invokes the associated toString() m
value the trace function invokes Boole

Event	Summary
⬆ **activate**	Dispatched becomes a
⬆ **add**	Dispatched addChild()
⬆ **added**	Dispatched
⬆ **addedToStage**	Dispatched through the
buttonDown	Dispatched
change	Dispatched
⬆ **click**	Dispatched over the sa

Chapter2_project.mxml

Original Source

```
        public var myText:String = "Welcome t
        public function addNumbers(number1:
        {
            var sum:int = number1 + number2;
            myText = "The sum of the numbers
        }
    ]]>
</mx:Script>
    <mx:TextInput id="inputNum1" width="50"
    <mx:TextInput id="inputNum2" width="50"
    <mx:Label text="{myText}" id="myLabel" /
    <mx:Button label="Add the Numbers" click
</mx:Application>
```

As you learned in Chapter 2, the main focus of Flex is using MXML. This allows you to write complex ActionScript code using simple and easily understood tags. However, as powerful as MXML is, there are going to be times when you will want to write ActionScript code. Those times will become apparent as we progress through this book.

An in-depth discussion of ActionScript would be a book within itself. For that reason, the goal of this chapter is to just give you a strong foundation.

> *For a more in-depth discussion of ActionScript 3.0, I recommend* Object-Oriented ActionScript 3.0 *by Peter Elst, Sas Jacobs, and Todd Yard (friends of ED, 2007). In addition, I strongly recommend* Foundation ActionScript 3.0 Animation: Making Things Move *by Keith Peters (friends of ED, 2007).*

In this chapter, you will

- Explore the fundamentals of object-oriented programming.
- Learn the ActionScript 3.0 syntax.
- Explore the structures of ActionScript 3.0.
- See how to combine ActionScript 3.0 and MXML.
- Use the Flex Debugging Perspective.
- See code refactoring and reference.

ActionScript programming concepts

Over several years, ActionScript has evolved from a fairly minor programming language that handled some Flash animation routines to its present form as a sophisticated object-oriented programming (OOP) language. However, before you can start analyzing and writing ActionScript 3.0, you will need to learn some fundamental concepts about OOP and what it is—this is what you will achieve in this section.

As you progress through this book, you will see these concepts in action. For this reason, the following explanations are just brief overviews.

Understanding what a class file is

In the early days of programming, developers relied on a technique called **procedural programming**. This meant that nearly all of the code needed for a project was contained in a relatively few files, each containing thousands, or sometimes hundreds of thousands, of lines of code that ran in pretty much a sequential fashion. This made coding, and the subsequent debugging, a nightmare sometimes. Among the early programming languages that relied on procedural programming were FORTRAN (FORmula TRANslator), Pascal, COBOL (Common Business Oriented Language), and Ada.

In the early 1970s, Dennis Ritchie of Bell Laboratories developed a fast-running procedural language called C. Approximately 10 years later, Bjarne Stroustrup, also of Bell Labs, developed the next generation of the C programming language called C++. With this, a new breed of programming was introduced called **object-oriented programming**. This served as the basis for several subsequent programming languages including Java, C# .NET, Visual Basic .NET, and now ActionScript.

> *ActionScript 2.0 was semi-object-oriented in that it used many of the concepts of OOP. However, because it was supporting ActionScript 1.0 (a decidedly non-OOP language), it didn't follow many of the accepted OOP practices.*

3

What distinguishes an OOP program from a procedural program is how the work is divided up. As I just mentioned, the procedural program uses long sequences of code. However, an OOP program breaks the work up into smaller, more specialized units called **class files**.

A class file is a self-contained program containing all the variables (called **properties**) and functions needed to perform one specialized task or a group of related tasks.

Think of your data as a car being built as it moves down an assembly line. Each station in that line performs one specialized task in the assembly of the vehicle. That station has all of the tools and information necessary to perform that one specialized task.

A class file could be analogous to one of those specialized work stations. It will perform a specialized task on your data. This task could be something like formatting the data, performing a calculation, routing the data to a different location, etc.

They also serve as the basis, or template, for something I will be discussing a lot throughout this book: **objects**. An object is a temporary copy of the class file that is stored in your computer's memory. In all projects, class files and the objects they create can work with each other as needed.

Since class files are self-contained and specialized, you can use them in any of your projects at any time. Essentially, ActionScript 3.0, like other OOP programming environments, is nothing more than a large collection of prebuilt class files. This requires a bit of explanation.

As I briefly mentioned in Chapter 2, the collection of prebuilt class files in any OOP program are referred to as the SDK, or Software Development Kit. For a programming environment like Java, the SDK comes with nearly 150,000 prebuilt class files. ActionScript 3.0 is not nearly as daunting at approximately 900 class files.

As you work with ActionScript 3.0, your library of class files will probably grow as you need to perform tasks specialized to your particular job. The ability to write your own class files is called **extensibility**. It means you are extending the abilities of the SDK. In addition, you will probably download additional class files from a variety of sources. You will find that, over time, you will be doing less coding and more research on what class files are available and how to use them. Less coding means faster project completion with fewer bugs. As you progress through this book, you will get to use a variety of class files. Bottom line: don't try to reinvent the wheel. If it is already available, use it!

All classes have two potential programming constructs attached to them: **properties** and **functions**. I say "potential" because a class file is not required to have either or both. The words "property" and "function" are OOP terms. A property is nothing more than a variable attached to a class file, and a function is a sequence of commands grouped together to perform an action that can be called upon as needed. We will refine these definitions as we progress through this chapter.

A simple example might be a class call AddNumbers. It could have two properties: num1 and num2. It could then have a function called addNumbers that takes the two properties, adds them together, and sends the result to whoever needs it.

> ActionScript 3.0 documentation identifies a third construct attached to a class file: an **event listener**, or simply **event**. It is my opinion that an event listener is just a specialized function.

Let me clarify a fine point in terminology:

In most OOP programming environments, the word **method** is more correct than function. Like a property is a variable connected with a class file, a method is a function connected with a class file. In ActionScript programming syntax, the term "function" is used in place of method. To add to the confusion, the ActionScript documentation uses the term "method" quite correctly. However, declaring a function in the code goes something like this:

```
public function createName():String
```

Thus ActionScript tends to use the terms "function" and "method" interchangeably.

To avoid confusion, I will use the word "function" throughout this book, even when referring to what most OOP environments call methods.

Compatibility with previous versions

ActionScript 3.0 is different architecturally from versions 1.0 and 2.0. Because of this, there are more than a few compatibility issues. While Flash Player 9 (the latest version of Flash Player as of the writing of this book) supports all three versions, there are some caveats.

When designing Flex or Flash applications, it is not unusual to have one SWF file call another SWF file. And it is not unusual to have one SWF file pass information to another SWF file. ActionScript 3.0–generated SWF files can have limited interaction with ActionScript 1.0 and 2.0 files. However, the ActionScript 3.0 SWF cannot read any of the functions or properties of the earlier versioned SWF files.

To communicate with SWF files created in Flash version 8, you will need to use the class file ExternalInterface to facilitate the communications. To communicate with SWF files generated with earlier versions of Flash, you will need the class file LocalConnection. If all of that sounds scary, don't worry: we are only going to work with ActionScript 3.0 in this book.

You cannot mix ActionScript 1.0/2.0 code with ActionScript 3.0.

Bottom line: if at all possible, try to avoid earlier versions of ActionScript.

Starting to use ActionScript 3.0

Time to get some hands-on practice using ActionScript 3.0:

1. If it isn't opened already, go ahead and open Flex Builder.

2. You probably created a project for Chapter 2 with the name Welcome. Since we won't be using those files in this book any longer, you have three choices for this next step:

   ■ You could just create a new MXML project, using the techniques shown in Chapter 2, supplying whatever name you choose.

   ■ You could close the Chapter 2 project as follows: Right/Ctrl-click the project name in the Flex Navigator View and select Close Project. Your screen should look like Figure 3-1.

Figure 3-1.
The closed project icon

By doing that, you can reopen the project at anytime by right-clicking it and selecting Open Project.

   ■ A third technique, if you do not need the files any longer, is to right-click the project name and select Delete. This will present you with the dialog box shown in Figure 3-2.

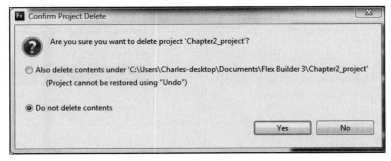

Figure 3-2. The Confirm Project Delete dialog box

Here you can disconnect the project from Flex Builder and decide whether you would want to delete the project files also. Again, this is up to you. For purposes of this book, I went ahead and selected the option that starts Also delete contents.

> *You can have multiple projects in Eclipse going on at the same time. Eclipse calls the collection of projects the **workspace**. You can create different workspaces for different collections of projects. Also, in a workspace, you can mix projects, such as a Flex project and a Java project. Throughout most of this book, we will be working with the default workspace.*

3. Using what you learned in Chapter 2, create a new project. For purposes of this exercise, call it Chapter3_project. You can accept the default settings.

You might have noticed something curious when creating the project. Flex Builder gave you the option of creating a new ActionScript Project as shown in Figure 3-3.

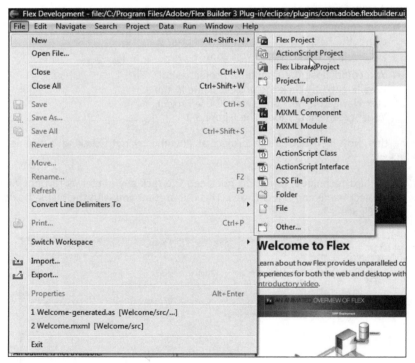

Figure 3-3. Project type options

You are probably saying to yourself, "If I am going to work with ActionScript in this chapter, wouldn't it make sense to start a new ActionScript project?"

The answer to that is NO! At least not at this stage of your learning.

If you create an ActionScript project, you preclude the use of any MXML code and can use only ActionScript. In Chapter 2, you saw a bit of the ActionScript code that MXML produces. Some programmers want to have more control over the finished code and, to accomplish that, choose this option. Since this is a book geared toward beginning users of Flex, we will not be getting into pure ActionScript environments. Instead, we will be focusing on mixing ActionScript with MXML code.

For that reason, throughout this book, we will be selecting Flex Project.

When you set up a new project for this chapter, you are once again presented with an MXML page with just a skeletal code structure.

```
<?xml version="1.0" encoding="utf-8"?>
<mx:Application xmlns:mx="http://www.adobe.com/2006/mxml" ➥
layout="absolute">

</mx:Application>
```

Let's see how this relates to our earlier discussion about class files.

MXML and ActionScript

As I stated in Chapter 2, when you convert an MXML file to a SWF file, known as **compiling it to a binary file**, Flex converts the MXML code to ActionScript 3.0. But how does it do that?

Nearly every one of the MXML tags you use has a corresponding ActionScript 3.0 class file it is tied to. Let's see a quick example of that by revisiting something we did in Chapter 2.

1. Between the two Application tags shown in the preceding section, insert a Label tag with a text attribute of "Welcome to Flex!" and an id property of "myLabel".

```
<?xml version="1.0" encoding="utf-8"?>
<mx:Applicatinx xlsm=ht:/whtp/wwaoecm20/xl CClyu=aslt"ml"
CClyulaot"bouaboueut"">
      <mx:Label text="Welcome to Flex!" id="myLabel" />
</mx:Application>
```

You saw the Label tag and got a brief explanation of the text attribute in Chapter 2. By using this simple tag, Flex actually wrote the following ActionScript code in the background:

```
var myLabel:Label = new Label();
myLabel.text = "Welcome to Flex!";
```

As I said earlier, an object is a copy of a class file in memory. You can almost think of it as a very sophisticated variable with properties and functions. When the object is created, we call that an **instance** of the class file. Since it is in memory, and we can have multiple objects in that memory, we have to have a way of identifying them. We call the identifying name the **object reference**.

*If you have used Flash, you may have seen the phrase (located in the Properties panel) called **instance name**. "Instance name" and "object reference" mean exactly the same thing.*

In the preceding example, myLabel would be the object reference. The only difference is that in MXML it is called the id. Beyond that, these MXML and ActionScript code examples accomplish exactly the same thing.

Notice that the MXML command is shorter than the ActionScript command. While saving one line of code may not seem like much to you, imagine the savings in increasingly complex situations. You will see that as you progress through this book.

Let's look at further evidence of the connection between ActionScript and MXML. You saw this in Chapter 2, but it is worth the review.

2. Click anywhere inside the Label tag,

3. Press the F1 key (on a Mac, use Shift+Cmd+?).

4. Click the Label (mx.controls.Label) link in the Help View.

This brings up the ActionScript 3.0 Label class. If you scroll down the Public Properties area, you will find the text property, as shown in Figure 3-4.

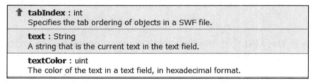

↑ tabIndex : int
Specifies the tab ordering of objects in a SWF file.

text : String
A string that is the current text in the text field.

textColor : uint
The color of the text in a text field, in hexadecimal format.

Figure 3-4. The text attribute

That entire list of properties is available to the Label MXML tag you are using, as well as an equally long list of functions, events, and styles. All the tag is doing is serving as a proxy for ActionScript code. For each tag, there is a corresponding ActionScript class file and, as you saw in Chapter 2, Flex is writing the intricacies of ActionScript code in the background.

Many beginners to Flex treat MXML and ActionScript as two separate subjects. However, as I hope you are starting to see, they are two means to the same end.

In a Flex environment, you can achieve the results you want in one of three ways:

- Using just MXML
- Using just ActionScript code
- Using a combination of MXML and ActionScript code

From my experience, the third option is the one most often used and where our focus will be in this book.

Let's see how to combine the two together.

5. Make the following alterations in bold to the code:

```
<?xml version="1.0" encoding="utf-8"?>
<mx:Application xmlns:mx="http://www.adobe.com/2006/mxml" ➥
layout="vertical">
    <mx:TextInput id="myName" />
    <mx:Label text="{myName.text}" id="myLabel" />
</mx:Application>
```

The first thing we did here was change the layout to vertical in the Application tag. We will be discussing that more in the next chapter. For now, however, just understand that we did that to avoid having to use x- and y-coordinates in our objects.

The MXML tag

```
<mx:TextInput id="myName" />
```

instantiates the TextInput class (a form control used to input text) into an object with the reference of myName. If you were to study the documentation of the TextInput class, like we did with the Label class earlier, you would discover that it has a text property also and that the property works as it did in the Label class (it contains the content of the object).

But notice that in the next line we set the text property of the Label object, myLabel, to equal the text property of the TextInput object, myName.

If you are new to OOP, you might be curious about the dot between myName and the text property. This is a standard OOP syntax called **dot notation**. In dot notation, the name of the object you are referencing is on the left side of the dot. On the right side of the dot is the name of the property or function within that object you are calling. So in this case, we are calling the TextInput object with the id (object reference) of myName and asking the text property of that object to send its result.

Notice that we surrounded the text property of myLabel with curly braces. This is called **data binding**, and it is how one object can ask for data from another object in MXML.

6. Go ahead and save your work, and then click the Run Application button in Flex Builder (just as a reminder, it is the green circle with the white arrow in it).

Figure 3-5 shows what happens when you type text into the TextInput object.

Figure 3-5. The results of the data binding

> *We will not be concerned about formatting until later on in the book.*

As you type in the TextInput object, the Label object reads the text property and makes its own text property equal to it in real time.

But what about mixing in ActionScript code?

Mixing MXML and ActionScript code

As powerful as MXML is, the real power of Flex isn't unleashed until you combine MXML and your own ActionScript 3.0 code. This will become obvious as you progress through this book. In this section, I am going to show you how you combine it.

As a quick note, you can place your own ActionScript code either within the MXML file or, if you prefer, in an external file with the file extension .as. For now, keep it within the MXML file.

> *Do not confuse writing your own custom ActionScript code with creating a class file. Those are two completely different processes. We will be talking about class files later on in this book.*

In order to add custom ActionScript code to our existing MXML file, we need to use an MXML tag called the Script tag. This in turn sets up a CDATA tag which tells the compiler to treat its contents with a different process.

> *CDATA is common to XML files. It indicates that there is programming code within it and to not treat its content as part of the XML file.*

The exact mechanics happen in the background and are really not important here. For now, you'll add a Script tag under the Application tag.

1. Under the opening Application tag, create the tag `<mx:Script>.<$I~<mx\:Script> tag>`.

> *The Script tag does not have to be placed right under the Application tag. This is just a practice that has emerged in Flex programming.*

```
<?xml version="1.0" encoding="utf-8"?>
<mx:Application xmlns:mx="http://www.adobe.com/2006/mxml" ➥
layout="vertical">
```

```
<mx:Script>
    <![CDATA[

    ]]>
</mx:Script>
<mx:TextInput id="myName" />
<mx:Label text="{myName.text}" id="myLabel" />
</mx:Application>
```

We will set up our ActionScript code inside of the CDATA tag. The first thing we will do is set a **variable**. A variable is a container in memory that holds data.

We begin naming a variable with the keyword var. A **keyword** is a word reserved by a program for specific use. Table 3-1 shows the keywords used by ActionScript.

Table 3-1. ActionScript keywords

break	final	namespace	super
case	finally	native	switch
catch	for	new	this
class	function	null	throw
const	get	override	to
continue	if	package	true
default	implements	private	try
delete	import	protected	typeof
do	in	public	use
dynamic	include	return	var
each	instanceof	set	void
else	interface	static	while
extends	internal	with	
false	is		

Note that because these words are reserved by ActionScript, you cannot use them as names for your own variables or functions. If you use one of these words, they should be color coded blue in Flex Builder 3.

   2. Within the CDATA section, type var.

After using the keyword var, we have to give the variable a name. For our purposes, let's call it myText.

3. After the keyword var, press the spacebar and type myText.

```
<mx:Script>
    <![CDATA[
        var myText
]><m:c</xSrp>ritt>
```

Logic would dictate that if you liken a variable to a container, and that a container is designed to hold only a specific type of item, then a variable should hold only a specific type of item. But how do you tell a variable to hold only certain types of items?

In programming terms, this is known as **strict typing**. It means that you assign the variable to a class file. The properties and functions of that class file tell the variable what it can and cannot do.

The most common class assignments are

- Strings: These are sequences of characters and spaces that are enclosed in double quotes (" "). For instance "Welcome to Flex!" or "Today is 6/19/2007".
- Numbers: This is a broad category that could mean an integer (a whole number) such as 12 or 5, or it could mean a decimal number such as 12.5 or 5.678.
- Boolean: This special type has only two values: true or false.

This has important meaning. Let's assume that you defined two variables, num1 and num2, as type Strings. Now, later on assume that you try to use the following formula:

```
num1 * num2;
```

> *If you are not familiar with arithmetic operators, + means add, - means sub-tract, * means multiply, and / means divide. If you want to use exponents, ^ denotes an exponent.*

ActionScript will not know what you are talking about because the class file, String, makes no provision for multiplication. The variable has no means of figuring it out on its own.

Older versions of programs like Visual Basic and the last version of ActionScript did not require strict typing. So if you wanted to multiply the two numbers, the program might use reasoning something like this:

"Well, let's see. num1 looks like a number, so maybe I can use the class Number. Same goes for num2. So if I use Number for the class for both, that might tell me what to do with the asterisk."

Needless to say, you can imagine that using reasoning like that for every variable operation can drink up an enormous amount of processing power and make your programs run far less efficiently. Also, it could make for a lot of programming errors. A formula may end up with a String when it is expecting a Number.

> ActionScript 3.0 does not absolutely require strict typing. However, for the reason stated previously, it is not a good idea to leave it out. Also, there are plans to make it strict in future updates.

So how do you tell it what type it is?

4. After typing your variable name, type a colon (:). This brings up a list of class files that can be used as data types (see Figure 3-6).

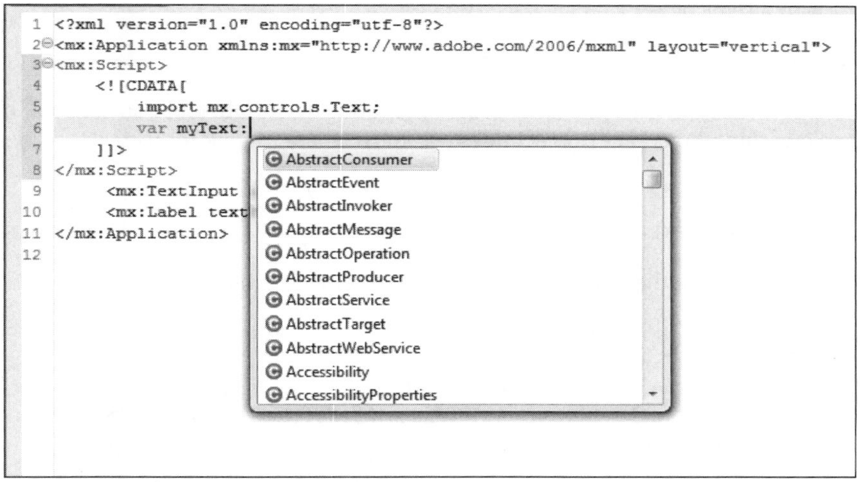

```
1 <?xml version="1.0" encoding="utf-8"?>
2 <mx:Application xmlns:mx="http://www.adobe.com/2006/mxml" layout="vertical">
3 <mx:Script>
4     <![CDATA[
5         import mx.controls.Text;
6         var myText:
7     ]]>
8 </mx:Script>
9     <mx:TextInput
10    <mx:Label text
11 </mx:Application>
12
```

AbstractConsumer
AbstractEvent
AbstractInvoker
AbstractMessage
AbstractOperation
AbstractProducer
AbstractService
AbstractTarget
AbstractWebService
Accessibility
AccessibilityProperties

Figure 3-6. The class file list

> A note about naming conventions here. By tradition, class files always begin with a capital letter. Names that you create, such as variable names, are all lowercase except for mid-capitalization, no spaces, begin with a letter (not a number), and can use the nonalphanumeric characters $ (dollar sign) or _ (underscore).

5. Select the String class by either scrolling down to it or just type str.

6. Once String is highlighted, you can press Enter to complete it.

Your variable should now look as follows:

```
var myText:String
```

Once the variable has been declared, it is a good idea to assign it an initial value. This is called **initialization**, and it is a good programming practice even though ActionScript assigns default values of 0 to numeric variables, empty strings (" ") to String variables, and false to Boolean variables.

7. Type = "*your name*".

```
<![CDATA[
    var myText:String = "Charles Brown";
]]>
```

The single equal sign (=) is often known as an **assignment operator**. This means that whatever is on the right side of the equal sign is assigned to the left side of the equal sign.

In programming, a **statement** is a command for the program to do something. Here we are commanding ActionScript to create a String variable called myText and assigning it a value of your name. While not strictly required, it is a good idea to end ActionScript statements with a semicolon (;).

8. Type a semicolon to end the statement.

You are now ready to give your little program a test. However, before you can, you must change one thing. Your Label object does not know where to look for its text.

9. Change the data binding so that it looks as follows:

```
<mx:Label text="{myText}" id="myLabel" />
```

The text property of the object will now use the String variable myText.

Your complete code should look as follows:

```
<?xml version="1.0" encoding="utf-8"?>
<mx:Application xmlns:mx="http://www.adobe.com/2006/mxml" ➥
layout="vertical">
    <mx:Script>
        <![CDATA[
            var myText:String = "Charles Brown";
        ]]>
    </mx:Script>
    <mx:TextInput id="myName" />
    <mx:Label text="{myText}" id="myLabel" />
</mx:Application>
```

10. Save and run your project. Your results should resemble Figure 3-7.

Figure 3-7. The results of our code

While the TextInput tag is still there, it is not being accessed by anything in the application. Normally, you would just delete or comment it out. Let's leave it for now for something we will be doing in a bit.

When you saved your file, before running it, you may have noticed two warning messages in the Problems View located at the bottom of Flex Builder (see Figure 3-8).

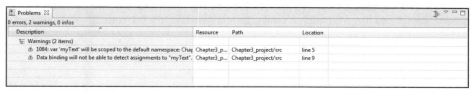

Figure 3-8. The Problems View with warnings

We will be discussing these a bit later in this chapter. However, just understand for now that when the warnings have an exclamation point in a yellow triangle beside them, and not a red x (which is known as an error), your application won't be prevented from running. For the time being, you can disregard them.

In Chapter 2, I spoke about the importance of the Outline View. As you start to build your applications, it is a good idea to keep an eye on your Outline View located in the lower-left side of Flex Builder. As you can see in Figure 3-9, this View gives you a visual representation of the hierarchy of the structure of your MXML page.

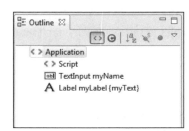

Figure 3-9.
The Outline View

Comments

It is always a good idea to comment your code. That way when either you or another programmer looks at your code, it is easy to see the purpose of various parts.

Commenting syntax is common to most programs, and two types of comments are supported:

- Single-line comments:

  ```
  // This is an example of a single-line comment
  ```

- Multiple-line comments:

  ```
  /* This is an example of a multiple-line comment,
  which encompasses several lines in one block */
  ```

It's a good practice to include a header comment indicating when and why your file was created.

```
/* This file was created on 6/20/2007
       by Charles E. Brown
       to demonstrate the parts of ActionScript 3.0 code */
```

You can also comment MXML tags. However, rather than use the two techniques just shown, you would use a technique similar to commenting XHTML code:

```
<!--       -->
```

Flex Builder will assist you in adding comments to MXML tags.

Normally you use comments, as shown here, to add explanations and descriptions to your code. However, they have a second use: to disable code temporarily not being used. This is very handy when testing. Rather than delete the code, you can just comment it out. Then, when you want to use it again, you just remove the comment. Here is an example:

1. Highlight the TextInput tag you created earlier.
2. Right/Ctrl-click and select Source ➤ Toggle Block Comment (or you could press Ctrl+Shift+C/Shift+Cmd+C). Your tag should now look as follows:

```
<!--<mx:TextInput id="myName" /> -->
```

When the file is converted to a SWF file, the comments are ignored and do not add to the size of the file.

If you are working along with the examples in this book, why don't you go ahead and add some comments to the code file now.

Using the trace() function

If you have ever done programming in Flash, you probably used the trace() function. This was a handy little tool that, during code development, would send an output of some sort to the Output window. You could use it to test whether variables had the proper values, whether a function was being called properly, and so on.

Happily, the trace() function is still available in ActionScript 3.0. However, because you are not working in Flash, there is no Output window. Instead, the output of the trace() function is sent to the **Console View** of Eclipse. In programming parlance, this is sometimes referred to as **console output**. In other words, this is the same as sending the output to the command prompt of the operating system. Eclipse is just doing the work for you by accessing the command prompt and handling all of the behind-the-scenes tasks for you.

Let's take a look at the documentation for this feature.

1. Select Help ➤ Find in Language Reference.
2. Click the Index link at the top of the library as shown in Figure 3-10.

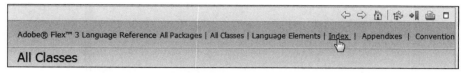

Figure 3-10. The Index link in the Language Reference

3. Click the letter T along the line marked Symbols.

As an alternative function, you can expand the Index *listing in the left pane and select* T *from there.*

4. Scroll down to the trace(. . . rest) function and click the link to go to details about using it. You should see the screen shown in Figure 3-11.

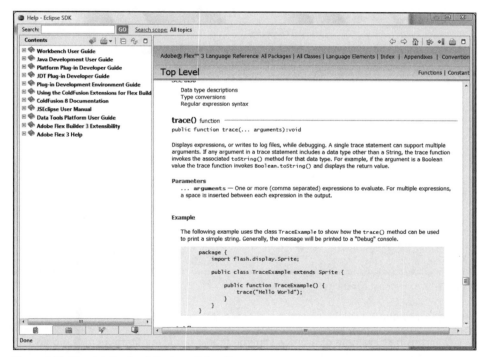

Figure 3-11. The details about the trace() function

From the example, you can see the that the trace() function is one of a group of functions called **top-level functions**. A top-level function is one that is available to all parts of your code automatically without the need to reference a class file or use an import statement.

> *You will learn more about* import *statements as you progress through this book.*

In other words, you can just call a top-level function whenever one is needed. They are sometimes referred to as **global functions**.

There are also **top-level constants**. These are values that never change and are global. For instance, when a value is not a number the constant NaN is called. If you look in the upper-right corner of the Language Reference, you will see the Constants hyperlink. Click it, and you will see the screen in Figure 3-12.

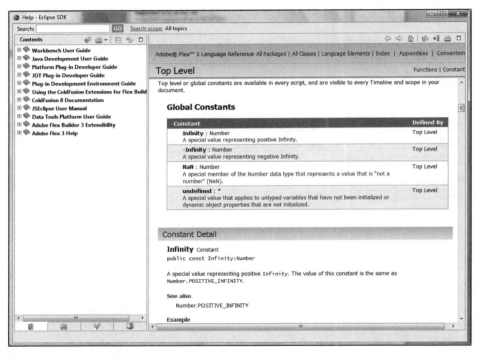

Figure 3-12. The global constants

Let's return to our Script block and put a trace statement into it.

5. In this first example of a trace statement, just put some literal text (the bold text enclosed in quotes) into it.

```
<mx:Script>
    <![CDATA[
        var myText:String = "Welcome to Flex!";
        trace("Welcome to Flex 3 and ActionScript 3.0");
    ]]>
</mx:Script>
```

To use the trace function, you need to use the Debug button and not the Run Application button. If you use the Run Application button, the trace statement will not run.

The Debug button is to the right of the Run Application button and has a little bug icon on it, as you can see in Figure 3-13.

Figure 3-13.
The Debug button

6. Save the file, and then click the Debug button.

You should see the browser open as if you clicked the Run button. However, if you return to Flex Builder, you should see the Console View, located along the bottom, with the contents of the trace() function, as shown in Figure 3-14.

```
Problems  Console ☒
Chapter3_project [Flex Application] file:/C:/Users/Charles-desktop/Documents/Flex%20Builder%203/Chapter3_project/bin/Chapter3_project.html
[SWF] C:\Users\Charles-desktop\Documents\Flex Builder 3\Chapter3_project\bin\Chapter3_project.swf - 536,074 bytes after dec
Welcome to Flex 3 and ActionScript 3.0
```

Figure 3-14. The Console View

We will be using the trace statement a great deal as we move through this book. I will also be showing you some useful techniques to use it to test your code.

Functions

Odds are pretty good that you want your ActionScript to do a bit more than fill in a label from a hardwired variable. The real workhorses of any program are the functions. A function is simply a block of code that does a specific job and can be called at anytime.

Imagine for a moment that you need to add two numbers together, and that this job needs to be done several times in the code. It would be terribly inefficient to keep writing the same code over and over again. Instead, you build a function once and then call it every time that particular job needs to be performed. While this seems like a relatively simple task, imagine needing to do it several hundred times in the application. We would need to write the same code over several hundred times. This could add a lot of unnecessary code, overhead, and debugging.

There are two basic types of functions: functions that just perform a job, and functions that return a value to whoever is calling it.

> As I have stated earlier in this chapter, ActionScript tends to use the word "function" instead of "method" in its syntax. However, most OOP programs use the word "method." They essentially mean the same thing, and I will be using the word "function" in the text.

The first line of a function is called the **signature**. After the signature, you put an opening and closing curly brace ({ }) that will group the code that the function needs to execute. This is called the function's **body**.

> *For many reasons, ActionScript 2.0 supported multiple syntaxes for declaring a function. This frequently led to confusion for programmers. ActionScript 3.0 has standardized to the syntax shown here.*

1. Below the variable declarations in the Script block, insert the following function declaration:

```
function createMyName():String
{

}
```

> *Flex Builder will automatically place a closing curly brace when you type an opening curly brace and press Enter.*

There is a lot to talk about here. The function, named createMyName, returns information of type String to whoever calls it. String is called the function's **return type**. If the function does not need to return anything, we would give it a return type of void.

> *In ActionScript 2.0, this return type required an initial capital letter (Void). In ActionScript 3.0, it is all lowercase.*

2. Let's add some code to the function's body.

```
function createMyName():String
{
    var myFirstName:String = "Charles";
    var myLastName:String = "Brown";
    return myFirstName + " " + myLastName;
}
```

The first two lines are just setting two String variables as we had before. The only difference is that we are setting them inside of the function. It is interesting to note that variables set inside of a function are called **local variables** and exist only as long as the function is running. Variables outside of a function are called **instance variables** and exist as long as the application is running.

The last line of the body uses the keyword return. When a function has a return type other than void, you must specify what is returned with the keyword return. If the return type is void, you cannot use the keyword return to return a value. They are mutually exclusive.

As an example, comment out the return line by using the single-line comment //.

   3. Save the application. You should see the error shown in Figure 3-15 in the Problems View.

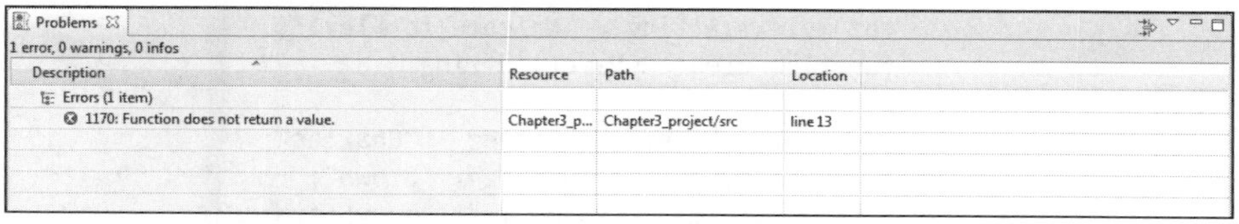

Figure 3-15. The Problems View showing a value not being returned by the function

   4. Remove the comment for the return line.

The code following the return line is an example of a **concatenation**. This is a fancy word for connecting multiple items together.

   5. Connect the first variable (myFirstName) to quotes with a space to put a space between the first and last names, and then connect that to the second variable (myLastName). The items are connected using the plus (+) character.

   Your finished Script block should look as follows:

```
<mx:Script>
    <![CDATA[
        public var myText:String = "Welcome to Flex!";
        function createMyName():String
        {
            var myFirstName:String = "Charles";
            var myLastName:String = "Brown";
            return myFirstName + " " + myLastName;
        }
    ]]>
</mx:Script>
```

In a concatenation, everything (whether it is a number or a string) is converted into type String.

We need to do one last thing before this will work properly. In order to do its job, a function must be called by something. The calling code simply uses the name of the function, followed by an open and closed parenthesis. (()). In the next section we will use the parentheses to pass arguments, or parameters, to the function.

6. Modify your Label object as follows:

```
<mx:Label text="{createMyName()}" id="myLabel" />
```

Your code should now look as follows:

```
<?xml version="1.0" encoding="utf-8"?>
<mx:Application xmlns:mx="http://www.adobe.com/2006/mxml" ➥
layout="vertical">
    <mx:Script>
        <![CDATA[
            var myText:String = "Welcome to Flex!";
            function createMyName():String
            {
                var myFirstName:String = "Charles";
                var myLastName:String = "Brown";
                return myFirstName + " " + myLastName;
            }
        ]]>
    </mx:Script>
    <mx:Label text="{createMyName()}" id="myLabel" />
</mx:Application>
```

7. Run the application now; you should see the returned values in the Label object (see Figure 3-16).

Figure 3-16.
The results of the function

That's great for simple functions, but what about if the function needs more information to do the job? Let's have a look at how we can pass values (usually called **parameters** or **arguments**) to a function to enable it to perform more complex tasks.

Passing parameters

A function often needs to be supplied with information before it can do its job properly. The caller needs to send it that information as parameters, and the function then needs to process them as necessary. Let's take a look at an example.

1. Change your function as follows:

```
<mx:Script>
    <![CDATA[
        var myText:String = "Welcome to Flex!";
        function createMyName(myFirstName:String, ➥
myLastName:String):String
        {
            return  myFirstName + " " + myLastName;
```

```
        }
    ]]>
</mx:Script>
```

Notice that in this case, you removed the two variables and replaced them with parameters inside of the parentheses. The parameters must specify not only the order in which they must be sent, but also the types. In this case, the function is expecting the first name and the last name, in that order, and both of them must be of type `String`. This requires an adjustment to your function call in the Label object.

2. Make the following changes to your Label object:

```
<mx:Label text="{createMyName('Charles', 'Brown')}" id="myLabel" />
```

Here the necessary parameters are in the function call in the order that they are expected. However, there is a small trap here that you are going to run into frequently. Normally, you would pass strings using double quotes (" "). When you select the text property in MXML, you see this:

```
text = " "
```

The text value is automatically a string.

> *MXML handles nearly all properties as a string.*

However, in this case, there would be a problem. The function is expecting two separate strings passed to it: one for first name and one for last name. Thus, you will need to have a smaller string within a larger string. In a situation like this, you will need to use the single quotes (' ') to identify the substrings.

If you were to surround the first and last names with double quotes, it would confuse the SWF compiler as to where the property ends, and you would get errors. If you did use the double quotes, you would get the message shown in Figure 3-17 in the Problems View.

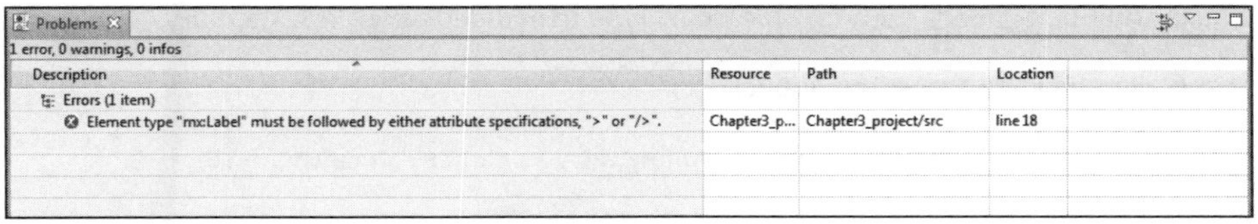

Description	Resource	Path	Location
Errors (1 item)			
Element type "mx:Label" must be followed by either attribute specifications, ">" or "/>".	Chapter3_p...	Chapter3_project/src	line 18

1 error, 0 warnings, 0 infos

Figure 3-17. Errors in the Problems View

Unlike the exclamations you saw earlier, and which we will be addressing again shortly, a red x means that there are serious errors that will prevent the SWF file from compiling properly. If you go to run it, you will get a further warning. If you bypass that warning by answering Yes to the "Continue Launch?" question, you end up just relaunching the previous version of the SWF.

If you made changes to your code to see this error, change the substrings in the function call back to single quotes.

3. Run the project now; it should compile fine, and you should see the name as you did before.

Let's adjust things a bit in order to further demonstrate some of the concepts we are discussing here.

4. Delete the existing function, and in its place put the following one (there will be an intentional error in it):

```
function addNumbers(number1:Number, number2:Number):Number
{
    var sum:int = number1 + number2;
    return "The sum of the numbers is: " + sum;
}
```

5. Change your Label object as follows:

```
<mx:Label text="{addNumbers(2, 3)}" id="myLabel" />
```

There are a few things worth mentioning here. First of all, since you are passing numbers, the quotes, either single or double, are not needed around the parameters in the function call. Also, the return type of the function is now Number.

Also, it is worth talking about the type int assigned to the sum variable. This is a new type for ActionScript 3.0. Types String, Number, Boolean, int (integer), and uint (unsigned integer) are referred to as the **primitive types**. We use the word "primitive" because they are the types that all other, more complex, types are built on.

Type int will allow you to save integers between approximately –2.14 million and 2.14 million. Type uint allows you to save values between 0 and 4.29 million.

You might be wondering why the three types Number, int, and uint are needed. It has to do with storage space. Type Number will block out enough room to hold a number up to 179 with over 300 zeros after it. That is one huge number! Type int, because it holds much smaller numbers, needs a lot less memory. Type uint needs even less memory.

6. Go ahead and save the application.

Whoops! Problems prevent it from compiling, as you can see in Figure 3-18.

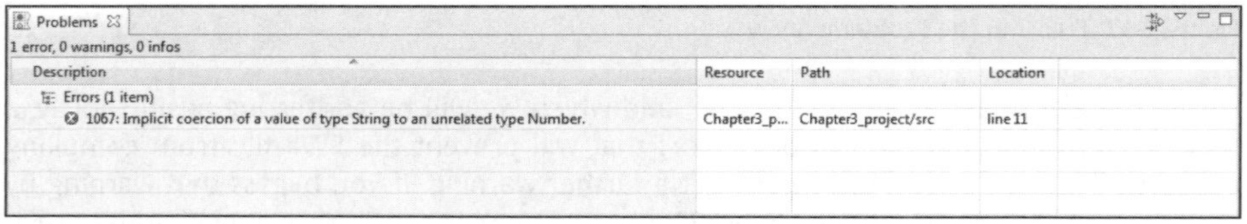

Problems ⊠				
1 error, 0 warnings, 0 infos				
Description	Resource	Path	Location	
⊟ Errors (1 item)				
⊗ 1067: Implicit coercion of a value of type String to an unrelated type Number.	Chapter3_p...	Chapter3_project/src	line 11	

Figure 3-18. Implicit coercion error

But what went wrong here?

Take a few moments and see if you can discover what the problem is.

Give up?

You will recall earlier that I said a concatenation turns the returned value into a string, even if there are nonstrings in it. So the function is now returning a string. However, if you look at the return type of the function, it is still declared as a Number. You need to change the return type to String if you are going to do a concatenation.

    7. Change the return type of the function to String.

Notice in the Problems View, shown in Figure 3-18, that this called an **implicit coercion**. This is fancy way of saying that you are trying to take one type of data (in this case, a String) and pass it as another type (in this case, a Number).

After making the change, run the application again. It should work fine.

As you can see, ActionScript 3.0 enforces the rules pretty strictly. The end result, however, is code that runs more efficiently and more bug free.

Handling events

Up to this point, all of your code has run as soon as you started the application. But many times, you may not want some of the code to run until an **event** has happened.

An event could be a click of the mouse button, a press of a key, a roll of the mouse over an object, an application loading, and so on. All events have to have two parts: an **event listener** and an **event handler**.

An event listener is something that is doing just as it says, listening for a certain event to happen. Once the event happens, the event listener needs to let a function know to do its job. That function is the event handler.

If we look at the ActionScript documentation, you will see that nearly all classes have a set of events particular to that class.

Let's go back to the Language Reference found in Help.

Locate the Button class and, once there, scroll down to the Events section shown in Figure 3-19.

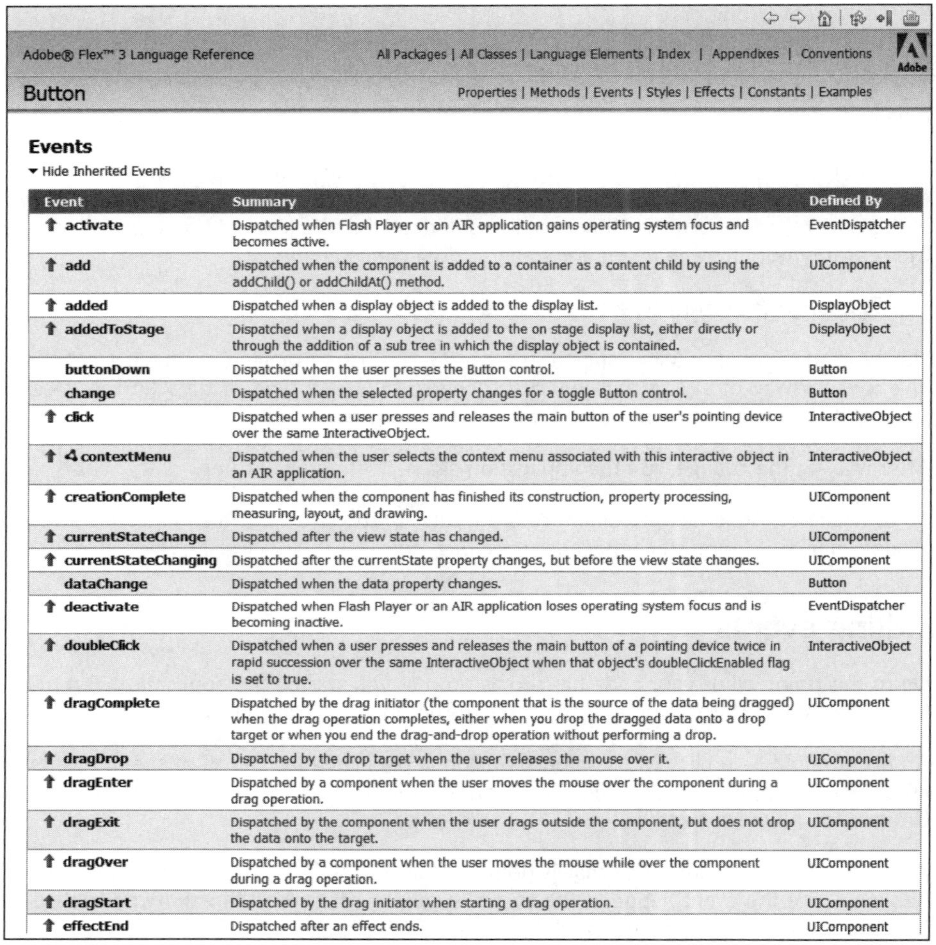

Adobe® Flex™ 3 Language Reference   All Packages | All Classes | Language Elements | Index | Appendixes | Conventions

Button   Properties | Methods | Events | Styles | Effects | Constants | Examples

Events

▼ Hide Inherited Events

Event	Summary	Defined By
↑ **activate**	Dispatched when Flash Player or an AIR application gains operating system focus and becomes active.	EventDispatcher
↑ **add**	Dispatched when the component is added to a container as a content child by using the addChild() or addChildAt() method.	UIComponent
↑ **added**	Dispatched when a display object is added to the display list.	DisplayObject
↑ **addedToStage**	Dispatched when a display object is added to the on stage display list, either directly or through the addition of a sub tree in which the display object is contained.	DisplayObject
buttonDown	Dispatched when the user presses the Button control.	Button
change	Dispatched when the selected property changes for a toggle Button control.	Button
↑ **click**	Dispatched when a user presses and releases the main button of the user's pointing device over the same InteractiveObject.	InteractiveObject
↑ **contextMenu**	Dispatched when the user selects the context menu associated with this interactive object in an AIR application.	InteractiveObject
↑ **creationComplete**	Dispatched when the component has finished its construction, property processing, measuring, layout, and drawing.	UIComponent
↑ **currentStateChange**	Dispatched after the view state has changed.	UIComponent
↑ **currentStateChanging**	Dispatched after the currentState property changes, but before the view state changes.	UIComponent
dataChange	Dispatched when the data property changes.	Button
↑ **deactivate**	Dispatched when Flash Player or an AIR application loses operating system focus and is becoming inactive.	EventDispatcher
↑ **doubleClick**	Dispatched when a user presses and releases the main button of a pointing device twice in rapid succession over the same InteractiveObject when that object's doubleClickEnabled flag is set to true.	InteractiveObject
↑ **dragComplete**	Dispatched by the drag initiator (the component that is the source of the data being dragged) when the drag operation completes, either when you drop the dragged data onto a drop target or when you end the drag-and-drop operation without performing a drop.	UIComponent
↑ **dragDrop**	Dispatched by the drop target when the user releases the mouse over it.	UIComponent
↑ **dragEnter**	Dispatched by a component when the user moves the mouse over the component during a drag operation.	UIComponent
↑ **dragExit**	Dispatched by the component when the user drags outside the component, but does not drop the data onto the target.	UIComponent
↑ **dragOver**	Dispatched by a component when the user moves the mouse while over the component during a drag operation.	UIComponent
↑ **dragStart**	Dispatched by the drag initiator when starting a drag operation.	UIComponent
↑ **effectEnd**	Dispatched after an effect ends.	UIComponent

Figure 3-19. The events associated with the Button class

> *I clicked the* Show Inherited Events *link before taking the screenshot shown in Figure 3-19. Class files fit into a hierarchy of other class files. Due to a feature of OOP called* ***inheritance****, you can access properties, functions, and events of other class files in the hierarchy. The rightmost column shows you what class the event, property, and function comes from.*

The most common event associated with the `Button` object is `click`, which is triggered when users press and release their mouse button.

Let's make some changes to our small application to see this in action.

1. Add a Button object under the Label object as follows:

```
<mx:Label text="{addSum(2, 3)}" id="myLabel" />
<mx:Button label="Add the Numbers"/>
```

If you researched the Button class, you would see that label property gives the button its text.

One of the quirks of ActionScript 3.0 is it sometimes gives the same name to a class file and a property of a class file. For instance, as we have seen, there is a class file called Label. However, in the Button class, there is a property called label. To tell the difference, remember class files begin with a capital letter (Label) and a property begins with a lowercase letter (label).

We will be talking extensively about events in Chapter 5. However, for the time being, MXML offers us a real easy way to handle events using an **inline handler**. This means we can embed the handler right into the MXML tag.

Just as a simple demonstration, say you wanted the text property of the Label object to change when the Button object is clicked.

2. Add the following code to the Button tag:

```
<mx:Button label="Add the Numbers" click="myLabel.text = ➥
'Button Has Been Clicked!'"/>
```

Notice that once again we have a situation of a string within a string and need to use the single quotes. In this case, we told the Button object that when the click event happens, send a message to the Label object to change its text property to the text "Button Has Been Clicked!".

3. Run the application and click the button. Your screen should resemble Figure 3-20.

Figure 3-20. After the Button object is clicked

The combination event listener/handler found inside of an MXML tag is good for simple tasks as you just saw. However, if you want to accomplish more complex tasks, you will need to write your own handler.

An event handler is really nothing more than a function that responds to an event. There are several different ways you can write a handler, and the next chapter will be discussing this in a bit more detail. For the time being, let's look at a simple example.

4. Modify the function so that it looks as follows:

```
<mx:Script>
    <![CDATA[
        var myText:String = "Welcome to Flex!";
        function addNumbers(number1:Number, number2:Number):void
        {
            var sum:int = number1 + number2;
            myText = "The sum of the numbers is" + " " + sum;
        }
    ]]>
</mx:Script>
```

Notice that inside of the function you didn't preface the variable myText with the keyword var. We only use var when creating a new variable. However, all we are doing here is assigning a value to the instance variable myText.

Two things are worth mentioning here: The results of the function will now be sent to the variable myText, which we declared earlier in this chapter. We have also set the return type of the function to be void. Isn't this a contradiction from what I stated earlier? Isn't the function returning a string?

The answer to that is no. It is not returning a value to the caller, and thus not modifying the caller in any way. All it is doing is sending the information to a variable that has already been declared.

In order to get this example to work, we need to make two additional modifications to the MXML tags. We need to bind the Label object to the myText variable, and we need to make the call to the addSum() function when the Button object is clicked.

```
<mx:Label text="{myText}" id="myLabel" />
<mx:Button label="Add the Numbers" click="addNumbers(2, 3)"/>
```

When the application starts to run the variable myText, it initializes with the String "Welcome to Flex!". Subsequently, the Label object sets its text property to equal myText.

When the Button object is clicked, it calls the addSum() function, sending it two numbers, 2 and 3.

When the function runs, it sends its results to the myText variable, replacing the string, which should subsequently change the text property of the Label object.

5. All seems in order. Go ahead and run the application and click the Button object.

Huh? Nothing changed?

You have just run into an interesting quirk of ActionScript 3.0 and one of the reasons for those exclamation points in the Problems View as shown in Figure 3-21.

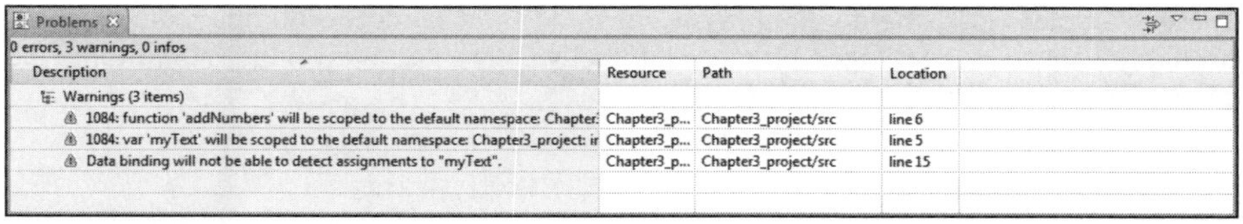

Figure 3-21. The bindable warnings in the Problems View

Using the [Bindable] tag

When the preceding application started, the variable myText broadcasted its original contents to whoever needed it (in this case, just the Label object myLabel). However, the variable does not automatically transmit changes to its value when it is updated unless you specifically tell it to do that. In order to accomplish that, we need to use an ActionScript **metadata tag** called [Bindable].

Simply put, a metadata tag is an instruction to ActionScript 3.0. When the ActionScript compiler sees the metadata tag, it automatically writes the necessary code, in the background, so that when the contents of the variable changes, the changes will be broadcast to anyone using that content.

You must put the [Bindable] metadata tag before each variable that will need to broadcast. If you don't, the Problems View will remind you with a warning with an exclamation point. This type of warning is just an advisory and will not stop the application from compiling into a SWF file.

1. Add the [Bindable] tag to the Script block as follows:

```
<mx:Script>
    <![CDATA[
        [Bindable]
        var myText:String = "Welcome to Flex!";
        function addSum(number1:Number, number2:Number):void
        {

            var sum:int = number1 + number2;
            myText = "The sum of the numbers is" + " " + sum;
        }
    ]]>
</mx:Script>
```

Once you save the application, the data binding advisory should disappear from the Problems View.

2. Run the application now.

The Label object should change to reflect the results of the function when you click the Button object. But you will notice that there are still warnings in the Problems View. Hold tight! We will be addressing those shortly.

These examples work fine if you always want to add the same two numbers. But you will probably want to make things a bit more interactive. With just a few minor alterations, you can easily accomplish that.

Adding interactivity

Let's create a way for users to enter the two numbers they want to add. For that, we will turn to a class file we briefly looked at earlier in this chapter: the TextInput class.

1. Right above the Label tag, add two new TextInput tags (remember, the tags reflect the corresponding class files). Since you will need to interact with them using ActionScript, you need to give them id properties. For the purposes of this example, inputNum1 and inputNum2 will do the job nicely. Also, set the width to 50 pixels.

```
<mx:TextInput id="inputNum1" width="50" />
<mx:TextInput id="inputNum2" width="50" />
<mx:Label text="{myText}" id="myLabel" />
<mx:Button label="Add the Numbers" click="addNumbers(2, 3)"/>
```

> *By default, all measurements in Flex are pixels.*

2. Run the application. Your form should look like Figure 3-22.

Figure 3-22. The finished form

Of course, if you click the button, it will still add just 2 and 3, regardless of what you put into the fields, because you never changed the event that the Button object broadcasts.

3. Return to the application and alter that event as follows:

```
<mx:Button label="Add the Numbers" click=➡
"addNumbers(inputNum1.text, inputNum2.text)"/>
```

4. Save your work.

You should see a red x pop up on the line of the code and in the Problems View (see Figure 3-23).

Description	Resource	Path	Location
⚠ Errors (1 item)			
⊗ 1067: Implicit coercion of a value of type String to an unrelated type Number.	Chapter3_p...	Chapter3_project/src	line 18

Figure 3-23. The error generated by the most recent code changes

Whoops again! Same problem as before: implicit coercion.

The text property is a string. You passed two strings into the Button object's event, and then you passed those strings into the function. But the two parameters of the function are defined as type Number. So somewhere you need to convert the contents of the two text properties (which by definition are strings) into type Number. This is easily accomplished with a simple modification.

5. Modify the code as follows:

```
<mx:Button label="Add the Numbers" click="addNumbers➡
(Number(inputNum1.text), Number(inputNum2.text))"/>
```

The Number and String classes are sometimes referred to as **wrapper classes**. The class looks and acts like a function. By wrapping a number that is a string in the Number class, the class converts the string to a number. You could also use the String class to convert a number to a string.

6. Run the code now.

It should work fine. Change the numbers and click the button again. You do not need to restart the application each time.

Flex has some remarkable ways of handling unexpected events, called **exceptions**. Try putting text strings into the two TextInput fields. Rather than crashing, as many programs do, the application simply returns 0 as shown in Figure 3-24.

Figure 3-24.
Putting strings in the number fields

> As an exercise, try building an application in which the user inputs two numbers and, when the button is clicked, the application returns the sum, difference, product, and quotient of the two numbers. Then try building an application that has separate buttons to get the sum, difference, product, and quotient. Here is a hint: for the second exercise, you will need to build separate functions for each calculation.

Everything seems to be working fine now. However, we still have some pesky warning messages in the Problems View.

Access modifiers

Both variables and functions should have something called an **access modifier**. This modifier will state who does, or doesn't, have access to it.

If you are new to programming, this may not make a lot of sense to you. But think of it this way: it decides what data should be restricted so that only other components in the file can see it, and what data should be accessible to the rest of the world.

The two most common access modifiers are private and public. private means only other functions and variables in this MXML file (and corresponding class file) can see it. public means it can be accessed by any other file in the project.

In the small example of this chapter, the access modifier we use is not critical since no other files are accessing it. Just for demonstration, we will use public. Later in the book, we will be delving into this a lot more deeply.

Change the modifiers for myText and addNumbers()as follows:

```
<![CDATA[
    [Bindable]
    public var myText:String = "Welcome to Flex!";
    public function addSum(number1:Number, number2:Number):void
    {
        var sum:int = number1 + number2;
        myText = "The sum of the numbers is" + " " + sum;
    }
```

Once you do this, the warnings in the Problems View should disappear.

Just to show a point, change the two public modifiers to private. The application should work exactly as before because no outside sources are trying to access the variable or function.

Refactoring

There are sometimes situations in which you may need to change the name of a variable. In a large project, where that variable is referenced many times, that could have enormous editing and debugging consequences.

Most modern integrated development environments have a handy tool for handling that: **refactoring**. This simply means that if you change the name in one place, the IDE will go through and change it everywhere else. It is a very sophisticated search-and-replace tool. Flex Builder 3 now includes a refactoring tool. Let's give it a try by changing the name of the variable myText to myNameText.

1. In the `Script` block, highlight the variable `myText`.

2. Select Source ➤ Refactor ➤ Rename as shown in Figure 3-25.

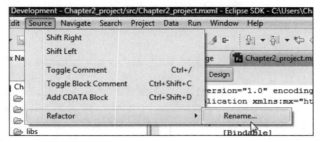

Figure 3-25. Selecting the refactoring tool

When you select Rename, the dialog box shown in Figure 3-26 should come up.

Figure 3-26. The Rename Variable dialog box

Notice that the highlighted variable name is already inserted in the New name field.

3. Change the name to myNameText.

While it is not necessary, you can preview the changes and even make some adjustments by clicking the now available Preview button.

4. Click the Preview button. You should see the dialog box shown in Figure 3-27.

It is strongly suggested not to make any changes here unless you are really an experienced programmer and understand the ramifications of your changes.

As you can see, it shows the original code on the left side (Original Source), and what the changes will be on the right side (Refactored Source). The top window has check boxes to help you determine which references you want to change or not change. Again, for now, I would strongly advise you not to make any changes here.

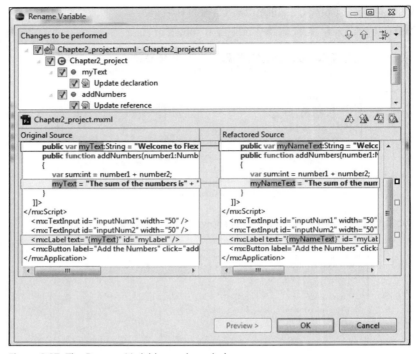

Figure 3-27. The Rename Variable preview window

5. Click OK.

You should have seen the reference in the function, as well as the Label control, change to reflect the new name: myNameText.

6. Run the application; it should run the same as before.

As you can see, this could be a powerful tool in complex programming scenarios that use many variable names, and where those names need to be adjusted for one reason or another.

We are now going to take refactoring one step further.

We briefly discussed components in Chapter 2, and will be discussing them in greater detail in Chapter 5. So, for this exercise, I am going to ask you to just follow the steps of creating a component for now. The construction of the component will not be our focus, refactoring will be.

1. In the application file, delete all the code between the opening and closing Application tags.

2. In the Flex Navigator, right-click the project name, Chapter3_project, and select New ➤ MXML Component. The dialog box shown in Figure 3-28 should open.

Figure 3-28. The New MXML Component dialog box

3. Give the component a file name of FirstComponent. The other settings can be left as they are.

4. Click Finish.

Your code should look as follows:

```
<?xml version="1.0" encoding="utf-8"?>
<mx:Canvas xmlns:mx="http://www.adobe.com/2006/mxml" ➥
width="400" height="300">

</mx:Canvas>
```

For now, that is all you need.

5. Return to the application file. Between the opening and closing Application tags, you will call up the component with the following tag. (After you type the < symbol to open the tag, just start to type the name of the component. Flex Builder should fill in the rest. Just press Enter when it does.)

```
<?xml version="1.0" encoding="utf-8"?>
<mx:Application xmlns:mx="http://www.adobe.com/2006/mxml" ➥
layout="absolute" xmlns:local="*">
    <local:FirstComponent/>
</mx:Application>
```

Again, don't be concerned about the rest of the code for now.

If you look in the Flex Navigator, you should notice that the name of the component is there as shown in Figure 3-29.

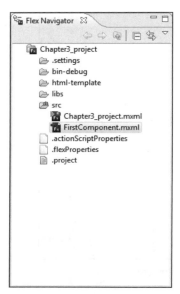

Figure 3-29.
The Flex Navigator with the new component

6. Right-click the component name, FirstComponent.mxml, and select Rename. The dialog box shown in Figure 3-30 should appear.

Figure 3-30. The Rename Class dialog box

As you will learn in Chapter 5, the words "Class" and "Component" mean about the same thing.

7. Rename the component to MyFirstComponent. Make sure that the Update references option is checked.

8. Click the OK button.

This may take a few moments to run. However, when it is complete, all references to the component will reflect the name change. Just look in Flex Navigator and the code in your application file.

```xml
<?xml version="1.0" encoding="utf-8"?>
<mx:Application xmlns:mx="http://www.adobe.com/2006/mxml" ➥
layout="absolute" xmlns:local="*">
        <local:MyFirstComponent/>
</mx:Application>
```

As you can see, Flex Builder 3 does its best to make sure that references are always correct. This will greatly decrease potential debugging time.

Let's take this out one step yet further.

1. Return to the MyFirstComponent file and put a Script block right under the opening Canvas tag.

2. Within the Script block, create the following variable:

```xml
<?xml version="1.0" encoding="utf-8"?>
<mx:Canvas xmlns:mx="http://www.adobe.com/2006/mxml" width="400" ➥
height="300">
    <mx:Script>
        <![CDATA[
            [Bindable]
            public var myProperty:String;
        ]]>
    </mx:Script>
</mx:Canvas>
```

3. Return to the application file and modify the call to the component by adding an id and sending a value to the property as follows:

```xml
<local:MyFirstComponent id="myComponent" myProperty="Welcome to Flex"/>
```

4. Under the call to the component, add the following Label tag:

```xml
<m:aellll tx="""{myopnn.yrpryyyyyyyyyyy}" i=mLbl"""""""/>
```

5. Under the opening Application tag, add the following Script block:

```xml
<mx:Script>
    <![CDATA[
        public var myProperty:String = myComponent.myProperty;
    ]]>
</mx:Script>
```

6. Return to MyFirstComponent.

7. Right-click the myProperty variable and select References ➤ Project.

Notice that Flex Builder 3 will allow you to search for references in the same file, within the same project, or across multiple projects in the same workspace.

A new View called Search should have opened along the bottom of the Perspective (see Figure 3-31).

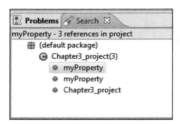

Figure 3-31.
The Search View

Notice that it is showing you that there are three references.

8. Double-click one of the references. You should be taken back to the application file with all of the references highlighted and arrows located along the left side of the editor as shown in Figure 3-32.

```
 1 <?xml version="1.0" encoding="utf-8"?>
 2 <mx:Application xmlns:mx="http://www.adobe.com/2006/mxml" layout="absolute" xmlns:local="*">
 3 <mx:Script>
 4     <![CDATA[
 5         public var myProperty:String = myComponent.myProperty;
 6     ]]>
 7 </mx:Script>
 8     <local:MyFirstComponent id="myComponent" myProperty="Welcome to Flex"/>
 9     <mx:Label text="{myComponent.myProperty}" id="myLabel"/>
10 </mx:Application>
11
```

Figure 3-32. The referenced variables

As you can see, you can now easily reference your properties. Again, this is significant in helping to reduce debugging time.

Let's try one final test here.

1. Return to MyFirstComponent.

2. Right-click myProperty and select Refactor ➤ Rename. The Rename dialog box should open.

3. Rename the property to myFirstProperty. Make sure the Update references option is checked.

4. Select OK.

If you return to the application file, all of the references should have been updated. As you can see, it is quite easy to work with.

Flex debugging

If you have done ActionScript programming in the Flash environment, I am sure you will agree that the programming environment is very basic, and its ability to debug the code is practically nonexistent. This, as you are about to see, is not the case with Flex Builder.

As I mentioned in the first two chapters, Flex Builder is built over the powerful Eclipse programming environment. This means that there are some powerful debugging tools available. We will be taking a brief look at it here. However, you will be returning to it periodically as you progress through the book. You will have plenty of opportunities to use it.

1. Make sure you are in the application file.

2. Change the myProperty variable as follows:

```
public var myProperty:String = "Welcome to Flex";
```

3. In the upper-right corner, you should see a small button with a larger one to the right of it that says Flex Development (or at least part of that name). This is shown in Figure 3-33.

Figure 3-33.
The Perspective buttons

As I said in Chapters 1 and 2, the arrangement of the Views in Eclipse is called a Perspective.

4. Click the small button on the left and select the Flex Debugging Perspective. Your environment should change to what you see in Figure 3-34.

Here we can set various breakpoints (places to stop the code and check values) and watches. You will see a simple demonstration here.

Notice that there is a View called Expressions. If you were a user of Flex Builder 2, you know that you would need to write an expression inside this View that would allow you to monitor a property. In Flex Builder 3, that is no longer the case. Let's take a look.

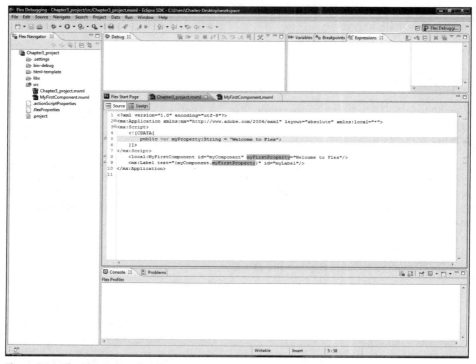

Figure 3-34. The Flex Debugging Perspective

5. Right-click myProperty in the Script block. Notice that there is now a new option: Watch "myProperty", as shown in Figure 3-35. Select it.

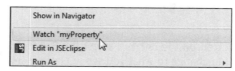

Figure 3-35. The Watch option

When you selected it, notice that the expression in now added automatically to the Expression View, as shown in Figure 3-36.

Figure 3-36. The expression added to the Expressions View

6. Debug the application by clicking the Debug button located just to the left of the Run Application button you have been using. The button looks like a small bug.

The browser should open as if you were running the application.

7. Leave the browser open, switch back to Flex Builder, and look at the Expressions View now (see Figure 3-37).

Figure 3-37. The watched expression populated

As you can see, the value of the watched variable was returned. This is a great way to test that the correct values are getting to where they are supposed to get at the proper times.

8. Return to the Development Perspective using the same button you used to switch to the Debugging Perspective.

As I stated, we will be returning to the Debugging Perspective several times in the course of this book.

Summary

You have just put a lot of the Flex puzzle together. Not only did you learn some of the basics of ActionScript 3.0 (such as variables, functions, and simple events), but you also used it to interact with MXML. You also learned that a well-designed Flex application uses a combination of MXML and ActionScript.

You learned how important it is to use the [Bindable] metatag and why strict typing is so important and what can happen when you don't pass the proper type.

Finally, you finished up by learning to use some of the powerful debugging and reference tools available in Flex Builder 3.

From here on in, we will build on the concepts you learned in this chapter as well as Chapter 2.

We will next turn our attention to the design aspects of Flex by using containers. We are also going to look at the power of components and how we can use components to model our applications.

So turn the page and let's start putting everything together.

4 CONTAINERS

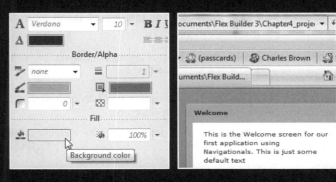

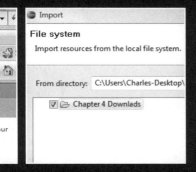

Now that you have installed Flex (and Flex Builder) and have had a chance to develop a familiarity with the environment, MXML, and ActionScript, we are now ready to dig into the heart of Flex design: containers.

As you will see in this chapter, there are different types of containers to handle different types of tasks. It is important that you select the proper container for the job that needs to be accomplished.

In addition, we will examine how we get from container to container through navigation and transitioning from one to the other.

In this chapter, we will look at

- Layout containers
- The Form container
- Navigation containers
- States
- Transitions

In many ways, this chapter will be the foundation for much of what you will be doing in Flex design. Take your time and make sure you understand each concept.

Application container

In 1995, Sun Microsystems introduced a new set of class files to its Java development environment: Swing classes. These classes allowed the programmer to design sophisticated **graphic user interfaces (GUIs)** in order to write and read data from the application.

The premise behind this set of classes was remarkably simple. The developer could use the classes to create containers, or boxes, of various sorts. Each container had a function called a **layout manager** that automatically arranged the contents of the container for it. The content could be typical form fields (such as text inputs, labels, buttons, etc.), or it could be other containers with additional content.

Flex uses exactly the same concept with its various **layout containers**. We will see these in action right after we take care of a few household chores.

1. Since you will no longer be using the project from Chapter 3, you can either close or delete it (with the file deletion option selected).
2. Create a new project called Chapter4_project. Use the default location and the default MXML application file name.

You will recall from Chapters 2 and 3 that all your code, MXML, and ActionScript must end up between the opening and closing Application tags. For that reason, the opening and closing Application tags together are referred to as the **root container**. The word "container" is used because it contains the rest of the components needed for our application, as well as other containers.

From here on in, we will be thinking of most work in Flex in terms of containers.

Layout manager

All containers have a built-in function called the **layout manager**. The layout manager decides how the content of the container will be placed. The three possibilities are

- **Absolute**: With absolute layout, you must specify the x- and y-position of the content.
- **Vertical**: With vertical layout, the content is placed vertically and centered.
- **Horizontal**: With the horizontal layout, the content is arranged from left to right.

Let's see an example of how this works.

If you look at the Application tag, you should see that the layout property is absolute. If it isn't, don't worry about that for now. We will fix that shortly.

```
<mx:Application xmlns:mx="http://www.adobe.com/2006/mxml" ➥
layout="absolute">
```

1. Switch over to Design Perspective.

2. Click anywhere in the Design area.

If you look in the Flex Properties View, you should see the field for Layout under the Layout section of the View, as shown in Figure 4-1.

Figure 4-1. The Layout section of the Flex Properties View

3. If necessary, set the layout to absolute. This will automatically make the change to the Application tag.

4. Go to the Controls section of the Components View and drag three Label controls onto the stage, as shown in Figure 4-2. Their position and text are not important.

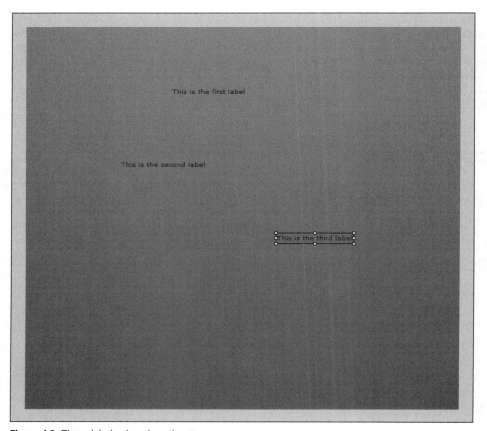

Figure 4-2. Three labels placed on the stage

As I just stated, when you use absolute layout, the x- and y-coordinates need to be stated. Flex Builder handled that for us when we positioned our labels on the stage.

5. Switch to Source View and look at the code.

```
<?xml version="1.0" encoding="utf-8"?>
<mx:Application xmlns:mx="http://www.adobe.com/2006/mxml" ➥
layout="absolute">
    <mx:Label x="162" y="139" text="This is the first label"/>
    <mx:Label x="285" y="212" text="This is the second label"/>
    <mx:Label x="195" y="285" text="This is the third label"/>
</mx:Application>
```

Here you can see the x and y properties.

6. Just to prove a point, delete the x and y properties of all three labels. After you delete them, run the application (or switch to Design View). Your results should appear as in Figure 4-3.

Figure 4-3. Absolute positioning without the x and y properties

Without the x and y properties, anything placed in a container with absolute layout defaults to 0,0.

> *Flex, as well as Flash, measures coordinates from the upper-left corner. Thus, 0, 0 is the upper-left corner.*

Let's take a look at the other two layouts. You can switch the layouts of a container in either Design View (using the technique shown previously) or in Source View.

7. If necessary, switch to Source View, and change the layout to horizontal.

> *You could also highlight the word "absolute" and press Ctrl+spacebar/Cmd+spacebar. This brings up a list of the three layouts, and you can select it from there.*

8. Rerun the application. Your results should resemble Figure 4-4.

Figure 4-4. The horizontal layout

As you can see, the labels are arranged left to right.

9. Go back to the code and change the layout to vertical.

10. Run the application. You should see results similar to Figure 4-5.

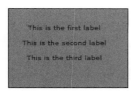

Figure 4-5.
The vertical layout

When you use either the vertical or horizontal layouts, the x and y properties are disabled. Instead, everything is handled by the layout manager.

> *Using absolute layout will result in slightly more efficient applications. This is because Flex doesn't need to work out the positioning of the content.*

Now that you have an understanding of layouts, you are ready to take the concept of containers to the next level.

Layout containers

A **layout container** draws a rectangular area that defines the size and positioning of child containers or child controls. If you are not sure what I mean by the word "child," don't worry; it will be abundantly clear to you in just a few minutes.

1. Switch to Design Perspective and delete the three Label controls you were just working with by selecting each one and pressing the Delete key.

Since these controls were within the Application container, they are considered to be children of that container.

OK, I am really going to confuse you on terminology now (well, not me, but Flex)!

We have already discussed in Chapters 2 and 3 how an MXML tag is a representation of an ActionScript class file. That is pretty easy to see. But here is where MXML uses its own terminology:

In MXML, an ActionScript class file is called a **component**. But MXML gets a little inconsistent in that it calls form items (like labels, buttons, text inputs, etc.) **controls**, despite the fact that they are MXML representations of ActionScript class files also. This was done in order to conform with XHTML terminology.

Bottom line: components, class files, and controls all mean pretty much the same thing. Now that we are past that, let's continue on.

2. Inside of the Components View, select the category called Layout to view the layout containers shown in Figure 4-6.

Figure 4-6. The layout containers

In the course of this book, we will be covering nearly all of these layout containers. However, for now, we are going to place our focus on the most commonly used of the containers: HBox and VBox.

HBox and VBox containers

You just had your first taste of using a layout manager. You changed the layout of the Application container from absolute, to horizontal, to vertical, and you saw the results. With the horizontal and vertical layouts, the components were automatically positioned for you, and the x and y properties were ignored.

The HBox and VBox containers come with a predefined layout manager that cannot be changed. It is probably obvious to you, but HBox has a layout manager predefined to horizontal, while VBox's layout manager is predefined to vertical.

Let's have a look:

1. Switch to the Design Perspective.

2. Change the layout of the Application container to horizontal.

3. From the Components View, drag an HBox container onto the stage.

You should see a dialog box open similar to the one shown in Figure 4-7.

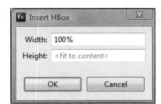

Figure 4-7. The Insert HBox dialog box

If your settings are different from those shown in Figure 4-7, don't worry; we are about to change them.

You can size your containers to a precise size measured in pixels or as a percentage of the size of the **parent container**, which is the next outer container. For instance, if you look at the dialog box shown in Figure 4-7, the width would be 100% the size of the Application container, which is the next outer container in this exercise.

There is one other possibility for sizing a container:

By not putting any measurement in, you automatically select <fit to content>. This means that the container will dynamically size depending on the content for any particular moment. We will see that demonstrated in a moment.

4. Set both the height and width to 100% and click OK. Your HBox component should now resemble what you see in Figure 4-8.

Figure 4-8. The placement of the HBox container

5. Using the Flex Properties View, change the background color, located at the bottom of the Style section, to a color of your choice (see Figure 4-9).

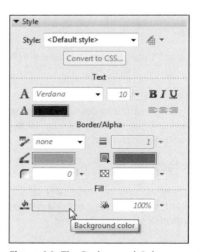

Figure 4-9. The Background Color property

6. Place a VBox container within the HBox container just created. Set the width to 50% and the height to 100%.

This VBox container is a child container of the outer HBox.

7. Change the background of the VBox container to a light and contrasting color.

Notice that placement is automatic due to the layout manager of the HBox container, as shown in Figure 4-10.

Figure 4-10. The VBox container as a child container of the HBox container

8. Place another VBox container to the right of the one you just created and use the same settings as the last VBox added. Change the background color to a light and contrasting color.

9. Within the right VBox container, which we just placed, put an HBox container with a width of 100% and a height of 50%.

10. Change the color of the new HBox container to whatever color you choose.

11. Finally, put an HBox with the same settings as the previous one below the HBox you just created. Change the color of the container (see Figure 4-11).

Figure 4-11. The finished layout

As you have seen, a lot of the concerns about placement are handled automatically by the parent container.

You can see the hierarchical relationships several ways:

12. First of all, click the Outline tab next to the Components tab, to bring up the Outline View (see Figure 4-12).

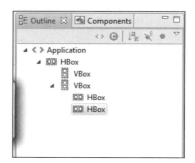

Figure 4-12. The Outline View

As you can see, there are two HBox containers within the second VBox container. The second VBox container is the second of two placed within an HBox container, which in turn is a child of the Application container. Within the Outline View, you can click any container, and that container will be selected on the stage.

If you look above the stage, just to the right of the Source and Design buttons, you will see a button to show surrounding containers.

13. Click the Show Surrounding Containers button (or press the F4 keyboard shortcut), shown in Figure 4-13.

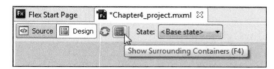

Figure 4-13. The Show Surrounding Containers button

By clicking this button, you will see the relationship of the containers on the stage (see Figure 4-14).

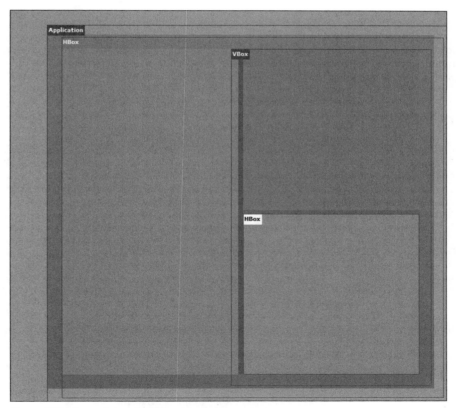

Figure 4-14. The containers' relationship

By clicking the various containers, you can see relationships for individual containers.

14. Click the Show Surrounding Container button (or press F4) to toggle it off.

15. Switch to Source View to see the code.

```
<?xml version="1.0" encoding="utf-8"?>
<mx:Application xmlns:mx="http://www.adobe.com/2006/mxml" ➥
layout="horizontal">
    <mx:HBox width="100%" height="100%" backgroundColor="#454FD9">
        <mx:VBox width="50%" height="100%" backgroundColor="#E69393">
        </mx:VBox>
        <mx:VBox width="50%" height="100%" backgroundColor="#AC713D">
            <mx:HBox width="100%" height="50%" ➥
backgroundColor="#E7DAA4">
            </mx:HBox>
            <mx:HBox width="100%" height="50%" ➥
backgroundColor="#822222">
            </mx:HBox>
        </mx:VBox>
    </mx:HBox>
</mx:Application>
```

Here you see the code for the embedded containers.

Now that you have a working knowledge of containers, you need to know how to place content within those containers. In order to accomplish that, we are going to turn to yet another layout container.

Form container

When you work with the HBox and VBox containers, you cannot change the layout property. By definition, an HBox uses horizontal layout and VBox uses vertical layout. While this can help us a lot with laying out the content, it can also create some problems.

Let's look at an example:

1. If necessary, switch back to Design Perspective.

2. In the Components View, switch to the Controls category.

3. Drag a Label control to the upper-right HBox container.

4. Change the text of the label to First Name:.

5. To the right of that, drag a TextInput control.

This is a pretty standard process in creating forms. Your form should resemble Figure 4-15 at this point.

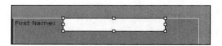

Figure 4-15. The HBox with child controls

The Label and TextInput controls are child controls of the HBox container.

6. Add another Label control (see Figure 4-16) and change the text to Last Name:.

Figure 4-16. Another control added

No matter where you place the new Label control, the HBox container's layout manager takes over and automatically places the control as the next horizontal item. Needless to say, this is not a desirable result.

7. Delete the three controls in the HBox container.

8. Return to the Layout category of the Components View and drag the Form container into the same HBox you just deleted the controls out of. Leave both the height and width set for <fit to content>.

The Form container allows us to easily lay out form controls in a logical format.

A word of explanation is needed here. If you have done HTML programming, you have used Form containers before. However, the functionality is very different. In HTML, the Form container is needed to gather the form's data and send it to the server with the proper variable names (decided by the name of the controls). However, in Flex, the Form container is used only for layout purposes. It does not have any data gathering functionality.

Before we add the controls to our form, it is a good idea to give our form a heading. We will use, you guessed it, yet another container.

Just below the Form container, in the Components View, you should see another layout container called FormHeading. This container will center the text in relationship to the width of the Form container (which will adjust to content).

9. Drag the FormHeading container into the Form container you just placed in the HBox.

During the last section of this chapter, you may have noticed a blue line while placing the various containers. The purpose of this line is to show you where the component will be placed. Notice that when you were dragging the FormHeading into the Form container, that blue line became horizontal and near the top of the container as shown in Figure 4-17.

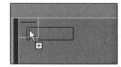

Figure 4-17. The placement of the FormHeading container

10. Change the text to Contact Form, as shown in Figure 4-18, by either double-clicking the text or using the Flex Properties View.

We will place three controls in our small form: one for the first name, one for the last name, and one for e-mail. Your

Figure 4-18. The completed FormHeading container

first instinct is probably to drag a Label control to the Form container. However, that is not quite how it works.

11. Drag a TextInput control to the container.

Once again, you can tell you are in the container by the small horizontal blue line under the FormHeading container (see Figure 4-19).

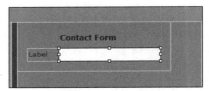

Figure 4-19. Adding the TextInput control

Notice that a label came right along with it. The Form container is handling all of this automatically.

12. Double-click the label and type First Name:.

13. When finished typing, press Enter.

When the label is set, the Form container adjusts its width and the FormHeading text automatically centers.

14. Go ahead and add two more TextInput controls for Last Name: and E-mail: (see Figure 4-20).

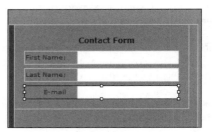

Figure 4-20. The Form container with three TextInput controls

After putting the TextInput controls in, notice that the labels automatically right-align. Once again, this is a function of the Form container. We will be looking into the code behind this in a moment.

Later on in this book, we will be talking about form validations and requirements. For now, we will let users enter whatever they want into the form fields.

If you create a form, chances are you will want to add a Submit button. Here there is a caveat with using the Form container.

15. Add a Button control as you did with the three TextIntput controls.

Notice the problem that occurs (see Figure 4-21).

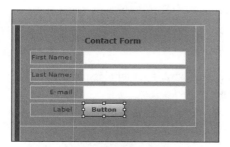

Figure 4-21. Adding a Button control

An unnecessary label for the Button control was added. There are a couple of different ways to handle this problem. The simplest way is to double-click the Label text, delete it, and then press Enter. The second way of handling it is slightly trickier, but more effective.

16. Delete the Button control you just added.

17. Drag another Button control to the container and notice the horizontal blue line (see Figure 4-22).

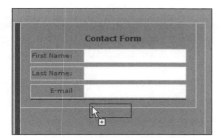

Figure 4-22. Normal positioning of the Button contol

The horizontal line is nearly the full width of the Form container. But if you drag the Button control a little higher, nearly on top of the previous TextInput control, the horizontal line shrinks to about the size of the TextInput control (see Figure 4-23).

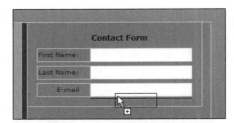

Figure 4-23. Better placement of the Button control

Not only does this resolve the extraneous label issue, but the Button control is now nicely centered, as shown in Figure 4-24.

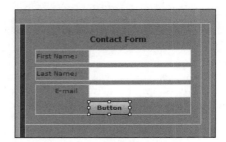

Figure 4-24. The proper positioning of the Button control

The borders around each of the controls will not show in the application when it runs. If you want, give it a try and see for yourself.

In order to fully understand how the Form container does its job, it is important to understand the code behind it.

18. Switch to Source View to look at the code.

Let's focus on the Form container code.

```
<mx:HBox width="100%" height="50%" backgroundColor="#E7DAA4">
    <mx:Form>
        <mx:FormHeading label="Contact Form"/>
            <mx:FormItem label="First Name:">
                <mx:TextInput/>
            </mx:FormItem>
            <mx:FormItem label="Last Name:">
                <mx:TextInput/>
            </mx:FormItem>
            <mx:FormItem label="E-mail:">
                <mx:TextInput/>
```

```
                          <mx:Button label="Button"/>
                    </mx:FormItem>
              </mx:Form>
        </mx:HBox>
```

The Form container places each control in another container called the FormItem. The FormItem has a property called label. So in theory we are not adding a Label control to the form, but are just utilizing the label property of the FormItem container.

The reason why we got the Button control to place properly is that we added the button as another item to the last FormItem container. We can rightly say that the TextInput and Button controls are children of the FormItem container.

Let's look at one other handy feature of the Form container.

19. Return to the Design Perspective.

20. Select the FormItem container labeled E-mail.

> *To select the entire container, click the label and not the* TextInput *control. If you click just the* TextInput *control, just that control will be selected, leaving the label unselected.*

If you look at the Flex Properties View, you will see a drop-down list for Required in the Common section of the View (see Figure 4-25).

Figure 4-25. The Required property

By setting that to true, an asterisk is automatically added to the control (see Figure 4-26).

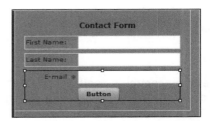

Figure 4-26. The Required asterisk added to the control

For the time being, all I want you to see here is that the Required property automatically adds an asterisk (*) to the field. As I mentioned earlier, later in the book we will be talking about handling the Required property and validation programmatically.

I am sure you are seeing the power of the Form control. But there are some additional possibilities for us to try. Let's turn our attention to a different layout container now.

Panel container

The Panel container is unique in that, like the Application container, it can handle all three layout modes. This gives you some flexibility as you will soon see. We will rebuild our small contact form using the Panel container in order for you to see the differences.

1. Delete the Form container and its contents.

2. Put a Panel container in place of the deleted Form container as shown in Figure 4-27.

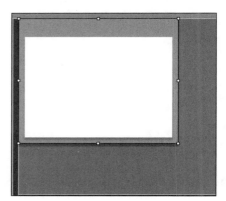

Figure 4-27. The Panel container

The Panel container has a semitransparent border around it that can hold a title property and, as you shall see in a bit, a control bar for buttons. Also, when we dragged it into the container, we did not get the dialog box to resize like we did with the HBox and VBox containers. We will set that shortly in the Flex Properties View.

3. Set the width to 50% in the Flex Properties View.

If you look in the Common section of the Flex Properties View, you should see an input box for Title.

> **4.** Type Contact Form in the Title field as shown in Figure 4-28.

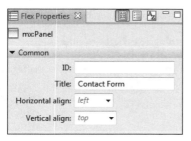

Figure 4-28. The Title field in Flex Properties

> **5.** After typing Contact Form, press Enter.

After you press the Enter key, you will see the other benefit to using the Panel container: a title property along the top of it as shown in Figure 4-29.

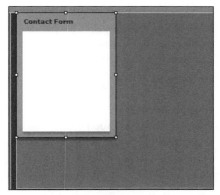

Figure 4-29. The title property in the Panel container

The white area is where you place your content.

Unlike the VBox and HBox containers, the Panel container can access all three layout managers: vertical, horizontal, and absolute.

> **6.** Set the layout for the Panel container to vertical. You can do this in the Flex Properties View as you did with the Application container.

In this exercise, we will be laying our form out a bit differently from before. Because of this, you will need to use combinations of VBox and HBox containers. Let's look at an example.

7. Drag an HBox into the white area of the Panel container.

8. Set both the width and height to <fit to content> by deleting any measurements. This will allow you to arrange the Label and TextInput controls from left to right.

9. Put a Label and TextInput control into the HBox control.

10. Change the Label control text to Last Name:.

Your form should look something like Figure 4-30.

Figure 4-30. The Panel container with controls added

Now is a good time to look at another control used in forms, the RadioButton. Since the Panel container is set to a layout of vertical, it won't be necessary to use another layout container. By placing them under the HBox container we placed in the previous steps, the Panel's vertical layout will take over.

Like XHTML, radio button controls in Flex can only be selected one at a time, as opposed to check boxes. In order to accomplish this, they are grouped together in yet another container called the RadioButtonGroup; which is located below the RadioButton control.

11. Drag a copy of the RadioButtonGroup below the HBox container in the Panel container.

The dialog box shown in Figure 4-31 should open up.

Figure 4-31. The Insert Radio Button Group dialog box

The group name should be used to properly identify the group. Later in the book, this will be important when we get deeper into programming applications.

12. Change the group name to contactType. Do not use a space.

13. Click Button 1 and change the text to Telephone.

14. Click Button 2 and change the text to E-mail.

15. Click the Add button to add a third button. A new dialog box should open to allow you to add a name.

16. Type No Contact and click OK.

17. When you are finished, click OK. Your form should resemble the one in Figure 4-32.

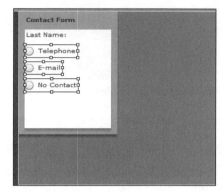

Figure 4-32. The RadioButton controls added

If you want, add a few more controls. The white area of the Panel container will automatically expand to accommodate the content.

Let's look at one more layout container that works in partnership with the Panel container.

ControlBar container

The ControlBar container automatically places itself in the bottom frame area of the Panel container. This is a handy container in that it allows you to arrange controls along the bottom of the Panel container. However, because it arranges itself along the bottom, there is one caveat you must be careful about: it must be the last child in the Panel container in order for it to work properly.

Let's see an example.

1. Return to the Layout category in the Components View.

2. Drag the ControlBar container to just under the last RadioButton control.

As soon as you let go of the mouse, notice where the container is placed: right in the bottom frame area.

You can now drag whatever controls you want into it.

3. Drag a couple of Button controls into the ControlBar container.

4. Change the labels of the buttons to Submit and Reset as shown in Figure 4-33.

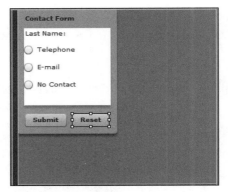

Figure 4-33. Buttons added to the ControlBar

As you can see, the ControlBar uses a layout manager set to horizontal.

There is one additional feature of the Panel container that makes it interesting to use.

5. Select the Panel container. You may find it easy to select the container by either clicking the title of the Panel or selecting it in Outline View.

In the Border/Alpha section of the Flex Properties View, there is a way to set the Corner Radius property of the container.

6. Set the corner radius to 35 as shown in Figure 4-34.

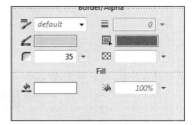

Figure 4-34. The Corner Radius field

7. Press Enter.

You should see the corners of the Panel adjust as shown in Figure 4-35.

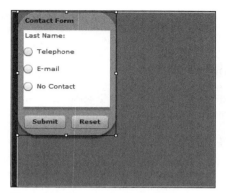

Figure 4-35. The Panel with rounded corners

I think you now understand the power of layout containers. As you can easily see, we only sampled the most commonly used ones here. However, as we progress through this book, you will have a chance to try some of the other containers.

We will now turn our attention to the navigation containers.

Navigation containers

Unlike HTML applications, you don't go to a brand-new page each time you click a link. Instead, all of your content is contained within a single SWF file and can be accessed when the appropriate link is selected. This will become very clear in just a few moments and again when we discuss states.

Like any application, you want to provide the user with an easy means of navigating the content. Flex helps us out by providing containers dedicated to just that. These containers are called **navigator containers**, or **navigators**, and can be found, like the layout containers, in the Components View (see Figure 4-36).

Figure 4-36. The navigators

Fundamental to navigators is an understanding of the ViewStack container, which we'll look at next.

ViewStack container

What we are going to do is build a very simple application from scratch so that you can understand the mechanics of navigators.

1. Close the existing MXML file you have open.

2. Select File ➤ New ➤ MXML Application to bring up the dialog box shown in Figure 4-37.

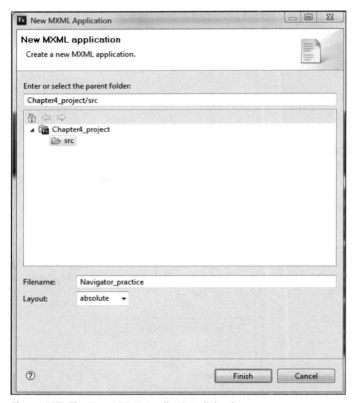

Figure 4-37. The New MXML Application dialog box

3. Name the MXML file Navigator_practice.

4. Set the layout to be vertical and click Finish.

5. If necessary, change to Design Perspective.

6. Drag a Panel container onto the stage.

7. Set the title to Welcome.

As you will see in a few moments, when designing containers to be used in navigation, it is a good idea to keep them all the same size. While it is not mandatory to do this, the reasons for making them the same size will be obvious in a bit.

8. Set the width to 250 and the height to 200. Remember, this measurement is in pixels.

Up to this point, we have not spoken a lot about the id property. As you start to get into more advanced techniques, it is important to give each item in your application a unique ID so that MXML/ActionScript can easily reference it.

Because MXML/ActionScript is case sensitive, it is important that we use the naming conventions we spoke of in Chapters 2 and 3. As a quick reminder:

- Must begin with a letter, underscore, or dollar sign, and not a number.
- No spaces.
- Everything in lowercase except for mid-word capitalizations (for example, myAddressBook).
- The only nonalphanumeric characters you can use are the underscore (_) or the dollar sign ($).

9. In the Flex Properties View, give this Panel container an ID of welcome.

Since we are focusing on learning how to build navigation here, we will keep the design aspect minimal. Just drag a Text control into the white area of the Panel and type in some text of your own choosing.

> *The* Label *control allows for only a single line of text, while the* Text *control allows for multiple lines of wrapping text.*

10. Adjust the width of the Text control to about 200 pixels and a height of about 120 pixels, and, using your mouse, position it in the content area of the Panel.

11. Type the text shown in Figure 4-38 (or any default text you want).

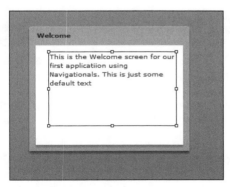

Figure 4-38. The Welcome panel

12. Drag another Panel container in the application. Because we set the layout to vertical, they should automatically position one under the other.

13. Give this Panel the title of Contact and an id property of contact.

14. Drag a Text control into the application using the same measurements as before and add some default text of your choosing.

15. Drag a third Panel container into the application.

You might notice a small problem here. The third Panel container seems to be overflowing the available real estate in the Design Perspective (see Figure 4-39).

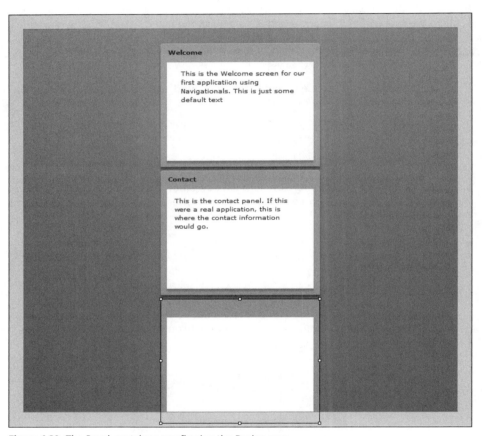

Figure 4-39. The Panel container overflowing the Design area

There are a couple of different ways we could approach this. Of course, we could switch to Source Perspective and finish it in code. But let's assume you want to stay in Design Perspective.

If you look along the top-right of the Design area, you will see a drop-down list that will allow you to adjust the area you are designing for, as shown in Figure 4-40. I often find this a convenient tool to just expand the Design area for situations like this one.

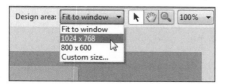

Figure 4-40. Setting the Design area

16. Set the Design area to 1024 x 768.

You can now use the scrollbars to get to the last Panel container easily.

17. Give the third Panel container a title of About Us and an ID of aboutUs.

18. As with the previous Panels, add a Text control with the same settings and fill it with default text of your choice.

Once completed, go ahead and run the application. It should look something like Figure 4-41. If it is not exact, don't worry, it doesn't need to be.

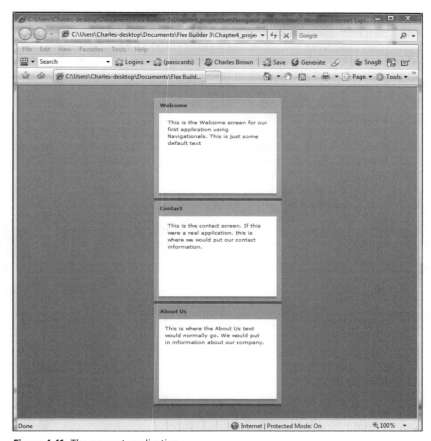

Figure 4-41. The present application

Needless to say, this is not the most desirable way to build an application. If you were creating this in HTML, you would probably create a separate HTML page for each of these topics with some sort of hyperlinked navigational design.

As I stated earlier, this is not necessary in Flex since everything is contained in a single SWF file. But in order to separate these three topics into separate sections, we need to do a bit of rather simple programming.

19. Switch to Source View to look at the code (if your text and measurements vary slightly from the code here, it is fine).

```
<?xml version="1.0" encoding="utf-8"?>
<mx:Application xmlns:mx="http://www.adobe.com/2006/mxml" ➡
layout="vertical">
    <mx:Panel width="250" height="200" layout="absolute" ➡
title="Welcome" id="welcome">
        <mx:Text x="10" y="28" text="This is the Welcome ➡
screen for our first application using Navigationals. This is ➡
just    some default text." width="200"/>
    </mx:Panel>
    <mx:Panel width="250" height="200" layout="absolute" ➡
id="contact" title="Contact">
        <mx:Text x="10" y="25" text="This is the Contact ➡
screen for our first application using Navigationals. ➡
In here we could put a contact form." width="200"/>
    </mx:Panel>
    <mx:Panel width="250" height="200" layout="absolute" ➡
id="aboutUs" title="About Us">
        <mx:Text x="10" y="10" text="This is where you ➡
could put information that would normally go into the ➡
About Us page. Enter information about who you are ➡
and what you do" width="200"/>
    </mx:Panel>
</mx:Application>
```

In order to create the appearance of separate pages, we can enclose the three Panels in the ViewStack navigator container.

20. Before the opening of the first Panel container, welcome, insert the following code:

```
<mx:ViewStack>
```

21. Cut and paste the closing </mx:ViewStack> tag after the close of the final Panel, aboutUs.

Your code should now look as follows:

```
<?xml version="1.0" encoding="utf-8"?>
<mx:Application xmlns:mx="http://www.adobe.com/2006/mxml" ➡
layout="vertical">
<mx:ViewStack>
    <mx:Panel width="250" height="200" layout="absolute" ➡
```

```
        title="Welcome" id="welcome">
                <mx:Text x="10" y="28" text="This is the Welcome ➥
screen for our first application using Navigationals. ➥
This is just some default text." width="200"/>
            </mx:Panel>
            <mx:Panel width="250" height="200" layout="absolute" ➥
id="contact" title="Contact">
                <mx:Text x="10" y="25" text="This is the Contact ➥
screen for our first application using Navigationals. ➥
In here we could put a contact form." width="200"/>
            </mx:Panel>
            <mx:Panel width="250" height="200" layout="absolute" ➥
id="aboutUs" title="About Us">
                <mx:Text x="10" y="10" text="This is where you could ➥
put information that would normally go into the About Us page. ➥
Enter information about who you are and what you do" width="200"/>
            </mx:Panel>
        </mx:ViewStack>
    </mx:Application>
```

22. Run the application. You should see a very different result from before, as shown in Figure 4-42.

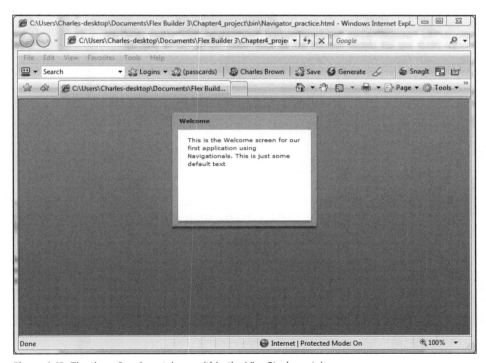

Figure 4-42. The three Panel containers within the ViewStack container

The three Panel containers are stacked vertically on top of each other. All you are seeing is just the first, or topmost, container.

This is also why I suggested that you make all of your containers the same size (although it is not critical that you do so) when creating navigation.

This completes the first part of creating the navigation. The next step is to create a means to navigating, such as links or buttons. To do that, we need to do a little more work. Let's return to our code.

Since the ViewStack contains the pages that need to be navigated, we need to have our navigational tools refer to it. However, in order to do so, we need to give it an id property. For purposes of this exercise, let's call it myPages.

23. Set the id property of the ViewStack container as follows. Notice that I use the proper naming conventions.

```
<mx:ViewStack id="myPages">
```

The navigational tools will be named automatically if you give each of the Panel containers within the ViewStack container a label property. The label should be given the value you want to see in the button or link.

24. Add the following labels to your Panels:

```
<?xml version="1.0" encoding="utf-8"?>
<mx:Application xmlns:mx="http://www.adobe.com/2006/mxml" ➡
layout="vertical">
<mx:ViewStack id="myPages">
    <mx:Panel width="250" height="200" layout="absolute" ➡
title="Welcome" id="welcome" label="Welcome">
        <mx:Text x="10" y="28" text="This is the Welcome ➡
screen for our first application using Navigationals. ➡
This is just some default text." width="200"/>
    </mx:Panel>
    <mx:Panel width="250" height="200" layout="absolute" ➡
id="contact" title="Contact" label="Contact Us">
        <mx:Text x="10" y="25" text="This is the Contact ➡
screen for our first application using Navigationals. ➡
In here we could put a contact form." width="200"/>
    </mx:Panel>
    <mx:Panel width="250" height="200" layout="absolute" ➡
id="aboutUs" title="About Us" label="About Us">
        <mx:Text x="10" y="10" text="This is where you could ➡
put information that would normally go into the About Us page. ➡
Enter information about who you are and what you do" width="200"/>
    </mx:Panel>
</mx:ViewStack>
</mx:Application>
```

Our final step is to create the buttons or links. As you are about to see, Flex handles that pretty easily also.

25. Put a blank line between the Application and ViewStack tags.

Among the navigation containers is the ButtonBar. When we put it into our application, we use the ID of the ViewStack container as the ButtonBar's dataProvider property. The ButtonBar will in turn create a Button control for each container within the ViewStack container. The label property of the Button control will be populated by the label property we added to the Panel containers earlier.

26. Put the following code in the blank line you just created. Notice that you use the ViewStack ID, myPages, as a binding with the curly braces for the dataProvider property.

```
<mx:ButtonBar dataProvider="{myPages}" />
```

27. Run your application; you should now have full navigation, as shown in Figure 4-43. Click the three buttons to test them.

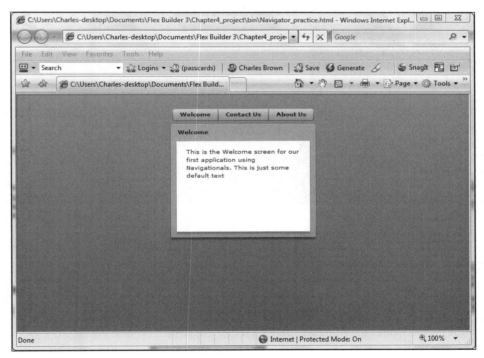

Figure 4-43. The completed ViewStack application

By just adding a container, a few properties, and a ButtonBar, you have a fully functioning navigational system. As you start to learn more advanced techniques, containers can be added to the ViewStack dynamically. Since the ButtonBar is adjusting itself according to the information provided by the ViewStack container, you will have a self-updating navigational system. We will be looking at scenarios like that later on in the book.

However, our flexibility does not stop here.

28. Return to the code and change the ButtonBar to a ToggleButtonBar.

```
<mx:ToggleButtonBar dataProvider="{myPages}" />
```

Nothing else changes.

29. Rerun the application. Your screen should resemble what you see in Figure 4-44.

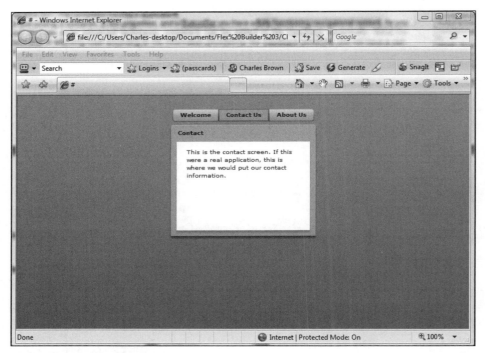

Figure 4-44. Using the ToggleButtonBar

Notice that with the ToggleButtonBar, the button that is associated with the page that the user is viewing appears depressed. This gives users a visual cue as to the page they are on.

You will find that when working with MXML, many features are easily interchangeable with only minor changes. You just saw that with the ButtonBar and the ToggleButtonBar. To highlight this concept even more, continue with these steps:

30. Change the ToggleButtonBar as follows:

```
<mx:LinkBar dataProvider="{myPages}" />
```

31. Once again, run the application. Your screen should appear as shown in Figure 4-45.

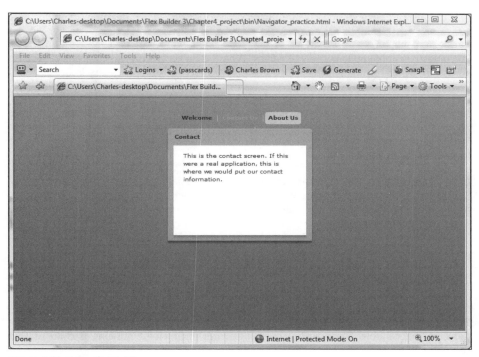

Figure 4-45. Using the LinkBar

This time, instead of having buttons, you now have a LinkBar with what looks like hyperlinks separated by vertical bars. Also, like the ToggleButtonBar, they give you a visual cue of what page the user is viewing.

Because of this interchangeability, it is easy to test alternatives without massive recoding.

Speaking of coding, let's talk about navigation and ActionScript a bit.

Using ActionScript with navigation

It is possible to easily use ActionScript syntax to create navigation. While we will be doing it in a relatively simple scenario here, these same simple concepts will be needed later on when we get into more advanced programming techniques.

1. Begin by creating an HBox container below the closing ViewStack tag and add three Button controls into it as follows:

```
</mx:ViewStack>
<mx:HBox>
    <mx:Button label="Welcome"/>
    <mx:Button label="Contact Us"/>
    <mx:Button label="About Us"/>
</mx:HBox>
</mx:Application>
```

2. Run the application; you should see the three buttons arranged horizontally along the bottom.

In the last section, you saw the ViewStack. What I didn't mention was that the ViewStack container, as well as many other class files in ActionScript 3.0, uses a very important programming tool: an **array**.

Normally, we think of a variable as holding a single value. For instance, a variable lastName might have a value of Smith. You probably wouldn't think of lastName having the values of Smith, Jones, and Brown. Yet, that is exactly what an array does: it allows a single variable to hold multiple values.

In an array, each value is called an **element**. So if our variable, lastName, had the values of Smith, Jones, and Brown, those would be its three elements. Each element is automatically assigned a number called an **index**. In most programming environments (including ActionScript 3.0), the first element is assigned the index number of 0.

> ColdFusion is a notable exception. It starts the first element of an array with the numeric value of 1.

To be consistent with other terminology I have used in this book regarding MXML, you can think of the variable name as the container, with each element being a child of that container.

In most programming environments, including ActionScript, an array is notated with the index numbers assigned to the elements in square brackets. For example:

```
Smith[0], Jones[1]. Brown[2]
```

Here, the variable is myPages, the ID of the ViewStack. The multiple values (children or elements) it holds are the IDs of the containers within it: welcome, contact, and aboutUs.

The ViewStack container has a property called selectedIndex. This property allows an element to be called by its index number.

Before we write the code, let's quickly review two concepts from Chapters 2 and 3.

Most OOP languages use something called **dot notation**. We discussed that in Chapter 3. With dot notation, we enter the name of the object (or variable name) on the left side of the dot and the name of the property or function need on the right side of the dot. So if you want to call element 0 of the ViewStack you created earlier, you would notate it as follows:

```
myPages.selectedIndex = 0;
```

Also recall from Chapters 2 and 3 that many Flex classes, or components, have events built into them. One of the most commonly used is the click event associated with the Button class.

3. Use these two concepts to create navigation by making the following alterations to the Button controls that you just added:

```
<mx:HBox>
    <mx:Button label="Welcome" click="myPages.selectedIndex = 0"/>
    <mx:Button label="Contact Us" click="myPages.selectedIndex = 1"/>
    <mx:Button label="About Us" click="myPages.selectedIndex = 2"/>
</mx:HBox>
```

4. Run the application now; the buttons you added at the bottom should be fully functional.

5. Return to the code.

You may find situations where referring to the index number of the element is not convenient. This could be especially true in dynamic situations in which the number of elements could be constantly changing. If that is the case, ViewStack helps us out a bit with an alternative property: selectedChild.

Recall earlier my statement that anything added to a container is a child of that container. Thus, our ViewStack container currently has three child elements.

The easy part about the selectedChild property is that you can refer to the child by its id property rather than its index number.

6. Modify the code as follows:

```
<mx:HBox>
    <mx:Button label="Welcome" click="myPages.selectedChild = welcome"/>
    <mx:Button label="Contact Us" click="myPages.selectedChild = ➥
contact"/>
    <mx:Button label="About Us" click="myPages.selectedChild = ➥
aboutUs"/>
</mx:HBox>
```

7. Run the application again. The buttons should work as before.

Let's now look at two other ways of creating some interesting navigation.

TabNavigator and Accordion containers

The TabNavigator and Accordion containers combine navigation with design aspects and are very easy to use.

To see a demonstration of these containers, let's do a little surgery on our code.

1. Remove the LinkBar tag and the HBox containing the three buttons you created earlier.

2. Change the opening and closing ViewStack tags to TabNavigator.

Your code should now look as follows:

```
<?xml version="1.0" encoding="utf-8"?>
<mx:Application xmlns:mx="http://www.adobe.com/2006/mxml" ➥
layout="vertical">
<mx:TabNavigator id="myPages">
     <mx:Panel width="250" height="200" layout="absolute" ➥
title="Welcome" id="welcome" label="Welcome">
          <mx:Text x="10" y="28" text="This is the Welcome ➥
screen for our first application using Navigationals. ➥
This is just some default text." width="200"/>
     </mx:Panel>
     <mx:Panel width="250" height="200" layout="absolute" ➥
id="contact" title="Contact" label="Contact Us">
          <mx:Text x="10" y="25" text="This is the Contact ➥
screen for our first application using Navigationals. ➥
In here we could put a contact form." width="200"/>
     </mx:Panel>
     <mx:Panel width="250" height="200" layout="absolute" ➥
id="aboutUs" title="About Us" label="About Us">
          <mx:Text x="10" y="10" text="This is where you could ➥
put information that would normally go into the About Us page. ➥
Enter information about who you are and what you do" width="200"/>
     </mx:Panel>
</mx:TabNavigator>
</mx:Application>
```

3. Run the application. Your results should appear similar to Figure 4-46.

As you can see, each child container within the outer TabNavigator container creates a tab. Like earlier, the label property of the tab is populated with the label property of the child container.

As I said earlier, many related components are easily interchangeable in Flex. Here is yet another example:

4. Change the opening and closing TabNavigator tags to Accordion tags and run the application. Your screen should resemble what you see in Figure 4-47.

Each child container creates another "fold" in the accordion. The container's label property provides the text for the navigation as before. All the user needs to do is click the bars separating the folds.

So far we have looked at a variety of navigational techniques. All have been fairly easy to use. However, one cannot discuss navigation without talking about one of the most important features of designing Flex applications: **state**.

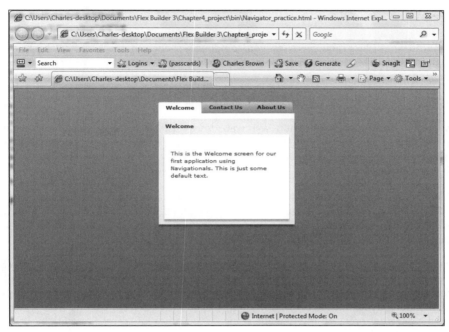

Figure 4-46. The TabNavigator container

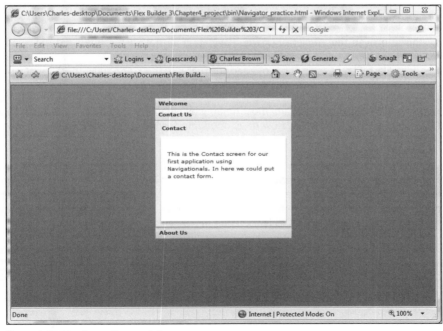

Figure 4-47. The Accordion container

State

In the previous navigation exercises, you completely changed the View of what you were looking at. However, what about a scenario in which only some of the information needs to change?

Let's step back to XHTML design for a moment.

As I noted earlier, traditional non-SWF web design usually consists of many individual XHTML pages, arranged in some sort of hierarchy, tied together by a common navigation system. The navigation system, at its most basic level, is a series of hyperlinks that moves users from page to page.

While this system works most of the time, it is very inefficient. Each time the user clicks a hyperlink, a request has to be sent to a web server, and the page has to be located by that server, sent over the Internet to the caller, and loaded into the browser. In some cases, a "Page Not Found" error occurs.

Flash addressed many of these issues by internalizing a complete website into one SWF file as we saw previously; in some very complex situations, two or three SWF files might be used and incorporated through various means into the main SWF file. In earlier versions of Flash, clicking a link in the navigation system moved the user from page to page by moving to a different point on the timeline or possibly a different scene. From Flash MX, you could dynamically change the interface right in the same frame. In later versions, rather than using the timeline or scenes, pages were created using multiple SWF files that could be encased within the library of the main SWF or loaded dynamically using tools such as empty movie clips.

All of this improved the efficiency of web navigation in that each request did not need to go back to the server and be returned over the Internet. Once the main SWF file was loaded into Flash Player, everything needed for that website to be fully operational would be loaded with it.

Flex suddenly changed things again, most notably by eliminating the now familiar timeline. But if the timeline is eliminated, how does one jump from page to page within the application?

One way is to use the navigation containers you saw in the previous sections. Another way is by employing state. Moving between states is similar to jumping to different points on a timeline. You'll get a better understanding of this as you work through the examples here. In the process of building these examples, you will have a chance to review some previously discussed concepts as well as learn some new ones.

Our first example will be a simple one: you will make panels appear by clicking hyperlinks.

1. Close the previous MXML file you were working on.
2. Create a new MXML application by choosing File ➤ New ➤ Flex Application.
3. Call your application State_practice.
4. If necessary, change the layout to absolute.

5. If necessary, switch to Design Perspective.

6. Drag a Panel container to the upper-left corner of the stage as shown in Figure 4-48.

Figure 4-48. The placement of the Panel container

7. Give the Panel container a title of Enemies of Ed, using either the Flex Properties View or by double-clicking in the header.

8. Drag a Text control into the white body area of the Panel container as you did earlier and add the following text:

We would like to hear from you. Please click on the link below to ➡ find out how to contact us.

9. Press Enter.

The Text control probably extends beyond the Panel container. Earlier, we changed the width of the Text control using the Flex Properties View. As an alternative, do the following:

10. Use the right-middle graphic handle to drag the right edge of the control back into the white area of the Panel container so that your screen resembles Figure 4-49.

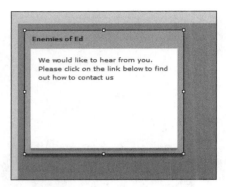

Figure 4-49. The adjusted Text control

You want to make a new panel appear when an event happens. In order to accomplish this, what you want to do is create an event to trigger the new state. This is a good chance to look at a control you haven't seen before: LinkButton.

The LinkButton control is, in my opinion, a rather unfortunate name, as the result is not a button at all. Instead, it is closer to a hyperlink in XHTML.

11. Drag a copy of the LinkButton control, found under the Controls category in the Components View, and place it under the text you just created (see Figure 4-50).

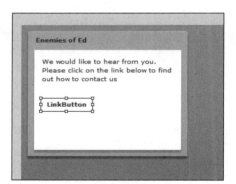

Figure 4-50. The LinkButton control added to the Panel container

12. Either double-click the control or use the Text field in the Flex Properties View to change the text. Type the text Click Here to E-mail Us.

13. Press Enter to lock in the changes.

Like all hyperlinks, you may want to change the color of the text to identify it as being a hyperlink. This can easily be done.

14. In the Flex Properties View, change the font color located in the Style section (see Figure 4-51).

Figure 4-51. Setting the font color

15. Test the application, and look at the LinkButton control.

The background color changes when you roll over the text, so you can easily see how this looks and feels more like a hyperlink than a button.

16. Close the browser and return to Flex Builder.

Changing the state

Now the next trick is to use the LinkButton control to change the state of the application. Notice that in the upper-right corner of Flex Builder, right above the Flex Properties View, is a View called States as shown in Figure 4-52.

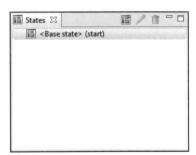

Figure 4-52. The States View

All Flex applications start in a base, or start, state. This is the default state. In other words, what you see in Flex Builder is what you get.

But now you are going to add an additional state.

1. Either right-click <Base state> in the States View and select New State or click the New State button located in the upper-right corner of the States View.

A dialog box will open that will allow you to name your state.

2. Call the new state contact, as shown in Figure 4-53.

Figure 4-53. The New State dialog box

The Based on list is where you specify which state you want to build the new state over. Since you have no other states built, we have to leave this set as <Base state>. You can also make this new state the default or start state. For now, however, leave the Set as start state option unchecked.

3. Click OK.

You should now see your new state appear in the States View (see Figure 4-54).

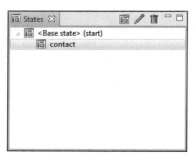

Figure 4-54. The new state added to the States View

Everything looks the same on the new state. But you are going to change that.

When working with multiple states, it is important to keep an eye on the States View to see what state is now active. It is the state that is highlighted in the States View.

4. Make sure that contact is selected in the States View.

5. Drag another Panel container onto the stage, place it to the right of the existing panel, and give it the title of Send Us a Question (see Figure 4-55).

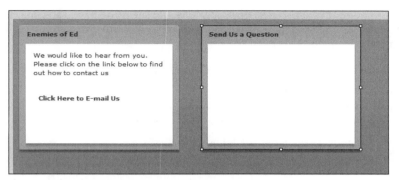

Figure 4-55. Adding a second panel in the contact state

Let's build a simple e-mail form in this new Panel container as shown in Figure 4-56. Since you will not be actually e-mailing it now, the details of the form are not important.

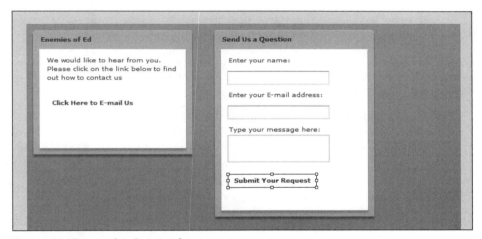

Figure 4-56. The completed contact form

6. Using Figure 4-56 as your guide, drag Label, TextInput, TextArea, and Button controls into the Panel container.

7. Change the text of the labels and button as shown in Figure 4-56.

8. Resize the Panel container to accommodate the form. For this example, I found that a height of 300 pixels worked well.

Once you have completed this second panel, let's see a little magic.

9. In the States View, click the <Base state> tag.

The Panel container you just created disappears. If you click the contact state again, your new Panel container returns.

    Welcome to State!

If you were to run the application now, all you would see is the base state. You now have to add some code so that the LinkButton and Button controls, located in the base and contact states, can change state.

10. If necessary, return to Flex Builder and click <Base state> in the States View.

11. Click the LinkButton control.

12. In the Flex Properties View, locate the On click field. Putting code here is the same as typing in a click event in Source View as you did in Chapter 3.

13. In the On click field, enter the following:

```
currentState = 'contact'
```

14. Press Enter.

As discussed in Chapter 3, the single quotes signify a string within a larger string. ActionScript needs this inner string to work properly. A quick look at the code in Source View will show the reason why.

```
<mx:LinkButton x="10" y="74" label="Click Here to Email Us" ➡
color="#0000FF" click="currentState = 'contact'"/>
```

You can see that currentState is the main string for the click event. The state that the event is triggering, contact, is the inner string. The command, currentState, is used by ActionScript to switch from state to state.

15. Give your code a test by saving and running the application. When you click the LinkButton control of the Panel container located in the base state, the contact panel should appear. This can create a pretty cool way of going from page to page.

You are not finished yet.

16. Close the browser and return to Design View in Flex Builder.

We now need to give the Button control, located in the Panel container in the contact state, some functionality.

17. Click the contact tag in the States View.

18. Click the Button control in the Panel container for contact.

19. In the On click field, type the following code:

```
currentState = ''
```

The empty single quotes signify the base state.

> When signifying the base state with the empty single quotes, do not put a space between the quotes. This could result in an error.

20. Save and run your application.

When you click the LinkButton control, the second panel should turn on. When you click the Button control on that panel, it should return you to the original panel and the base state.

I am sure you are now seeing a lot of possibilities opening up. Keeping that in mind, let's take this concept one step even further.

21. Return to Flex Builder and select the contact state in the States View.

22. Click the New State button again.

Notice that this time you are asked whether you want to base your new state on the contact state. Flex will always ask whether you want to build on whatever state you have selected. In our case, we are basing it on the contact state.

23. Name your new state thankYou as shown in Figure 4-57. Remember, do not use any spaces.

Figure 4-57. The New State dialog box for a state built over the contact state

24. Click OK. Your States View should now resemble Figure 4-58.

Figure 4-58. The States View with a hierarchy of states

Notice that your new state, since it is built over the contact state, is indented in the States View. This makes it easy to see the hierarchy that is created by various states, as well as which states are built upon what others.

25. With the thankYou state selected, bring a third Panel container into the Design View.

26. Give this Panel container a title of Thank you for Contacting Us.

27. In the body of the Panel container, using a Text control, add the following text:

Thank you for sending us your inquiries. We will try to answer ➡
your question in the next year or so.

28. Drag a Button control into the Panel container and give it the label of OK as shown in Figure 4-59.

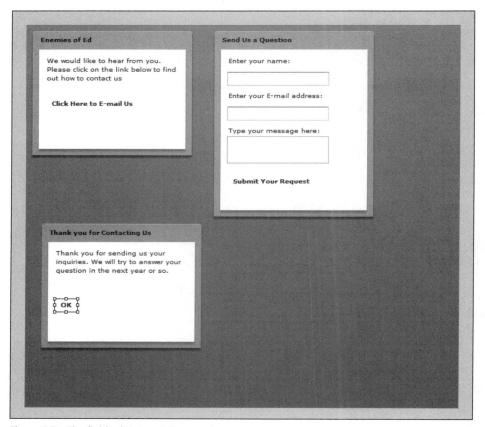

Figure 4-59. The finished states of the exercise

29. Click the Button control you just created and set the On click event to return to the base state:

currentState = ''

30. Return to the contact state and change the On click event of the Submit Your Request button to go to the thankYou state.

currentState = 'thankYou'

31. Save and test your application. You should see the application change appearance when you click the various buttons.

Needless to say, there are any number of variations you can try using these same ideas. For instance, you could have based the thankYou state on the base state. By doing that, the e-mail form would become invisible when the Submit Your Request button is clicked.

This also supports a statement I made toward the beginning of this chapter: in Flex applications, you pretty well confine most of your application to a single SWF file rather than go from page to page like you would do using XHTML.

It is worth spending a bit of time looking at the Source code behind what you just created in Design View.

States and code

Throughout most of this book, I will make every attempt to show you both the Design and Source (code) way of doing things. In my opinion, this gives you maximum control in creating your application. That being said, when creating states, Design View is unquestionably the better choice because the code can be daunting for a beginner. However, there are a couple of interesting concepts going on that you haven't seen yet. Take a look at the following code (or switch to Source View):

```
<?xml version="1.0" encoding="utf-8"?>
<mx:Application xmlns:mx="http://www.adobe.com/2006/mxml" ➡
layout="absolute">
    <mx:states>
        <mx:State name="contact">
            <mx:AddChild position="lastChild">
                <mx:Panel x="307" y="10" width="250" ➡
height="300" layout="absolute" title="Send Us a Question">
                    <mx:Label x="10" y="10" ➡
text="Enter your name:"/>
                    <mx:TextInput x="10" y="36"/>
                    <mx:Label x="10" y="66" ➡
text="Enter your e-mail address"/>
                    <mx:TextInput x="10" y="92"/>
                    <mx:Label x="10" y="122" ➡
text="Type your message here:"/>
                    <mx:TextArea x="10" y="138"/>
                    <mx:Button x="10" y="210" ➡
label="Submit Your Request" click="currentState = 'thankYou'"/>
                </mx:Panel>
            </mx:AddChild>
        </mx:State>
        <mx:State name="thankYou" basedOn="contact">
            <mx:AddChild position="lastChild">
                <mx:Panel x="71" y="331" width="250" ➡
height="200" layout="absolute" title="Thank You for Contacting Us">
                    <mx:Text x="10" y="10" text="Thank you ➡
for sending us your inquiry. We will try to answer your question ➡
in the next  year or so." width="198"/>
```

```
                              <mx:Button x="82" y="73" label="OK" ➡
            click="currentState = ''"/>
                          </mx:Panel>
                      </mx:AddChild>
                  </mx:State>
              </mx:states>
              <mx:Panel x="10" y="10" width="250" height="200" ➡
          layout="absolute" title="Enemies of Ed">
                  <mx:Text x="10" y="12" text="We would like to hear ➡
          from you. Please click on the link below to find out how to ➡
          contact us." width="210"/>
                  <mx:LinkButton x="10" y="74" label="Click Here to ➡
          E-mail Us" color="#0000FF" click="currentState = 'contact'"/>
              </mx:Panel>
          </mx:Application>
```

If you look carefully, you will see what appears to be a contradiction from what I said earlier. The entire state structure is enclosed in an opening and closing tag called

```
<mx:states>
```

Yet in Chapter 2, I stated that the MXML tags are based on ActionScript class files, and that a class file always begins with a capital letter.

This opening tag is not a contradiction. Instead, it is an interesting concept in MXML that we will see several times in the course of this book.

If you do a little research on the Application class, you will discover that one of its properties is states. MXML sometimes allows you to break out a property to its own separate tag to allow for more precise definitions. In this case, we are saying that the property states will have two state instances attached to it.

Each state that we define, in this case two (we do not count the base state), calls a new instance of the State class and gives it a name property. If you look at the code, you will see a State class with the name of contact and a State class with the name of thankYou.

So, in summary, all the states are wrapped in a property of the Application tag called states, and the particulars of each state are wrapped in a tag called State.

As soon as you click the control that calls the currentState handler, the AddChild class calls the <mx:states> property to find the appropriate <mx:State> class.

The AddChild class does just what its name implies: it will add a child to a container. When using MXML, the AddChild class is called automatically when a new state is created.

The AddChild class then takes over and creates a new container. The AddChild class has a property called position, which has a default value of lastChild. This puts the new container after any previous AddChild containers that might exist.

When the child container is no longer needed, `<mx:states>` calls a class called RemoveChild automatically. This class has the appropriate methods for removing the container.

As I said at the outset, this can be a bit daunting for a novice programmer. However, to help you get your toes a bit wet, let's try a small exercise involving rollover effects.

Rollovers and states

In traditional XHTML design, JavaScript can be used to create rollover effects. As soon as a mouse rolls over text or an image, an event handler in JavaScript catches the event, and the code instructs the browser to swap out one item for another. This process, as easy and commonplace as it is by today's web standards, requires a lot of resources.

Flash handled the process much more efficiently by compiling and compressing all the necessary graphics and code into a single SWF file. Again, like the previous examples, much of this was handled with the timeline. However, the timeline is no longer present in Flex.

Once again, states come to the rescue. Let's try a simple example. This time, rather than use Design View as before, you will create the code for this example in Source View. But before we do that, we need to import some assets into our small project.

Importing assets into a project

Follow these steps to import assets into your project:

1. Download the Chapter 4 files from www.friendsofed.com. This is just a picture of one of our many books and, as an alternative, you can use any image you want.

2. Unzip the download to any folder you choose.

3. Go to the Flex Navigator View in Flex Builder.

4. Right-click the src folder and select New ➤ Folder to bring up the dialog box shown in Figure 4-60.

5. Name the folder assets.

6. Click Finish.

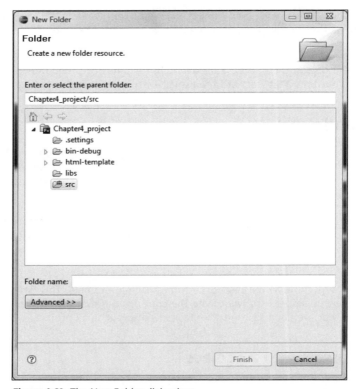

Figure 4-60. The New Folder dialog box

You should now see the folder in the Navigator View, as shown in Figure 4-61.

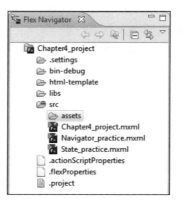

Figure 4-61. The Navigator View with
the assets folder

The next step is to import the desired files into that folder.

7. Right-click the new assets folder. This time select Import to bring up the dialog box shown in Figure 4-62.

Figure 4-62. The Import dialog box

8. Under the General category, select File System.

9. Click Next.

10. Click the Browse button, to the right of the From directory field, and navigate to the folder you unzipped the downloaded files to (see Figure 4-63).

Notice that there are two windows in the Import dialog box. The left window shows the folder, and the right window shows the files contained within that folder (on a Mac, you need to highlight the folder name in the left window before the right window is populated). You can either click the check box to the left of the folder to select all the files within that folder or click the check boxes for the specific files you desire.

11. Since there is only one file, jacobs.jpg, select it.

12. The Into folder field should have the src/assets folder selected. If not, use the Browse button to navigate to there.

13. Once everything is selected, click the Finish button.

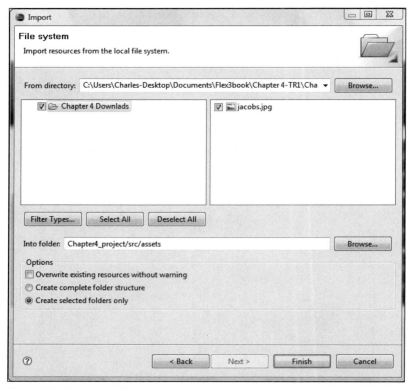

Figure 4-63. The Import dialog box

The file, or files, should be in the assets folder. You can check this in the Flex Navigator View (see Figure 4-64).

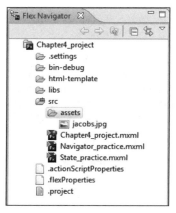

Figure 4-64. The Navigator View with the file imported

Now that the file is imported, we are ready to get back to the rollover example using states.

14. Close any MXML files you may still have open in the project.

15. Create a new MXML application and call it RollOver_practice.

16. Set the layout of the application to absolute.

While we could easily insert the graphic we just imported in Design mode, let's get our hands a little dirty and do some coding.

17. If necessary, switch to Source Perspective.

18. Between the Application tags, put an Image tag in with the properties shown here:

```
<?xml version="1.0" encoding="utf-8"?>
<mx:Application xmlns:mx="http://www.adobe.com/2006/mxml" ➡
layout="absolute">
    <mx:Image x="180" y="25" source="assets/jacobs.jpg"/>
</mx:Application>
```

Even though Flash and Flex are both working in ActionScript, the Image tag highlights one of the differences between Flash and Flex.

In Flash, when you insert an image on the stage, the image is embedded into the SWF file. That is not the case the with Image tag. The Image tag is calling the image from the server in much the same way that XHTML does. If you want to embed the image, you would need to modify the source property as follows:

```
<mx:Image x="180" y="25" source="@Embed('assets/jacobs.jpg')" />
```

Once again, notice the single quotes to designate a string within a string.

You can switch to Design View momentarily to ensure that the image was inserted properly, as shown in Figure 4-65.

19. We are now going to start coding the states by hand, so return to Source View.

Recall from our earlier example that each state uses the State class, and that all the State class instances need to be enclosed within the states property of the Application tag.

20. Break the states property out to its own container as follows:

```
<?xml version="1.0" encoding="utf-8"?>
<mx:Application xmlns:mx="http://www.adobe.com/2006/mxml" ➡
layout="absolute">
<mx:states>

</mx:states>
    <mx:Image x="180" y="25" source="assets/jacobs.jpg"/>
</mx:Application>
```

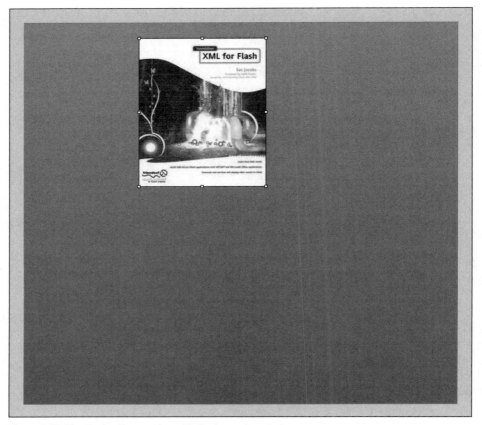

Figure 4-65. The Design Perspective with the image inserted

Notice that we put the code right below the Application tag. While this is not absolutely necessary, it makes for clearer coding since it is a property of the Application tag.

   21. Enter the code if you hadn't already.

Each state must now use the State class with a unique name.

   22. Add the following State and give the name property a value of bookDetails:

```
<?xml version="1.0" encoding="utf-8"?>
<mx:Application xmlns:mx="http://www.adobe.com/2006/mxml" ➥
layout="absolute">
<mx:states>
    <mx:State name="bookDetails">

    </mx:State>
</mx:states>
    <mx:Image x="180" y="25" source="../assets/jacobs.jpg"/>
</mx:Application>
```

Just to prove a point, return to Design View and look at the States View (see Figure 4-66). The state you just created with the <mx:State> tag should be listed in the View. Each subsequent state added will be listed.

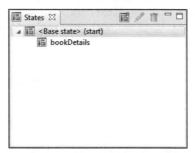

Figure 4-66. The bookDetails state listed

Returning to the code, the new state is added by creating a new container. The AddChild class is used to create the new container. This class also decides the position of this new container. The default position, as mentioned earlier, is lastChild. This means that it will be positioned after any other child containers added, which in this case is none.

23. Add the AddChild class as follows:

```
<?xml version="1.0" encoding="utf-8"?>
<mx:Application xmlns:mx="http://www.adobe.com/2006/mxml" ➡
layout="absolute">
<mx:states>
    <mx:State name="bookDetails">
        <mx:AddChild position="lastChild">

        </mx:AddChild>
    </mx:State>
</mx:states>
        <mx:Image x="180" y="25" source="assets/jacobs.jpg"/>
</mx:Application>
```

Within the AddChild tags, we add the required content for the container. That content could be anything from text to additional containers and images.

> If you don't want to type the following text, I have included a text file, RollOver_practice_text.txt, for you to use with the downloads for this chapter.

24. In this case, add a Text tag as follows:

```
<mx:State name="bookDetails">
    <mx:AddChild position="lastChild">
        <mx:Text width="385" x="110" y="275" fontWeight="bold" ➡
text="XML is a completely platform agnostic data medium. Flash is ➡
```

```
        able to make use of XML data, which is very useful when you are ➡
        creating Rich Internet Applications - it allows you to populate ➡
        Flash web interfaces with data from pretty much any source that ➡
        supports XML as a data medium, be it databases, raw XML files, ➡
        or more excitingly, .NET applications, web services, and even ➡
        Microsoft Office applications such as Excel and Word"/>
            </mx:AddChild>
        </mx:State>
```

25. Switch to Design View and click bookDetails in the States View; you should see the placement of your text, as shown in Figure 4-67.

Figure 4-67. The new child container with text

We can go back to Source View and create a second container using the AddChild class. In this one, we will add a container with a Text control for the book's ISBN number.

26. Add another AddChild instance right under the existing AddChild container. Again, show its position as lastChild and add the following Text control:

```
</mx:AddChild>
<mx:AddChild position="lastChild">
    <mx:Text width="135" fontWeight="bold" ➡
text="ISBN: 1590595432" x="236" y="380"/>
</mx:AddChild>
```

Hopefully, you are now beginning to see how the AddChild class adds containers within the State container.

You may be thinking that you could have added these Text controls directly into the State container. However, I strongly suggest that you do not do that. It you do, you will sacrifice some interesting design possibilities. You will see some of these possibilities as you progress through this book.

It is now time to give your application some functionality.

Recall that earlier in this chapter, you assigned the currentState handler to the click event. You will do a slight variation here and assign this handler to a rollOver event for the image.

27. Make the following modifications to the Image MXML tag:

```
<mx:Image id="jacobsBook" x="180" y="25" source=➡
"../assets/jacobs.jpg" rollOver="currentState = 'bookDetails' " />
```

> *Please remember to enclose* bookDetails *in single quotes as discussed earlier.*

28. Save and test the application.

As soon as you roll over the image, your AddChild containers and their contents should appear.

You now have one slight problem. When you roll off of the image, the content in the AddChild containers remain.

As you probably guessed, we can easily remedy this by adding a second event to the Image control as follows:

29. Make the following additional modification to the Image tag:

```
<mx:Image id="jacobsBook" x="181" y="25" source=➡
"../assets/jacobs.jpg"rollOver="currentState = ➡
'bookDetails' " rollOut="currentState = '' " />
```

30. Save and run your application now. You should see the text disappear after you roll the mouse away from the image.

Let's try a small variation in order to see an interesting programming tool in Flex 3.

31. Delete the rollOut event you just created in the Image control.

Before the closing </ mx:State> tag, we will create a SetEventHandler tag. The SetEventHandler class allows you to define events outside of the component creating the event. This class can be used only within an <mx:State> container. While this will be a relatively simple example, you will be using this in increasingly complex situations—for instance, assigning multiple events and transitions to a state.

The SetEventHandler class has three important properties:

- The name property is the name of the event you are setting the handler for. In this case, it will be rollOut.

- The target property is the name of the component that will be dispatching the event. In this case, it will be the Image control with the ID of jacobsBook. You need to set the target using the binding syntax with curly braces ({}).

- The handler property is what to do when the event occurs. In this case, it will be returning to the base state.

32. Put this code before the closing State tag:

```
<mx:SetEventHandler name="rollOut" target="{jacobsBook}" ➥
handler="currentState = '' "/>
```

33. Test your application now. It should work exactly the same way when you roll your mouse out.

When I give Flex seminars, I show the power of the SetEventHandler using an example similar to the one I just showed here. Invariably, I am asked whether the rollover event can be set up the same way. I have the attendees set it up and, when they go to test it, nothing happens. Can you guess why?

The reason can be understood with a bit of logic. The SetEventHandler class is invoked within the State container. This means that it is not active until the State it is in is active. In this case, the State is not active until the rollover event occurs. So you would be trying to call something that programmatically does not exist yet. It is a bit of cyclical thinking.

Along with the SetEventHandler, there is the SetProperty event. The syntax for this is very similar in that the target attribute will be the component whose properties you want to change. Like the SetEventHandler, the name property is the property you want to change. Unlike the SetEventHandler, you will use value to assign a value to the property you are changing.

In this example, you want to reduce the size of the image by 50% when the state bookDetails is activated. This will require that you add two SetProperty tags: one for the scaleX property and one for the scaleY property.

The scaleX and scaleY properties are multipliers of the width and the height, respectively. So if you set a scaleX property to 2, it will multiply the present width by 2. Likewise, if you were to set a scaleY property by .5, it will reduce the height by half.

34. Give it a try by putting the following two tags below the SetEventHandler tag:

```
<mx:SetEventHandler name="rollOut" target="{jacobsBook}" ➥
handler="currentState = '' "/>
<mx:SetProperty target="{jacobsBook}" name="scaleX" value=".50"/>
<mx:SetProperty target="{jacobsBook}" name="scaleY" value=".50"/>
```

35. Run the application. When you roll over the image, it should reduce its size by 50% (see Figure 4-68).

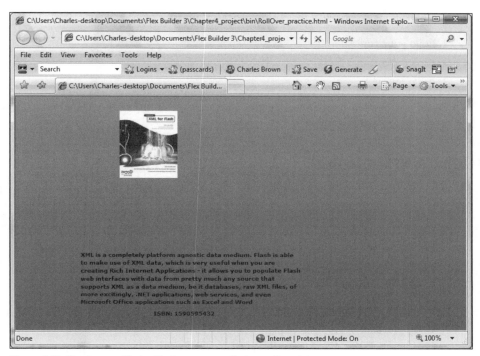

Figure 4-68. The image effect with the mouse rolled over the picture

> *When you run this application, you may have some erratic behaviors with the image size. This is due to the target area changing. Don't be concerned about that now. Our main goal here is for you to understand the concepts. As you progress through this book, you will be fine-tuning much of your code.*

In all of these examples, the states seem to be making a rather ungraceful entrance and exit. Let's see how you can smooth things up a little bit.

Transitions

A **transition** is a way to gracefully turn a state on or off. There is no way to set transitions up in Design View, and, as you are about to see, they require a bit of MXML coding. The subject of transitions could be a large one, and a detailed discussion of them is outside the scope of this book. The following example will hopefully give you a solid introduction.

Building transitions is actually a three-step process:

1. Build your container.

2. Create the states.

3. Program the transitions.

In this exercise, you are going to work with a slightly more complex scenario. You will give the container some animation with transitions.

Building the container

You'll start this exercise by building the container you will eventually use the transition with.

1. Start a new MXML application and give it a name of Transition_practice. The layout will be absolute.

You are going to build a container to hold the information for the Sas Jacob's XML book. This part will be pretty straightforward.

2. In Source View, create the following code:

```
<?xml version="1.0" encoding="utf-8"?>
<mx:Application xmlns:mx="http://www.adobe.com/2006/mxml" ➥
layout="absolute">
      <mx:Panel title="XML Book" id="book" horizontalScrollPolicy=➥
"off" verticalScrollPolicy="off">
           <mx:Form id="bookForm">
                 <mx:FormItem label="Foundation XML for Flash" ➥
fontWeight="bold"/>
                 <mx:FormItem label="Sas Jacobs" fontStyle="italic"/>
           </mx:Form>
      </mx:Panel>
</mx:Application>
```

Here we see two properties we have not addressed yet: horizontalScrollPolicy and verticalScrollPolicy. Many of the visual classes contain these properties, and they handle the functionality of the scrollbars in the application. There are three possible values you can assign to these properties: auto, off, or on. The auto value will switch the scrollbars on when needed. The off or on values will leave them off or on no matter what the circumstances.

3. Switch to Design View; your initial Panel container should appear as shown Figure 4-69.

Figure 4-69. The initial Panel container

Next, you need to add a LinkButton and Label control to the Panel container. As you saw earlier in this chapter, the easiest way to do that is with a ControlBar. The purpose of the ControlBar is to provide a container for adding any controls you might need along the bottom of the Panel container.

You want to be certain that there is a space between the LinkButton and Label controls. In order to do this, you are going to call on a class in Flex called Spacer. In situations where the size of that parent container could be variable, the Spacer class has a number of properties for setting height, width, maximum height and width, minimum height and width, percent height and width, and so on. It would be well worth your time to study the documentation for this class. I find that it comes in handy for a variety of situations.

4. Add the following code to the Panel container you just created:

```
<mx:Panel title="XML Book" id="book" horizontalScrollPolicy=➡
"off" verticalScrollPolicy="off">
     <mx:Form id="bookForm">
          <mx:FormItem label="Foundation XML for Flash" ➡
fontWeight="bold"/>
          <mx:FormItem label="Sas Jacobs" fontStyle="italic"/>
     </mx:Form>
     <mx:ControlBar>
          <mx:LinkButton label="Book Details" id="bookLink"/>
          <mx:Spacer width="100%" id="spacer1"/>
          <mx:Label text="Book Title" id="title"/>
     </mx:ControlBar>
</mx:Panel>
```

Your Panel container should now look like Figure 4-70.

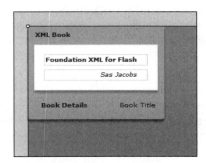

Figure 4-70. The completed Panel container

Now that the container is completed, your next step is to build the state for it.

Building the state

Recall from earlier in this chapter that states must be enclosed within the <mx:states> tag that creates an array of containers. Each of these containers represents a different state and must be enclosed in the <mx:State> tag, which represents the State class.

Most of the following code example is similar to the previous states you built. However, there will be some interesting additions, which we will discuss after we enter the code.

1. Place the following code right after the opening Application tag:

```
<mx:states>
    <mx:State name="bookDetails" basedOn="">
        <mx:AddChild relativeTo="{bookForm}" ➥
position="lastChild" creationPolicy="all">
            <mx:FormItem id="isbn" label="ISBN: 1590595432"/>
        </mx:AddChild>
        <mx:SetProperty target="{book}" name="title" ➥
value="Book Details"/>
        <mx:SetProperty target="{title}" name="text" ➥
value="Book Details"/>
        <mx:RemoveChild target="{bookLink}"/>
        <mx:AddChild relativeTo="{spacer1}" position="before">
            <mx:LinkButton label="Collapse Book Details" ➥
click="currentState = ''"/>
        </mx:AddChild>
    </mx:State>
</mx:states>
```

After the opening <mx:states> tag, you create the state, named bookDetails, using the <mx:State> tag.

As mentioned previously, the AddChild class adds a new container, and each container can contain any content that you might need. However, here you are using it a bit differently from the earlier examples.

In this example, you are adding the relativeTo attribute to the AddChild class to add the container to the bookForm Form container you created earlier. You are also telling it to position this container, containing the form items, as the last child (or container) in the form.

The creationPolicy property decides when the child container is created.

> Notice I said "created" and not "added." When it is created, it is just held in memory until it is called.

The creationPolicy property has three possible values. The default is auto. An auto value means that the container is created when the state is activated. The all value, which you use in this example, means that the container is created when the application is started. When doing transitions (which are basically animations), you might find that caching the child containers will facilitate smoother transitions since the pieces will be in place already. The none value means that the child will not be created until a function, createInstance(), is called to specifically create it. This can be handy in certain advanced programming scenarios.

You are using the `all` value here to help make for a smoother transition later on.

After the `AddChild` container is created, you use the `SetProperty` class discussed earlier in the chapter. Notice that, in this case, you are using two instances of the class to change the title value of the `Panel` container, book, and the text attribute of the `Label` control, `title`, in the `ControlBar` container. Remember, these actions will not occur until the state is activated.

The next few lines are where things start to become a bit different.

Remember, whenever you add something to a container, including another container, you are adding a child to that container. The class `RemoveChild` removes child containers and controls from the user interface. In this case, you are telling it to remove the `LinkButton` control, `bookLink`, in the `ControlBar` container.

Once the initial `LinkButton` is removed, you put a whole new one in its place. Notice that you position the new control before the `Spacer`, `spacer1`, using a combination of the `relativeTo` and `position` properties. This raises an interesting programming issue: could you have used the `SetProperty` and `SetEventHandler` classes to do the same thing?

The answer to that is yes!

In this case, either technique would have worked. The decision as to which technique should be used is largely a matter of programming style and needs. As you progress through this book, and as you learn new techniques, you may want to go through previous exercises and modify them using your newfound knowledge.

2. Switch to Design View and activate the `bookDetails` state; your UI should look something like Figure 4-71.

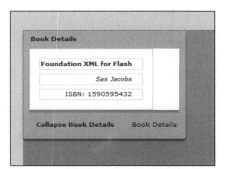

Figure 4-71. The layout of the bookDetails state

Notice the change in the panel's title and the label's text. Also, there is additional content, the ISBN number, in the form.

You have one more small thing to do. You need to tell the initial `LinkButton` control, located in the `ControlBar`, to switch to the `bookDetails` state when clicked.

3. Add the following code to the LinkButton tag:

```
<mx:LinkButton label="Book Details" id="bookLink" ➥
click="currentState = 'bookDetails' "/>
```

Again, do not forget to use the single quotes around the name of the state.

At this point, your code should look as follows:

```
<?xml version="1.0" encoding="utf-8"?>
<mx:Application xmlns:mx="http://www.adobe.com/2006/mxml" ➥
layout="absolute">
<mx:states>
    <mx:State name="bookDetails" basedOn="">
        <mx:AddChild relativeTo="{bookForm}" ➥
position="lastChild" creationPolicy="all">
            <mx:FormItem id="isbn" label="ISBN: 1590595432"/>
        </mx:AddChild>
        <mx:SetProperty target="{book}" name="title" ➥
value="Book Details"/>
        <mx:SetProperty target="{title}" name="text" ➥
value="Book Details"/>
        <mx:RemoveChild target="{bookLink}"/>
        <mx:AddChild relativeTo="{spacer1}" position="before">
            <mx:LinkButton label="Collapse Book Details" ➥
click="currentState = ''"/>
        </mx:AddChild>
    </mx:State>
</mx:states>
    <mx:Panel title="XML Book" id="book" horizontalScrollPolicy=➥
"off" verticalScrollPolicy="off">
        <mx:Form id="bookForm">
            <mx:FormItem label="Foundation XML for Flash" ➥
fontWeight="bold"/>
            <mx:FormItem label="Sas Jacobs" fontStyle="italic"/>
        </mx:Form>
        <mx:ControlBar>
            <mx:LinkButton label="Book Details" id="bookLink" ➥
click="currentState = 'bookDetails' "/>
            <mx:Spacer width="100%" id="spacer1"/>
            <mx:Label text="Book Title" id="title"/>
        </mx:ControlBar>
    </mx:Panel>
</mx:Application>
```

Your next step is to start creating a transition so your state enters and exits gracefully.

Creating transitions

In many respects, the syntax for creating transitions is similar to the syntax for states. You are going to use a tag, <mx:transitions>, to create an array of transitions. Like <mx:states>, transitions is a property of the Application tag, which we will break out to its own container. You can create as many transition effects as you want. In addition, you can make a decision whether you want them to play sequentially or parallel.

1. Enter the following transition code under the closing </mx:states> tag. We will discuss it line by line after you enter it.

```
<mx:transitions>
    <mx:Transition fromState="*" toState="*">
        <mx:Parallel targets="{[book, bookLink, title, isbn]}">
            <mx:Resize duration="5000" easingFunction=➡
"Bounce.easeOut"/>
            <mx:Sequence target="{isbn}">
                <mx:Blur duration="2000" blurYFrom="0.0" ➡
blurYTo="20.0"/>
                <mx:Blur duration="2000" blurYFrom="20.0" ➡
blurYTo="0.0"/>
            </mx:Sequence>
        </mx:Parallel>
    </mx:Transition>
</mx:transitions>
```

Just as the <mx:states> tag creates an array of states, the <mx:transitions> tag creates an array of transitions within it. And just as the <mx:State> tag creates a new state, <mx:Transition> creates a new transition. However, the fromState and toState properties create an interesting programming possibility.

Let's create a hypothetical situation here and say that your application has four states: stateA, stateB, stateC, and stateD. You could specify to use this particular transition only when going from stateB to stateC as follows:

```
<mxTransition fromState = "stateB" toState = "stateC" >
```

By using the asterisk (*) in the project code, you are telling Flex to use this transition when it switches from any state to any state.

With transitions, you can choose whether they perform all together, in **parallel**, or one after the other, in **sequence**.

In this example, you choose to have parallel performance by selecting the Parallel class. But now you have to tell Flex what components you want to run in parallel. If you are transitioning just a single component, you use the target property. However, if you are transitioning multiple components, you use the targets property with array syntax.

```
<mx:Parallel targets="{[book, bookLink, title, isbn]}">
```

4

By using the Parallel class, you are telling Flex to resize all of the components contained in the square brackets (array syntax) to perform the transition together.

The syntax is important here. Since we are using multiple targets, the Parallel class is setting up its own array of components. The square brackets ([ ]) is array syntax. So the components book, bookLink, title, and isbn will transition all at the same time, or in parallel.

Within that Parallel container, you now need to specify the actions these components will perform. You have a choice of either the Resize or Move class. For this example, we are using the Resize class.

```
<mx:Resize duration="5000" easingFunction="Bounce.easeOut"/>
```

The first attribute you see is the duration property. This will decide how long the resizing transition will take to complete. It is measured in milliseconds, so 5000 milliseconds translates to 5 seconds.

> In this exercise, I purposely slowed down the transition in order to show the effect. In an actual project, 2–3 seconds would probably be more realistic.

The easingFunction property varies the speed of the transition animation and goes back to a feature of Flash. The best analogy is that of a ball. If you ever follow the calculus of throwing a ball in the air, gravity will cause it to slow as it rises and accelerate as it descends. The variation of velocity is called **easing**. Rather than specify a value directly, you are going to let the value of the easingFunction be controlled by yet another class: Bounce.

The Bounce class does just as it says: it causes the easing to bounce like a ball. The easeOut function causes the bounce to begin quickly and then slow down. So, in this case, the resize transition will last 5 seconds (5000 milliseconds) and end with a bounce that will begin quickly and then slow down.

There is one quirk to using the Bounce class that you need to know. The Bounce class is part of the mx.effects.easing package. As I discussed in Chapter 2, a **package** is a directory structure for storing related class files. Before ActionScript can use class files from another package (or directory structure), it has to be able to find that package. There are two ways of accomplishing that: In MXML you would use a namespace property in the Application tag. Within ActionScript itself, you would use the import command. Since both options get you to exactly the same place, they are interchangeable. The only difference is that the import command must be within the Script tag.

2. Under the Application tag, create a Script block as follows:

```
<mx:Application xmlns:mx="http://www.adobe.com/2006/mxml" ➡
layout="absolute">
<mx:Script>
    <![CDATA[
        import mx.effects.easing.Bounce;
    ]]>
</mx:Script>
```

ActionScript can now find the Bounce class.

While all of this is going on, we will run a second animation in the isbn label.

3. Use the Sequence class instead of the Parallel class so that the two animations will perform one after the other:

```
<mx:Sequence target="{isbn}">
     <mx:Blur duration="2000" blurYFrom="0.0" blurYTo="20.0"/>
     <mx:Blur duration="2000" blurYFrom="20.0" blurYTo="0.0"/>
</mx:Sequence>
```

An old trick of animators is to create a sense of motion by blurring an object and then bringing it back into focus. The Blur class does just that by creating a graphic effect called a Gaussian blur.

Looking at the preceding code, it should be fairly obvious why you did this sequentially. You first change the blur of the control from 0.0 to 20.0 over a time of 2 seconds, and then change back from 20 to 0 over another 2 seconds to bring it back into focus.

Now that you have the transitions all set, take a quick review of all of your code.

```
<?xml version="1.0" encoding="utf-8"?>
<mx:Application xmlns:mx="http://www.adobe.com/2006/mxml" ➥
layout="absolute">
<mx:Script>
     <![CDATA[
          import mx.effects.easing.Bounce;
     ]]>
</mx:Script>
<mx:states>
     <mx:State name="bookDetails" basedOn="">
          <mx:AddChild relativeTo="{bookForm}" position=➥
"lastChild" creationPolicy="all">
               <mx:FormItem id="isbn" label="ISBN: 1590595432"/>
          </mx:AddChild>
          <mx:SetProperty target="{book}" name="title" ➥
value="Book Details"/>
          <mx:SetProperty target="{title}" name="text" ➥
value="Book Details"/>
          <mx:RemoveChild target="{bookLink}"/>
          <mx:AddChild relativeTo="{spacer1}" position="before">
               <mx:LinkButton label="Collapse Book Details" ➥
click="currentState = ''"/>
          </mx:AddChild>
     </mx:State>
</mx:states>
<mx:transitions>
     <mx:Transition fromState="*" toState="*">
          <mx:Parallel targets="{[book, bookLink, title, isbn]}">
               <mx:Resize duration="5000" easingFunction=➥
```

4

```
                        "Bounce.easeOut"/>
                                <mx:Sequence target="{isbn}">
                                        <mx:Blur duration="2000" blurYFrom="0.0" ➥
            blurYTo="20.0"/>
                                        <mx:Blur duration="2000" blurYFrom="20.0" ➥
            blurYTo="0.0"/>
                                </mx:Sequence>
                        </mx:Parallel>
                </mx:Transition>
        </mx:transitions>
                <mx:Panel title="XML Book" id="book" horizontalScrollPolicy=➥
        "off" verticalScrollPolicy="off">
                        <mx:Form id="bookForm">
                                <mx:FormItem label="Foundation XML for Flash" ➥
            fontWeight="bold"/>
                                <mx:FormItem label="Sas Jacobs" fontStyle="italic"/>
                        </mx:Form>
                        <mx:ControlBar>
                                <mx:LinkButton label="Book Details" id="bookLink" ➥
            click="currentState = 'bookDetails' "/>
                                <mx:Spacer width="100%" id="spacer1"/>
                                <mx:Label text="Book Title" id="title"/>
                        </mx:ControlBar>
                </mx:Panel>
        </mx:Application>
```

If all looks well, go ahead and give the code a test drive.

When you click the LinkButton control, you should see all the changes of the new state taking place. When you return to the base state, the changes reverse.

While these transitions are fun and, once you get the idea, easy to program, I strongly recommend that you plan them out before you start to program. In very complex situations, they can get quite involved.

And you thought you lost the timeline from Flash?

Summary

We just covered a lot of ground here. you learned about the two types of containers: layout and navigation. Once you had the concept of containers under control, we then discussed how to smoothly activate containers only when needed by using states. But, as you learned, we don't need to just turn these states on and off like a switch; we can smoothly transition these containers on and off by using transitions. I often liken transitions to using the timeline in Flash.

I hope you now see how the whole concept of containers lies at the heart of Flex application design. From this point on, we will be building on these very important concepts and will frequently be referring to this chapter. But our discussion of containers does not end here.

Up to this point, we have only briefly touched on components and events. The next chapter will drill into them a lot deeper and show you how they work together.

4

5 EVENTS AND COMPONENTS

Now that you know the mechanics of Flex, we need to start talking about design models.

What do I mean by that?

Essentially, it means how to design your applications. These designs will include techniques for making your application modular and dividing up the workflow.

In this chapter, we will begin by discussing events differently from the previous chapters. Instead of building simple events into the MXML code, we will use ActionScript 3.0. As you will see, this will open many more possibilities for us.

Then we will look at how to build specialized components. While this may seem, on the surface, to be unrelated to events, they are actually connected, as you will learn while progressing through this book.

We will discuss Model-View-Controller, a design pattern that will help you plan many of your projects.

Finally, we will return to events so you can learn how to create custom events that will either trigger actions or pass data while triggering actions.

Trust me, by the time you reach the end of this chapter, your understanding of Flex application design will forever be changed. Let's get started.

Events

As I stated earlier in the book, an event could be anything that causes an action to happen. For example, it could be a mouse click or a key press.

> *While tossing your computer against the wall could be considered an event, it is not one that can be easily handled by ActionScript 3.0. However, Adobe engineers are working on it for a future update.*

It could also be something unseen, such as the application completely loading, data loading, a connection being made, etc. ActionScript can handle hundreds of seen or unseen events.

While ActionScript 2.0 also had these capabilities, ActionScript 3.0 has streamlined and made the ability to handle these functions easier than ever.

We will begin by building a simple graphical user interface (GUI) to test event handling.

1. Close and/or delete any projects you may have open in Flex Builder 3.
2. Start a new Flex project of any name of your choice. I am using the name Chapter5_project.
3. Set your layout for the application to absolute.

4. Create a Panel container with the x property set to 320, y set to 130, width property to 250, and height will equal 200. Set the layout to be absolute and the title to Testing Events.

```xml
<?xml version="1.0" encoding="utf-8"?>
<mx:Application xmlns:mx="http://www.adobe.com/2006/mxml" ➥
layout="absolute">
    <mx:Panel x="320" y="130" width="250" height="200" ➥
layout="absolute" title="Testing Events">

        </mx:Panel>
</mx:Application>
```

5. Within the Panel container, put a Label component with an id of myLabel and a Button with a label of Test and an id property of myButton. While position is not important, I gave the Label an x-position of 55 and a y-position of 45. I gave the Button an x-position of 90 and a y-position of 96 (see Figure 5-1).

Figure 5-1. The basic GUI setup

Your finished code should look as follows:

```xml
<?xml version="1.0" encoding="utf-8"?>
<mx:Application xmlns:mx="http://www.adobe.com/2006/mxml" ➥
layout="absolute">
    <mx:Panel x="320" y="127" width="250" height="200" ➥
layout="absolute" title="Testing Events">
        <mx:Label x="55" y="45" id="myLabel"/>
        <mx:Button label="Test" id="myButton" x="90" y="96"/>
    </mx:Panel>
</mx:Application>
```

Let's do a quick review.

We could simply give the Button an inline event as follows:

```xml
<mx:Button label="Test" id="myButton" x="90" y="96" ➥
click="myLabel.text = 'The button is clicked' "/>
```

> *Please remember that the text is enclosed in single quotes because the entire* click *event has to be enclosed in double quotes. This is how most programming environments define a string within a string.*

6. Run the application and click the button; the label should look something like what appears in Figure 5-2.

Figure 5-2. The initial application

Getting that label text to appear is pretty easy, with little coding involved other than the MXML tags. That ease comes at a bit of a price. The price is flexibility.

Let's start handling things a bit differently now.

7. Right under the Application tag, build a Script block with the following code for a private function:

```
<mx:Script>
    <![CDATA[
        private function fillLabel():void
        {
            myLabel.text = "The Button is Clicked!";
        }
    ]]>
</mx:Script>
```

8. Change the click event in the Button component as follows:

```
<mx:Button label="Test" id="myButton" x="90" y="96" ➥
click="fillLabel()"/>
```

Here, rather than call the Label control directly, we pass it through the fillLabel() function in the Script block.

> *Recall that the "private scope" means that only this file can see and use the* fillLabel() *function.*

9. Run the application again; it should work exactly the same as before.

So how does this make things more flexible? Hold tight! A bit of terminology is in order here.

The click event in the Button component is actually referred to in most programming environments as the **event listener**. This means its only job is to listen for its assigned event to happen. This term is going to take on an increased importance shortly. Once the event happens, it tells the assigned code (in this case, the fillLabel() function) to go ahead and do its job. That code is the **event handler**.

Coding such as this allows you to build events easily. However, there is a third, and very powerful, way to handle events: the **event object**.

The event object

When an event happens in ActionScript, as is true of most programming environments today, an object is generated called the **event object**. This object contains two very important pieces of information: the **target** and the **type**.

The target property contains nearly all of the information about who generated the event. For instance, it could return the ID, x-position, y-position, etc., of our Button component. The type property returns what type of event was generated. In our small case, it would be a click event. But in more complex situations, there could be many different types of events.

> *In more precise terminology, the* target *property is creating a pointer to the broadcaster of the event. As you get into more advanced programming scenarios, that small distinction will be quite important.*

Let's see how the event object works by modifying the code a bit.

1. First of all, modify the Button component's event as follows:

```
<mx:Button label="Test" id="myButton" x="90" y="96" ➥
click="fillLabel(event)"/>
```

Notice that when the click event now calls the event handler, in this case fillLabel(), it is now passing a parameter. The name of that parameter, event, is actually the name of the event, and that name is important. You cannot use any name other than that.

2. Now turn your attention to the fillLabel() handler. Modify the code as follows:

```
private function fillLabel(evt:Event):void
{
    myLabel.text = evt.target.id + " is pressed";
}
```

5

Notice that we received the event object with a reference called evt. Here we could have called it anything. It is just a name so that the function can reference it. Recall, however, that when a function receives a parameter, it must have a data type (which is a class file) associated with it. The class best suited to handle most events is class Event. In this case, you could have used MouseEvent as the type or even Object. We will keep things pretty generic for now, however.

If you bring up the documentation of the Event class, you can see its many properties and functions. There is a new part to it called **constants**, and we will talk about them a little later in this chapter in the section "addEventListener."

As you can see, the Event class is part of the flash.events package and has the ability to capture and handle events.

> As we progress through this book, we will be seeing different types of events and the classes associated with them.

Once the event object is "caught" by the function (event handler), the function has access to all of the properties of the event originator (sometimes called the **event dispatcher**) through the target property. The function can also see what type of event it was through the type property.

The code

```
myLabel.text = evt.target.id + " is pressed";
```

is calling the id property of the event dispatcher, in this case myButton, by using the target property.

3. Give it a try. You should get the same result shown in Figure 5-3.

Figure 5-3. The changed label

I am sure you are starting to see the potential here. For instance, as you will shortly see, you could build decision structures based on who triggered the event or what the event was.

Let's see an example by adding a second Button control beneath the original one like so:

4. Add the following second Button:

```
<mx:Button label="Test" id="myButton" x="90" y="96" ➡
click="fillLabel(event)"/>
 <mx:Button label="Test 2" id="myButton2" x="90" y="126" ➡
click="fillLabel(event)"/>
```

5. Run the application again, and click back and forth on the buttons.

You see that the one event handler, fillLabel(evt:Event), can now handle the click event generated by either button. You don't need to write a separate handler for each component.

Now take this even further with a slight variation.

6. Change the code so that it decides who is generating the event and responds differently as follows:

```
private function fillLabel(evt:Event):void
{
    if(evt.target.id == "myButton")
    {
        myLabel.text = "Button 1 is pressed";
    }
    if(evt.target.id == "myButton2")
    {
        myLabel.text = "Button 2 is pressed";
    }
}
```

Here you see the syntax for building a **decision** statement. The decision it needs to make is referred to as a **Boolean statement**. It is enclosed in parentheses and returns a value of either true or false. The body of code that will run if the Boolean statement returns true, like functions, is enclosed in curly braces.

Here you are building two decision statements to test which component is broadcasting the event.

> Note that a double equal sign is used here instead of a single one. The double equal sign means compare what is on the left side of the equal sign to what is on the right side. A single equal sign, called an **assignment operator**, assigns what is on the right side of the equal sign to what is on the left side. The double equal sign is called the **comparison operator**. For example, a = b means the value of b will be assigned to a. However, a == b is testing to see whether a is equal to b. If it is, it returns true. If not, it returns false.

7. Go ahead and run the application. You should see the label text change for each button as expected.

Up to this point, we have only used the target property. But you will recall that I mentioned a second property earlier: type. This returns the type of event that was generated.

8. Delete the two if statements in the handler and replace the code as follows:

```
private function fillLabel(evt:Event):void
{
        myLabel.text = evt.type;
}
```

If you run the code now, both buttons return the same event: click (see Figure 5-4).

Figure 5-4. The function showing a click event

Hopefully, you are beginning to see a huge number of possibilities here. However, you still do not have the whole picture; there is one other feature that will open an even greater world of possibilities: the addEventListener.

addEventListener

An event listener takes up a fair amount of memory. In the small applications you have been creating here, it is not a large factor. However, in large and complex applications, you want to minimize the resources used as much as possible. You do not want to add an event listener until it is actually needed. We can do that programmatically as follows.

The addEventListener function is found in many of the class files within ActionScript 3.0. This function allows you to assign events to a component when they are needed. Because of this, you can completely change the results of an event as needed, as well as preserve resources by assigning an event listener only when it is needed.

To better understand this, here's an example that would be common in application construction:

1. Begin by removing the click event in myButton2. The button now has no way of accessing the handler fillLabel().

2. Inside of the handler, change the code so that the label property of the calling button will be displayed as follows:

```
private function fillLabel(evt:Event):void
{
    myLabel.text = evt.target.label;
}
```

We are now going to add the addEventListener function. Let's do this one step at a time.

3. Immediately below the line of code you just edited, add the following code:

```
myButton2.addEventListener(
```

When you type the open parenthesis, Flex Builder gives you code hinting as to what arguments will be needed. The first one is a box that shows you the type of events available, as shown in Figure 5-5.

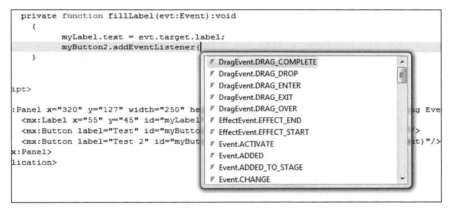

Figure 5-5. The list of available events

In actuality, it is in two parts: the first part is the type of event, and after the dot, the name of the event itself appears in capital letters. It is in capital letters for a reason. Recall earlier that when we looked at the documentation for the Event class, there was a category called **constants**. A constant means a property that does not change. A common example would be the mathematical property of PI in the Math class. PI never changes. In OOP environments, constants are usually designated with all capital letters.

4. CLICK is a MouseEvent. So scroll down to MouseEvent.CLICK (or press the M key) and select it.

5. Type in a comma.

Now you need to enter the second argument, which is the name of the handler, fillLabel. Here is where things get a little strange: even though we are making a function call, we don't use parentheses like we did earlier. We use the parentheses to pass parameters. However, here, all of that is being handled in the background for us.

6. After the comma, just type fillLabel. Your finished handler should look as follows:

```
private function fillLabel(evt:Event):void
{
    myLabel.text = evt.target.label;
    myButton2.addEventListener(MouseEvent.CLICK,fillLabel);
}
```

Your complete code should look like this:

```
<?xml version="1.0" encoding="utf-8"?>
<mx:Application xmlns:mx="http://www.adobe.com/2006/mxml" ➥
layout="absolute">
<mx:Script>
    <![CDATA[
        private function fillLabel(evt:Event):void
        {
            myLabel.text = evt.target.label;
            myButton2.addEventListener(MouseEvent.CLICK,fillLabel);
        }
    ]]>
</mx:Script>
    <mx:Panel x="320" y="127" width="250" height="200" ➥
layout="absolute" title="Testing Events">
        <mx:Label x="55" y="45" id="myLabel"/>
        <mx:Button label="Test" id="myButton" x="90" y="96" ➥
click="fillLabel(event)"/>
        <mx:Button label="Test 2" id="myButton2" x="90" y="126"/>
    </mx:Panel>
</mx:Application>
```

7. Run the application.

8. Click the Test 2 button first. Nothing should happen.

9. Click the Test button, and the button's label property should appear in the Label (see Figure 5-6).

Figure 5-6. The result of pressing the Test button

10. Now click the Test 2 button again. The label property should display as shown in Figure 5-7.

Figure 5-7. The Test 2 button results

As soon as you clicked the Test button, you accessed the handler. The code then assigned a MouseEvent click event to the Test 2 button and tells the event to use the fillHandler method when the event occurs. We actually assigned the event while the application is running. This is called a **runtime** assignment. This also means that, depending on what is going on, you can assign events as they are needed. You may be wondering why this is important. Do you need to click button A before button B will work? Not very useful if that is the case.

If you are thinking that, then you're missing the point, which is that events can be initialized during runtime as they are needed. In this example, we had one button initialize the event of another button. But we could easily have set up a scenario, as just one example, in which the event handler the button selects depends on a check box the user might select. I could list endless permutations and combinations. But hopefully you are getting the idea.

As you progress through the book, you will be frequently revisiting events. Further, you will learn a concept called a **custom event** a little later in this chapter. However, we will now turn our attention in a slightly different direction.

Components

Until this point, we have put everything into a single MXML file and have run that file. However, if you have ever done OOP coding, you probably know that it is better to divide things out into more specialized units of programming called **class files**. Class files make the application more modular. This feature, in turn, improves both the maintainability and reusability of the code. Each class does only one specialized job. If necessary, it can call upon other class files when it needs additional operations completed in order for it to do its job.

We have used class files quite a bit to this point in that MXML serves as a surrogate to those class files. As we have seen, each MXML tag is accessing the properties, functions, and events of a related class file.

In this section, we are going to create our own class files. However, rather than create the code in ActionScript 3.0, we will create the MXML equivalent called **components**.

In OOP, studies have shown that nearly all applications fall into a limited number of coding techniques called **design patterns**. Once you become familiar with these patterns, it is easy to pick one of them in order to accomplish a certain task.

One of the most frequently used design patterns in Flex is the **Model-View-Controller** pattern (often referred to as MVC). I will keep the explanation brief here because, as you progress, the meaning behind this will become crystal clear.

As we start to work with data, we may want to see different aspects of that data. For instance, at one point we may want to see input forms; at another, just the names and departments of employees; and at yet another, perhaps just the employment history. We place each "View" of this data into a specialized component that "Models" how the data should be presented, including formatting, order, etc. From there, these Views are called upon when needed by the main MXML file (the MXML file that contains the Application tags). This main file is called the "Controller." So rather than have tons of code in the main file, all that is there is the code necessary to call upon these specialized components.

I am certain by now you can see many of the advantages that this could offer in terms of maintainability and reusability.

1. Delete all the code between the opening and closing Application tags in the Chapter 5 project file you have been working with.

In MXML application design, only one file should have those Application tags. We refer to that file as the Controller or **Application** file.

While it is not necessary, it is a good idea to place your components into one or more specialized folders just as you would probably place your images in a folder marked images. This makes it easier to find things. In the case of components, we call these folders **packages**, and, as you will shortly see, these packages will require a little extra coding and preparation.

You are first going to need to decide whether you want to put the component inside the src folder, with the application MXML file, or create a separate folder to hold your components. The decision is purely organizational. The components will function the same either way. However, if you do choose separate folders, you will shortly see that there is a little extra coding necessary for Flex to find those folders and the components they hold.

For the purposes of these exercises, let's create a folder called components under the src folder.

2. In the Navigator View, right-click the src folder.

3. Select New ➤ Folder.

A dialog box should open that will allow the folder to be named, as shown in Figure 5-8.

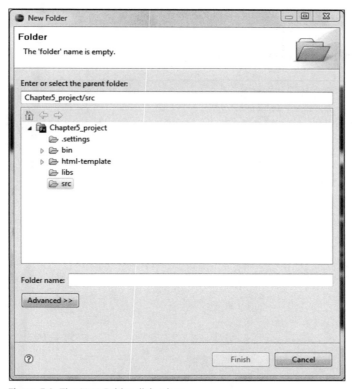

Figure 5-8. The New Folder dialog box

4. In the Folder name field, I used the name components. However, you can choose any name you like.

5. Once the name is entered, press Finish. Look at your Navigator View; it should resemble Figure 5-9.

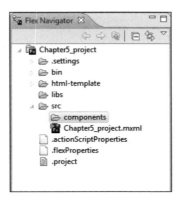

Figure 5-9. The Navigator View in Flex Builder

We will be placing our components in this new folder or package.

6. Now Right/Ctrl-click the new folder, components, and select New ➤ MXML Component to bring up the dialog box shown in Figure 5-10.

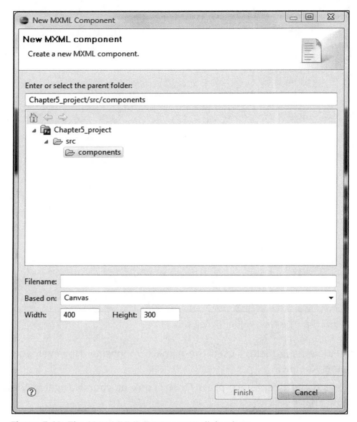

Figure 5-10. The New MXML Component dialog box

Notice that the folder is selected in the Enter or select the parent folder field.

The new component needs a name.

7. In the Filename field, enter MyForm as the component name.

> As I mentioned in several locations, in OOP environments, class file names traditionally begin with a capital letter. Since components are the MXML equivalents of class files, you should begin their names with a capital letter.

Up to this point, all of our MXML files have used the Application tag as the main container. However, as I mentioned earlier in this chapters, only the MXML file that is serving as the main, or controller, file can have the Application container. If any other file with an Application container is referenced, an error will occur. For that reason, we use a different type of container when we create a component.

> As you will see later on in this book, we could even base a component on a control such as the Image tag.

If you look at the Based on drop-down menu, you'll see all the containers, as well as the other built-in components for Flex, are listed.

8. For the purposes of this exercise, select the VBox container.

Notice that you could also set the Width and Height properties of the component. However, it is a common practice to delete the numbers in these fields. By doing that, the container will size automatically based on the content. Of course, this is a design issue you will need to consider. But, for the purposes of this exercise, let's delete the numbers.

9. Delete the numbers in the Width and Height text boxes.

10. Click Finish

A new tab should open in Flex Builder with your component. Notice that the component is using the VBox container in place of the Application tag.

```
<?xml version="1.0" encoding="utf-8"?>
<mx:VBox xmlns:mx="http://www.adobe.com/2006/mxml">

</mx:VBox>
```

Also, you should see the component saved under the components folder in the Navigator View as shown in Figure 5-11.

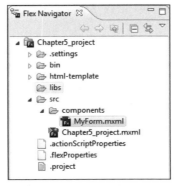

Figure 5-11. The new component under the components folder

For this first example, we will keep it simple and just add a couple of Label tags to our component. We will make later examples more functional, with the ability to pass data back and forth.

11. Add the following labels to the MyForm component:

```
<?xml version="1.0" encoding="utf-8"?>
<mx:VBox xmlns:mx="http://www.adobe.com/2006/mxml">
    <mx:Label text="This is a test of our first component"/>
    <mx:Label text="You will quickly see how easy components ➡
are to use"/>
</mx:VBox>
```

12. Save your work and switch back to the main MXML file which, in this example, is Chapter5_project.mxml.

13. Delete all of the code except for the opening and closing Application tags.

Adding a component

There are a couple of ways of adding a component to the main application file. Let's start by doing it the hard way.

As I mentioned earlier, the folder you place the component (or class file) into is called the **package**. In order to include a component in the finished application, the compiler needs to be able to find it and then include it as part of the compiled SWF file. But how does the compiler know to look in a package or directory structure?

In all OOP programs, one of two syntaxes is used: **namespace** or **import**. While the syntax of the two techniques varies slightly, they essentially do the same thing: point the compiler to the proper directory (package) and find the component (class file).

You have already seen the import statement in Chapter 4. In Flex, ActionScript uses import, while MXML uses a namespace property in the opening Application tag. As a matter of fact, there is one that comes automatically in the opening Application tag:

```
<mx:Application xmlns:mx="http://www.adobe.com/2006/mxml" ➡
layout="absolute">
```

While this looks like a reference to a website URL, it is actually an internal reference that points to the location of the ActionScript library of class files.

Notice that the namespace property begins with the designation xmlns (XML namespace). After the colon, you use a proxy name in place of having to type out the path each time the component is needed. In the default xmlns, the letters mx are used—thus, the reason all the tags begin with mx.

Now here is the good news!

New to Flex Builder 3, the namespace will be built automatically for you.

1. Between the opening and closing Application tags, type < as if you were creating any other tag. Start to type comp. As you do, you should see your components package pop up automatically, as shown in Figure 5-12.

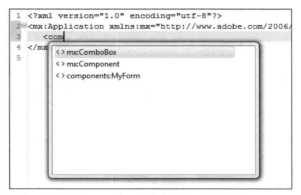

Figure 5-12. The component coming up on the list

2. You can either complete the typing or scroll down and press Enter.

After you select the package, you should see the namespace automatically built in the Application tag.

```
<mx:Application xmlns:mx="http://www.adobe.com/2006/mxml" ➡
layout="absolute" xmlns:component="components.*">
```

If your layout is set for absolute, you will want to add an x and y property like you would for any other component. Your code should look as follows:

```
<?xml version="1.0" encoding="utf-8"?>
<mx:Application xmlns:mx="http://www.adobe.com/2006/mxml" ➡
layout="absolute" xmlns:components="components.*">
    <components:MyForm x="225" y="260"/>
</mx:Application>
```

3. Go ahead and give the application a try. You should see the two labels of your component embedded into the application, as shown in Figure 5-13.

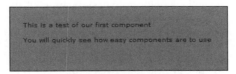

Figure 5-13. The embedded component

You cannot run a component by itself. In order for any Flex application to work, the opening and closing Application tags must be present.

5

As I said at the beginning of this exercise, this is the difficult way of doing it. Let me show you a far easier way.

4. Close any files you have open.

5. Create a new MXML application file. You can use any name you want. For this exercise, I used ComponentTest.

6. If necessary, switch to Design View.

If you look in the Components View, usually located on the lower-left side of Flex Builder, you should see a folder called Custom. Expand it if necessary using the small arrows to the left of the folder icon (see Figure 5-14).

Figure 5-14. The Components View with our custom component

Flex Builder automatically finds any custom components we create and places them inside of the Custom folder.

If you want to use this component, just drag it right into your application MXML file. Flex Builder will automatically build the namespace and tag for you.

7. Drag MyForm into your MXML file and switch to Source View.

```
<?xml version="1.0" encoding="utf-8"?>
<mx:Application xmlns:mx="http://www.adobe.com/2006/mxml" ➥
layout="absolute" xmlns:ns1="components.*">
    <ns1:MyForm x="217.5" y="258">
    </ns1:MyForm>
</mx:Application>
```

Notice that Flex Builder automatically built a namespace called ns1 and then used that to create an instance of the component into the application.

> The word "instance" is an object-oriented programming word. Recall earlier in the book that I said an object is a copy of the class file in memory. Since a component is really an ActionScript class file, we are just creating a copy of it in our application. We call this copy an instance of the class file.

8. Run the application, and it should work exactly the same as before. Could you want it any easier?

This small example highlights another important concept: the reusability of components. Notice that we just used the same component in two different application files. As you progress through Flex, this concept will start to take on an increasing importance.

Of course, a component with just labels in it probably would not be very useful for you. Let's take a look at how to pass data back and forth between components and the application file.

Components and data

Let's start by creating a new component:

1. As before, Right/Ctrl-click the components folder in the Navigator View.

2. Select New ➤ MXML Component.

For the purposes of this exercise, I am going to use the VBox container without any height or width numbers. I am calling the component MyForm2. In order to pass data back and forth, we need to create a variable in ActionScript for each property we want to pass.

3. In your new component, begin by creating a Script block and putting two variables into it called myFirstName and myLastName. Both variables are of type String.

```
<?xml version="1.0" encoding="utf-8"?>
<mx:VBox xmlns:mx="http://www.adobe.com/2006/mxml">
    <mx:Script>
        <![CDATA[
            [Bindable]
            public var myFirstName:String;
            [Bindable]
            public var myLastName:String;
        ]]>
    </mx:Script>
</mx:VBox>
```

Notice that I made both variables public because they will need to be accessed from outside of the component. They should both be [Bindable].

4. Create two Label components that are bound to the two variables. Also add a small concatenation as shown here:

```
<?xml version="1.0" encoding="utf-8"?>
<mx:VBox xmlns:mx="http://www.adobe.com/2006/mxml">
    <mx:Script>
        <![CDATA[
            [Bindable]
            public var myFirstName:String;
            [Bindable]
            public var myLastName:String;
        ]]>
    </mx:Script>
    <mx:Label id="txtFirstName" text="Your first name ➥
is {myFirstName}" />
    <mx:Label id="txtLastName" text="Your last name is ➥
{myLastName}" />
</mx:VBox>
```

5

185

> *Notice that, unlike ActionScript, MXML does not need to use the + symbol for concatenations. This is yet another example of how MXML can save you time and programming effort.*

5. Save the component and start a new MXML application file. Again, you can use any name you would like. I am calling this MyNameData.

6. Create a Script block and add two private variables that are [Bindable] and of type String. Assign each of them a value; I called them fName and lName.

```
<mx:Script>
    <![CDATA[
        [Bindable]
        private var fName:String = "John";
        [Bindable]
        private var lName:String = "Smith";
    ]]>
</mx:Script>
```

7. After the Script block, instantiate the component. Give it an x-position of 250 and a y-position of 125. Do not complete the tag; you need to do a couple of extra steps here.

8. Press the spacebar and select the id property.

When instantiating components in anything but the simplest of situations, such as the first example, it is important to give them an id property so that they can be identified by ActionScript code or other MXML tags when passing data. In these initial examples, you are using just a single component. But as you progress through this book, you will be using multiple components, all speaking to each other. Without the id property, this would not be possible.

> *In Chapter 3, I talk about the terms "object reference" and "instance name" (they mean the same thing). Giving the component an ID is the MXML equivalent of giving the object an instance name.*

9. For this example, I used the id property of names. You could use any name you want.

10. Press the spacebar again for the list of properties and scroll down until you find the two public properties, myFirstName and myLastName, that you declared in the component (see Figure 5-15).

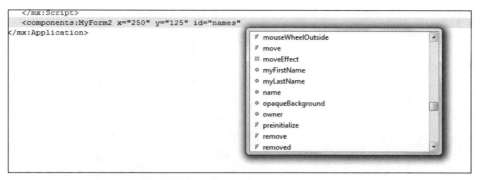

Figure 5-15. The two public properties of the component

11. Select the myFirstName property and bind it to the variable fName.

12. Do the same with myLastName to lName.

Your finished code should look as follows:

```
<?xml version="1.0" encoding="utf-8"?>
<mx:Application xmlns:mx="http://www.adobe.com/2006/mxml" ➥
layout="absolute" xmlns:components="components.*">
<mx:Script>
    <![CDATA[
        [Bindable]
        private var fName:String = "John";

        [Bindable]
        private var lName:String = "Smith";
    ]]>
</mx:Script>
    <components:MyForm2 id="names" x="250" y="125" ➥
myFirstName="{fName}" myLastName="{lName}"/>
</mx:Application>
```

13. Give it a run to see if it is working so far. Your screen should resemble what you see in Figure 5-16.

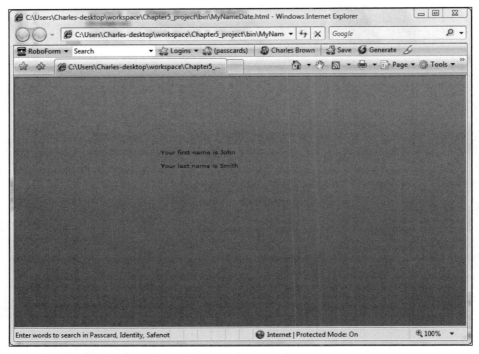

Figure 5-16. Passing data from the application to the component

Now that we know the data is being passed successfully from the application file to the component, let's take a look at how to reverse the process.

14. In the application file, MyNameData.mxml, place a Label component below the instantiation. Give it an x- and y-position of 350 and 200, respectively.

15. Bind the text property to the two public properties in the component, which has the id property of names, as follows (I used a concatenation):

```
<mx:Label x="350" y="200" text="My full name is ➡
{names.myFirstName} {names.myLastName}"/>
```

Notice that the properties of the component pop up as before.

16. Run the application again; you should see the label fully populated as shown in Figure 5-17.

I am sure that you see the enormous capabilities here. We could create many reusable components, each doing a specialized job, passing data back and forth as needed.

Now that you are somewhat familiar with events and components, the question is what the two have to do with other.

Components and events come together with a programming process called a **custom event**.

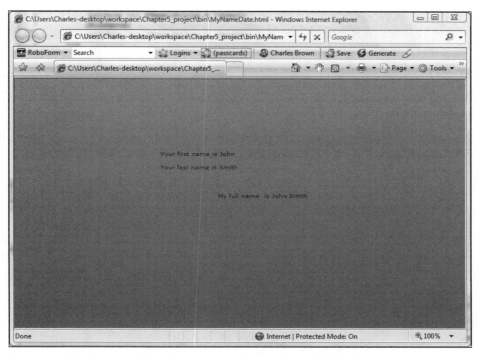

Figure 5-17. The data passed from the component back to the application file

Custom events

I am going to say, right from the beginning, that a custom event is, from a programming perspective, very easy to do. However, if you are new to programming, this could be a tough concept to understand. I have even seen experienced programmers have trouble with the concept. So please don't be discouraged if you don't understand the uses for it right away.

As you have seen already, very little happens without an event of some sort to trigger a process. An event happens, which in turn triggers a function called an event handler. That part is pretty clear.

In OOP, we sometimes refer to objects as **black boxes**. You put data into one end of it and get the result out the other side without being aware of how the result was arrived at.

I often use the analogy of a bank ATM machine. You place your card into the ATM and punch in your PIN, and the cash is dispensed to complete the transaction. You are probably not interested in what programming language the ATM uses, what computers it communicates with, or any of the other processes involved. All you care is that you give it the necessary information, and it dispenses the cash you request.

If you were the bank, would you want the general public to know how the ATM did its job? Most likely not! That information could compromise the security or integrity of the operation.

As you build web-based systems, you will most likely want to hide how your components do their jobs. In OOP environments, we call this **encapsulation**. We sometimes refer to this as **loose coupling architecture** in which each component knows nothing of the processes in another component.

ActionScript 3.0 takes the concept of encapsulation one step further with custom events. What this means is that the component could let an event handler in the main application file know that an event happened and for the event handler to do its job. But the dispatcher and type of event can be completely hidden. This would completely encapsulate the operation of the component. All the event handler knows is that an event of some sort happened and to do its job.

OK, that was the tough part. Building the custom event is the easy part; or at least easier.

There are three parts to creating a custom event:

1. Declare the event using the Event meta tag.

2. Create the event.

3. Dispatch the event.

We will look at these steps one at a time.

Declaring a custom event

In this exercise, we are going to build an MXML application file and two Flex components. What will be interesting is that the components, initially, will have absolutely no relationship to the application file or to each other. Later on, we will link them all up. This is a very real-world scenario. In a typical project, you select the components that perform the tasks you need accomplished and make them all work with each other.

Let's begin by doing a little setup here:

1. Close any files you may have open and create a new main application. For the purposes of this exercise, I am going to call it NameMain.mxml.

2. Under the opening Application tag, place a Script block and put a [Bindable], private variable into it called sharedNameData. Make it of type String, and give it an initial value of Default Name.

3. Under the variable, create a private function called sharedNameDataHandler that accepts one parameter of type event and has a return type of void.

Your completed code should look as follows:

```
<?xml version="1.0" encoding="utf-8"?>
<mx:Application xmlns:mx="http://www.adobe.com/2006/mxml" ➡
layout="absolute" xmlns:components="components.*">
    <mx:Script>
        <![CDATA[
            [Bindable]
            private var sharedNameData:String = "Default Name";

            private function sharedNameDataHander(evt:Event):void
            {

            }
        ]]>
    </mx:Script>
</mx:Application>
```

We will be returning to this file in a bit. But now we need to create a component that will create (dispatch) the event.

4. Right/Ctrl-click the components folder created earlier and create a new MXML component, named NameDispatcher, based on the VBox container with no width or height numbers.

5. Create a Script block below the opening VBox container and place into it a private function called clickHandler that accepts no parameters and has a return type of void.

6. Below the Script block, create a Label component with the text property of Name Dispatcher and a font size of 16.

7. Below the label, create a button with a label property of Click Me and a click event that calls the clickHandler function created previously.

Your code should look as follows.

```
<?xml version="1.0" encoding="utf-8"?>
<mx:VBox xmlns:mx="http://www.adobe.com/2006/mxml">
    <mx:Script>
        <![CDATA[
            private function clickHandler():void
            {

            }
        ]]>
    </mx:Script>
    <mx:Label text="Name Dispatcher" fontSize="16"/>
    <mx:Button label="Click Me" click="clickHandler()"/>
</mx:VBox>
```

We are now going to start to build the custom event that will let other components know that an event has happened. We will go through this in a very step-by-step fashion.

5

191

Creating the event

To begin building our custom event, follow these steps:

1. Just below the Script block, but before the Label tag, put an opening and closing Metadata tag.

```
<mx:Metadata>

</mx:Metadata>
<mx:Label text="Name Dispatcher" fontSize="16"/>
```

Metadata tags provide information to the Flex compiler that describes how your MXML components are used in a Flex application. Metadata tags do not get compiled into executable code, but provide information to control how portions of your code get compiled.

Now keep in mind, you cannot put ActionScript or MXML code into a Metadata tag, only special instructions.

Inside of the Metadata tag, we need to tell the compiler that we are creating a custom event and then give that event a name of our choice. You do this declaration using the square brackets in the same way you declare a variable as [Bindable]. The square brackets are called a **meta tag**.

2. Enter the Event meta tag as follows:

```
<mx:Metadata>
    [Event(name="nameDataShared")]
</mx:Metadata>
```

Notice that the name property is enclosed in parentheses, and the actual name is a string in quotes.

Inside the clickHandler() function, we need to instantiate the event class that matches the type of event being generated. For instance, this would be a click event with the button. However, when you are not passing data, such as the case here, you can simply use the Event class itself. In the parentheses, you pass the name you gave the event earlier.

3. Enter the following code inside of the clickHandler function:

```
<mx:Script>
    <![CDATA[
            private function clickHandler():void
        {
            var myEvent:Event = new Event("nameDataShared");
        }
    ]]>
</mx:Script>
```

We now need to do the final step, dispatching the event.

Dispatching the event

Finally, we need to send the event on its way. Fortunately, most of the visual components in Flex (or actually ActionScript 3.0) have a handy little function called dispatchEvent(). The event we are going to dispatch is going to be our new object called myEvent, and myEvent will bring along the custom event name of nameDataShared.

1. Add the dispatchEvent() function after the instantiation of the Event class as follows:

```
private function clickHandler():void
{
    var myEvent:Event = new Event("nameDataShared");
    dispatchEvent(myEvent);
}
```

So, just to recap, when the button gets pressed, all that any other components are concerned about is that an event called nameDataShared occurred. What that event was, who generated it, etc., is completely hidden.

OK, we are finished here for now.

2. Switch back to the NameMain application file.

Here we would instantiate the components we just created in the same way we did in previous exercises. However, there will be one slight variation.

3. Below the closing Script tag, instantiate the NameDispatcher component. Give it an x- and y-position of 35 and 40, respectively. However, do not close the tag.

Normally, as we have seen many times already, the events available for a component can be listed in the MXML tag. We have used this often with the Button component employing the click event. Our custom event, which we just created, is every bit as legitimate as the click event in the Button.

4. Press the spacebar and type the letter n; you will see the event nameDataShared. You can tell it is an event because of the little thunderbolt symbol to the left of it (see Figure 5-18).

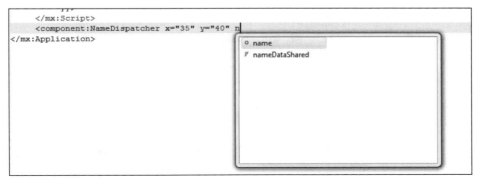

Figure 5-18. The nameDataShared event

5. Select nameDataShared.

Now, as you have probably figured out already, you are going to have this event call the sharedNameDataHandler(evt:Event) function in much the same way you would if you were using a click event. We will need to pass the event parameter because we said this is of type Event when we defined it in the component.

> *Later on in the book, we will be passing other types of events.*

6. Complete the event as follows:

```
<components:NameDispatcher x="35" y="40" nameDataShared=➥
"sharedNameDataHandler(event)"/>
```

We should be back in familiar territory now.

7. Inside the sharedNameDataHandler, place code that will change the variable sharedNameData to a name.

```
private function sharedNameDataHandler(evt:Event):void
{
    sharedNameData = "Charles E. Brown";
}
```

The last step will be a simple one. We will build a simple component to receive the new data from sharedNameData.

8. Create a new component called ReceiveName using the VBox container with no height or width specified.

9. Create a Script block and put into it a [Bindable], public variable called myName of type String.

10. After the Script block, put a Label component with its text property bound to myName and give it a fontSize property of 16.

```
<?xml version="1.0" encoding="utf-8"?>
<mx:VBox xmlns:mx="http://www.adobe.com/2006/mxml">
    <mx:Script>
        <![CDATA[
            [Bindable]
            public var myName:String;
        ]]>
    </mx:Script>
    <mx:Label text="{myName}" fontSize="16"/>
</mx:VBox>
```

11. Return to NameMain and instantiate the ReceiveName component under the DispatchName component. Give it an x and y property of 35 and 120, respectively. Finally, bind the myName property of the component to the sharedNameData property of the application file.

The finished code in the application file should be as follows:

```
<?xml version="1.0" encoding="utf-8"?>
<mx:Application xmlns:mx="http://www.adobe.com/2006/mxml" ➥
layout="absolute" xmlns:components="components.*">
    <mx:Script>
        <![CDATA[
            [Bindable]
            private var sharedNameData:String = "Default Name";

            private function sharedNameDataHandler(evt:Event):void
            {
                sharedNameData = "Charles E. Brown";
            }
        ]]>
    </mx:Script>
    <components:NameDispatcher x="35" y="40" nameDataShared=➥
"sharedNameDataHandler(event)"/>
    <components:ReceiveName x="35" y="120" myName="{sharedNameData}"/>
</mx:Application>
```

We should be ready to give it a try.

12. Start the application; it should like Figure 5-19.

Figure 5-19.
When the application is first started

13. Click the button; you should see the name change as shown in Figure 5-20.

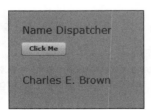

Figure 5-20.
After the custom event is triggered

Notice how easy it was to plug the component into the application file and have the component trigger an event. The application file, or any other components, didn't have to have any knowledge of the inner workings of the component.

I am sure you are not going to want to always pass a static piece of data. Let's make a few modifications to our code so that we can pass changing data from the component.

Passing data

To pass changing data to our component, start with these steps:

1. Return to the NameDispatcher component.

2. Right below the Label component and before the Button, insert an HBox container.

3. Inside of the HBox container, add a Label component with the text property of Enter Your Name.

4. Below that, put a TextInput component with an id property of myNameInput.

The HBox code should appear as follows:

```
<mx:HBox>
    <mx:Label text="Enter Your Name"/>
    <mx:TextInput id="myNameInput"/>
</mx:HBox>
```

Because we are now going to be passing data, we can no longer pass it as a simple event. In other words, more than an action is going to happen. As a result, we need to find an event class that will be able to handle the passing of text data (I am choosing my words carefully here).

If you go into the ActionScript documentation and bring up the Event class, you will find something interesting (see Figure 5-21).

Notice that the Event class is at the top of many specialized event classes. For instance, there are classes for handling things like video events, keyboard events, calendar events, and so forth. As I stated earlier, if you are just triggering an action, like we did in the last exercise, then you can use the generic Event class. But when you are passing data, you have to match the event class to the kind of data you are passing.

Like I said, I choose my words carefully. In this case, we are passing text, so we need to do the work with the TextEvent class. Notice that the event classes are part of the package flash.events. This is going to be important to us shortly.

Let's start making some modifications.

5. Go up to where we declared the name of our custom event in the MetaData tag. When we use any event class other than the Event class, we need to declare the type as shown here:

```
<mx:Metadata>
    [Event(name="nameDataShared", type="flash.events.TextEvent")]
</mx:Metadata>
```

Figure 5-21. The documentation for class Event

Notice that I put a comma after the name property and used the full package name when declaring the type.

> In OOP, we call using the full package name a **fully qualified name**.

6. Next, you need to go to the clickHandler function and change the instantiation from type Event to type TextEvent. Make sure you do it on both sides.

```
private function clickHandler():void
{
    var myEvent:TextEvent = new TextEvent("nameDataShared");
    dispatchEvent(myEvent);
}
```

The TextEvent class offers us the ability to transfer text from any field. We placed a TextInput field called myNameInput into this component. We now need to pass that text into the TextInput object's text property.

7. Pass the TextInput's text property as follows:

```
private function clickHandler():void
{
    var myEvent:TextEvent = new TextEvent("nameDataShared");
    myEvent.text = myNameInput.text;
    dispatchEvent(myEvent);
}
```

Finally, as I have said before, when using a class from a different package, we need to import that package so the compiler will know where to find it.

8. Import the TextEvent class:

```
<mx:Script>
    <![CDATA[
        import flash.events.TextEvent;

        private function clickHandler():void
        {
            var myEvent:TextEvent = new TextEvent("nameDataShared");
            myEvent.text = myNameInput.text;
            dispatchEvent(myEvent);
        }
    ]]>
</mx:Script>
```

9. Save the changes and return to the NameMain application files. We need to make a couple of minor modifications here.

Notice that the sharedNameDataHandler is expecting an Event passed to it. However, what is really now being passed is a TextEvent.

10. Change the code so that sharedNameDataHandler expects a TextEvent, and then use the import statement at the top of the Script block as you did in the component.

11. Make the variable sharedNameData equal to evt.text.

Here is the full code:

```
<?xml version="1.0" encoding="utf-8"?>
<mx:Application xmlns:mx="http://www.adobe.com/2006/mxml"
layout="absolute" xmlns:components="components.*">
    <mx:Script>
        <![CDATA[
            import flash.events.TextEvent;
            [Bindable]
            private var sharedNameData:String = "Default Name";
```

```
            private function sharedNameDataHandler➤
(evt:TextEvent):void
            {
                    sharedNameData = evt.text;
            }
        ]]>
    </mx:Script>
    <components:NameDispatcher x="35" ➤
y="40" nameDataShared="sharedNameDataHandler(event)"/>
    <components:ReceiveName x="35" y="120" myName="{sharedNameData}"/>
</mx:Application>
```

12. Give it a run and type a name into the field. After you click the button, the name should appear in the ReceiveName component instance.

Once again, notice that neither NameMain nor ReceiveName has to look at the properties or functions inside of NameDispatcher. In other words, the operation of NameDispatcher is completely hidden.

5

Summary

The material presented on events and components in this chapter was a lot to digest in one sitting, especially if you are relatively new to programming. I strongly advise you to go over these concepts a few times until they are very clear in your mind. You will find that you can repeat the steps shown here in a variety of situations.

We are now going to turn our attention to data and how Flex handles XML.

6 FLEX AND XML

faultCode = "Server.Error.Request"
faultDetail = "Error: [IOErrorEvent type="]
bubbles=false cancelable=false eventPhas
text="Error #2032: Stream Error. URL:
file:///C:/Users/Charles-
desktop/My%20Documents/Flex%20Builde
oxie/Chapter6_project/bin/assets/book.xm
URL: assets/book.xml"
faultString = "HTTP request error"
headers = (Object)#2
messageId = "BE334F96-6B42-75B8-0D8
AD0F5CD328E2"
rootCause = (flash.events::IOErrorEvent)
    bubbles = false
    cancelable = false
    currentTarget = (flash.net::URLLoader)
        bytesLoaded = 0
        bytesTotal = 0

Value
Chapter6_project (@464a0a1)
mx.rpc.events.ResultEvent (@46e2e01)
false
true
mx.rpc.http.mxml.HTTPService (@4551dc1)
2
mx.messaging.messages.AcknowledgeMess.
"68EE3C4A-42B7-48FB-8DC9-AE463846A3C8"
mx.utils.ObjectProxy (@468be51)
mx.utils.ObjectProxy (@468be09)
Object (@4620a39)
mx.collections.ArrayCollection (@46e4101)

Software	Big Gates
ns of Money	Donald Rump

Now that you have a good handle on building rich Internet application GUIs, you will need to start to focus on putting content into them. After all, what good are all these tools if they are not tied into a data source?

In this chapter, you will

- Understand what an XML file is.
- Connect Flex to an XML file.
- Learn about reading XML data using E4X syntax.
- See how the DataGrid component works.
- Explore security in Flash Player.
- Explore the new AdvancedDataGrid control.
- Examine the Tree control.

While you work through this chapter, I strongly suggest experimenting with the GUI building techniques you have learned up to this point when connecting with XML. As you will soon see, what applies to one control applies equally to many controls.

This chapter will start to bring a lot of little pieces together.

Data sources

Let's being begin with a simple question: what is a data source?

If you had asked this question 6 or 7 years ago, the answer would probably be a database. If you ever did programming in one of the earliest dynamic web technologies, ASP, you would have programmed direct references to a database, such as Microsoft Access or SQL Server, right into the dynamic page template. While some of today's dynamic technologies, such as ColdFusion, still have that capability, the trend is to move away from that toward XML and web services. Let's see a simple example to demonstrate why this is happening.

Let's assume you want to build an online travel site where the user can compare flights and make a reservation. Let's further say that a user wants a flight between Newark, NJ, and Orlando, FL, on a given day.

The user enters the dates, cities, preferred flight times, etc., and then presses the Submit button. That site then "polls" all airlines such as Continental, American, JetBlue, and so on to see whether they have flights that match the specifications requested. If you followed the dynamic page model of ASP I mentioned previously, your site would need to have a direct connection to the databases of dozens of airlines in order to work. Furthermore, it would have to take into account the individual database servers and structures for each of those airlines. Finally, if you were the airlines, would you want websites having direct connections to your data without any filtering? I am sure you can easily see why this would not be very practical. You need some sort of standardized way to allow your website to access the information from all the airlines easily.

XML is the standard to do just that: to exchange data easily over the Internet. Since it is a text-based format, it can be read without difficulty by both man and computer. Plus, it is flexible enough to adapt to a number of scenarios easily. Today's dynamic technologies (PHP, ColdFusion, .NET, JSP, and the older ASP) can work easily with XML.

This new model is so prevalent that Macromedia (which made the decision before Adobe acquired the company) stripped the capability of Flex and Flash to access a database directly. In its place are a number of class files that allow for the easy access of XML files.

> *In this book, I will be focusing on using XML as the data source. While this is the easiest technique, it is not the only one. When you get into advanced Flex techniques, you can use the LiveCycle Data Services server, the ability to read ColdFusion and Java files directly (Flex Remoting), and web services. Many of these advanced techniques are covered in the book* Foundation Flex for Developers: Data-Driven Applications with PHP, ASP.NET, ColdFusion, and LCDS *by Sas Jacobs and Koen De Weggheleir (friends of ED, 2007).*

Let's discuss the mechanics of an XML file a bit.

6

XML: A very brief introduction

You need to understand a few things first before we get into an overview of XML.

As I just stated in the previous paragraph, Flex, or for that matter Flash, cannot connect directly with a database; nor do you want it to. The purpose of Flex, or Flash, is to present the data in a user-friendly manner. It's the responsibility of the business logic level to establish what is and is not permissible in accessing that data. **Business logic** simply means using a programming environment like Java, ColdFusion, .NET, or PHP to establish all the rules for connecting to a database, inserting data, deleting data, reading data, distributing data, and so on. The purpose of Flex, or Flash, is to present the data in a user-friendly manner. However, the business logic level establishes what is and is not permissible in accessing that data.

An extensive discussion of the mechanics of XML is out of the scope of this book. If you are interested, I strongly suggest picking up copies of *Foundation XML for Flash* by Sas Jacobs (friends of ED, 2005) and *Beginning XML with DOM and Ajax: From Novice to Professional*, also by Sas Jacobs (Apress, 2006).

That said, it's time for your look at XML. The specifications for XML were first released by the W3C in 1998.

> *In case you don't know, the W3C is the **World Wide Web Consortium**. Its purpose is to set standards for the various programming and markup languages used on the Web. If you want to learn more about these specifications, just go to* www.w3.org.

Like XHTML, XML is a markup language, meaning that it is text-based and its purpose is to describe data. As a matter of fact, XML means **Extensible Markup Language**. But what does "Extensible" mean?

If you have done any design work with XHTML, you know you have a well-defined set of tags to work with—for example, <p>, <h1>, and <head> are tags that describe the way text should be styled on a web page, and so on. XML allows you to define your own set of tags depending on the particular needs of the data. As a matter of fact, there are libraries, or **vocabularies**, of XML tags for specific industries. One such example is Chemical Markup Language (CML) for the chemical engineering community, which has tags for defining the layout of chemical formulas, among other things.

Let's look at a small example. Say you wanted to represent a small fictional bookstore in XML. The structure might look something like this:

```
<?xml version="1.0" encoding="iso-8859-1"?>
<foed>
   <book isbn="8909123456">
      <book_name>XML for Flash</book_name>
       <author>Sas Jacobs</author>
       <cover>assets/jacobs.jpg</cover>
   </book>
   <book isbn="890998765">
      <book_name>Foundation Flash 8 Video</book_name>
       <author>Tom Green</author>
       <cover>assets/green.jpg</cover>
   </book>
   <book isbn="8909435876">
      <book_name>Object Oriented Programming for Flash 8</book_name>
       <author>Peter Elst</author>
       <cover>assets/elst.jpg</cover>
   </book>
   <book isbn="890929435">
      <book_name>Foundation ActionScript Animation: ➥
Making Things Move</book_name>
       <author>Keith Peters</author>
       <cover>assets/peters.jpg</cover>
   </book>
</foed>
```

You will notice several things about the XML structure.

First of all, the tag names are very descriptive of the data they contain. Second, notice that for every opening tag, there is a corresponding closing tag (signified by a / at the beginning of the tag). Third, there is a strict hierarchy. And fourth, they are case sensitive.

Notice that there are four book **elements**, which are known as **nodes**. Each one of these nodes has three child elements: <book_name>, <author>, and <cover>. In addition to the child elements, each of the book nodes has an attribute called isbn. Everything is contained within the root node called <foed>.

When Flex accesses the XML file, each node becomes a new object in memory.

I know you are asking how programs like Java or ColdFusion create or use the XML files. Sorry, but that discussion is way outside the scope of this book. If you want to know more, consider picking up the books I mentioned at the beginning of this section.

Using XML in Flex

For starters, if you haven't done so yet, please download the XML files for this chapter from the downloads section of www.friendsofed.com. Unzip them into a folder in a location of your choice. With that done, let's get down to business and run through an example of using XML in Flex. By the end of this chapter, you will be amazed at how easily this can be done!

1. If necessary, delete or close the Chapter5_project.
2. Create a new Flex Project called Chapter6_project in the default location.
3. Create an assets folder, under the src folder, and import the books.xml file (creating the folder and importing the assets are discussed in Chapter 4) from the Chapter 6 downloads into the new folder.

Before we get started, open the books.xml file in the assets folder and examine it.

```
<?xml version="1.0" encoding="iso-8859-1"?>
<books>
   <stock>
      <name>The Picasso Code</name>
       <author>Dan Blue</author>
       <category>Fiction</category>
       <description>Cubist paintings reveal a secret society ➥
of people who really look like that</description>
   </stock>
   <stock>
      <name>Here With the Wind</name>
       <author>Margaret Middle</author>
       <category>Fiction</category>
       <description>In this edition, nobody in the south ➥
really gives a damn</description>
   </stock>
   <stock>
      <name>Harry Potluck and the Chamber of Money</name>
       <author>J.K. Roughly</author>
       <category>Fiction</category>
       <description>Young wizard finds the real pot-of-gold ➥
and retires</description>
   </stock>
   <stock>
      <name>No Expectations</name>
```

```
                <author>Chuck Dickens</author>
                <category>Fiction</category>
                <description>Dickens finally reveals what he really ➡
        thinks of people</description>
            </stock>
            <stock>
                <name>Atlas Stretched</name>
                <author>Ann Rind</author>
                <category>Fiction</category>
                <description>Great inventors finally just take the ➡
        money and run</description>
            </stock>
            <stock>
                <name>Recycling Software</name>
                <author>Big Gates</author>
                <category>Nonfiction</category>
                <description>How to just change the name and interface of ➡
        the same old software and sell it as new</description>
            </stock>
            <stock>
                <name>Make Tons of Money</name>
                <author>Donald Rump</author>
                <category>Nonfiction</category>
                <description>Rump explains how he became a billionaire ➡
        while constantly declaring bankruptcy</description>
            </stock>
            <stock>
                <name>How to Win Enemies and Lose Friends</name>
                <author>Dale Crochety</author>
                <category>Nonfiction</category>
                <description>The Ultimate how-to book for people who ➡
        want to stay loners</description>
            </stock>
            <stock>
                <name>My Lies</name>
                <author>Swill Clinton</author>
                <category>Nonfiction</category>
                <description>This former American president tries to ➡
        define what a lie is</description>
            </stock>
            <stock>
                <name>The Complete History of the World</name>
                <author>David McClutz</author>
                <category>Nonfiction</category>
                <description>McClutz gives you the entire history of ➡
        all civilization is less than 300 pages</description>
            </stock>
        </books>
```

Normally, if you were working on a full system and getting data from a database, you would not see this data filled in. Instead, you would just see a basic XML structure. So how does data get used in it? I will give you a brief and generic insight.

When I teach XML, I usually tell my students to think of the outermost container, in this case <books </books>, as a giant container. Within that container, there are smaller containers, in this case ten called <stock> </stock>. Each one of those stock containers holds the information about one book: the name, author, category, and description.

In truth, the technical explanation isn't much different. In this example, if a request were sent to a database that met all of the business logic rules, the database would return the data through the XML file. An object called books would be created. The books object in this case would refer to ten other objects called stock. Each stock object would have name, author, category, and description properties. All Flex needs to do is access these ten objects through the book object.

> If you are an XML expert, remember that this is just a quick explanation and not meant to cover all of the technical issues of XML. So please don't send me a nasty e-mail!

6

You can keep the XML file open, if you wish, for reference.

Using the HTTPService tag

If you ever programmed an XML connection in ActionScript 2.0, you may have had to use code something similar to this:

```
myData = this.firstChild.childNodes[2].firstChild.firstChild.nodeValue
```

Words such as "firstChild" and "childNodes" can be a bit cryptic when trying to write and debug code. They don't tell us much about what data they are calling up. Happily, thanks to MXML, as well as a newly rewritten XML ActionScript class, much of that sort of coding is now gone.

> In ActionScript 3.0, the XML class is completely rewritten. What was the XML class in ActionScript 2.0 is now called the XMLDocument class.

MXML gives us a very handy tag, once again related to an ActionScript class, called HTTPService. In MXML, the HTTPService tag reads XML dynamically. By that, I mean that each time a given event occurs, the SWF is requesting the latest data from an XML file. This is sometimes referred to as an **asynchronous request**. The term "asynchronous" is usually used to describe communications in which data can be transmitted intermittently rather than in a steady stream. In this case, the intermittent cause is an event of some sort.

1. Return to the MXML file created when you set up this project.

2. Under the opening `Application` tag, start an `HTTPService` tag with an `id` attribute of bookData.

```
<mx:HTTPService id="bookData"
```

The next attribute you want to add in is an important one: the URL of the XML file.

In this example, the URL target is located on the local drive. But it could just as easily be an `http://` address in another location that uses a web service. The `HTTPService` class does not make a distinction.

3. Add the `url` attribute, as shown in the following code example, and close off the tag:

```
<?xml version="1.0" encoding="utf-8"?>
<mx:Application xmlns:mx="http://www.adobe.com/2006/mxml" ➥
layout="absolute">
    <mx:HTTPService id="bookData" url="../assets/books.xml"/>
</mx:Application>
```

As I stated in Chapter 5, very little happens in code without an event to trigger it of some kind. Just using the `HTTPService` class to connect with the XML file is not an event. An event would be the clicking of a button, the pressing of a key, or, as you have learned in previous chapters, the completion of the loading of the SWF file.

While we could use any event to trigger the loading of the XML data, for purposes of these examples, we will use the `creationComplete` event The `creationComplete` event is commonly included inside the opening `<mx:Application>` tag; however, it could be used inside any of the containers. What it does is report when the container (in this case the Application container) is completely loaded. When it does report, it will run whatever instructions we instruct it to run.

In this case, when the `creationComplete` event occurs, the `HTTPService` class is alerted to trigger the `send()` function to send a request to the XML file which, in turn, will return its latest data. The `HTTPService` class handles all of the mechanics in the background. All you need to do is set up the code as I am showing here. Note the `creationComplete` event in the Application tag that calls the `send()` function is bookData, which is the `id` of our `HTTPService` tag.

4. Add a `creationComplete` event to the opening Application tag as follows:

```
<?xml version="1.0" encoding="utf-8"?>
<mx:Application xmlns:mx="http://www.adobe.com/2006/mxml" ➥
layout="absolute" creationComplete="bookData.send()">
    <mx:HTTPService id="bookData" url="assets/books.xml"/>
</mx:Application>
```

It is probably not a bad idea to test the connection at this point. If you are looking down at the Problems View, not seeing any errors or warnings, you are thinking you are in good shape. However, there is one problem: Flash Player does not make the connection until the request is actually made. That request is not made until the application is running. This is called a **runtime process**.

5. Run the application just to make sure there are no problems. If you just see a blank browser, you are probably in good shape.

Just to show you what can happen, let's deliberately break the URL.

6. In the HTTPService tag, change the URL to request book.xml instead of books.xml.

7. Run the application again, and you should see the error shown in Figure 6-1.

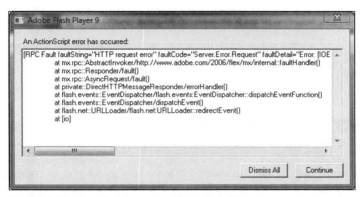

Figure 6-1. The error being returned from Flash Player

Flash Player returns a fault in the HTTPService request. Since there is nothing else going on in this application yet, it is a pretty safe bet that the XML connection is the fault.

8. Click either the Dismiss All or Continue button, and then close the browser.

9. Change the url attribute back to what it was, and retest your application to make sure everything is working fine.

Displaying data

Now that you have connected Flex to an XML data source, you will want to display the data. There are a number of ways to do that, which will be covered as you progress through the rest of this book. However, one of the easiest ways is to use the DataGrid component.

With a minimum of effort and virtually no programming, the DataGrid component can read the properties of XML objects and display the data in a user-friendly format with some additional benefits, as you will see shortly.

1. Start by setting up a DataGrid control. Modify the code as follows:

```
<?xml version="1.0" encoding="utf-8"?>
<mx:Application xmlns:mx="http://www.adobe.com/2006/mxml" ➥
layout="absolute" creationComplete="bookData.send()">
    <mx:HTTPService id="bookData" url="assets/books.xml"/>
    <mx:DataGrid x="56" y="250" width="950"/>
</mx:Application>
```

I purposely had you make the grid a bit wide to accommodate the data it will need to display.

2. Run the application now; you should get something that looks like Figure 6-2.

Figure 6-2. The empty DataGrid control

Unless you like the look of a big, blank box, it is not very useful as is. In order to fill it with data, you need to add another property called the dataProvider. I want to spend a few minutes talking about this property. It may be helpful if you refer to the contents of the books.xml file listed earlier while I do so.

Remember, the connection to the XML file, as well as the setting up of the objects, is all being handled by the <HTTPService> tag<$I~<HTTPService> tag> (bookData), which you just set up. That service is going to be your data provider.

3. Modify the DataGrid tag as follows:

```
<mx:DataGrid x="56" y="250" width="950" dataProvider=➥
"{bookData.lastResult.books.stock}"/>
```

We need to look at this a bit more closely.

Notice, as you have done with other ActionScript bindings, that you enclose it in curly braces ({ }). But what is going on inside of those curly braces?

We know that bookData is the id property of our HTTPService class. HTTPService stores the data returned from the XML file to a property called lastResult.

Once that much is established, we have to drill down to the "repeating data" we want to display. Following the container analogy I used earlier, the repeating data is within the stock container, which is within the books container. The stock container contains the name, author, category, and description of the books we want to display. As I stated earlier, syntax like lastChild and childNodes is gone. Instead, we can use the actual names of the XML nodes.

4. Run the application. It should look like Figure 6-3.

author	category	description	name
Dan Blue	Fiction	Cubist paintings reveal a secret society	The Picasso Code
Margaret Middle	Fiction	In this edition, nobody in the south real	Here With the Wind
J.K. Roughly	Fiction	Young wizard finds the real pot-of-gold	Harry Potluck and the Chamber of Mone
Chuck Dickens	Fiction	Dickens finally reveals what he really thi	No Expectations
Ann Rind	Fiction	Great inventors finally just take the mor	Atlas Stretched
Big Gates	Nonfiction	How to just change the name and interf	Recycling Software

Figure 6-3. The populated DataGrid control

The DataGrid component did most of the work. Notice that it uses the node names as headers. It brings them in alphabetically. All of this can be modified with code, but for now let's look at the more user-friendly features of the DataGrid control.

Click one of the headings; notice the data is sorted on that criterion. For instance, if the user clicks the name header, the data will be sorted by the book names. Click the header again, and the data is sorted in descending order.

This control even gives the user the chance to rearrange columns and adjust their width using the same techniques you might use if you were in Excel. Give it a try by clicking the name column heading and dragging it over to the first column. Then click between the category and description column headers and make the description column wider.

All of this gives end users a tremendous amount of control over how they display the data.

We will be talking about modifying and controlling the DataGrid control a bit more later in this chapter. But, for now, let's take a look at how to accomplish an XML connection using ActionScript 3.0.

XML and ActionScript 3.0

Throughout this book, I have been making every effort to show you how to do things with MXML and then accomplish the same ideas with ActionScript. As you have probably seen already, MXML is the easy way to do things. However, as you have probably seen also, easy does not always equate to most flexible or efficient.

If you are working with simple data, as you are here, the way I showed you earlier doesn't present much of a problem, and the preceding techniques are fine. But if you are working in more complex situations, you may prefer to employ the power of ActionScript programming. As an example, let's say you need to call different XML files depending on a user response. You would need to program that in ActionScript.

As was shown with events in the last chapter, learning a few basic ActionScript techniques can go a long way in covering a lot of potential situations. The same will be true here.

Let's start by examining the most important of these concepts: the ArrayCollection class. In learning this, you will reproduce programmatically what you just did in MXML. While this may seem a bit silly, it will help you in understanding the underlying ActionScript code, which in turn will aid you as you get into increasingly complex situations.

The ArrayCollection class

One of the first things any programming student learns is the definition of an **array**.

Normally, you associate a variable with a single piece of data. For instance:

```
var fName:String = "John";
```

or

```
var myAge:Number = 35;
```

However, an array means multiple values associated with a single variable. This is not exact syntax, but it would look something like this:

```
var myName:Array ={ "John", "Mary", "Chris", "Tom"};
```

Each value (called an **element**) is assigned a number called the **index**. In a typical array, the first index number is 0.

Like everything else in ActionScript, an array is handled by an ActionScript class. If you go to the ActionScript documentation and scroll down, you'll find the Array class. It is worth taking a few minutes to study it over. There are some subtleties that may be easy to miss.

If you look at the list of methods, you will see that they are all geared toward manipulating the elements of the array itself. For instance, sorting the elements, adding an element to the end of the array (push()), creating a subset of the array (slice()), and so on. While this may seem fine, what is not obvious is that it has no way to perform operations on the data that is making up the elements of the array. For instance, let's say you needed to add additional records or delete records.

For that reason, XML data uses a second class that wraps itself around the Array class: ArrayCollection.

It is worth taking a look at the documentation for this class now.

As an example, a method such as removeItemAt() will delete the record rather than just removing it from the array. With the ArrayCollection class, you work on the actual underlying data.

The HTTPService tag, which you used in the last section, automatically converted the XML data to type ArrayCollection. However, if you manually program things in ActionScript, some setup will be required.

1. Within the same file you just worked on, create a Script block under the opening Application tag.

2. Create a private and [Bindable] variable called bookStock as type ArrayCollection.

```
<?xml version="1.0" encoding="utf-8"?>
<mx:Application xmlns:mx="http://www.adobe.com/2006/mxml" ➥
layout="absolute" creationComplete="bookData.send()">
<mx:Script>
    <![CDATA[

        [Bindable]
        private var bookStock:ArrayCollection;
    ]]>
</mx:Script>
```

Notice that Flex Builder automatically created the necessary import statement to use the ArrayCollection class.

All that remains now is for you to write a method to handle the XML data. This method will accept only one argument: the event object, which you saw in Chapter 5. When handling XML events, the event object is of type ResultEvent. The ResultEvent class is part of the mx.rpc (remote procedure call) package. This package contains many of the class files associated with the handling of XML and web services.

You are going to create a function to set the bookStock variable, which in turn will become the dataProvider to the DataGrid control. Add the following highlighted lines to your code (the second import statement should be written automatically).

3. Within the Script block, create the following function called bookHandler:

```
<mx:Script>
    <![CDATA[
        import mx.rpc.events.ResultEvent;
        import mx.collections.ArrayCollection;
        [Bindable]
        private var bookStock:ArrayCollection;

        private function bookHandler(evt:ResultEvent):void
        {

        }
    ]]>
</mx:Script>
```

Your last step is to fill in the functionality of the function. Recall that when an event object is passed, the target property contains the information about who sent the object, In the case of a ResultEvent, rather than pass a target, you pass a **result**. The result property contains the XML data, which will then be saved to the ArrayCollection variable we created: bookStock.

4. Add the following code to the body of the bookHandler function:

```
private function bookHandler(evt:ResultEvent)
     {
          bookStock = evt.result.books.stock;
     }
```

The ArrayCollection, bookStock, will now be the dataProvider and not the HTTPService class. However, the HTTPService class still needs to make the actual connection and then pass the result up to the function.

5. Make the following modification to the <HTTPService> tag (you will modify the DataGrid control in a moment):

```
<mx:HTTPService id="bookData" url="assets/books.xml" ➥
result="bookHandler(event)"/>
```

In the HTTPService class, result is an event that occurs when the data is successfully returned. This sends the result of the XML connection to the bookHandler function by passing the event object of type ResultEvent that contains the result property.

It is easy to get the word result confused in its functionality. In the case of the HTTPService class, it is an event, and with the ResultEvent class, it is a property.

6. Modify the DataGrid tag as follows:

```
<mx:DataGrid x="56" y="250" width="950" dataProvider="{bookStock}"/>
```

7. Run your application; it should work exactly the same as before.

As I said from the outset, the purpose of this exercise was to show you the basic skeletal structure of programmatically connecting to an XML file. From here, you have the powerful programming capabilities of ActionScript, mixed with MXML, to use wherever you need it.

When good code goes bad

Earlier in this chapter, when you misnamed your XML file, you saw an error message returned by Flash Player. Unfortunately, this is not a very graceful way of handling things.

In most programming environments, error handling is done programmatically. However, the HTTPService class can handle it simply through a simple, built-in event.

Let's look at how this works now.

You'll start by writing a function to handle the error. The event object you are going to use is a FaultEvent, which is a class file and, conveniently, also part of the mx.rpc.events package you saw in the last exercise. Its purpose is to report an error connecting to a remote component or XML file.

1. Modify your Script block as follows. The additional import statement should be added automatically:

```
<mx:Script>
    <![CDATA[
        import mx.rpc.events.FaultEvent;
        import mx.rpc.events.ResultEvent;
        import mx.collections.ArrayCollection;
        [Bindable]
        private var bookStock:ArrayCollection;

        private function bookHandler(evt:ResultEvent):void
        {
            bookStock = evt.result.books.stock;
        }

        private function faultHandler(evt:FaultEvent):void
        {

        }
    ]]>
</mx:Script>
```

> The import *statements could be consolidated to* import mx.rpc.events.*. *If you want you could do this. However, other than adding a couple of extra lines of code, having separate* import *statements for each class in a package adds no additional overhead to the application.*

The next thing you will do is construct a variable to hold your message.

2. Add the following to the faultHandler function:

```
private function faultHandler(evt:FaultEvent):void
{
    var faultMessage:String = "Could not connect with XML file";
}
```

We are going to send this string message to be displayed in an **alert box**. Alerts are part of the mx.controls package.

3. Add the following import statement to the other import statements:

```
import mx.controls.*;
```

Once that is completed, set up the Alert class using its show() function:

4. Add the following code body to the faultHandler function:

```
private function faultHandler(evt:FaultEvent):void
{
    var faultMessage:String = "Could not connect with XML file";
    Alert.show(faultMessage, "Error opening file");
}
```

The first argument in the show() function is the message to be displayed (which was the string in the previous variable you created), and the second is the title of the pop-up box.

All that remains to be done is to have the HTTPService call the method when a fault is encountered. The <HTTPService> class<$I~<HTTPService> class> has an event called fault which will handle this for us.

5. Add the following fault event to the HTTPService tag:

```
<mx:HTTPService id="bookData" url="assets/books.xml" result=➡
"bookHandler(event)" fault="faultHandler(event)"/>
```

Notice that if a fault occurs, the faultHandler function you just created will be called, and the FaultEvent event object will be passed.

6. As you did earlier in the chapter, misspell the name of the XML file in the <HTTPService> tag and run the application. You should get the output shown in Figure 6-4.

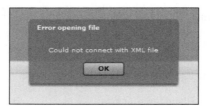

Figure 6-4.
The fault message

You can easily see where the message and title properties are placed.

7. Click OK and shut down the browser session.

Let's take a look at a couple of other message possibilities.

Recall that an event object has a property called target that identifies who is broadcasting the event. The FaultEvent object can use this property. Let's give it a look.

8. Change your fault message string to the following:

```
var faultMessage:String = "The origin of the fault is: " + evt.target;
```

9. Run the code now; you should see that HTTPService broadcasted the event, as shown in Figure 6-5.

Figure 6-5. Dialog box showing the target property

While the first fault message we generated would be friendly for an end user, this last message would probably only be used in a debugging situation. The end user probably doesn't care that the origin of the fault is the HTTPService request.

10. There are a number of messages you can generate during the coding and debugging process. To have a quick look at them, change the fault message as follows:

```
var faultMessage:String = "The origin of the fault is: " + evt.message;
```

This will list all the messages as shown in Figure 6-6.

Figure 6-6. The message property generating all error messages

Notice the line about two-thirds of the way down:

    faultString = "HTTP request error"

Make a note of that. You will see something interesting in the next section.

I am sure you wouldn't want your users to see this. As a suggestion, you may want to stick with the first dialog box you generated.

11. Change the broken URL link in the HTTPService tag back to books.xml.

If you are going to connect to the outside world, you have to be very conscious of security. This is a good place to take a look at this issue.

Flash Player security

Flash Player security is pretty tight. Like most plug-in players (sometimes referred to as ActiveX controls), it has a **sandbox** around it. In other words, to spin a phrase from a commercial for Las Vegas, what goes on in Flash Player stays in Flash Player.

Let's take a look at how the security features in Flash Player 9 work. For this part, you may want to just read through the text. However, if you want to try this out, you will need to have ColdFusion 8 installed with the web server feature that is available in the Developer Edition. You could have one of the other server technologies installed. If you do, the ColdFusion steps I have listed here should be easy to translate to a different server.

> For instructions on installing the ColdFusion 8 Developer Edition (with the web server feature), please see the Appendix.
>
> If you know how to do it, you could try out this example in any web server such as Apache or IIS.

Here are the steps to follow for this demonstration:

1. Set up a folder (I called it test) under the wwwroot directory of ColdFusion 8 (ColdFusion8 directory).

When you have ColdFusion running locally, for testing purposes, its address is localhost:8500. The name localhost is the name of the server, and the 8500 is the port that it runs on.

2. Don't forget to change the name of the XML file back to books.xml from the previous exercise.

3. Place a copy of the books.xml file in the ColdFusion8\wwwroot\test directory you just created.

4. Change the url property in the <HTTPService> tag as follows:

```
<mx:HTTPService id="bookData" url="http://localhost:8500/test/➥
books.xml" result="bookHandler(event)" fault="faultHandler(event)"/>
```

5. Run the application; it should work fine. If this is the first time you are running it in ColdFusion, it may take a few moments for the data to appear in the DataGrid. This is because ColdFusion is handling all the mechanics of connecting with Flex and using the XML file. Subsequent runs should be a lot faster.

The newly generated SWF file now knows to talk only to localhost:8500/test.

Now, we are going to try a little experiment.

6. Copy the Chapter6_project.swf file (or whatever you called the underlying MXML file) and paste it into the wwwroot\test directory of ColdFusion 8. This is the same folder that books.xml is located in.

7. Open a browser session and input the following URL:

http://localhost:8500/test/Chapter6_project.swf

It should work exactly as before. This is nearly the same process you would use to deploy it to a server.

As you may know, the web address of 127.0.0.1 is the more formal way of saying localhost.

8. Change your browser's URL to the following:

http://127.0.0.1:8500/test/Chapter6_project.swf

In essence, this is the same URL as earlier. However, when you run it, the faultHandler triggers. Look once more at the faultString you first saw in the last section (see Figure 6-7).

Figure 6-7. The new faultString

This time the faultString is reporting a "Security error accessing url." Even a minor change in the URL is enough to cause the security features of Flash Player to trigger.

But what happens if you need the SWF file to access a URL different from its domain? You can override this security feature by creating an XML file in the root directory of the web server. You must name this file crossdomain.xml and save it in the root folder of the web server, not the application folder—in the case of ColdFusion, it would be in the wwwroot folder. If you are using Apache on a Mac, locate crossdomain.xml in Macintosh HD:Library:WebServer:Documents. Placing it in the root level of your Sites folder won't work.

Here is a sample of the syntax that needs to be used. I created this using Dreamweaver CS3. However, you can use any text editor.

```
<?xml version="1.0" encoding="utf-8"?>
<!DOCTYPE cross-domain-policy SYSTEM "http://www.adobe.com/xml/➥
dtds/cross-domain-policy.dtd">
<cross-domain-policy>
     <allow-access-from domain="127.0.0.1" />
</cross-domain-policy>
```

9. After creating crossdomain.xml and placing it in the server's root directory, rerun the previous URL.

If everything was done correctly, 127.0.0.1 should have no trouble accessing the generated SWF file now.

You could have substituted an asterisk (*) for the domain name in the crossdomain.xml file. However, this means that all domains will have access to the SWF file. I strongly recommend not doing this for obvious reasons.

Now that you know how to work with XML in Flex, let's change the rules a bit.

Introducing E4X

Until now, ActionScript had no way of directly working with XML data except to convert it into an ArrayCollection, as you just saw.

E4X (which stands for **ECMAScript for XML**) is an emerging standard for reading and querying XML data in a simplified manner that bypasses the need to use the ArrayCollection.

As I stated earlier in the chapter, the ArrayCollection converts each of the nodes of the XML file into separate objects. We can see an example of this by using the Flex Builder debugging feature.

1. If necessary, change the URL in the HTTPService tag back to assets/books.xml:

```
<mx:HTTPService id="bookData" url="assets/books.xml" result=➥
"bookHandler(event)" fault="faultHandler(event)"/>
```

You may want to give it a quick test to make sure all is working fine.

2. On the same line as the closing curly brace for the bookHandler function, right/Ctrl-click in the left margin and select Toggle Breakpoint (see Figure 6-8).

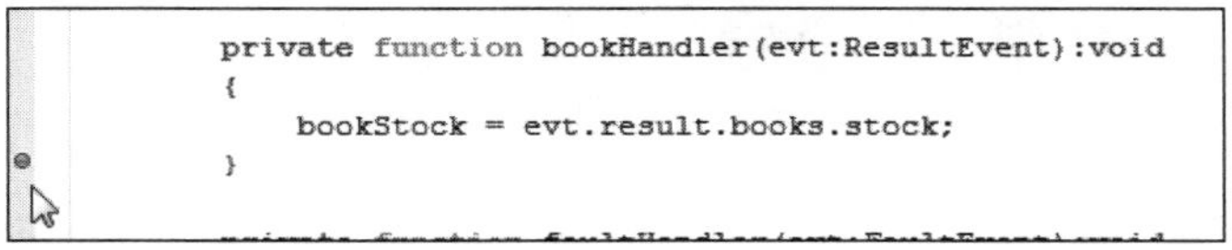

```
private function bookHandler(evt:ResultEvent):void
{
    bookStock = evt.result.books.stock;
}
```

Figure 6-8. The placement of the breakpoint

3. Run Flex in Debugging mode by clicking the Debug button located just to the right of the Run Application button you have been using all along.

4. After the browser opens, switch back to Flex Builder. You should see a dialog box telling you that it needs to switch to the Debugging Perspective, as shown in Figure 6-9.

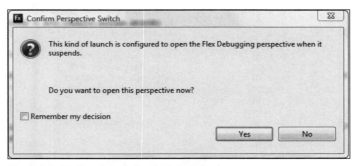

Figure 6-9. Confirm Perspective Switch dialog box

5. Click Yes.

You are now in Flex Debugging Perspective.

6. In the upper-right corner, you should see the Variables View. Double-click the Variables tab to maximize it.

7. Expand the evt branch. This corresponds to the ResultHandler event you set in the function.

8. Expand the result branch under evt.

9. Expand books and then stock. Notice how everything is in sync to how you set up the function and requested the XML data (see Figure 6-10).

6

Figure 6-10. The representation of the XML data in the Variables View

You can see that `result.books.stock` was made into an `ArrayCollection`, there are 10 elements beginning with index number 0, and that each element is an `Object` (Flex uses the class `mx.utils.ObjectProxy`). This matches everything I have said up to this point.

10. To stop debugging, close the browser.

11. Double-click the Variables View to restore it to its normal size.

Stay in Debugging Perspective.

12. Go the `HTTPService` tag and add the property `resultFormat = "e4x"`.

```
<mx:HTTPService id="bookData" url="assets/books.xml" result=➥
"bookHandler(event)" fault="faultHandler(event)" resultFormat="e4x"/>
```

13. Run the debugger again and return to the Variables View.

Now when you drill down, as before, you see actual data instead of cryptic code, as shown in Figure 6-11.

Figure 6-11. The Variables View in E4X format

As a matter of fact, notice that ArrayCollection is missing.

When you use the E4X format, Flex does not use class ArrayCollection. Instead, the data is converted to a format that is native to ActionScript and which can be easily used for query and display.

14. If necessary, return the Variables View back to normal size by double-clicking the Variables tab.

15. End the debugging session by either clicking the red square button in the Debugging View or closing the browser session (on a Mac, you can also press Cmd+F2).

16. Return to the Development Perspective.

17. Toggle off the breakpoint.

In order to use the E4X format, we need to make a few minor changes. First of all, our variable bookStock cannot be of type ArrayCollection because ArrayCollection is not used with E4X.

18. Change the type of the bookStock variable to XMLList.

Class XMLList is used when working with multiple XML elements or nodes. If you try to use multiple objects with class XML, you will get an error. Class XML is used to manipulate individual elements within the XML file as well as handling the new E4X standard, which we are discussing. The differences between XML and XMLLIst will become apparent as you progress through this chapter.

Let's see a few examples on how E4X can help us. We will use the DataGrid to display our data for now.

Let's say we want to see only the book names, <name>.

19. Modify the function as follows:

```
private function bookHandler(evt:ResultEvent):void
{
    bookStock = evt.result..name;
}
```

The two dots between result and name are called the **descendant accessor**. This means access any data associated with the <name> node no matter how deeply it is descended from the root node. In other words, you don't need to specifically drill down to the data like we did before and certainly in ActionScript 2.0.

20. Run the code; you should see a list of the books.

21. If you wanted to see just a list of the authors, you would substitute author for name and run the application.

Where the real power of E4X comes into play is in the ability to query the XML data based on criteria. As an example, let's say you wanted to see only the books with the category of Fiction (this is case sensitive).

22. Change your code as follows:

```
private function bookHandler(evt:ResultEvent):void
{
    bookStock = evt.result.stock.(category=="Fiction").name;
}
```

Notice that you use the double equal sign (comparative operator) as if you were writing an if statement in ActionScript.

23. Run the code now; you should see only the requested books.

> *Please remember that this is case sensitive. As a result, if you used "fiction", you would have gotten an empty result.*

An entire book could be written about the various aspects of E4X syntax. While we will be revisiting various aspects of this subject throughout this remainder of this book, you can learn more about it at

www.ecma-international.org/publications/files/ECMA-ST/Ecma-357.pdf

For now, let's look at yet another aspect of XML data.

The Model tag

The Model tag is one of the few MXML tags that does not have a corresponding ActionScript class file. The purpose behind it is to do just as its name states, to model data that will be used in the application without the use of a live XML file. Usually, what you do is create a small XML file, right in the MXML file, with just two or three records, that will mimic the actual XML data you will be working with.

Let's try an example. Let's say you wanted to model the XML data we have been working with.

1. In the MXML file you have been working with, remove the Script block, the HTTPService tag, and the creationComplete event in the opening Application tag. All that should be left is the DataGrid control.

2. Under the opening Application tag, set up an opening and closing Model tag with the id property of bookStock.

```
<?xml version="1.0" encoding="utf-8"?>
<mx:Application xmlns:mx="http://www.adobe.com/2006/mxml" ➡
layout="absolute">
<mx:Model id="bookStock">

</mx:Model>

<mx:DataGrid x="56" y="250" width="950" dataProvider="{bookStock}"/>
</mx:Application>
```

3. Within the opening and closing Model tags, build the following simple XML model:

```
<?xml version="1.0" encoding="utf-8"?>
<mx:Application xmlns:mx="http://www.adobe.com/2006/mxml" ➡
layout="absolute">
<mx:Model id="bookStock">
    <stock>
        <name>The Picasso Code</name>
        <author>Dan Blue</author>
        <category>Fiction</category>
        <description>Cubist paintings reveal a secret society ➡
of people who really look like that</description>
    </stock>
</mx:Model>
<mx:DataGrid x="56" y="250" width="950" dataProvider="{bookStock}"/>
</mx:Application>
```

The DataGrid control should still have bookStock as its dataProvider. If not, enter it in as shown.

4. Run your application; you should see your sole record in the DataGrid, as shown in Figure 6-12.

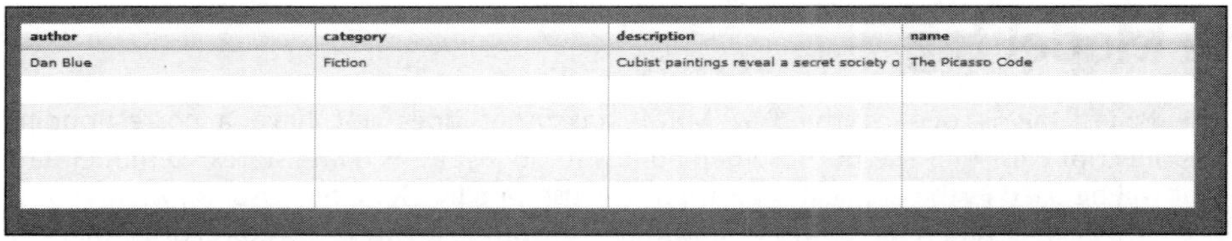

author	category	description	name
Dan Blue	Fiction	Cubist paintings reveal a secret society o	The Picasso Code

Figure 6-12. The data from the Model tag

The Model tag also has a property called source that will allow you to call an XML file from an external source. Knowing that, you are probably asking yourself why that can't be used in place of the HTTPService tag. The answer is easy: the data used in the Model tag is actually embedded into the SWF file. This means that if the data in the external XML file changes for any reason, those changes would not be reflected in the SWF. For that reason, the Model tag should be used for just that: modeling and testing data during design.

> *I know several designers who use this tag for small amounts of unchanging data, such as office locations or state abbreviations.*

Well, we have been using the DataGrid up to this point in this chapter. And I am sure you are quite impressed with it. However, we have only looked at a fraction of its capabilities. Let's turn our attention to it to see how we can unleash its power.

The DataGrid control

When the DataGrid control was introduced with Flash MX 2004, I was astonished at its power and capabilities. Unfortunately, most Flash websites I have seen have not taken advantage of its power. Here, you will learn how, and hopefully incorporate that power into your own site.

1. If necessary, import the books2.xml file that was in your Chapter 6 download files.

This file is similar to the book.xml file with the additional field of <publish_date>.

```
<books>
    <stock>
        <name>The Picasso Code</name>
        <author>Dan Blue</author>
        <category>Fiction</category>
        <description>Cubist paintings reveal a secret society of ➥
people who really look like that</description>
        <publish_date>2005-06-03</publish_date>
    </stock>
```

This is a good time to do a quick test to see how much you have learned.

2. Go ahead and connect this XML file with the HTTPService tag, and use the results as the dataProvider for the DataGrid control. Don't forget the creationComplete event in the opening Application tag.

No ActionScript handlers are necessary for this exercise.

If you need to check yourself, here is the finished code:

```
<?xml version="1.0" encoding="utf-8"?>
<mx:Application xmlns:mx="http://www.adobe.com/2006/mxml" ➥
layout="absolute" creationComplete="bookStock.send()">
<mx:HTTPService id="bookStock" url="assets/books2.xml"/>
<mx:DataGrid x="56" y="250" width="950" dataProvider=➥
"{bookStock.lastResult.books.stock}"/>
</mx:Application>
```

You DataGrid should look like the one in Figure 6-13.

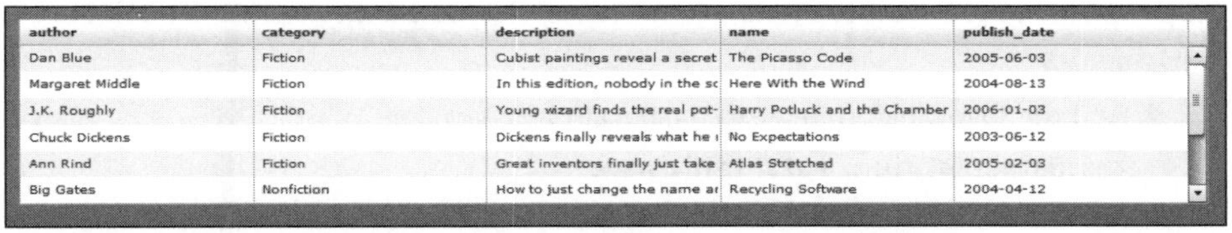

author	category	description	name	publish_date
Dan Blue	Fiction	Cubist paintings reveal a secret	The Picasso Code	2005-06-03
Margaret Middle	Fiction	In this edition, nobody in the sc	Here With the Wind	2004-08-13
J.K. Roughly	Fiction	Young wizard finds the real pot-	Harry Potluck and the Chamber	2006-01-03
Chuck Dickens	Fiction	Dickens finally reveals what he	No Expectations	2003-06-12
Ann Rind	Fiction	Great inventors finally just take	Atlas Stretched	2005-02-03
Big Gates	Nonfiction	How to just change the name ar	Recycling Software	2004-04-12

Figure 6-13. The DataGrid after the initial setup

While it is not bad looking, you may want to make some alterations. For instance, they may not be in the order that you want, nor will they necessarily have the header text that you want. All the header controls did was pick up the node names.

Modifying DataGrid columns

Let's go ahead and alter the columns a bit.

1. At the end of the DataGrid tag, delete the /> and replace it with just the > character. Flex Builder should build a closing tag. As I have said in earlier chapters, this would be analogous to turning the control into a container.

```
<mx:DataGrid x="56" y="250" width="950" dataProvider=➥
"{bookStock.lastResult.books.stock}">

</mx:DataGrid>
```

The DataGrid control has a property called columns. Recall from our discussion of states and transitions in Chapter 4 that MXML has the ability to turn a property into its own container. This gives us the ability to add multiple items, or control additional properties, within that property. We will do that here with the DataGrid control's columns property.

2. Add the columns property as follows:

```
<mx:DataGrid x="56" y="250" width="950" dataProvider=➡
"{bookStock.lastResult.books.stock}">
    <mx:columns>

    </mx:columns>
</mx:DataGrid>
```

Within the columns property container, we can now set up an array of DataGridColumns that we can control the look of as well as their content.

3. Within the columns container, begin the first tag as follows:

```
<mx:DataGridColumn
```

The DataGridColumn control allows complete control of the format, heading, and content of the column. One warning here: once you define one of the columns of the DataGrid with this tag, you must define all of the columns using a separate tag for each column.

The first property you want to add is the dataField property. This allows you to specify which XML node you want to display. For instance, say you want to show the book's name first.

4. Add the following property to the DataGridColumn tag:

```
<mx:DataGridColumn dataField="name"
```

> You may want to have the XML file open to refer to the names as you go through these exercises.

Often the node names are not user friendly. You may want to specify what text you want users to actually see. You can do so with the headerText property.

5. Add the following headerText property to the DataGridColumn tag:

```
<mx:DataGridColumn dataField="name" headerText="Book Name"
```

6. Close the tag by adding />. Your code should look like this:

```
<mx:DataGrid x="56" y="250" width="950" dataProvider=➡
"{bookStock.lastResult.books.stock}">
    <mx:columns>
        <mx:DataGridColumn dataField="name" headerText="Book Name"/>
    </mx:columns>
</mx:DataGrid>
```

As I just said, when you define one column using the DataGridColumn control, you have to define all of them with it.

7. Run the application right now; your DataGrid will show only one column (see Figure 6-14).

Figure 6-14. The reformatted DataGrid column

Notice that the header text reflects what we put into the DataGridColumn control.

8. Set up DataGridColumn controls for author, description, and publish_date.

```
<mx:DataGrid x="56" y="250" width="950" dataProvider=➥
"{bookStock.lastResult.books.stock}">
    <mx:columns>
        <mx:DataGridColumn dataField="name" headerText="Book Name"/>
        <mx:DataGridColumn dataField="author" ➥
headerText="Author Text"/>
        <mx:DataGridColumn dataField="description" ➥
headerText="Description"/>
        <mx:DataGridColumn dataField="publish_date" ➥
headerText="Publish Date"/>
    </mx:columns>
</mx:DataGrid>
```

9. Run the application; you should see the results shown in Figure 6-15.

Book Name	Author Text	Description	Publish Date
The Picasso Code	Dan Blue	Cubist paintings reveal a secret society	2005-06-03
Here With the Wind	Margaret Middle	In this edition, nobody in the south real	2004-08-13
Harry Potluck and the Chamber of Mone	J.K. Roughly	Young wizard finds the real pot-of-gold	2006-01-03
No Expectations	Chuck Dickens	Dickens finally reveals what he really thi	2003-06-12
Atlas Stretched	Ann Rind	Great inventors finally just take the mor	2005-02-03
Recycling Software	Big Gates	How to just change the name and interf	2004-04-12

Figure 6-15. The completed DataGrid

You may not like how the Publish Date column is formatted. Let's make some changes to it.

The DateFormatter class

ActionScript has five class files known as the formatter classes: CurrencyFormatter, DateFormatter, NumberFormatter, PhoneFormatter, and ZipCodeFormatter.

The DateFormatter class has a property called formatString that allows you set a mask for, as you guessed, dates.

1. Under the opening Application tag, start a DateFormatter tag and give it an id of publishDate.

```
<mx:DateFormatter id="publishDate"
```

As I just stated, the formatString property allows you to set a mask for formatting the date. If you research the documentation for the class, which I always say to do, you will see the various formats that are available. For now, we are going to use a common one: MMMM DD, YYYY. This will produce a date that will look like March 02, 2008.

Like everything else in Flex, the date format is case sensitive. You must use all capital letters when formatting the date in the formatString property.

2. Set the formatString property of the DateFormatter tag as shown here. Close the tag on completion.

```
<mx:DateFormatter id="publishDate" formatString="MMMM DD, YYYY"/>
```

Now here is where things get a little tricky. You now need to tell the DataGrid control to use this format for the publish_date field. Unfortunately, you cannot do this directly, only through a function.

3. Create a Script block and add a function called dateFormat().

This function will need to accept two arguments. The first argument you call is the dateItem (you could use any name you want), which has to be of type Object. This represents each line of data. The second argument is the name of the column you want to format. I used the name dateColumn. It must be of type DataGridColumn. The return type of the function is String.

4. Add the following arguments to the dateFormat function:

```
<mx:Script>
    <![CDATA[

        private function dateFormat(dateItem:Object, ➡
dateColumn:DataGridColumn):String
        {

        }
    ]]>
</mx:Script>
```

Once again, Flex Builder should have built the import statement automatically.

Since there is a return type, as we have discussed earlier, you must use the keyword return in the function. But you have to decide what to return. The syntax I am about to show you is pretty boilerplate and can be used in nearly any situation.

```
    private function dateFormat(dateItem:Object, ➡
    dateColumn:DataGridColumn):String
    {
        return publishDate.format(dateItem[dateColumn.dataField]);
    }
```

The date is passed from the DataGrid to the DateFormatter (which you called publishDate) through the dateItem argument. The DateFormatter returns this formatted date, through its format function, to the dataField of the column whose name was passed through the dateColumn argument. If you found that a bit confusing, just follow the reasoning slowly. Trust me, it will make sense!

The only thing left to do is to instruct the DataGridColumn to pass the necessary arguments to the dateFormat function we just created.

5. Go to the DataGridColumn for publish_date and add the labelFunction property. This will call the dateFormat function as follows:

```
<mx:columns>
    <mx:DataGridColumn dataField="name" headerText="Book Name"/>
    <mx:DataGridColumn dataField="author" headerText="Author Text"/>
    <mx:DataGridColumn dataField="description" ➡
headerText="Description"/>
    <mx:DataGridColumn dataField="publish_date" ➡
headerText="Publish Date" labelFunction="dateFormat"/>
</mx:columns>
```

Notice that we don't need to specify the two arguments that need to be passed to the function. The DataGridColumn class handles all of this automatically. You just have to have the function set up to receive two arguments, the first of type Object and the second of type DataGridColumn, as you did previously.

6. Give the application a test. If all was set up properly, you should get the results shown in Figure 6-16.

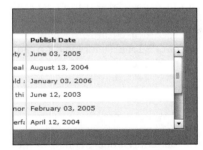

Figure 6-16. The formatted dates

Well, we have expanded the already powerful capabilities of the DataGrid control. Now let's make it really fly.

Editing and rendering data

The DataGrid control is not just for displaying data. It can also be used to edit existing data or enter new data. Let's take a look at this feature. Say you want to make the description field editable.

First, you must switch the editable feature of the entire DataGrid on.

1. Add the editable property to the DataGrid control, like so:

```
<mx:DataGrid x="56" y="250" width="950" dataProvider=➡
"{bookStock.lastResult.books.stock}" editable="true">
```

This has one rather unfortunate side effect: it makes all of the fields editable.

2. Run the application and click in each field. As you can see, you can change any data you want in the DataGrid columns.

> *The changes you make to data will not be written back to the XML file at this point. We will be discussing that later on in the book.*

If you only want the description field to be editable, you have to set the editable property of the fields you don't want to be editable to false.

3. Change the DataGridColumns as follows:

```
<mx:DataGrid x="56" y="250" width="950" dataProvider=➡
"{bookStock.lastResult.books.stock}" editable="true">
    <mx:columns>
        <mx:DataGridColumn dataField="name" ➡
headerText="Book Name" editable="false"/>
        <mx:DataGridColumn dataField="author" ➡
headerText="Author Text" editable="false"/>
        <mx:DataGridColumn dataField="description" ➡
headerText="Description"/>
        <mx:DataGridColumn dataField="publish_date" ➡
headerText="Publish Date" labelFunction="dateFormat"➡
            editable="false"/>
    </mx:columns>
</mx:DataGrid>
```

4. Run the application now. You should be able to change only the description field.

The next steps should change your entire understanding of the DataGrid control and open up powerful design possibilities.

5. Change the structure of your DataGrid by adding a new column that isn't part of the underlying XML file. Once again, we will not be saving this data for now, but just using it to show design possibilities.

```
<mx:DataGrid x="56" y="250" width="950" dataProvider=➥
"{bookStock.lastResult.books.stock}" editable="true">
    <mx:columns>
        <mx:DataGridColumn dataField="name" headerText=➥
"Book Name" editable="false"/>
        <mx:DataGridColumn dataField="author" ➥
headerText="Author Text" editable="false"/>
        <mx:DataGridColumn dataField="description" ➥
headerText="Description"/>
        <mx:DataGridColumn dataField="publish_date" headerText=➥
"Publish Date" labelFunction="dateFormat" editable="false"/>
        <mx:DataGridColumn dataField="review" ➥
headerText="Your Review" editable="true"/>
    </mx:columns>
</mx:DataGrid>
```

6. Try out the code. The changes should result in a new column in which users can write their own reviews, as shown in Figure 6-17.

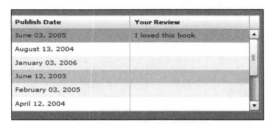

Figure 6-17. The DataGrid control with a new column

The DataGrid control allows you to embed other components, either from Action-Script 3.0 or those you have created, into cells. For instance, let's assume you want to put a TextArea control into the cells of the column you just created in order to allow users to more easily write their reviews. You could go two possible routes: ItemEditor or ItemRenderer. Both properties will allow you to place components into the cell. However, these two properties have slightly different functionality. This difference is more easily seen than explained. So let's have a look.

For starters, the column's editable property must be true.

As you have seen earlier, the controls built into ActionScript 3.0 are in the package mx.controls.

7. Add the following property to your new column:

```
<mx:DataGridColumn dataField="review" headerText="Your Review" ➥
editable="true" itemEditor="mx.controls.TextArea"/>
```

Notice that you not only specified to put a TextArea into the field, but also defined the package that contains it (mx.controls). You combined the import and control into one simple MXML statement.

8. Run your application. Something will look wrong at first blush (see Figure 6-18).

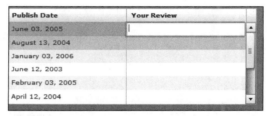

Figure 6-18. When the ItemEditor first loads

It looks like nothing happened.

9. Click a cell and watch what happens—you should see a change, as shown in Figure 6-19.

Publish Date	Your Review
June 03, 2005	
August 13, 2004	
January 03, 2006	
June 12, 2003	
February 03, 2005	
April 12, 2004	

Figure 6-19. The clicked itemEditor

When you click a cell, the `itemEditor` property turns on the `TextArea` control and allows you to type an entry.

10. Now change the `itemEditor` property to `itemRenderer`.

```
<mx:DataGridColumn dataField="review" headerText="Your Review" ➥
editable="true" itemRenderer="mx.controls.TextArea"/>
```

11. Run your code now. You should see a significant difference in the results, as shown in Figure 6-20. The TextArea control is automatically turned on for each row in the cell.

Deciding between `itemEditor` and `itemRenderer` is a matter of style and of appropriateness.

There is one drawback to the techniques you just saw. A cell can contain only one control at a time. What happens if you want the cell to contain several controls?

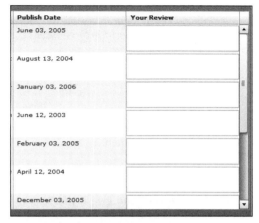

Figure 6-20. DataGrid with the itemRenderer control added

You can turn to a concept you have learned already: components.

6

12. Right-click the src folder and select File ➤ New ➤ MXML Component to bring up the New MXML Component dialog box shown in Figure 6-21.

Figure 6-21. The New MXML Component dialog box

235

I am purposely not placing this component in a separate folder for this exercise in order to reduce having to add a path, using xmlns, later on. I am doing it just to keep things simple.

13. Name this component ReviewForm.

14. Use the VBox as the underlying basis and set the Width and Height properties to 400 and 300, respectively. (This is one time where you want to control the size. The reason for this will be obvious in a moment.)

15. Click Finish.

16. Switch to Design View, if you are not already in it.

17. Drag a Label control into the VBox and give it the Text property of Please enter your Email address (see Figure 6-22).

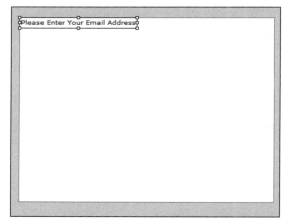

Figure 6-22. The VBox with the Label control added

18. Underneath this, add a TextInput control to enter the e-mail address, as shown in Figure 6-23.

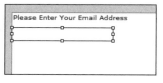

Figure 6-23.
The TextInput control added

For purposes of this exercise, you are not going to add an id property because you are not going to do any coding.

19. Add another Label control and give it the text Please enter your review, as shown in Figure 6-24.

Figure 6-24.
The Label control added

20. Next, add a TextArea control to write the review in, as shown in Figure 6-25.

Figure 6-25. The TextArea control added

We want to now make the component as small as possible to fit comfortably inside of a cell of the DataGrid and not make the DataGrid overly large.

21. Click the VBox container itself and, using the resizing handles, get rid of as much wasted space as possible as shown in Figure 6-26.

Figure 6-26.
The finished component

If you want to play it by the numbers, you could go into Source View and set the width and height of the VBox container to around 190 and 140, respectively.

22. Save your component and, if you want, close it. If you don't save the component, the application will not function properly.

23. Return to the application file.

24. Replace `mx.controls.TextArea` with the name of your component, `ReviewForm`. Since you saved it in the same directory, there does not need to be any package named.

```
<mx:DataGridColumn dataField="review" headerText="Your Review" ➥
editable="true" itemRenderer="ReviewForm"/>
```

25. Run the application. You should see the result shown in Figure 6-27.

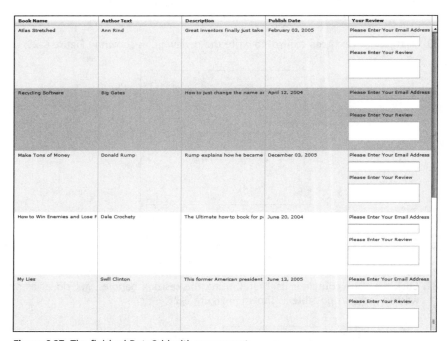

Figure 6-27. The finished DataGrid with component

We have a few things going wrong here. Let's treat them one step at a time.

First of all, you may have horizontal and vertical scrollbars turned on for each instance of the component. This is easily remedied.

Scrollbar functionality is handled with the properties `horizontalScrollPolicy` and `verticalScrollPolicy`.

26. Close the browser and return to the `ReviewForm` component.

27. Modify the outer VBox container as follows:

```
<mx:VBox xmlns:mx="http://www.adobe.com/2006/mxml" width="190" ➥
height="140" horizontalScrollPolicy="off" verticalScrollPolicy="off">
```

Notice that the scroll policy properties offer three options: off—which means they never come on, on—which keeps the scrollbars turned on, and auto—they are turned on or off as needed.

28. Save the component and run the application again. That scrollbar problem should be remedied (see Figure 6-28).

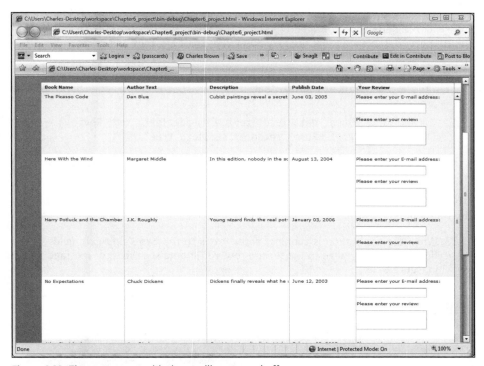

Figure 6-28. The component with the scrollbars turned off

OK, first problem easily solved. However, two more to go.

29. With the application running, click one of the TextInput fields in the component. You should get a strange-looking message in the field (see Figure 6-29).

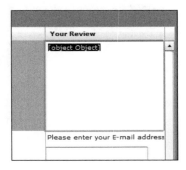

Figure 6-29.
The "[object Object]" message

You are going to run into cryptic message "[object Object]" from time to time in Flex. This is ActionScript's way of telling you it is not sure what you are talking about.

If this component was providing read-only data, this would not be an issue. However, in this case, we are asking the DataGrid control to use the component within the itemRenderer and to be able to write data into the component. In other words, the itemRenderer will need to serve as an editor. In MXML, you must explicitly give the itemRenderer permission to function in both roles with the rendererIsEditor property. This property is Boolean in that the only two values for it are true and false.

30. Close the browser and return to the application file.

31. On the DataGridColumn tag that uses the itemRenderer, add the following property:

```
<mx:DataGridColumn dataField="review" headerText="Your Review" ➥
itemRenderer="ReviewForm" rendererIsEditor="true" />
```

32. Save the component and run the application again. The "[object Object]" problem should be gone now.

Two of the problems solved. The next one is a bit trickier, and here I will provide a temporary solution.

33. While the application is running, enter text into the two TextInput fields of the first row. When you go to the second row, you should see the error message shown in Figure 6-30.

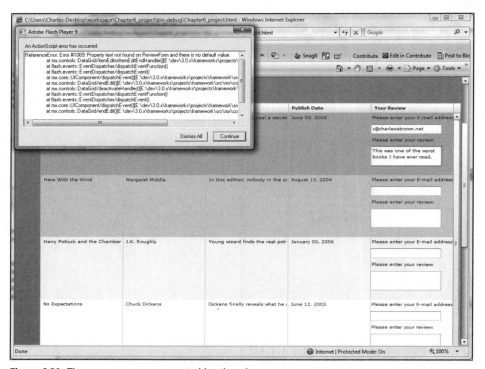

Figure 6-30. The error message generated by changing rows

When you change rows, ActionScript is going to try to trigger a deactivate event on the row you are working on. When it deactivates, the event attempts to save the data to a property called text. From there on in, text will attempt to write the data to wherever it needs to be written to.

In our small example, we are not yet using any dynamic technology. However, this problem can be temporarily resolved by returning to the component, adding a Script block, and creating a bindable, public property called text.

34. Close the browser and return to the component. Add the following Script block to it:

```
<mx:Script>
    <![CDATA[
        [Bindable]
        public var text:String = "";

    ]]>
</mx:Script>
```

35. Save your work and rerun the application. All problems should be solved now.

As you can see, the component, with multiple controls, worked beautifully inside the cell of the DataGrid column. You can set up all sorts of complex design scenarios and programming situations by using this powerful feature. I have even seen applications where an embedded component contains a secondary DataGrid or other components.

A favorite trick of mine is to create a component with an Image control, tie that into the URL of the image in the XML file, and then bring the component into the DataGrid control. In that spirit, let's see what you can do with images.

Flex can pass data to a component. The DataGrid *control has a property called* data *that will pass information to the properties of the component. We will be looking at that a little later in this book.*

6

Images in the DataGrid container

Included with the download files for Chapter 6, you should see a file called foed.xml, as well as four JPG files.

1. If necessary, import these files into your project's assets folder.

The XML file is fairly simple for this exercise and looks as follows:

```
<?xml version="1.0" encoding="iso-8859-1"?>
<foed>
    <book>
        <book_name>XML for Flash</book_name>
            <author>Sas Jacobs</author>
            <cover>assets/jacobs.jpg</cover>
    </book>
    <book>
        <book_name>Foundation Flash 8 Video</book_name>
         <author>Tom Green</author>
          <cover>assets/green.jpg</cover>
    </book>
    <book>
        <book_name>Object Oriented Programming for Flash 8</book_name>
         <author>Peter Elst</author>
          <cover>assets/elst.jpg</cover>
    </book>
    <book>
        <book_name>Foundation ActionScript Animation: ➥
Making Things Move</book_name>
            <author>Keith Peters</author>
            <cover>assets/peters.jpg</cover>
    </book>
</foed>
```

2. Create a new MXML application file called Image_practice.mxml.

3. Connect to the XML file and pass just the book_name to the dataGrid control. Your code should look as follows:

```
<?xml version="1.0" encoding="utf-8"?>
<mx:Application xmlns:mx="http://www.adobe.com/2006/mxml" ➥
layout="absolute" creationComplete="bookStock.send()">
<mx:HTTPService id="bookStock" url="assets/foed.xml"/>
 <mx:DataGrid width="400" dataProvider=➥
"{bookStock.lastResult.foed.book}" x="345" y="30">
    <mx:columns>
        <mx:DataGridColumn dataField="book_name" headerText=➥
"Book Name" />
    </mx:columns>
</mx:DataGrid>
</mx:Application>
```

Here you see something we have bumped into a couple of times (when talking about states and transitions). Notice that you broke out the column property to its own container. You will sometimes do that when a property needs to hold multiple values.

4. Run the application—you should see the results shown in Figure 6-31.

Figure 6-31. The DataGrid control with book titles

Notice that there are some blank lines under the last title. The DataGrid control has a property that will allow you to specify how many lines you want displayed at a time: rowCount.

5. Because there are four titles, you need to set the row count to 4 as follows:

```
<mx:DataGrid width="400" dataProvider=➡
"{bookStock.lastResult.foed.book}" x="345" y="30" rowCount="4">
```

Your DataGrid should look like Figure 6-32.

Figure 6-32. The adjusted DataGrid control

Now you'll do a little design work.

6. Switch to Design View.

7. Drag a Label control under the DataGrid control and align the left edge with the left edge of the DataGrid.

8. Use the Flex Properties View to give it an id property of bookName.

9. Delete the default text of the Label, as shown in Figure 6-33.

Figure 6-33. Placement of the Label control

10. Drag another Label control under the previous one. Give it an id property of authorName and, again, delete the default text.

11. Finally, drag an Image control under the DataGrid and line up the right edge with the right edge of the DataGrid, as shown in Figure 6-34. Give it an id of coverPicture.

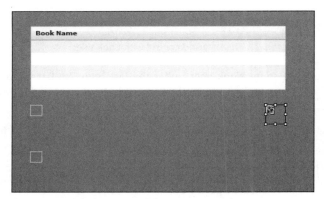

Figure 6-34. The placement of the Image control

12. Now that you have everything in place, return to the Source Perspective.

You have probably guessed what I am cooking up here. When you click the name in the DataGrid, the book_name and author are assigned to the respective labels. Then the image path is assigned to the source property of the Image control which, in turns, displays the cover image.

In order to accomplish this, we need to revisit, as we have been doing frequently, events.

Many of the controls that make lists of objects, such as DataGrid, ComboBox, and List, allow you to click items on the list. The item you select is called the selectedItem.

> There is also a second property called the selectedIndex. Since items in a list are internally arrays, the selectedIndex selects the index number of the element. In many programming scenarios, with an adjustment to the code, selectedIndex and selectedItem are interchangeable. However, if you are new to programming, you may find selectedItem easier to work with.
>
> If the control allows the possibility of selecting multiple items on the list, the properties become selectedItemsd selectedIndices.

Moving from one selectedItem, or index, to another triggers the change event (which is of type Event). Because of this, you need to create a function, as you have done before, to handle the change object. For the purposes of this exercise, let's call the function changeHandler and pass it the change event of type Event.

13. Create the following function in a Script block:

```
<mx:Script>
    <![CDATA[
        private function changeHandler(evt:Event):void
        {

        }
    ]]>
</mx:Script>
```

As I have mentioned several times, the event object contains a property called target. The target property contains the name of the control broadcasting the event, as well as most of the information about the event. In this case, it also has the identification of the selectedItem selected in the DataGrid control. However, selectedItem goes one step further: it contains all the data for that particular record. In this case, selectedItem contains the book_name, author, and cover data.

From here on in, the rest is easy. All we do is assign the information to the proper controls.

14. Add the following code to the changeHandler function:

```
private function changeHandler(evt:Event):void
{
    bookName.text = evt.target.selectedItem.book_name;
    authorName.text = evt.target.selectedItem.author;
    coverPicture.source = evt.target.selectedItem.cover;
}
```

15. Now you need to tell the DataGrid control to call the changeHandler function when a change event occurs.

```
<mx:DataGrid width="400" dataProvider=➡
"{bookStock.lastResult.foed.book} ➡
"x="345" y="30" rowCount="5" change="changeHandler(event)">
```

16. Test the application again. Click a title, and you will be greeted with a display similar to the one shown in Figure 6-35.

6

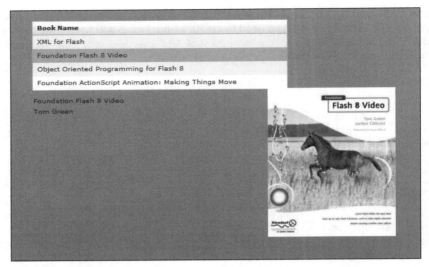

Figure 6-35. The filled-in fields

As you can see, the event object is once again the glue that ties a lot together.

17. Using the Flex Properties View, change the font and size of the two Label controls.

```
<mx:Label x="345" y="150" id="bookName" fontFamily="Arial" ➥
fontWeight="bold" fontSize="30"/>
 <mx:Label x="345" y="187" id="authorName" fontFamily="Arial" ➥
fontSize="24"/>
```

The result should be something like Figure 6-36.

Figure 6-36. Results of further changing the Label control properties

In the preceding example, the longer titles may hide partially behind the image. Feel free to rearrange the components any way that you want.

As powerful as all of the features of the DataGrid control are, there is a control that is geared to work with the parent-child relationship of XML data. Let's have a look.

The Tree control

As you have seen already, XML has a strong hierarchical relationship with regards to data. In other words, there is a parent-child relationship.

The Tree control is used in situations where this parent-child relationship regarding data exists. It is a little tough to describe the Tree control. So let's do a couple of exercises that will introduce this control. Along the way, we will revisit a few concepts you learned earlier with some variations, as well as a few brand new concepts.

1. Close any files you might have open and create a new MXML application called Tree_demonstration.mxml.

Earlier in this chapter, you got to try the Model tag for modeling data during development and testing. However, as you have seen many times by now, there is an ActionScript 3.0 equivalent for the MXML tags you use. The MXML equivalent of using the Model tag is to set up a variable of type XML and enter the modeled XML structure into that.

2. Create a Script block.

3. In the Script block, create a private and bindable variable called myData and make it of type XML. However, do not close it with a semicolon. Instead, put an equal sign in to add data.

```
<?xml version="1.0" encoding="utf-8"?>
<mx:Application xmlns:mx="http://www.adobe.com/2006/mxml" ➥
layout="absolute">
    <mx:Script>
        <![CDATA[
            [Bindable]
            private var myData:XML =

        ]]>
    </mx:Script>
</mx:Application>
```

We will now create a simple XML structure much like we did when we used the Model tag earlier.

4. Add the following data to the myData:XML property:

```
<?xml version="1.0" encoding="utf-8"?>
<mx:Application xmlns:mx="http://www.adobe.com/2006/mxml" ➥
layout="absolute">
    <mx:Script>
        <![CDATA[
            [Bindable]
            private var myData:XML =
            <stock name="In stock">
                <category name="Fiction"></category>
                <category name="Nonfiction">
                    <title name="Flash CS3 for Designers"></title>
                    <title name=➥
"Flex 3 with ActionScript 3.0"></title>
                    <title name=➥
"Dreamweaver CS3 with CSS, Ajax, and PHP"></title>
                </category>
            </stock>
        ]]>
    </mx:Script>
</mx:Script>
```

As you can see, the parent-child relationship is stock—category—title. However, notice that each of the nodes has an attribute called name (we discussed XML structure and attributes toward the beginning of this chapter). The Tree control needs this common attribute in order to properly function. For that reason, if you are planning to use this control, you will need to plan the structure of your XML files carefully, and it may not be appropriate in all situations.

> *There are a number of different ways you can structure the XML data. The ones we look at here are the more common techniques.*

The Tree control does not care about the names of the XML tags. All it concerns itself with is the parent-child relationship. Let's see an example.

5. Beneath the Script block, enter the following MXML tag for the Tree control:

```
<mx:Tree dataProvider="{myData}" width="400"/>
```

Notice that we made the XML variable, myData, the dataProvider property. Like binding properties we have seen in the past, it is surrounded by curly braces. Also, we set a width property. While this is not mandatory, it is strongly suggested with using the Tree control. The reason is that the Tree control has no way of automatically adjusting its width to accommodate different data lengths.

6. Run the application. As you can see in Figure 6-37, it will not look right.

```
<stock name="In stock">
    <category name="Fiction"/>
    <category name="Nonfiction">
▶ ☐  <title name="Flash CS3 for Designers"/>
        <title name="Flex 3 with ActionScript 3.0"/>
        <title name="Dreamweaver CS3 with CSS, Ajax, and PHP"/>
    </category>
</stock>
```

Figure 6-37. Running the initial Tree control

Rather than show us a well-structured tree, it just displayed the underlying XML. That is not the result we wanted.

What we need to do is tell the Tree control how we want the branches created. In order to accomplish that, we are going to return to another topic we discussed earlier in this chapter: E4X.

We took a quick look at the syntax for using E4X earlier. However, we didn't discuss how to access attributes within an XML file. To request the attributes, we use the @ symbol. So if you wanted to access the name attribute, you would use @name.

Notice that all of the tags in our small XML model have the attribute of name. We can leverage this to tell the Tree control to base the branches on that attribute by using a property of the Tree control called labelField.

7. Add the labelField to the Tree control and tell it to use the name attribute as follows:

```
<mx:Tree dataProvider="{myData}" width="400" labelField="@name"/>
```

8. Run the application now to see the difference, as shown in Figure 6-38.

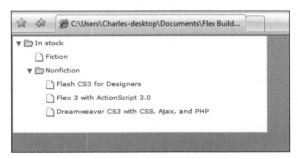

Figure 6-38. The properly functioning Tree control

Notice that we can twirl down the branches and, in the process, clearly see the parent-child relationship from the underlying XML file. This will allow the user to easily navigate to the desired data.

There are some visual cues here to help the user. Notice that In stock and Nonfiction are represented by folder icons. This is because there are child elements associated with them. When using the Tree control, these are called **branches**. However, notice that the icons for Fiction and each of the Nonfiction titles look like sheets of paper with the upper-right corner turned down. These icons, called **leaves**, mean that they terminate, or have no child elements associated with them.

Let's take this into a more "real-life" situation.

9. Close the existing MXML application and start a new one named Tree2_demonstration.

10. If necessary, import bookTree.xml into the assets folder. This file should be included with your chapter downloads.

Let's stop for a moment and look at the structure of bookTree.xml.

```
<?xml version="1.0" encoding="utf-8"?>
<stock>
    <title name="Flash CS3 for Designers" isbn="159059861">
        <author name="Tom Green" />
    </title>
    <title name="Flex 3 with ActionScript 3.0" isbn="1590597338">
        <author name="Charles E. Brown" />
    </title>
    <title name="Dreamweaver CS3 with CSS, Ajax, and PHP" ➥
isbn="1590598598">
        <author name="David Powers" />
    </title>
</stock>
```

The root is stock with no attributes. Each of the title nodes has two attributes: name and isbn. Finally, the child of title, author, has one attribute: name. Again, you see the common attribute of name. Also, you can clearly see the parent-child relationship.

11. In the MXML application, create an HTTPService tag. Give it an id property of treeData, a url property of ../assets/bookTree.xml, and a resultFormat of e4x.

```
<?xml version="1.0" encoding="utf-8"?>
<mx:Application xmlns:mx="http://www.adobe.com/2006/mxml" ➥
layout="absolute">
    <mx:HTTPService id="treeData" url="../assets/bookTree.xml" ➥
resultFormat="e4x"/>
</mx:Application>
```

We are also going to do a little cosmetic work to make our application look pretty.

12. Beneath the HTTPService tag, create an HBox container whose width is 900 pixels.

13. Within the HBox container, create two Panel containers with the id properties of leftPanel and rightPanel, respectively.

14. Give the left Panel container a title property of Friends of ED Adobe Library.

15. Give the right Panel container a height property that binds it to the height of the left Panel container.

I am pulling a little sleight-of-hand here. When we created the left Panel container, we gave it no width or height. It will automatically adjust to the height and width of its contents; which in this case will be a Tree control. We told the right container to make its height whatever the height of the left container is.

Your code should look as follows:

```
<?xml version="1.0" encoding="utf-8"?>
<mx:Application xmlns:mx="http://www.adobe.com/2006/mxml" ➥
layout="absolute">
    <mx:HTTPService id="treeData" url="../assets/bookTree.xml" ➥
resultFormat="e4x"/>
    <mx:HBox width="900">
        <mx:Panel id="leftPanel" title="Friends of ED Adobe Series">

        </mx:Panel>
        <mx:Panel id="rightPanel" height="{leftPanel.height}">

        </mx:Panel>
    </mx:HBox>
</mx:Application>
```

16. Above the HTTPService tag, create a Script block with two bindable and private variables: treeXML of type XMLList and selectedData of type XML.

```
<mx:Script>
    <![CDATA[
        [Bindable]
        private var treeXML:XMLList;

        [Bindable]
        private var selectedData:XML;
    ]]>
</mx:Script>
```

17. Create a private function called resultEvent that accepts one parameter, evt, that is of type ResultEvent. The return type is void.

```
private function resultHandler(evt:ResultEvent):void
{

}
```

Things are going to get a little tricky here. Recall from earlier in this chapter that a ResultEvent uses the property result to return the data, as opposed to target, which is used by the Event class. What we need to do is bring in the results of the HTTPService class as an XML type and then have the XML class send the result to the XMLList variable. If you are new to programming, or even just ActionScript programming, this may seem a bit

6

251

convoluted to you. However, passing data through multiple types is not uncommon in OOP environments. If you use the following syntax, it should work fine each time.

18. Add the following to the function you just created:

```
private function resultHandler(evt:ResultEvent):void
{
    var result:XML = evt.result as XML;
}
```

19. Pass the XML result to the XMLList variable using the descendant accessor discussed previously in the "Introducing E4X" section of this chapter.

```
private function resultHandler(evt:ResultEvent):void
{
    var result:XML = evt.result as XML;
    treeXML = result..title as XMLList;
}
```

There is a strange new operator here: as. In Chapter 3, we talked about some OOP concepts, and that everything is an object and that all objects have a type or class file associated with it. In OOP parlance, we call this a **casting operator**. Essentially, what it means is that you are taking data of one type and converting it to another type. In this case, we are converting the data coming into the function first to XML and then converting it to type XMLList before saving it to treeXML.

20. As you did when we first discussed the HTTPService, you need to create a result event in the tag as follows:

```
<mx:HTTPService id="treeData" url="assets/bookTree.xml" ➥
resultFormat="e4x" result="resultHandler(event)"/>
```

21. Finally, create a creationComplete event in the opening Application tag using the id of the HTTPService tag. To review, this is to trigger the HTTPService to make a call to the XML file.

```
<mx:Application xmlns:mx="http://www.adobe.com/2006/mxml" ➥
layout="absolute" creationComplete="treeData.send()">
```

> *If you wanted, you could check the connection using the Debugging Perspective as discussed earlier in this chapter.*

We now have the connection all set. What we need to do next is set up the Tree control and have a means of selecting data. When you select data in the Tree control, you are triggering a change event.

22. To accommodate the change, build the following skeletal structure for a changeEvent handler function in the Script block:

```
private function changeHandler(evt:Event): void
{

}
```

We will now build the Tree control in the left Panel container.

23. Create the Tree control in the left Panel container. Give it an id property of myTree and use the change event to call the changeHandler function you just created. Also, set the dataProvider to be bound to the XMLList variable you created, treeXML, and give it a width of 400 pixels. Finally, add a labelField property to find the name attribute. The code should look as follows:

```
<mx:Panel id="leftPanel" title="Friends of ED Adobe Library">
    <mx:Tree id="myTree" dataProvider="{treeXML}" ➥
labelField="@name" width="400" change="changeHandler(event)" />
</mx:Panel>
```

If you give your application a run, you can test to make sure the data is getting to the Tree control.

24. Run the application. Your screen should resemble Figure 6-39.

Figure 6-39. The functioning Tree control

Earlier in this chapter, while discussing the DataGrid control, we talked about arrays. Recall that when you select an item in an array, you set the property selectedItem. We are going to use that now.

Since selectedItem selects only one item at a time, we will send the data to the XML variable selectedData. Remember, individual pieces of data get sent to class XML, and multiple records get sent to XMLList. If we were not using E4X, it would all be sent to class ArrayCollection. These distinctions are very important in that you need to select the correct class for the job.

25. Return to the changeHandler function and add the following code:

```
private function changeHandler(evt:Event): void
{
    selectedData = myTree.selectedItem as XML;
}
```

Remember the passed parameter, event, is carrying all the data with it. We discussed that in Chapter 5.

We now have to have a place to send our data to. We will use the right Panel container for that.

26. Inside of the right Panel container, put a Form container. Give it a width of 400 pixels.

```
<mx:Panel id="rightPanel" height="{leftPanel.height}">
    <mx:Form width="400">

    </mx:Form>
</mx:Panel>
```

Now here is where we work a little programming magic. We will add a FormItem with a label property of Book Name, and within that FormItem we will put a Label control with an empty text property.

27. Add the following FormItem:

```
<mx:Panel id="rightPanel" height="{leftPanel.height}">
    <mx:Form width="400">
        <mx:FormItem label="Book Name">
            <mx:Label text=""/>
        </mx:FormItem>
    </mx:Form>
</mx:Panel>
```

This is a good place to review the flow of data.

HTTPService is sending the XML file results to the resultHandler function in E4X format. The resultHandler function is converting the result (title) data to type XMLList and sending it to the treeXML variable. The treeXML variable is sending the multiple rows of data to the Tree control, which is parsing the data out into branches based on the name attribute. When you select a branch in the Tree control, it causes a change event to be sent to the changeHandler function and, because it is just one record, the changeHandler function sends it to the XML variable selectedData.

I hope you are starting to see the logical flow.

The only thing left to do is to have the text property of the Label control in the Form container read that XML variable and select the data it needs. Remember, when selecting an attribute using E4X, you use the @ symbol.

28. Add the following binding to the text property of the Label control:

```
<mx:Form width="400">
    <mx:FormItem label="Book Name">
        <mx:Label text="{selectedData.@name}"/>
    </mx:FormItem>
</mx:Form>
```

29. Run the application and click the book names in the Tree control (see Figure 6-40).

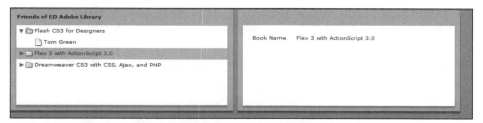

Figure 6-40. Clicking the book name and populating the Label control

If you click the author name in the tree, you will get the author name in the Book Name *field. We will be addressing that in a bit.*

30. Add another FormItem and populate it with the ISBN number as follows:

```
<mx:Panel id="rightPanel" height="{leftPanel.height}">
    <mx:Form width="400">
        <mx:FormItem label="Book Name">
            <mx:Label text="{selectedData.@name}"/>
        </mx:FormItem>
        <mx:FormItem label="ISBN Number">
            <mx:Label text="{selectedData.@isbn}"/>
        </mx:FormItem>
    </mx:Form>
</mx:Panel>
```

When you run the application, you should now see the ISBN number added. However, we still have a problem in that if you select the name of the author, the Book Name field gets populated improperly with that data. What we need to do is test the parent-child relationship so that if the author name is selected, the selectedItem will be sent back up to the parent branch.

In order to accomplish this, we need to build a conditional statement in the changeHandler. We want to test to see whether the title node is selected. If not, we want to force it to be selected.

The XML class has a function called name() that returns the name of the node selected. We will begin by setting a variable, of type String, to equal the name of the node selected.

31. Inside of the changeHandler function, set a variable called nodeName of type String and make it equal to the name() function of the XML variable.

```
private function changeHandler(evt:Event): void
{
    selectedData = myTree.selectedItem as XML;
    var nodeName:String = selectedData.name();
}
```

Now we will build an if statement that will test to see whether we are NOT on the title node. In ActionScript, as well as most programming environments, the syntax for not is !. So != means not equal to.

32. Build the following if statement below the variable you just set:

```
private function changeHandler(evt:Event): void
{
    selectedData = myTree.selectedItem as XML;
    var nodeName:String = selectedData.name();

    if(nodeName != "title")
    {

    }
}
```

This conditional statement will run if the title is not selected. In our example, the only other choice would be the author node.

The XML class has another function, called parent(), that selects the parent of the selected node. We can use that within our if statement to select the parent node if it isn't selected.

33. Fill the following code in the body of the if statement.

```
if(nodeName != "title")
{
    selectedData = selectedData.parent();
}
```

Notice that we told it to look at the existing XML record and then go to the parent of that record.

This may be a good point to look at our finished code.

```
<?xml version="1.0" encoding="utf-8"?>
<mx:Application xmlns:mx="http://www.adobe.com/2006/mxml" ➥
layout="absolute" creationComplete="treeData.send()">
<mx:Script>
    <![CDATA[
        import mx.rpc.events.ResultEvent;
        [Bindable]
        private var treeXML:XMLList;

        [Bindable]
        private var selectedData:XML;

        private function resultHandler(evt:ResultEvent):void
        {
            var result:XML = evt.result as XML;
            treeXML = result..title as XMLList;
        }
```

```
            private function changeHandler(evt:Event): void
            {
                 selectedData = myTree.selectedItem as XML;
                 var nodeName:String = selectedData.name();

                 if(nodeName != "title")
                 {
                      selectedData = selectedData.parent();
                 }
            }
      ]]>
</mx:Script>
      <mx:HTTPService id="treeData" url="../assets/bookTree.xml" ➥
resultFormat="e4x" result="resultHandler(event)"/>
      <mx:HBox width="900">
           <mx:Panel id="leftPanel" title="Friends of ED Adobe Library">
                <mx:Tree id="myTree" dataProvider="{treeXML}" ➥
labelField="@name" width="400" change="changeHandler(event)" />
           </mx:Panel>
           <mx:Panel id="rightPanel" height="{leftPanel.height}">
                <mx:Form width="400">
                     <mx:FormItem label="Book Name">
                          <mx:Label text="{selectedData.@name}"/>
                     </mx:FormItem>
                     <mx:FormItem label="ISBN Number">
                          <mx:Label text="{selectedData.@isbn}"/>
                     </mx:FormItem>
                </mx:Form>
           </mx:Panel>
      </mx:HBox>
</mx:Application>
```

34. Run the application. It should work fine when you click an author name.

We have one other small problem here. If you run the application and click the twirl arrow, rather than the item itself, the data will not be selected. This is easily fixed by creating another handler function and passing it an event of type TreeEvent (I warned you in Chapter 5 that you would be using a lot of different events).

35. In the Script block, add another event handler called openTree and pass it one argument of type TreeEvent. The return type is void.

```
private function openTree(evt:TreeEvent):void
{

}
```

The Tree control has an ItemOpen event.

36. In the Tree control, set the itemOpen event as follows:

```
<mx:Tree id="myTree" dataProvider="{treeXML}" labelField="@name" ➥
width="400" change="changeHandler(event)" itemOpen="openTree(event)" />
```

We set the body of the openTree handler much like the changeHandler function. However, we don't need to worry about a child being selected because if the twirl arrow is selected, the branch, and not the leaf, must be selected.

37. Add the following code to the body of the openTree handler:

```
private function openTree(evt:TreeEvent):void
{
    selectedData = evt.item as XML;
}
```

38. Run the application. The data should be selected when you click the twirl arrow.

As I hope you see, the Tree control offers some powerful navigation possibilities for XML data.

We are now going to return to the DataGrid control, or at least a variation on it.

The AdvancedDataGrid component

With Flex 3, Adobe introduced a new control: the AdvancedDataGrid control.

This new control incorporates many features that users of Flex 2 expressed a desire for. As of this writing, it is unclear as to why Adobe decided not to incorporate these features into the existing DataGrid control. Also, it is unclear how these two controls will coexist in the future. However, in Flex 3, these are the tools we have to work with.

The AdvancedDataGrid has all of the same functionality as the standard DataGrid control with some notable additions. Most notable of these is the ability to summarize data within the grid. It is that feature that I will demonstrate here.

1. Delete all the code between the opening and closing Application tags in the existing application file.

2. Create an HTTPService tag, with an ID of bookStock, that will access the books.xml file located in the assets folder. The result event will call a function, bookHandler(), in the Script block, and the bookHandler() function will assign the value to a bindable variable, called bookData, of type ArrayCollection. The necessary import statements should be written automatically. Also, in the opening Application tag, there should be a creationComplete event for the HTTPService. Since all of this has been discussed already, you should be able to code it on your own. Once you're done, your code should look as follows:

```
<?xml version="1.0" encoding="utf-8"?>
<mx:Application xmlns:mx="http://www.adobe.com/2006/mxml" ➥
layout="absolute" creationComplete="bookStock.send()">
<mx:Script>
    <![CDATA[
        import mx.rpc.events.ResultEvent;
        import mx.collections.ArrayCollection;

        [Bindable]
        private var bookData:ArrayCollection;

        private function bookHandler(evt:ResultEvent):void
        {
            bookData = evt.result.books.stock;
        }
    ]]>
</mx:Script>
    <mx:HTTPService id="bookStock" url="assets/books.xml" ➥
result="bookHandler(event)"/>

</mx:Application>
```

You will now set up the AdvancedDataGrid control. The syntax will be nearly identical, except that instead of using DataGrid and DataGridColumn, you will use AdvancedDataGrid and AdvancedDataGridColumn.

3. Set up the AdvancedDataGrid control as follows under the HTTPService tag:

```
<mx:AdvancedDataGrid dataProvider="{bookData}" width="70%">
    <mx:columns>
        <mx:AdvancedDataGridColumn dataField="category" ➥
headerText="Category" width="125"/>
        <mx:AdvancedDataGridColumn dataField="author" ➥
headerText="Book Author" width="225"/>
        <mx:AdvancedDataGridColumn dataField="name" ➥
headerText="Book Name" width="500"/>
    </mx:columns>
</mx:AdvancedDataGrid>
```

4. Go ahead and run the application. It should look similar to Figure 6-41, with some minor differences.

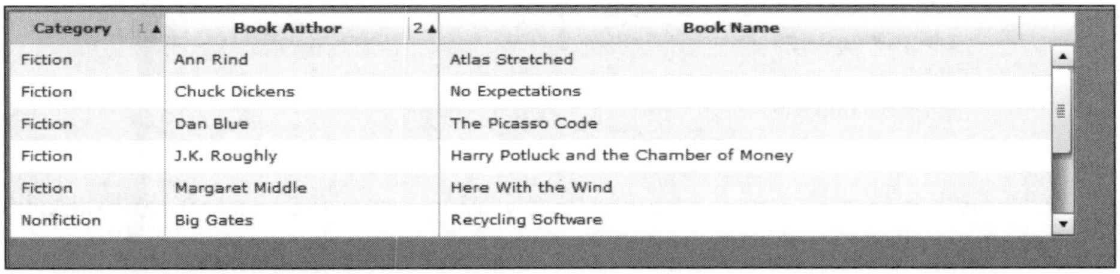

Category	1 ▲	Book Author	2 ▲	Book Name
Fiction		Ann Rind		Atlas Stretched
Fiction		Chuck Dickens		No Expectations
Fiction		Dan Blue		The Picasso Code
Fiction		J.K. Roughly		Harry Potluck and the Chamber of Money
Fiction		Margaret Middle		Here With the Wind
Nonfiction		Big Gates		Recycling Software

Figure 6-41. The AdvancedDataGrid control

Notice that there is an extra control area to the right of each column heading. When you roll over these areas, numbers appear that you can click. You can use these numbers to do multiple sorts. For instance, you could select Category for the initial sort, and then Book Author for the secondary sort. This feature is available only in the AdvancedDataGrid control.

The real power, however, is the ability of the AdvancedDataGrid control to group data together. For instance, let's say you wanted to group data based on category. In order to accomplish this, a bit of coding is involved in both the AdvancedDataGrid control and in ActionScript.

5. In the AdvancedDataGrid control, delete the dataProvider property.

6. Under the opening AdvancedDataGrid control, break the dataProvider out into its own container. Remember from previous discussions that you can break a property out into its own container to facilitate it hold multiple values.

```
<mx:AdvancedDataGrid width="70%">
    <mx:dataProvider>

    </mx:dataProvider>
    <mx:columns>
        <mx:AdvancedDataGridColumn dataField="category" ➡
headerText="Category" width="125"/>
        <mx:AdvancedDataGridColumn dataField="author" ➡
headerText="Book Author" width="225"/>
        <mx:AdvancedDataGridColumn dataField="name" ➡
headerText="Book Name" width="500"/>
    </mx:columns>
</mx:AdvancedDataGrid>
```

7. Within the dataProvider container, create another container called GroupingCollection. You must give the GroupingCollection container a unique ID so ActionScript can access it. Here, you will call it bookGroup.

```
<mx:AdvancedDataGrid width="70%">
    <mx:dataProvider>
        <mx:GroupingCollection id="bookGroup">

        </mx:GroupingCollection>
    </mx:dataProvider>
```

8. Within that container, create yet another container called Grouping.

```
<mx:GroupingCollection id="bookGroup">
    <mx:Grouping>

    </mx:Grouping>
</mx:GroupingCollection>
```

9. Name the field you want to group on by using the new GroupingField tag and name it using the field you want to group on.

```
<mx:GroupingCollection id="bookGroup">
    <mx:Grouping>
        <mx:GroupingField name="category"/>
    </mx:Grouping>
</mx:GroupingCollection>
```

You may be wondering now how the data is going to get into the AdvancedDataGrid control. After all, we are no longer referencing the ArrayCollection as we did earlier.

In the AdvancedDataGrid control, you will add a second property to the GroupingCollection tag called source. The source property will bind to the ArrayCollection.

10. Add the source property to the GroupingCollection tag:

```
<mx:GroupingCollection id="bookGroup" source="{bookData}">
```

If you run the application now, you will just get a blank DataGrid. The reason for this is that the GroupingCollection needs to refresh in order to display the data. This is one of the reasons you gave it an ID.

11. Return to the bookHandler() function and add a second line of code. This line will call the refresh() function of the GroupingCollection class.

```
private function bookHandler(evt:ResultEvent):void
{
    bookData = evt.result.books.stock;
    bookGroup.refresh();
}
```

> *The documentation for the* AdvancedDataGrid *control shows that the* refresh() *function can be put into the* AdvancedDataGrid *tag by using the* initialize *property. As of the writing of this book, I had some problems getting consistent results using that technique. I found that by placing it in the handler, the results were much more consistent.*

12. Run the application. You should see a tree-like control similar to Figure 6-42. You can open the tree and drill down to the data within that category.

Figure 6-42. The data grouped in the AdvanceDataGrid control

Of course, you can group on multiple columns if you want by adding more GroupingField tags.

Will the AdvancedDataGrid eventually replace the DataGrid? Or will the features of the AdvancedDataGrid eventually just be incorporated into the DataGrid control? Only time will tell.

Summary

This chapter covered a lot of ground. We first took a brief look at XML data and structure. We then saw how to connect to that data using the HTTPService class. From there on in we looked at some of the ways of displaying data including the powerful DataGrid and Tree controls. Along the way, you learned a bit more about using ActionScript 3.0, especially arrays, as well as the XML and XMLList classes and their related properties and functions. Finally, we took a look at the powerful new AdvancedDataGrid control.

In the next chapter, we will look at how to format our data with Cascading Style Sheets, as well as some of the internal formatting abilities of Flex.

7 FORMATTING AND CASCADING STYLE SHEETS

Style	Descripti
⬆ baseline	**CSS Inher** The vertica
⬆ bottom	**CSS Inher** The vertica
color	**Type:** uint Color of te
disabledColor	**Type:** uint Color of te
⬆ errorColor	**Type:** uint Color of th
fontAntiAliasType	**Type:** Stri

Odds are you are coming to Flex with some sort of web designing background. Assuming that you do have some web design experience, you more than likely have used **Cascading Style Sheets** (**CSS**) to format your HTML documents. That formatting could include selecting the fonts, size, color, placement of various elements of the page, and so on.

The good news is that your knowledge of CSS is not deemed obsolete with Flex. Instead, as you will see, it will just be used a little differently.

In this chapter, we will be

- Discussing some of the fundamentals for using CSS
- Discovering how Flex uses CSS, including the new features of Flex Builder 3
- Using the Validator and Formatter classes
- Combining MXML and ActionScript 3.0 to perform validation

Don't worry, if you don't have a background in CSS, you will not be lost here. I will explain each step along the way.

Flex and CSS

Most modern web designers have worked with Cascading Style Sheets. As a matter of fact, good XHTML design calls for the separation of content, presentation, and structure as follows:

In modern XHTML and CSS web design, XHTML handles the structure of the website. The content is either static, contained within the XHTML, or handled by a data source of some sort. Finally, the look of the site (the background color and images, colors, fonts, and so on) is handled by CSS. This division of work dramatically increases the site's flexibility and maintainability.

I am about to give you good news, without any corresponding bad news: you can use CSS in Flex. As a matter of fact, you can use CSS two ways: you can create an external style sheet like you would do for most site designs, or you can use the Style class (or the corresponding MXML tag) to define the styles internally.

You will be using the latter technique here for the sake of convenience only.

In light of what I just said in the preceding paragraphs, the function of CSS is limited compared to its use in HTML. For instance, CSS is frequently used in web design to position the various objects within an XHTML page. As you have seen in previous chapters, though, you can already position items within a Flex application very easily without using CSS. You may initially look upon that as a limitation in using CSS in Flex. However, my technical editor, David Powers, said it best: "Readers will discover very quickly that Flex offers a wide range of properties and styles that are impossible in XHTML."

Keeping these limitations in mind, let's discuss some basic terminology and syntax of CSS.

CSS: The basics

If you ever developed an XHTML page, without using CSS, you probably noticed that the page might look slightly different depending on the web browser it is being viewed in. For instance, the margins in a page may look a little different in Internet Explorer than in Firefox. The reason for this is that each browser has a set of built-in rules on how to present the various parts of the XHTML document.

Simply put, a Cascading Style Sheet overrides these browser rules by telling the browser that if you have an <h1> tag, it should use the font, color, size, and so on of your designation. That way, there is a greater consistency of appearance within the various browsers.

Keeping this in mind, a Cascading Style Sheet is simply a collection of rules telling the browser how the various elements of the XHTML document should look. These rules, however, must have a precise syntax. Let's look at that syntax here with a basic example of CSS:

```
h1 {color:red;}
```

The h1 part of this rule is called the **selector**—this is the element you are applying the rule to. The {color:red;} portion is called the **declaration**.

Within the declaration, the word color is called the **property**, and the red designation is the **value** you are assigning to the property. Notice that the declaration is surrounded by curly braces ({ }). Also, notice that the property and value are separated by a colon (:).

Within a declaration, you could set multiple properties as follows:

```
h1 {
        color:red;
        font:Arial;
        font-style:italic;
        text-align:center;
    }
```

Notice that each declaration is ended with a semicolon (;).

You could also assign the same rule to multiple elements as follows:

```
h1, h2, h3{color:red;}
```

Of course, this is saying that any time you have an <h1>, <h2>, or <h3> element, color the text red.

So far, you have only seen these rules applied to a specific tag. However, there is another type of rule called a **class rule**. A class rule begins with a dot and any name that you would want. For instance:

```
.myStyle{color;red;}
```

The advantage of a class rule is that it can be applied to any element at any time. In XHTML, an element is any tag on the page.

So where do you put these rules?

In XHTML, you can put CSS rules in one of three places: in a text document that can be referenced by any page in the site, in the heading of a particular page where the rules would apply only to that page, or on a specific line where the rules would only apply to that line of markup. If you put a rule in an external file, this is called a **linked** or **external** style sheet; if that rule is called within the heading of a particular document, this is called an **embedded** style sheet. A rule on a particular line is called an **inline** style.

Embedded styles get priority over the rules in external styles, and inline styles get priority over everything else. So if you had an external CSS that had

```
h1{color:red;}
```

and an embedded style that had

```
h1{color:blue;}
```

the latter would override the former, so you would see blue headings, not red.

By now, it may be becoming obvious why the function of CSS is limited in Flex. Flex does not use the browser except to call Flash Player. So, because Flex applications display within Flash Player (as SWF files), the issues regarding browser differences are simply not there.

Instead, you can use CSS to handle some general formatting issues that might apply to various components of your application. Let's take a look at how you would do this.

Working with CSS in Flex

If necessary, fire up Flex Builder 3.

Since we will not be using the practice application files from Chapter 6 again, you can either close or delete them using the techniques we discussed in previous chapters.

1. Create a new Flex project called Chapter7_project. You can keep the default name for the MXML application file.

2. In the opening Application tag, change the layout to vertical.

3. Between the opening and closing Application tags, create three Label tags with default text of your choice, and two Button tags with label text of your choice.

```
<?xml version="1.0" encoding="utf-8"?>
<mx:Application xmlns:mx="http://www.adobe.com/2006/mxml" ➥
layout="vertical">
    <mx:Label text="This is label 1"/>
    <mx:Label text="This is Label 2"/>
    <mx:Label text="This is Label 3"/>
    <mx:Button label="This is Button 1"/>
    <mx:Button label="This is Button 2"/>
</mx:Application>
```

4. Save your application and run it. Your screen should resemble what you see in Figure 7-1.

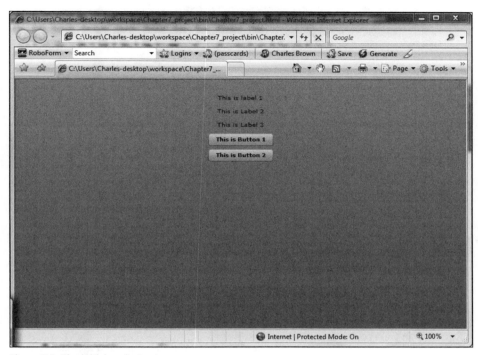

Figure 7-1. The initial project setup

By default, Labels have a default font size of 10 pixels and Buttons use a font weight of bold with 10 pixels.

5. Close the browser and return to the application.

6. Under the opening Application tag, type <mx:Style. Don't close the tag yet.

If you press the spacebar, you will notice that the Style class has one property: source. You would use the source property if you were linking your application to an external CSS file. Since we won't be doing that here, just go ahead and close the tag as a container using the > character. You should now have an opening and closing Style tag.

It is within the Style container that we put our CSS rules.

Before we do that, let's take a look at something interesting.

7. Like you have done in previous chapters, open the documentation for the Label class by clicking the word "Label" in one of the three Label tags you created, and pressing the F1 key. (In the Mac version, go to Help ➤ Dynamic Help to display the Related Topics panel.) Once you open the documentation, scroll down to the Styles section, shown in Figure 7-2.

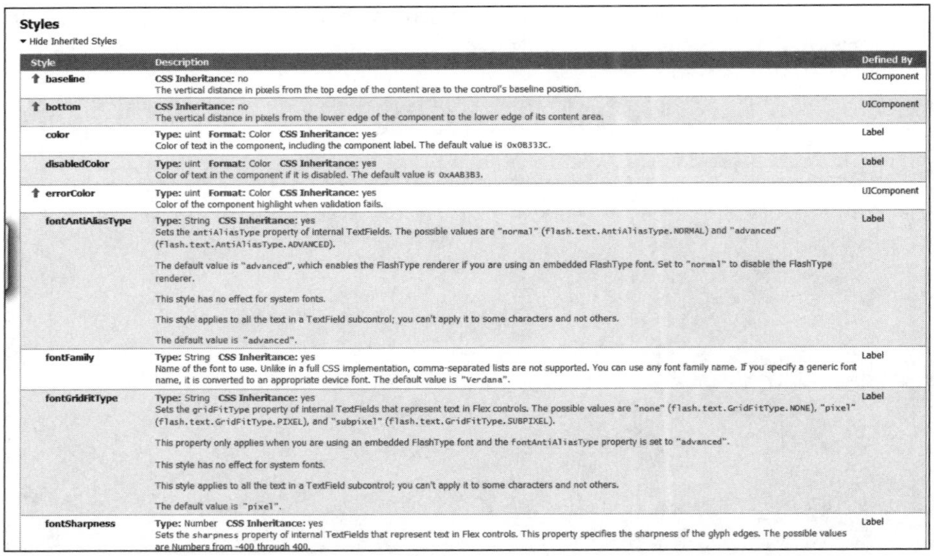

Styles

▾ Hide Inherited Styles

Style	Description	Defined By
↑ **baseline**	**CSS Inheritance:** no The vertical distance in pixels from the top edge of the content area to the control's baseline position.	UIComponent
↑ **bottom**	**CSS Inheritance:** no The vertical distance in pixels from the lower edge of the component to the lower edge of its content area.	UIComponent
color	**Type:** uint **Format:** Color **CSS Inheritance:** yes Color of text in the component, including the component label. The default value is `0x0B333C`.	Label
disabledColor	**Type:** uint **Format:** Color **CSS Inheritance:** yes Color of text in the component if it is disabled. The default value is `0xAAB3B3`.	Label
↑ **errorColor**	**Type:** uint **Format:** Color **CSS Inheritance:** yes Color of the component highlight when validation fails.	UIComponent
fontAntiAliasType	**Type:** String **CSS Inheritance:** yes Sets the `antiAliasType` property of internal TextFields. The possible values are `"normal"` (`flash.text.AntiAliasType.NORMAL`) and `"advanced"` (`flash.text.AntiAliasType.ADVANCED`). The default value is `"advanced"`, which enables the FlashType renderer if you are using an embedded FlashType font. Set to `"normal"` to disable the FlashType renderer. This style has no effect for system fonts. This style applies to all the text in a TextField subcontrol; you can't apply it to some characters and not others. The default value is `"advanced"`.	Label
fontFamily	**Type:** String **CSS Inheritance:** yes Name of the font to use. Unlike in a full CSS implementation, comma-separated lists are not supported. You can use any font family name. If you specify a generic font name, it is converted to an appropriate device font. The default value is `"Verdana"`.	Label
fontGridFitType	**Type:** String **CSS Inheritance:** yes Sets the `gridFitType` property of internal TextFields that represent text in Flex controls. The possible values are `"none"` (`flash.text.GridFitType.NONE`), `"pixel"` (`flash.text.GridFitType.PIXEL`), and `"subpixel"` (`flash.text.GridFitType.SUBPIXEL`). This property only applies when you are using an embedded FlashType font and the `fontAntiAliasType` property is set to `"advanced"`. This style has no effect for system fonts. This style applies to all the text in a TextField subcontrol; you can't apply it to some characters and not others. The default value is `"pixel"`.	Label
fontSharpness	**Type:** Number **CSS Inheritance:** yes Sets the `sharpness` property of internal TextFields that represent text in Flex controls. This property specifies the sharpness of the glyph edges. The possible values are Numbers from -400 through 400.	Label

Figure 7-2. The documentation for styles available to the Label class

Here we see the styles that are available to the `Label` class and that can be used by CSS. Each of the visual component classes has a similar section. Take a few moments and look at the styles available to the `Label` and `Button` classes. As you can see, there are many style properties that you normally do not see when using CSS with XHTML environments.

8. If you want, close the documentation and return to the application. Click between the opening and closing `Style` tags.

Referring to the earlier discussion about CSS syntax, Flex uses three different types of selectors:

- **Global selectors** apply to all classes in the application.
- **Type selectors** apply to particular classes.
- **Class selectors** work nearly identically to the way we discussed earlier in that they can be applied to any class at any time.

> *Do not get the term "class selectors," when using CSS in Flex, confused with an ActionScript class. As you will see, as you progress through this chapter, one has absolutely nothing to do with the other.*

You will get a chance to use all three here.

Let's assume we want to apply styles to all instances of the `Label` class. In that case, we would use a type selector with the word `Label`. Note that it is case sensitive.

9. Set it up as follows:

```
<mx:Style>
    Label{
            }
</mx:Style>
```

> *As of this writing, Flex Builder does not automatically indent the curly braces within the* Style *tags. You can adjust this by pressing the spacebar so they are indented evenly if you want.*

From here on in, our declarations will be pretty much the same as you saw earlier, with only a few minor variations.

For instance, let's say you wanted the text in the three Label instances to be 18 pixels and bold.

10. Enter the following declarations:

```
<mx:Style>
    Label{
                    font-size:18;
                    font-weight:bold;
            }
</mx:Style>
```

Notice that the syntax is nearly identical to the earlier discussion of using CSS in XHTML. However, there is one slight difference. In XHTML, you could use a variety of measurements for font size. For instance, you could use pixels, points, ems, etc. In Flex, the only measurement is pixels. So it isn't necessary to specify what unit of measurement is used for the font size.

11. Save your application and run it now. Your screen should look like what appears in Figure 7-3.

Notice that one CSS rule handled all three instances of the Label class in one shot. This is where the power of CSS in Flex is.

Flex allows us to use an alternative syntax in CSS declarations that looks a little more like ActionScript.

```
<mx:Style>
    Label{
                    fontSize:18;
                    fontWeight:bold;
            }
</mx:Style>
```

7

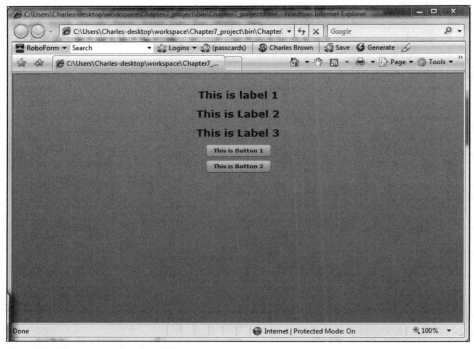

Figure 7-3. The application using CSS

Notice that the hyphen in the property names was replaced with camelcase notation. The result is exactly the same. Use whichever one you are most comfortable with. Remember, however, that like everything else in Flex, style names are case sensitive. For the most part, throughout the rest of this book, I will be using the camelcase notation for the sake of consistency. However, for examples, I may occasionally show the other notation. Remember that either notation gives you the same result.

Let's say you wanted to change the text size to 8 pixels inside of the Button class. The procedure would be similar. You would create a second type selector for the Button class as follows:

```
<mx:Style>
    Label{
                    fontSize:18;
                        fontWeight:bold;
            }
    Button{
                    fontSize:8;
            }
</mx:Style>
```

If you save and run the application, you should see the difference in the text Button size.

12. Open the documentation for the Button class and go to the Styles section. Look for the fillColors style, shown in Figure 7-4.

fillAlphas	Type: Array CSS Inheritance: no Alphas used for the background fill of controls. Use [1, 1] to make the control background opaque. The default value is [0.6, 0.4].
fillColors	Type: Array Format: Color CSS Inheritance: no Colors used to tint the background of the control. Pass the same color for both values for a flat-looking control. The default value is [0xFFFFFF, 0xCCCCCC].
focusAlpha	Type: Number CSS Inheritance: no

Figure 7-4. The fillColors style

Notice that it is of type Array. This means we can give the Button instances a gradient look. For instance, let's say we wanted to give the Button a vertical gradient from white to blue (not the prettiest of combinations, but it will allow you to see the gradient easily). As of this writing, there do not appear to be any options to create a horizontal gradient unless you use a graphics program such as Fireworks, Illustrator, or Photoshop.

You could use either hex code or color keywords of principal colors. You separate each color with a comma.

13. Add the following code to the Button type selector. In this example, you use both hex code and keywords for colors. I am having you use both just to show how to use them.

```
Button{
        fontSize:8;
        fillColors:#FFFFFF, blue;
    }
```

14. Save and run the application. You should see the button's fill gradient.

Let's try one more styling property: cornerRadius. This will allow you to round the corners of the instances of the Button class.

15. Add the following style to the Button selector declaration:

```
Button{
            fontSize:8;
            fillColors:#FFFFFF, blue;
            cornerRadius:20;
        }
```

16. Save and run the application. It should now appear as shown in Figure 7-5.

7

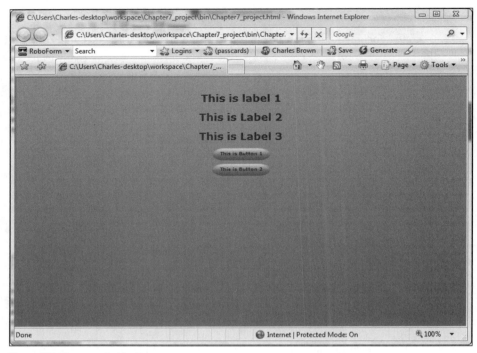

Figure 7-5. The rounded buttons

Now let's say you wanted all of your objects to have a Comic Sans MS font (you could use any font you want). You could easily do that using the **global** selector. Note that the "g" of global is lowercase. Past that, everything is exactly the same as if you used a type selector.

17. Enter the following global selector:

```
<mx:Style>
    Label{
                    fontSize:18;
                    fontWeight:bold;


            }

    Button{
                    fontSize:8;
                    fillColors:#FFFFFF, blue;
                    cornerRadius:20;
                }

    global{
                    fontFamily: "Comic Sans MS";
                }
</mx:Style>
```

> Note that the font name is enclosed in quotes. If the font name is a single word, such as Arial, the quotes are not necessary. However, the quotes are needed for a font with multiple words in its name. For the sake of consistency, it is probably not a bad idea to enclose all font names in quotes.

18. Save the application and give it a try (see Figure 7-6).

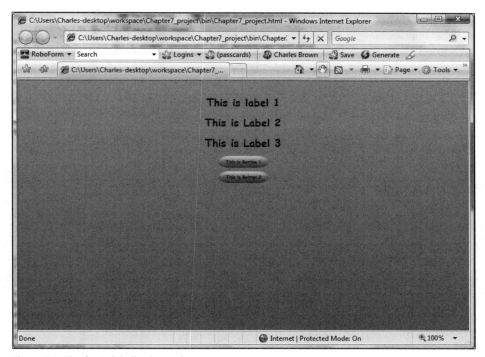

Figure 7-6. The font globally changed

Finally, let's say you want the second label instance to be blue. We can use a class selector much like we would in XHTML in that you can use a selector name of your own choosing. However, it must begin with a period.

Let's say you want to create a class selector called `.blueColor`; you would enter it as follows within the opening and closing Style tags.

```
.blueColor{
        color:#0000FF;
    }
```

Here is where things start to change a little. If you want to assign this class to the second Label instance, you use the property `styleName` rather than the class attribute you would have used if this were XHTML.

19. Modify the second label as follows:

```
<mx:Label text="This is Label 2" styleName="blueColor"/>
```

You do not use the dot when referencing the class name, and the reference is case sensitive.

If you save and run the application, the second label's text should now be blue.

One final caveat should be mentioned here. If you place your rules in an external CSS file, it does not load at runtime like it would in an XHTML environment. Instead, it is compiled into the final SWF file. This means that if you make changes to the CSS rules, you would need to recompile the SWF file before those changes would take effect. There is a way to have it load at runtime using the setStyle function available to most components. However, it is very resource intensive, and I strongly recommend staying clear of it unless there is a very unusual circumstance.

Now that you have a basic foundation in creating CSS rules in Flex, I am going to pull the rug out from under you a bit, but in a good way. Flex 3 offers a couple of new tools to help you create CSS rules in Design Perspective.

Flex 3 and CSS

Flex 3 brings us some new tools to assist with CSS. Well, actually, one new tool and one that was around for Flex2, but not well known. We look at the latter tool first.

Flex Style Explorer

The **Flex Style Explorer** is an online tool that will visually create the CSS rules for you, and then allow you to copy and paste those rules into the application. Since this is an online application, you will need to have an Internet connection to try it.

The Flex Style Explorer can be found at

```
http://examples.adobe.com/flex3/consulting/styleexplorer/➥
Flex3StyleExplorer.html#
```

Leave it open and return to your application code.

1. Either start a new Flex application or delete all of your code between the opening and closing Application tags.

2. Between the opening and closing tags, add a Panel container. Give it a title of Testing CSS.

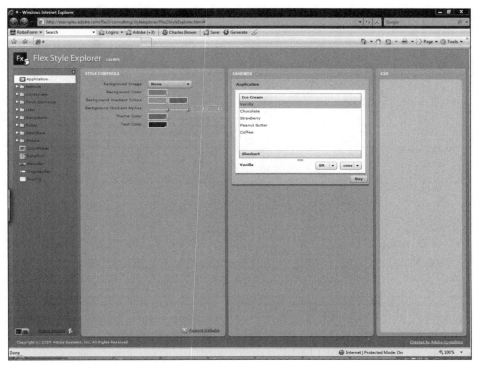

Figure 7-7. The Flex Style Explorer

3. Inside the Panel container, put a Text MXML tag and give it some default text.

```
<?xml version="1.0" encoding="utf-8"?>
<mx:Application xmlns:mx="http://www.adobe.com/2006/mxml" ➥
layout="vertical">
    <mx:Panel title="Testing CSS">
        <mx:Text text="This is a test of the Flex Style Explorer.➥
 Wait till you see how easy it is to use"/>
    </mx:Panel>
</mx:Application>
```

4. Save and run the application. It should look pretty standard (see Figure 7-8).

5. Return to your code and add a Style tag under the opening Application tag.

6. Return to the Flex Style Explorer.

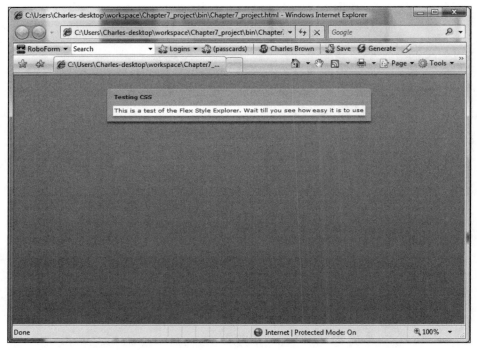

Figure 7-8. The Panel container

Notice that the Flex Style Explorer is divided into four panels. The first one allows you to select the component you want to style. The second (Style Controls) is for setting colors. The third (Sandbox) allows you to preview your CSS rules. And, finally, the last panel contains the created CSS code that you will copy and paste.

7. In the first panel, under the Containers category, select the Panel component. As soon as you select it, you will start to see a change in the preview panel.

We will make some changes.

8. Go ahead and experiment with different settings. You can see the result right in the Sandbox panel. Notice that there is also a second tab, in the Style Controls panel, for adjusting the style of the title property. Make some adjustments with that also. As you do, you should see the results in the Sandbox panel and the CSS code written as shown in Figure 7-9.

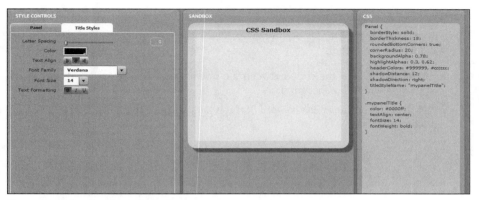

Figure 7-9. Using the Flex Style Explorer

Notice that it even creates a link between the titleStyleName property and the .mypanelTitle class rule.

9. Once you get the style rules the way you want them, go to the link at the bottom of the first panel that says Export All CSS. When you click the link, you should get a message telling you that your code has been saved to the clipboard (see Figure 7-10).

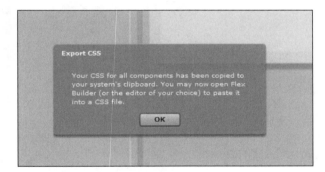

Figure 7-10. The Export CSS message

10. Return to the application and paste the CSS rules between the opening and closing Style tags. Save and run your application. It should now reflect all of your new style rules.

Yep, it is just that easy!

Converting to CSS

There is yet another tool that is brand new in Flex 3 to help you create CSS rules. To see how it works, try these steps:

1. Either delete all of the code between the opening and closing Application tags or start a new MXML application.

2. Put three labels between the Application tags and give them some simple default text (see Figure 7-11).

Figure 7-11.
The initial practice setup

3. Switch to Design Perspective and click the first Label.

Let's turn our attention to the Flex Properties View on the right side of Flex Builder 3 (see Figure 7-12).

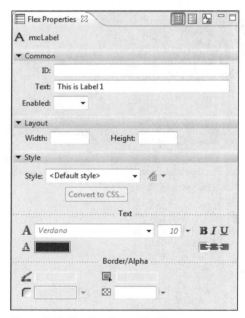

Figure 7-12. The Flex Properties View

Notice that the bottom area of the Flex Properties View is the Style area. We already had some experience with this in Chapter 4. But we will be doing sometime new and unique here.

4. Go to the Text section of the Style area and set the font to Verdana, the size to 18, and the weight to bold. Then, on the next line, change the font to a color of your choice.

As soon as you made changes, you should see the button marked Convert to CSS is now available.

5. Click the Convert to CSS button.

6. You may be prompted to save your MXML file. If you are, go ahead and save it. A new dialog box will open, as shown in Figure 7-13.

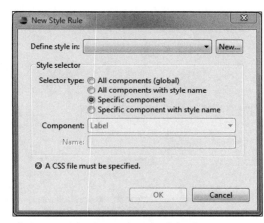

Figure 7-13. The New Style Rule dialog box

The New Style Rule dialog box will allow you to define an external style sheet and then save all of your changes to it.

7. Click the New button at the top of the dialog box.

A new dialog box will open that will allow you to give your external CSS document a name (see Figure 7-14). For the purposes of this exercise, use the name MyStyles. Flex Builder will look to save it right under the src folder.

8. Click Finish when your document is named. Notice in both the Flex Navigator View and the New Style Rule dialog box that the new document has the file extension of .css.

The four choices of the selector type tie into the discussion we had earlier. We can use the global selector to apply the change to everything, every component that uses a specific type name (which is basically a class selector), the type selector, or a combination of the type and class selector.

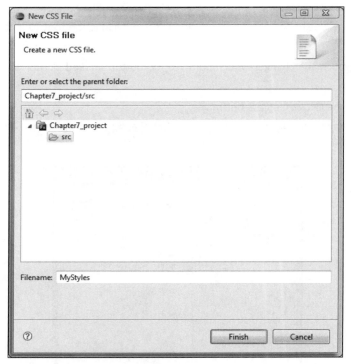

Figure 7-14. The New CSS dialog box

9. For the purposes of this exercise, use the default type selector. Since you were working with a Label component, the Component field is automatically set for Label.

10. Click OK. A lot is about to happen.

First of all, a new tab should have opened up in Design Perspective. It shows you a generic preview of what is in your CSS document (see Figure 7-15).

If you go to the Source Perspective, you will see the CSS written.

```
/* CSS file */

Label
{
    color: #0F3CE3;
    fontFamily: Verdana;
    fontSize: 18;
    fontWeight: bold;
}
```

Here you can make any adjustments you might want to make.

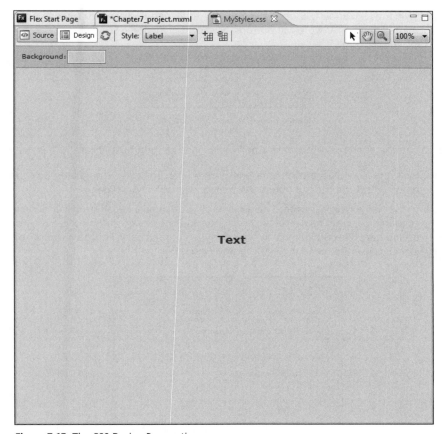

Figure 7-15. The CSS Design Perspective

11. Return to the application file. You will see that the Style tag is written with the source linked to the new CSS document.

```
<?xml version="1.0" encoding="utf-8"?>
<mx:Application xmlns:mx="http://www.adobe.com/2006/mxml" ➥
layout="vertical">
<mx:Label text="This is Label 1"/>
<mx:Label text="This is Label 2"/>
<mx:Label text="This is Label 3"/>
     <mx:Style source="MyStyles.css"/>
</mx:Application>
```

All of that was done for you automatically. If you save and run your application, it should now reflect the new style rules.

Let's take this one step even further.

12. Switch back to the CSS document and go to Design Perspective. You will notice at the top there are two small buttons, as shown in Figure 7-16.

Figure 7-16. The New Style button

The left button allows you to create a new style, and the right button deletes a style.

13. Click the New Style button (the one on the left). The New Style dialog box should open. Select the second option: All components with style name.

14. In the Name field, give the style a name of your choice. Recall from our earlier discussion that class names begin with a period. However, if you forget to put the period here, Flex Builder will insert it for you automatically. For the purposes of this exercise, use the name myTextStyle (see Figure 7-17).

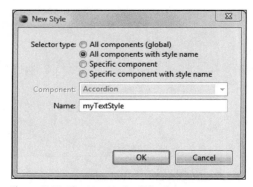

Figure 7-17. The New Style dialog box

15. Click OK.

16. You will next be prompted to what container you want to see your style in. This is for preview only. For the purposes of this exercise, select Label.

17. The Flex Properties View now reflects the style class name. Set it to Verdana, 16 pixels, bold, and the color of your choice.

18. Save the CSS document. If you don't, your class name will not be available for your application.

If you look in the Source Perspective, you should now have two rules: one for the Label you created earlier and one for the class .myTextStyle.

19. Switch to the application in Design Perspective.

20. Under the three instances of the Label component, drag a Button component.

21. Click the Style drop-down list, which now says <Default Style> (see Figure 7-18).

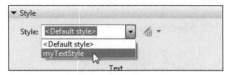

Figure 7-18. Selecting the class style

The class selectors in your CSS document, in this case just one, will come up on this list. By selecting it, you can assign any class to any component.

22. Select myTextStyle. The text in the button should now reflect the style changes, as shown in Figure 7-19.

Figure 7-19.
The Button component reflecting the style change

Well, hopefully you now see the powerful features available in Flex Builder 3 for creating and maintaining CSS style rules. We will now turn our attention to a different way of formatting. However, before we can format, we will validate to make sure we are working with the correct data.

Validating and Formatting

ActionScript has a number of classes called Validators and Formatters. The purpose of these classes is to ascertain that the correct information was entered into a form and that the resulting output is properly formatted.

While these appear to be two entirely different topics, with validating not related to the chapter topic of formatting, you will soon see that they frequently work together.

A complete list of the Validators and what they do can be found (as of this printing) at

```
http://livedocs.adobe.com/livecycle/es/sdkHelp/common/langref/mx/➥
validators/package-detail.html
```

A complete list of the Formatters can be found at

```
http://livedocs.adobe.com/livecycle/es/sdkHelp/common/langref/mx/➥
formatters/package-detail.html
```

285

While we certainly will not be going through every Validator and Formatter, we will take a look at a few of the more commonly used ones. Also, functionality between the Validators and Formatters has a great deal of commonality. So, by learning the most common ones, you will get a good overview of nearly all of them.

NumberValidator

Most developers I know agree that the most commonly used Validator is the NumberValidator. This particular one is quite handy in that it looks to see whether a number has been entered into a field and, if you want, it could test to see whether that number falls into a defined range.

To see this in action, we will start by building a simple form to enter a number into.

1. Either delete all the code between the opening and closing Application tags or, if you prefer, start a new MXML application file. The name is not important.

2. Below the Application tag, enter an opening and closing Form tag.

3. Enter two FormItem containers. The code should look as follows:

```
<?xml version="1.0" encoding="utf-8"?>
<mx:Application xmlns:mx="http://www.adobe.com/2006/mxml" ➥
layout="vertical">
<mx:Form>
    <mx:FormItem label="Enter a number between 1 and 10:">
        <mx:TextInput id="numberInput"/>
    </mx:FormItem>
    <mx:FormItem>
        <mx:Button label="Submit"/>
    </mx:FormItem>
</mx:Form>
</mx:Application>
```

Figure 7-20 shows how your form should look.

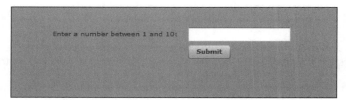

Figure 7-20. The form to validate

Of course, there is nothing here you haven't seen already, and the MXML code is pretty simple. But now we want to create some Validators for the TextInput field, numberInput.

You can place the NumberValidator tag anywhere in the MXML code. For our purposes, we will place it under the opening Application tag.

4. Put a couple of blank lines between the opening Application tag and the opening Form tag.

We will go through this step-by-step.

5. Start the following tag:

```
<mx:NumberValidator id="numValidate"
```

Here, obviously, we are just defining the tag and giving it an id. We will next use the source property to tell the Validator what field we are going to validate. Obviously, in this case, it is going to be numberInput and it will need to be done as an MXML binding.

6. Add the source property to the NumberValidator as follows:

```
<mx:NumberValidator id="numValidate" source="{numberInput}"
```

As you have learned already, ActionScript classes (and the corresponding MXML tags) have many properties. So we now have to tell the Validator which property of the TextInput instance it has to validate. Since we are checking the content of the field, the property we are checking for is the text property.

7. Add the following attribute to the NumberValidator and then close the tag:

```
<mx:NumberValidator id="numValidate" source="{numberInput}" ➥
property="text" />
```

8. Save and run your application.

9. Click in the TextInput field and press Submit. You should notice that the outline of the TextInput field turns red. Roll your mouse over it now (see Figure 7-21).

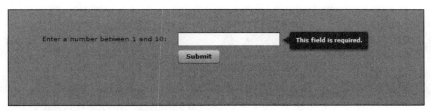

Figure 7-21. The required field error message

A little explanation is on order here.

First of all, using the Validator automatically makes the field required. There is a way of overriding this that you will see shortly.

Secondly, you have to have the focus in the field at least once before validation can occur. We will refine that in a bit with ActionScript.

While the application is running, let's try something else.

10. Type abc into the field, click Submit, and roll over the field again (see Figure 7-22).

287

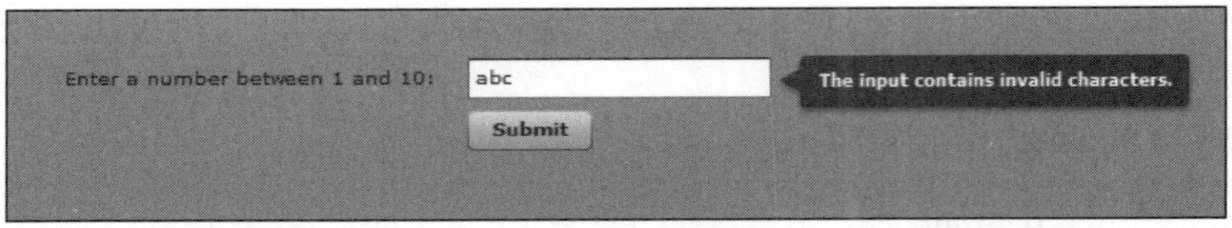

Enter a number between 1 and 10: abc   The input contains invalid characters.

Submit

Figure 7-22. The improper character error message

Notice that this time you receive a different error message. While the message about the field being required is pretty clear, the message about the input characters being invalid is a bit cryptic. Let's close the browser and return to our code.

If you click at the end of the NumberValidator and press the spacebar, you will see the properties pop up as expected.

Scroll down, for a moment, to the two properties required and requiredFieldError.

The property required will allow you to toggle the required attribute, which you just saw, on or off. However, in Validators, wherever you see the word "Error" at the end of a property name, it means that you can customize the error message that will be displayed.

Let's see an example.

11. Add an invalidCharError to the NumberValidator as follows:

```
<mx:NumberValidator id="numValidate" source="{numberInput}" ➥
property="text" invalidCharError="You must enter an ➥
integer between 1 and 10" />
```

12. Save and run the application. Trigger the error, as you did before, by typing abc into the field (see Figure 7-23).

Enter a number between 1 and 10: abc   You must enter an integer between 1 and 10

Submit

Figure 7-23. The customized error message

We will handle the integer factor in a bit.

Let's examine another problem now.

13. Type 20 into the field and click Submit.

No error was triggered, despite the fact that we instructed the user to enter a number between 1 and 10. This is because we instructed the NumberValidator to check only to see whether the data is an integer. We will fix that next.

14. Close the browser and return to your code.

The NumberValidator offers two properties, minValue and maxValue, that allow you to set a minimum and maximum range. The properties lowerThanMinError and exceedsMaxError allow you to set the corresponding messages (notice, once again, that they end with the word "Error").

15. Change the NumberValidator as follows:

```
<mx:NumberValidator id="numValidate" source="{numberInput}" ➥
property="text" invalidCharError="You must enter an integer ➥
between 1 and 10" minValue="1" maxValue="10" lowerThanMinError=➥
"The minimum number is 1" exceedsMaxError="The number must ➥
not exceed 10" />
```

16. Save, run, and test the errors in the application.

While we have the application running, we can test for yet another potential problem.

17. Type a number with a decimal, like "9.1", and click the Submit button. No error should be triggered.

The NumberValidator has a property called domain that allows you to set a numeric field for either int (without decimal places) or real (with decimal place). The corresponding error message can be set with the integerError property.

18. Add the following to your NumberValidator, and then save, run, and test the error in your application.

```
<mx:NumberValidator id="numValidate" source="{numberInput}" ➥
property="text" invalidCharError="You must enter an integer ➥
between 1 and 10" minValue="1" maxValue="10" lowerThanMinError=➥
"The minimum number is 1" exceedsMaxError="The number must not ➥
exceed 10" domain="int" integerError="Must be an integer" />
```

As you can see, we packed a lot of error checking into a single tag and even included custom messages. If we were to stop right here, it would be a pretty good error-checking mechanism without the complexities of JavaScript you may have experienced in XHTML environments. But we can take this even further using ActionScript 3.0. Let's take a look at that and then add formatting into the equation.

ActionScript and validation

The nice part of using ActionScript is that it is usually used in conjunction with, and not instead of, a Validator tag. We will walk through some code that will enhance the NumberValidator we just used. Then we will do some formatting using the CurrencyFormatter.

1. If necessary, close your browser and return to your code.

Recall from our previous exercise that the Validator triggers when we interact with it. We had to click inside the field before it would trigger the validation. Once we clicked inside, the Validator did its job. If you are going to use ActionScript, you need to turn that feature off. We do this by putting the triggerEvent attribute in the Validator tag and then leaving it blank as follows:

```
<mx:NumberValidator id="numValidate" source="{numberInput}" ➥
property="text" invalidCharError="You must enter an integer ➥
between 1 and 10" minValue="1" maxValue="10" lowerThanMinError=➥
"The minimum number is 1" exceedsMaxError="The number must ➥
not exceed 10" domain="int" integerError=➥
"Must be an integer" triggerEvent="" />
```

If you were to test the application now, none of the validations would work.

2. Under the opening Application tag, create a Script block.

3. Within the Script block, create a private function called validateNumber with no parameters and a return type of void.

```
<mx:Script>
    <![CDATA[
        private function validateNumber():void
        {

        }
    ]]>
</mx:Script>
```

4. Go to your Submit button tag and add a click event that will call the validateNumber function.

```
<mx:Button id="submit" label="Submit" click="validateNumber()"/>
```

So far, nothing too terribly new here.

ActionScript has a class called Validator. The Validator class has a function called validate(). The validate() function returns an object called ValidationResultEvent. Within the function we just created, you need to set a property to be of type ValidationResultEvent. For our purposes, let's call that property validNumber.

5. Add the following to the validateNumber() function:

```
<![CDATA[
    import mx.events.ValidationResultEvent;
    private function validateNumber():void
    {
        var validNumber:ValidationResultEvent;
    }
]]>
```

Flex Builder should automatically add the import statement above the function.

Here is where we call the validate() function.

Your NumberValidator tag should have the id property of numValidate from the last exercise. (If not, add it in.) We make the new property we just created equal to that id and the validate method.

6. Add the following to the property in the function:

```
private function validateNumber():void
{
    var validNumber:ValidationResultEvent = numValidate.validate();
}
```

The ValidationResultEvent object returns a property called type. The type property can have one of two possible results, both of which are constants: VALID or INVALID.

You need to set up an if structure, within the private function, to test whether the validation is VALID or INVALID. In this case, we are going to test for INVALID.

7. Add the following to the function:

```
private function validateNumber():void
{
    var validNumber:ValidationResultEvent = numValidate.validate();
    if (validNumber.type == ValidationResultEvent.INVALID)
    {

    }
}
```

For now, within the if structure, we will just include an alert that show will show the form is invalid.

8. Add the following to the if structure:

```
if (validNumber.type == ValidationResultEvent.INVALID);
{
    Alert.show("The form has errors");
}
```

9. Finally, we need to build an import statement, below the existing one, to be able to use the Alert class as follows:

```
import mx.controls.Alert;
```

Just to check yourself, your finished Script block should look as follows:

```
<mx:Script>
    <![CDATA[
        import mx.events.ValidationResultEvent;
        import mx.controls.Alert;
        private function validateNumber():void
        {
            var validNumber:ValidationResultEvent = ➥
numValidate.validate();
```

```
                    if (validNumber.type == ValidationResultEvent.INVALID);
                    {
                         Alert.show("The form has errors");
                    }
              }
       ]]>
    </mx:Script>
```

10. Save your application and run it. Do not worry now about first clicking in the InputText field. Instead, just click the Submit button (see Figure 7-24).

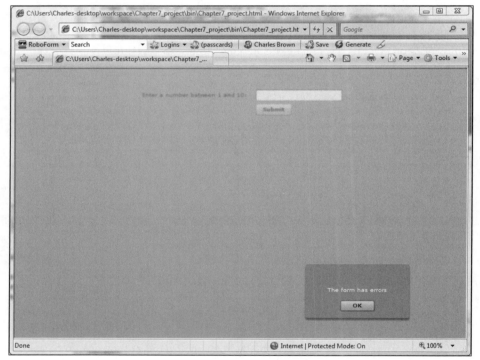

Figure 7-24. The error alert box

Once you dismiss the alert box by clicking OK, you can roll over the field and see the error messages you set earlier. For instance, type 20 into the field, or a decimal number, or letters. The validation will work as before when you roll over it. You now have the best of both worlds: ActionScript code allows you to trigger the validation without first interacting with the field, and you can easily set the multiple validations in the MXML tag.

Let's now take this several steps even further.

11. Go to the Form area of your application and add the following FormItem above the Submit button:

```
<mx:Form>
        <mx:FormItem label="Enter a number between 1 and 10:">
                <mx:TextInput id="numberInput"/>
        </mx:FormItem>
        <mx:FormItem label="Your total purchase is: ">
                <mx:Label id="myPurchase"/>
        </mx:FormItem>
        <mx:FormItem>
                <mx:Button id="submit" label="Submit" click=➥
"validateNumber()"/>
        </mx:FormItem>
</mx:Form>
```

12. Return to your Script block, and, just below the if structure, add an else structure.

```
private function validateNumber():void
{
        var validNumber:ValidationResultEvent = numValid.validate();
        if (validNumber.type == ValidationResultEvent.INVALID)
        {
        Alert.show("The form has errors");
        }
        else
        {

        }
}
```

Let's use our imagination a bit and set up a hypothetical situation. Assume that this is a site to make purchases. For the purposes of this exercise, we are going to assume that all of our purchases are $2.00. This means that we need to take the contents of the text property from the InputText field, numberInput, multiply it by 2, and send the result back to the text property of the myPurchase label. While this sounds pretty straightforward, there are a couple of caveats here we need to review.

The text property of a field sends out and receives strings. You cannot perform math operations on a string without first converting the string to a number. Further, the resulting calculation must be converted back to a string before sending it to the text property of the Label. Fortunately, ActionScript helps us out here.

Both the String and Number classes are sometimes referred to as **wrapper classes**. This means they can convert the type. As an example, let's say we wanted to convert the text content of the numberInput TextInput field. The syntax would be as follows:

```
Number(numberInput.text);
```

Likewise, let's assume we set a property called calcResult and wanted to send that value back to the myPurchase label. The syntax would be

```
myPurchase.text = String(calcResult);
```

Since we want to trigger this when the form validation is valid, we will put the code into the else structure we created a few moments ago.

13. Enter the following code into the else structure:

```
else
{
    var calcResult:Number;
    calcResult = Number(numberInput.text) * 2;
    myPurchase.text = String(calcResult);
}
```

This code should be pretty straightforward in light of the previous discussion.

14. Go ahead and run your application, and, provided you don't violate any of the validations, you should see a result similar to Figure 7-25.

Figure 7-25. The result

If all of the rules are met, the ValidationResultEvent type will return the constant VALID, which will trigger the else structure, resulting in the calculation being performed and sent to the label. However, we now want to format that result with a currency format.

Earlier in this chapter, I gave you links to the Validator and Formatter classes. One of the Formatter classes is CurrencyFormatter. That is the one we will use here.

15. Just below the close of the Script block, insert a CurrencyFormatter tag and give it an id of resultFormat.

```
<mx:CurrencyFormatter id="resultFormat"/>
```

We now need to return to the else block. The CurrencyFormatter class has a function called format that will take a numeric object or property, convert it into a string, and add a dollar sign to it (or whatever currency you are working in). This means that we no longer have to do that String conversion in the else structure.

16. Make the following change to your else statement:

```
else
{
    var calcResult:Number;
    calcResult = Number(numberInput.text) * 2;
    myPurchase.text = resultFormat.format(calcResult);
}
```

17. Save and run the application; you should see a dollar sign now, as shown in Figure 7-26.

Figure 7-26. The dollar sign added

You probably want to display the result in standard currency format with two decimal places. This can be easily done by using the precision property of the CurrencyFormatter. The precision property sets the number of decimal places.

18. Return to the CurrencyFormatter tag and add the following precision property:

```
<mx:CurrencyFormatter id="resultFormat" precision="2"/>
```

19. Save and run the application; you should see results similar to Figure 7-27.

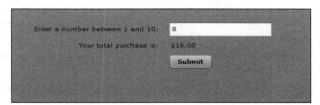

Figure 7-27. Adding two decimal places

Earlier, I stated that I would show you a couple of the most used Validator classes. In the next section, I am going to do a quick demonstration of the StringValidator. I am doing this just to show you how the process is nearly identical to the NumberValidator we just used.

Again, we will use both MXML tags and ActionScript code. I won't go into as much discussion of the steps because most of the concepts have been discussed already in this chapter.

The StringValidator

To see how to use StringValidator, follow these steps:

1. Either start a new Flex application or delete the code between the opening and closing Application tags.

2. Create a form with two FormItems as follows:

```
<?xml version="1.0" encoding="utf-8"?>
<mx:Application xmlns:mx="http://www.adobe.com/2006/mxml" ➥
layout="vertical">
<mx:Form>
    <mx:FormItem label="Enter Your Name: ">
        <mx:TextInput id="myName"/>
    </mx:FormItem>
    <mx:FormItem label="Enter your Password ➥
(between 3 - 6 characters)">
        <mx:TextInput id="myPassword" displayAsPassword="true"/>
    </mx:FormItem>
    <mx:FormItem>
        <mx:Button label="Submit"/>
    </mx:FormItem>
</mx:Form>
</mx:Application>
```

Notice that we use the displayAsPassword property for the second TextInput instance. This causes any typed content to show as asterisks.

3. Below the opening Application tag create a StringValidator tag and give it an id of validUserName. Bind it to myName as the source. Also, set the property to text.

4. Below, create another StringValidator with the id of validPassword and bind it to myPassword as the source. Again, set the property to text.

5. In both Validators, set the triggerEvent to empty, as you did before, because you will be using ActionScript code.

```
<mx:StringValidator id="validUserName" source="{myName}" ➥
property="text" triggerEvent=""/>
<mx:StringValidator id="validPassword" source="{myPassword}" ➥
property="text" triggerEvent=""/>
```

6. Above the two StringValidators, create a new Script block.

7. In the Script block, create a private function called validateUser with a return type of void.

```
<mx:Script>
    <![CDATA[
        private function validateUser():void
        {
```

```
        }
    ]]>
</mx:Script>
```

So far everything is about the same as before.

8. Within the function, create two properties, userValidation and passwordValidation, of type ValidationEventResult and make them equal to the respective StringValidators' validate function.

```
private function validateUser():void
{
    var userValidation:ValidationResultEvent = ➡
validUserName.validate();
    var passwordValidation:ValidationResultEvent = ➡
validPassword.validate();
}
```

As before, we now need to build an if structure to test whether the type property in the ValidationResultEvent object returns VALID or INVALID constants. In this case, we are going to test for two conditions. In most object-oriented languages, including Action-Script 3.0, we use a double ampersand (&&) to create an AND operator within an if structure. An OR test is done with the double pipe symbols (||).

9. Create the following if structure:

```
private function validateUser():void
{
    var userValidation:ValidationResultEvent = ➡
validUserName.validate();
    var passwordValidation:ValidationResultEvent = ➡
validPassword.validate();
    if(userValidation.type == ValidationResultEvent.VALID ➡
&& passwordValidation.type == ValidationResultEvent.VALID)
    {

    }
}
```

10. Within the if structure, keep it simple and just put an Alert statement in it telling the user that the information he entered was valid.

11. Create an else statement with an alert box showing invalid data.

```
if(userValidation.type == ValidationResultEvent.VALID && ➡
passwordValidation.type == ValidationResultEvent.VALID)
{
    Alert.show("You have entered valid information");
}
else
{
    Alert.show("You have entered invalid information");
}
```

12. Finally, create the second import statement for the Alert class.

13. We have one last thing we need to do. Go down to the Submit button and create a click event that calls the validateUser() function.

```
<mx:Button label="Submit" click="validateUser()"/>
```

14. Save and test the application. If you do not enter text into the two fields, you should get an INVALID result. If you enter text into both fields, you should get a VALID result.

So far, everything is nearly identical to our earlier exercise. But we have one more thing we need to fix. The password needs to be 3–6 characters. To handle that, let's return to the StringValidator for the password.

15. The StringValidator has two properties, maxLength and minLength. Needless to say, you should set these to 6 and 3, respectively. Also, to set the error message, set the properties tooShortError and tooLongError.

```
<mx:StringValidator id="validPassword" source="{myPassword}" ➡
property="text" triggerEvent="" minLength="3" maxLength="6" ➡
tooShortError="The password must be at least 3 characters" ➡
tooLongError="The password is maximum of 6 characters"/>
```

16. Save the application and run it.

You will see that everything works the same as in the previous exercise. In addition, the syntax hardly changed at all. As I have said in previous chapters, there is a lot of consistency in MXML and ActionScript 3.0.

Summary

In this chapter, you learned a lot about formatting and validating data. You formatted using both CSS and the Formatter classes. In addition, you learned the various options that Flex Builder 3 gives you when using CSS. You also learned how to validate the data using the NumberValidator and the StringValidator.

We are next going to take a look at the Repeater and Tile components. This will be the equivalent of writing loops in ActionScript and will allow you to repeat components for each data item.

8 THE REPEATER COMPONENT

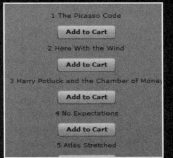

As I have said many times throughout this book, MXML is a convenient way to write ActionScript and is analogous to the way Adobe ColdFusion 8 writes Java code. You use a simple, tag-based language to write more complex syntax in the background.

This will be very obvious in this chapter. We are going to use an MXML component, the Repeater, to write ActionScript 3.0 loops. In my opinion, this is one of the most powerful components in Flex in that this component will tie into a data source and will repeat whatever is contained within the container for each instance of data.

As an example, let's say you want a button labeled Add (*name of book*) to cart in your e-commerce application. You could use the Repeater component for each book that comes up to add a button and add the name of that book to an array. You may think that is a lot of extra effort if you were selling only five books. But what if you had 300 books, and the books kept changing every week? The Repeater code could stay the same and generate all the buttons for you dynamically, no matter how many books were in the data source and how often they changed.

In this chapter, you will

- Learn about the Repeater component.
- Pass data with the Repeater component.
- Create an event using the Repeater component.

This chapter will be a relatively short one compared to the last chapter. But the information in it will be essential to your understanding of building Flex applications.

Understanding the Repeater component

When you use the Repeater component, what you are doing is creating an MXML container that will repeat its contents for each record in the data source. If you are a little confused by what I meant by that, it will become abundantly clear in just a few minutes. Before you get started, however, you need to do a little bit of housekeeping.

1. If you have the project from Chapter 7 open yet, either close or delete it. We will not be using its files again.

2. Create a new Flex project called Chapter8_project. You can accept the default MXML application name (which is the same as the project).

In order to have some data to work with, you will keep it simple and just create a short data structure using the Model tag. We discussed the Model tag in Chapter 6. As a short review, it is used primarily as the name says, a modeling tool where you set up a representative XML structure for testing purposes. You usually just put a few records into it for testing purposes. As I stated in Chapter 6, this is one of the few MXML tags that does not represent an ActionScript class file.

3. Just beneath the opening Application tag, set up the following Model tag:

```
<?xml version="1.0" encoding="utf-8"?>
<mx:Application xmlns:mx="http://www.adobe.com/2006/mxml" ➥
layout="absolute">
     <mx:Model id="bookData">
          <books>
               <bookName>The Essential Guide to Dreamweaver ➥
CS3</bookName>
               <bookName>Foundation Flex for Developers: ➥
Data-Driven Applications</bookName>
               <bookName>Flash CS3 for Designers</bookName>
          </books>
     </mx:Model>
</mx:Application>
```

Recall from the discussion of XML, in Chapter 6, that Flex converts XML data to the type ArrayCollection. Even though you used the Model tag in this example, you created an XML structure within it to structure the data. So you need to convert the data to an ArrayCollection.

Once again, we can use MXML to represent the ActionScript processes we saw in Chapter 6.

4. Add the following tag under the Model tag structure you just defined:

```
<mx:ArrayCollection id="bookArray" source="{bookData.bookName}"/>
```

In this case, the source is going to be the repeating node, bookName, of the Model tag bookData. Since the Model tag converts its contents to an MXML structure, you don't need to mention the root, books, at all. In addition, it must be done as a data binding using the curly braces.

Now that the Model structure is converted to an ArrayCollection, you are ready to start working with the Repeater component.

5. Create a Repeater structure using the ArrayCollection, bookArray, as the dataProvider. You will give the Repeater component an id of bookRepeater. Place it right underneath the ArrayCollection you just defined:

```
<mx:ArrayCollection id="bookArray" source="{bookData.bookName}"/>
<mx:Repeater id="bookRepeater" dataProvider="{bookArray}">

</mx:Repeater>
```

Once the Repeater component is set up, all you need to do is decide what you want to place inside of the container. Let's start with a very simple example.

8

6. Within the Repeater structure, add a Label control and give it the text property value of Place Book Title Here.

```
<mx:Repeater id="bookRepeater" dataProvider="{bookArray}">
    <mx:Label text="Place Book Title Here"/>
</mx:Repeater>
```

One final point you need to check was one we have discussed several times in this book already: the layout property of the Application tag. If it is set to absolute, you would need to set the position yourself. However, by changing it to vertical, this simple exercise should work fine.

Your finished code should look as follows:

```
<?xml version="1.0" encoding="utf-8"?>
<mx:Application xmlns:mx="http://www.adobe.com/2006/mxml" ➥
layout="vertical">
    <mx:Model id="bookData">
        <books>
            <bookName>The Essential Guide to Dreamweaver ➥
CS3</bookName>
            <bookName>Foundation Flex for Developers: ➥
Data-Driven Applications</bookName>
            <bookName>Flash CS3 for Designers</bookName>
        </books>
    </mx:Model>

    <mx:ArrayCollection id="bookArray" source="{bookData.bookName}"/>
    <mx:Repeater id="bookRepeater" dataProvider="{bookArray}">
        <mx:Label text="Place Book Title Here"/>
    </mx:Repeater>
</mx:Application>
```

7. Go ahead and run your code. The results should look like Figure 8-1.

Figure 8-1. The Repeater component

You can see that the Label control, placed inside of the Repeater container, repeats for each record. In this case, it repeats three times.

8. Now you are going to take this one step further and add a Button control with the label property set to Add to Cart. Add it inside of the Repeater container, right below the Label control.

```
<mx:ArrayCollection id="bookArray" source="{bookData.bookName}"/>
 <mx:Repeater id="bookRepeater" dataProvider="{bookArray}">
     <mx:Label text="Place Book Title Here"/>
     <mx:Button label="Add to Cart"/>
 </mx:Repeater>
```

9. Run your code. It should look something like Figure 8-2.

Figure 8-2.
The Repeater component with a Button
control added

Quite obviously, you don't want your finished label to say Place Book Title Here. You will want to add the actual name of the book. In order to accommodate that, you will need to make some modifications to your code.

Passing data in a Repeater component

Each time the Repeater component creates a new repetition, it is advancing to the next element of the Array. The Repeater class has two important properties you should be familiar with: currentIndex and currentItem. The currentIndex returns the index number, beginning with 0, of the item selected. The currentItem returns the actual data of the selected item. These properties are standard in most programming environments today.

If you were to open the documentation for the Repeater class, you would see these two items listed under properties, as shown in Figure 8-3.

Figure 8-3. Repeater class properties

As you can see, the currentIndex returns the array index number of the item the Repeater component is processing. The currentItem is returning the actual data of the processed item.

Let's see an example:

1. Make an adjustment to the text property of the Label control as follows:

```
<mx:Label text="{bookRepeater.currentItem}"/>
```

Here the Label control is making a call back to the Repeater component. It is asking that Repeater what the currentItem or data is. The Repeater component then returns the data in the current element back to the caller, which in this case is the text property of the Label control.

2. Save and run your code after making the change to the Label component. Your results should look like Figure 8-4.

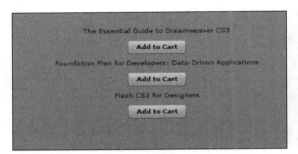

Figure 8-4. The data added to the Label control

The currentIndex property returns the index number, beginning with 0, of the element being processed by the Repeater component. This can be helpful when you want to number something.

3. Next, you will create a simple concatenation in the Label's text property. Make the following change:

```
<mx:Label text="{bookRepeater.currentIndex} ➡
{bookRepeater.currentItem}"/>
```

Notice that, unlike programming languages such as ActionScript, C++, Java, and so on, you don't need to set up a concatenation using the + character. In MXML, all you need to do is make the two calls and put a space between them.

4. Save and run the application. Your screen should look similar to Figure 8-5.

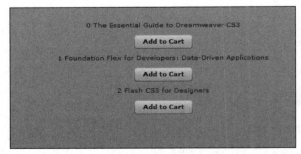

Figure 8-5. The Repeater component with numbering added

Whoops! Remember that arrays begin with the number 0. If you were running this application, I am sure you wouldn't want to see something numbered as 0.

5. Solve this problem with the following adjustment to your code:

```
<mx:Label text="{bookRepeater.currentIndex + 1} ➥
{bookRepeater.currentItem}"/>
```

6. Try running the application again—Figure 8-6 shows the problem fixed.

Figure 8-6. The fixed numbering in the Repeater component

The Button class, as well as many of the classes involving form items, have a method called getRepeaterItem() (see Figure 8-7). This works the same as the currentItem in that a control outside of the Repeater container can call the Repeater and request the item it is processing.

⬆ **getRepeaterItem**(whichRepeater:int = -1):Object	UIComponent
Returns the item in the dataProvider that was used by the specified Repeater to produce this Repeater, or null if this Repeater isn't repeated.	

Figure 8-7. The getRepeaterItem() function documentation

> currentItem *cannot be used outside of the* Repeater *component because it is referring to an item being currently processed by the* Repeater. *By the time you see everything displayed, the* Repeater *is done with its job, and* currentItem *is no longer accessible.*

7. Add a click item to the Button control and pass the event object to a function, which you will create shortly, called getBookData().

```
<mx:Button label="Add to Cart" click="getBookData(event)"/>
```

8. As you have done in previous chapters, create a Script block and, within that block, a function called getBookData(). Pass the event to that function as type Event.

```
<mx:Script>
    <![CDATA[
        private function getBookData(evt:Event):void
        {

        }
    ]]>
</mx:Script>
```

Recall that the target property of the event object allows you to access all of the properties and functions of the broadcaster of that event (in this case, the Button control). In this exercise, you will get the item from the Repeater component using the Button's getRepeaterItem() and pass that information to a Label control, called nameLabel, that we will create in a bit.

9. Add the following code to the getBookData() function you just created:

```
private function getBookData(evt:Event):void
{
    nameLabel.text = evt.target.getRepeaterItem();
}
```

10. Below the Repeater control, insert a Label control with the id property of nameLabel. So it will stand out, set the fontSize property to 14.

```
<mx:Label id="nameLabel" fontSize="14"/>
```

The complete code should look as follows:

```
<?xml version="1.0" encoding="utf-8"?>
<mx:Application xmlns:mx="http://www.adobe.com/2006/mxml" ➥
layout="vertical">
<mx:Script>
    <![CDATA[
        private function getBookData(evt:Event):void
        {
            nameLabel.text = evt.target.getRepeaterItem();
        }
    ]]>
</mx:Script>
    <mx:Model id="bookData">
        <books>
            <bookName>The Essential Guide to ➥
Dreamweaver CS3</bookName>
            <bookName>Foundation Flex for Developers: ➥
Data-Driven Applications</bookName>
            <bookName>Flash CS3 for Designers</bookName>
        </books>
    </mx:Model>

    <mx:ArrayCollection id="bookArray" source="{bookData.bookName}"/>
    <mx:Repeater id="bookRepeater" dataProvider="{bookArray}">
        <mx:Label text="{bookRepeater.currentIndex + 1} ➥
{bookRepeater.currentItem}"/>
```

```
            <mx:Button label="Add to Cart" click="getBookData(event)"/>
        </mx:Repeater>
        <mx:Label id="nameLabel" fontSize="14"/>
    </mx:Application>
```

11. Save and run the application. You should see the Label control reflect the book title when you click any of the three buttons (see Figure 8-8).

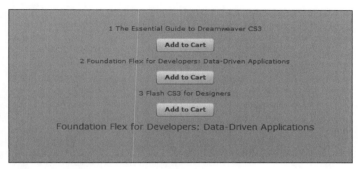

Figure 8-8. The new Label control populated

You are now going to turn your attention to bringing in your data from an XML file. As you will see, this will just be a variation on a theme.

Using XML data

In this section, you will pull your data from an XML file. This will give you a chance to review a few of the concepts covered in Chapter 6 and apply them to the Repeater component.

1. If you haven't done so already, download the XML file for this chapter from www.friendsofed.com. Unzip it to the directory of your choice.

2. In Flex Builder, using the Flex Navigator View, right-click the src folder and select New ➤ Folder to bring up the dialog box shown in Figure 8-9.

8

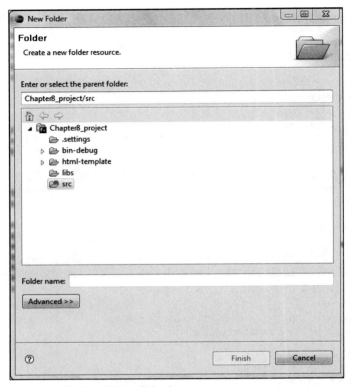

Figure 8-9. The New Folder dialog box

3. Give the new folder the name assets and click Finish. You should now see the folder under the src folder in the Flex Navigator View (see Figure 8-10).

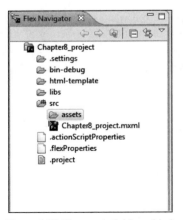

Figure 8-10. The assets folder added

4. In the Flex Navigator View, right-click the newly created assets folder and select Import. This brings up the Import dialog box, shown in Figure 8-11.

Figure 8-11. The Import dialog box

5. Twirl down the General category and select File System.

6. Click Next to bring up the dialog box shown in Figure 8-12.

7. Using the Browse button to the right of the From directory field, navigate to the directory where you unzipped the Chapter 9 download. You want to import the books.xml file by selecting the check box to the left of it.

8. Click Finish when selected. The file should now be seen in the assets folder you created in the Flex Navigator View after you twirl the assets folder open.

8

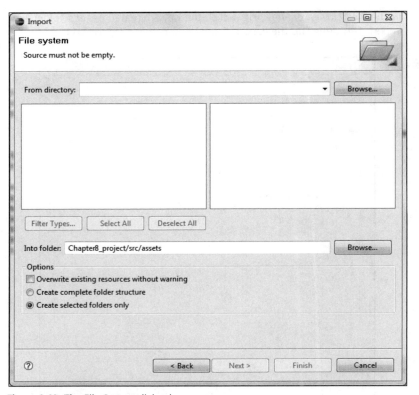

Figure 8-12. The File System dialog box

Open the books.xml file and briefly review its contents.

```xml
<?xml version="1.0" encoding="iso-8859-1"?>

<books>
   <stock>
      <name>The Picasso Code</name>
      <author>Dan Blue</author>
      <category>Fiction</category>
      <description>Cubist paintings reveal a secret society of ➡
people who really look like that</description>
   </stock>
   <stock>
      <name>Here With the Wind</name>
      <author>Margaret Middle</author>
      <category>Fiction</category>
      <description>In this edition, nobody in the south really ➡
gives a damn</description>
   </stock>
   <stock>
```

```
      <name>Harry Potluck and the Chamber of Money</name>
      <author>J.K. Roughly</author>
      <category>Fiction</category>
      <description>Young wizard finds the real pot-of-gold ➥
and retires</description>
   </stock>
   <stock>
      <name>No Expectations</name>
      <author>Chuck Dickens</author>
      <category>Fiction</category>
      <description>Dickens finally reveals what he really thinks ➥
of people</description>
   </stock>
   <stock>
      <name>Atlas Stretched</name>
      <author>Ann Rind</author>
      <category>Fiction</category>
      <description>Great inventors finally just take the money ➥
and run</description>
   </stock>
   <stock>
      <name>Recycling Software</name>
      <author>Big Gates</author>
      <category>Nonfiction</category>
      <description>How to just change the name and interface ➥
of the same old software and sell it as new</description>
   </stock>
   <stock>
      <name>Make Tons of Money</name>
      <author>Donald Rump</author>
      <category>Nonfiction</category>
      <description>Rump explains how he became a billionaire ➥
while constantly declaring bankruptcy</description>
   </stock>
   <stock>
      <name>How to Win Enemies and Lose Friends</name>
      <author>Dale Crochety</author>
      <category>Nonfiction</category>
      <description>The Ultimate how-to book for people who ➥
want to stay loners</description>
   </stock>
   <stock>
      <name>My Lies</name>
      <author>Swill Clinton</author>
      <category>Nonfiction</category>
       <description>This former American president tries to ➥
define what a lie is</description>
   </stock>
   <stock>
```

8

```
        <name>The Complete History of the World</name>
        <author>David McClutz</author>
        <category>Nonfiction</category>
        <description>McClutz gives you the entire history of all ➥
    civilization is less than 300 pages</description>
      </stock>
  </books>
```

9. Return to the application file you were working with earlier. Since you are bringing your data in from the XML file, you no longer need the Model tag and its contents. So go ahead and delete it. However, remember the name you gave it: bookData. That will save you some programming later on. Since we will be using the HTTPService class in a moment, we will not need the ArrayCollection tag. As discussed in Chapter 6, HTTPService automatically converts the data into an ArrayCollection.

As you may remember from Chapter 6, you need to use the HTTPService class to call the XML file.

10. In the place of the original Model tag, insert an HTTPService tag. Give it an id property of bookData and make the url property assets/books.xml.

```
<mx:HTTPService id="bookData" url="assets/books.xml"/>
```

You will need to adjust the dataProvider property of the Repeater component to reflect the new source. Recall from Chapter 6 that you need to use the lastResult property to build the data objects and keep them updated. In addition, you need to drill down the nodes of the XML file to get to the data you need.

11. Make the following modification to the Repeater component:

```
<mx:Repeater id="bookRepeater" dataProvider="➥
{bookData.lastResult.books.stock}">
```

Finally, an HTTPService does not happen automatically as soon as the application is run. There must be an event that triggers it. While you can use any event, the common practice is to place a creationComplete event in the Application tag that instructs the HTTPService to send the request for data to the XML file.

12. Add the following to the Application tag:

```
<mx:Application xmlns:mx="http://www.adobe.com/2006/mxml" ➥
layout="vertical" creationComplete="bookData.send()">
```

Since you made quite a few changes, please take a moment and review your completed code against the code shown here.

```
<?xml version="1.0" encoding="utf-8"?>
<mx:Application xmlns:mx="http://www.adobe.com/2006/mxml" ➥
layout="vertical" creationComplete="bookData.send()">
<mx:Script>
    <![CDATA[
        private function getBookData(evt:Event):void
```

```
            {
                    nameLabel.text = evt.target.getRepeaterItem();
            }
        ]]>
    </mx:Script>

    <mx:HTTPService id="bookData" url="assets/books.xml"/>
    <mx:Repeater id="bookRepeater" dataProvider=➥
    "{bookData.lastResult.books.stock}">
        <mx:Label text="{bookRepeater.currentIndex + 1} ➥
    {bookRepeater.currentItem}"/>
        <mx:Button label="Add to Cart" click="getBookData(event)"/>
    </mx:Repeater>
    <mx:Label id="nameLabel" fontSize="14"/>
    </mx:Application>
```

13. Save and run the application. You will get a very odd result as shown in Figure 8-13.

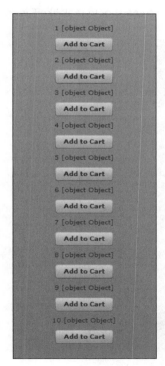

Figure 8-13.
The results of publishing the XML file in the Repeater component

Things did not quite work out as planned, as you can see.

When you used the Model tag, the Repeater component had an easy job. There was only one piece of data, bookName, that it needed to be concerned with. So the currentItem property was populated easily. However, if you look at the structure of the XML file, you will see that currentItem can be any one of three potential data items: name, author, or description.

The "[object Object]" response is ActionScript's way of telling you that it created the object for each data item, but it doesn't know which of the data items you want to use as the currentItem. You have to give ActionScript more specific instructions. Happily, this is not hard.

14. Make a small addition to the Label control in the Repeater structure:

```
<mx:Repeater id="bookRepeater" dataProvider=➡
"{bookData.lastResult.books.stock}">
        <mx:Label text="{bookRepeater.currentIndex + 1} ➡
{bookRepeater.currentItem.name}"/>
        <mx:Button label="Add to Cart" click="getBookData(event)"/>
</mx:Repeater>
```

You told the Label control which node to use to populate the text property.

15. Save and run the application now, and your screen should look like Figure 8-14.

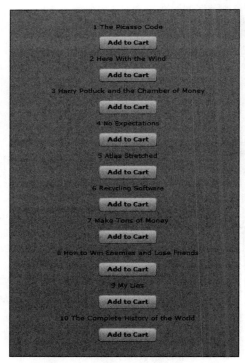

Figure 8-14. The proper data displayed in the Repeater structure

As you can see, the proper data is now being displayed. However, if you now click one of the Button controls, you are still getting the "[object Object]" in the Label control below the Repeater component. This can be easily remedied by making the same change to the body of the getBookData() function located in the Script block. However, we can make this a little more interesting by using a different data item.

16. Make the following modification to the body of the getBookData() function:

```
private function getBookData(evt:Event):void
{
    nameLabel.text = evt.target.getRepeaterItem().description;
}
```

17. Save and run the application and click one of the buttons. You should now see the description data in the Label control (see Figure 8-15).

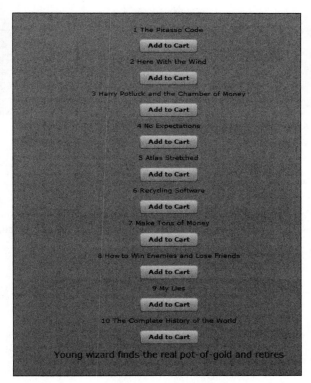

Figure 8-15. The description appearing in the bottom Label control

Let's look at one additional little touch. Assume you wanted the Button component to indicate that the book has been added to the shopping cart. You can accomplish that by using the target property of the event object a little differently from the way we have been using it up to this point.

18. In the getBookData() function, add the following line of code:

```
private function getBookData(evt:Event):void
{
    nameLabel.text = evt.target.getRepeaterItem().description;
    evt.target.label = "Added";
}
```

This code changes label property of whatever button is broadcasting the event to the word "Added".

19. Save and give it a try (see Figure 8-16).

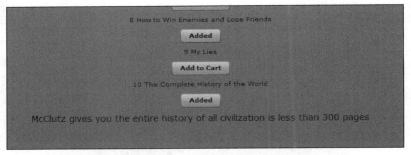

Figure 8-16. The changed label property of the broadcasting button

Summary

You discovered a lot of potential power in this discussion of the Repeater component. You can create incredibly complex structures that will repeat for each new incidence of data.

We are now going to turn to another powerful feature of Flex, the ability to drag and drop components.

9 DRAG AND DROP

NAME	AUT
The Picasso Code	Dan
Here With the Wind	Marg
Harry Potluck and the Chamber of N	J.K.
No Expectations	Chuc
Atlas Stretched	Ann
Recycling Software	Big (

	NAME	CATEGORY

AUTHOR	CA
Dan Blue	Fict
Margaret Middle	Fict
J.K. Roughly	Fict
Chuck Dickens	Fict
Ann Rind	Fict
Big Gates	Nor

TEGORY

NAME	AUTH(
The Picasso Code	Dan Bl
Here With the Wind	Marga
Harry Potluck and the Chamber of N	J.K. R(
No Expectations	Chuck
Atlas Stretched	Ann R
Recycling Software	Big Ga

[object Object]
[object Object]

When I teach Flex, one of the first questions I receive, nearly all of the time, is how to create the drag-and-drop scenario seen in the Flex Store sample application on the Adobe site. You saw this site in Chapter 1. In this sample application, each cell phone is in a separate component. That component can then be dragged and dropped into either a container to compare models or a shopping cart.

How often do you drag and drop desktop applications? You are probably thinking that it is common. Now here is a second question: how often do you drag and drop a web application? The answer? Not often (although it is becoming more commonplace on the modern Web).

Throughout this book, I have made frequent references to the distinction between desktop and web applications becoming blurred. Hopefully, you are now seeing that for yourself. This chapter will blur that distinction even more.

You will be learning how to use one of the most unique classes of ActionScript: DragManager.

As you will soon see, all the Flex visual components support the ability to drag and drop. In other words, by calling on a single property, you can grab a visual aspect of the web application and drop it into a different container within the application.

In this chapter, you will

- Implement dragging from a DataGrid to a DataGrid.
- Implement dragging from a DataGrid to a List.
- Implement dragging with ActionScript programming.
- Understand the classes associated with drag-and-drop operations.

You will need to learn some concepts and terminology first. So let's get started.

Understanding drag-and-drop concepts

Let's begin by thinking about the process of drag and drop.

A user initiates a drag-and-drop operation by selecting an item within a Flex component, such as the cell phones you see in the Flex Store sample application. The user then holds down the mouse button as he moves the selected item around the screen. Finally, the user moves the item to another component (usually a container) and releases the mouse button to drop the item into that component.

Of course, like anything, you have to understand some terminology associated with this process.

The component from which the user is dragging the cell phone image is called the **drag initiator**. The cell phone image itself would be the data that is being moved. This is called the **drag source**. While dragging the drag source around the screen, you will need to display the image being dragged. This image is called the **drag proxy**. Finally, the component you drop the drag source into is called the **drop target**.

Just to see how easy it is to set up drag and drop, let's go to the documentation for the DataGrid class.

If you scroll down, you will see two properties, dragEnabled and dropEnabled (as shown in Figures 9-1 and 9-2). You may need to click the Show Inherited Public Properties link located at the top of the Public Properties area. Notice that both of these properties come to the DataGrid class from the ListBase class. If you click the property links, they will take you to the ListBase class.

dragEnabled property

dragEnabled:Boolean [read-write]

A flag that indicates whether you can drag items out of this control and drop them on other controls. If true, dragging is enabled for the control. If the dropEnabled property is also true, you can drag items and drop them within this control to reorder the items.

The default value is false.

Implementation
        public function get dragEnabled():Boolean
        public function set dragEnabled(value:Boolean):void

Figure 9-1. The dragEnabled property

dropEnabled property

dropEnabled:Boolean [read-write]

A flag that indicates whether dragged items can be dropped onto the control.

If you set this property to true, the control accepts all data formats, and assumes that the dragged data matches the format of the data in the data provider. If you want to explicitly check the data format of the data being dragged, you must handle one or more of the drag events, such as dragOver, and call the DragEvent's preventDefault() method to customize the way the list class accepts dropped data.

When you set dropEnabled to true, Flex automatically calls the showDropFeedback() and hideDropFeedback() methods to display the drop indicator.

The default value is false.

Implementation
        public function get dropEnabled():Boolean
        public function set dropEnabled(value:Boolean):void

Figure 9-2. The dropEnabled property

I find that many students misunderstand these properties. Many feel that these properties enable the component to be dragged and dropped. However, that is not the case, at least not directly.

The dragEnabled property makes a component, usually a container, a drag initiator. The dropEnabled property makes the component a drop target.

Both are properties that use a Boolean type that defaults to false.

I am sure you are anxious to give this a little try. As I have done in previous chapters, I will show you the concept in a relatively simple setting.

Dragging to a DataGrid component

By far, the easiest way to handle drag and drop is to drag something to a DataGrid. This will become obvious as you progress. If you follow the steps I give you here, it should work each and every time.

If you have not done so already, please download the Chapter 9 files from www.friendsofed.com. Unzip them to the directory of your choice.

If necessary, delete or close the Chapter 8 project. We will not be using those files again.

1. Start a new Flex basic project as you have in previous chapters. For the purposes of these exercises, call it Chapter9_project.

2. As you did in the last chapter, set up an assets folder under the src folder in the Flex Navigator View.

3. As you have in the previous chapter, use the File ➤ Import feature to import the Chapter 9 download from the folder you unzipped it to into the assets folder you just created. The import is a single XML file and is the same XML file you used in the previous chapter.

4. In the application MXML file, enter the following code. There is nothing here you have not seen before. However, take a moment and peruse the code as a review.

```
<?xml version="1.0" encoding="utf-8"?>
<mx:Application xmlns:mx="http://www.adobe.com/2006/mxml" ➡
layout="absolute" creationComplete="bookStock.send()">
    <mx:Script>
        <![CDATA[
            import mx.collections.ArrayCollection;
            import mx.rpc.events.ResultEvent;

            [Bindable]
            private var books:ArrayCollection;

            private function bookHandler(evt:ResultEvent):void
            {
                books = evt.result.books.stock;
            }
        ]]>
    </mx:Script>

    <mx:HTTPService url="assets/books.xml" id="bookStock" ➡
result="bookHandler(event)"/>

    <mx:DataGrid x="158" y="62" dataProvider="{books}" ➡
id="dgInitiator" width="50%">
        <mx:columns>
            <mx:DataGridColumn headerText="NAME" dataField="name" />
            <mx:DataGridColumn headerText="AUTHOR" ➡
dataField="author"/>
            <mx:DataGridColumn headerText="CATEGORY" ➡
dataField="category"/>
        </mx:columns>
    </mx:DataGrid>
</mx:Application>
```

5. Save your application and give it a run. It should look like Figure 9-3.

NAME	AUTHOR	CATEGORY
The Picasso Code	Dan Blue	Fiction
Here With the Wind	Margaret Middle	Fiction
Harry Potluck and the Chamber of M	J.K. Roughly	Fiction
No Expectations	Chuck Dickens	Fiction
Atlas Stretched	Ann Rind	Fiction
Recycling Software	Big Gates	Nonfiction

Figure 9-3. The results of the entered code

Notice that we gave the DataGrid component an id property of dgInitiator. We also didn't use the description field from the XML file because it is not really needed for this exercise.

You will now need to add a second DataGrid control that will receive the dragged data. For the purposes of this exercise, this second DataGrid will have only two columns, one each for the book name and the category.

6. Add the second DataGrid.

```
<mx:DataGrid x="158" y="62" dataProvider="{books}" id="dgInitiator" ➥
width="50%">
     <mx:columns>
          <mx:DataGridColumn headerText="NAME" dataField="name" />
          <mx:DataGridColumn headerText="AUTHOR" dataField="author"/>
          <mx:DataGridColumn headerText="CATEGORY" ➥
dataField="category"/>
     </mx:columns>
</mx:DataGrid>

<mx:DataGrid id="dgTarget" x="228" y="269">
     <mx:columns>
          <mx:DataGridColumn dataField="name" headerText="NAME"/>
          <mx:DataGridColumn dataField="category" ➥
headerText="CATEGORY"/>
     </mx:columns>
</mx:DataGrid>
```

7. Run your code. Your result should now look like Figure 9-4.

9

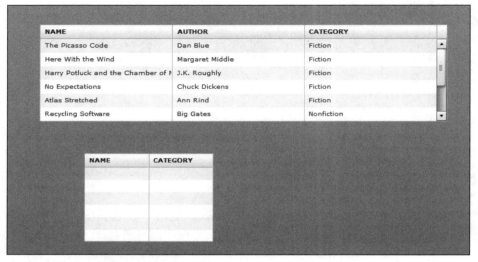

Figure 9-4. The result up to this point

Since we will be dragging data from the first DataGrid component, dgInitiator, we need to set its dragEnabled property to true.

8. Set the dragEnabled property of the first DataGrid to true.

```
<mx:DataGrid x="158" y="62" dataProvider="{books}" id="dgInitiator" ➥
width="50%" dragEnabled="true">
```

9. Save and run the application. You will be able to drag the information, but will have no place to drop it yet, as shown in Figure 9-5.

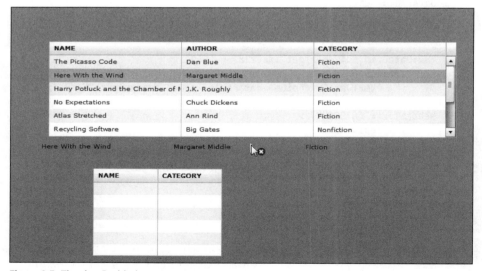

Figure 9-5. The dragEnabled property set to true

Notice that the cursor has a small circle with an x in it. The x indicates that you have dragged the data into a nondroppable area.

10. Set the dropEnabled property of the dgTarget DataGrid to true.

```
<mx:DataGrid id="dgTarget" x="228" y="269" dropEnabled="true">
```

11. Now test the application, and you should be able to drag and drop data items from one grid to another, as shown in Figure 9-6.

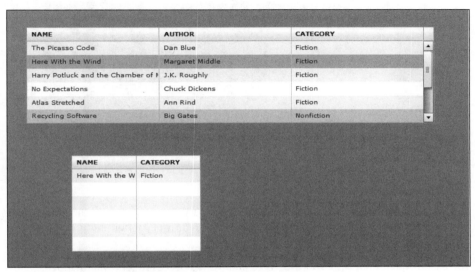

Figure 9-6. The data being dragged and dropped from one DataGrid to another

In the background, the DragManager class is being invoked and handles all of the mechanics involved. Other than setting up the DataGrids and enabling the drag-and-drop properties, you didn't need to do another thing in terms of coding.

Notice that when you drag and drop, the original data is left in the DataGrid intact. But let's assume that you want to remove the original data. You need to add another property to the dgInitiator DataGrid: dragMoveEnabled. This is also a Boolean property and will need to be set to true.

12. Set the dragMoveEnabled property of the first DataGrid.

```
<mx:DataGrid x="158" y="62" dataProvider="{books}" ➥
id="dgInitiator" width="50%" dragEnabled="true" dragMoveEnabled="true">
```

13. Run your code. The data should be moved, rather than copied, to the second DataGrid control (see Figure 9-7).

9

327

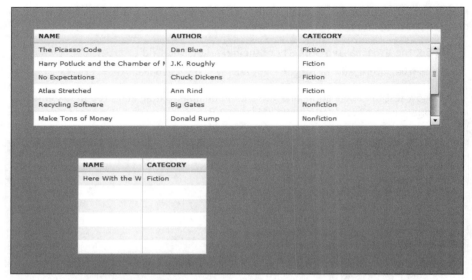

Figure 9-7. Moving rather than copying data

It is as easy as that.

You we progress through the rest of this chapter, as well as the rest of this book, I will introduce some additional complexities. But all of them will be built upon these simple concepts.

The easiest way to use drag and drop is to and from a DataGrid. But what happens if you want to drag to a List control where things aren't as clear cut as before?

Dragging to a List control

In the last example, dragging to and from a DataGrid control was easy because the column names between the dgInitiator DataGrid and the dgTarget DataGrid matched. But when you drag to a List control, there aren't any names to match. Instead, you have to save the data, which will be called **items**, from the DataGrid to a separate ArrayCollection, and then make that new ArrayCollection the dataProvider of the List. Since anything could come from the DataGrid, we will make the new ArrayCollection a collection of type Object.

Let's see how to do this.

1. Remove the dgTarget DataGrid from the previous example.

2. Replace the removed DataGrid with a List control as follows:

   ```
   <mx:List id="liTarget" width="225" dropEnabled="true" x="217" ➥
   y="244" />
   ```

3. Go ahead and run the application. Drag and drop a few items into the List control; you should see a result similar to Figure 9-8.

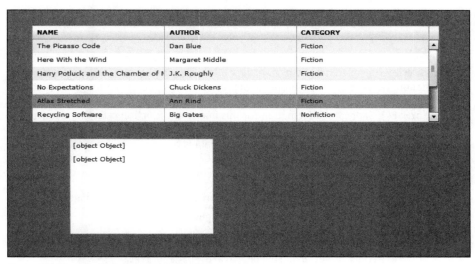

Figure 9-8. The result of dropping to the List control

Recall in Chapter 6 that I said "[object Object]" is ActionScript's polite way of telling you that it doesn't know which data to use. You have three items coming over from the DataGrid: NAME, AUTHOR, and CATEGORY. Which one do you want to use in the List control? You need to do a little programming to help it out.

4. Add the following event to the List control:

```
<mx:List id="liTarget" width="225" dropEnabled="true" x="217" ➥
y="244" dragDrop="testDragDrop(event)" />
```

The dragDrop event is dispatched when the user releases the mouse button over the List control. In this case, we are going to have it call a function, which we will write in the next step, called testDragDrop(). We pass it the event object.

5. In the Script block, create a private function called testDragDrop. It will accept the event object with a reference called evt. That reference will be of type DragEvent. The import statement should be written automatically with the other import statements.

```
private function testDragDrop(evt:DragEvent):void
{

}
```

As I stated a few moments ago, you are going to save each item dragged into the List control as an item of type Object.

6. Instantiate a new Object within the body of the function.

```
private function testDragDrop(evt:DragEvent):void
{
    var targetRow:Object = new Object();
}
```

As soon as you drag from an initiator, you are using the DragEvent class. The DragEvent class has a property called dragSource. At first blush, the name dragSource sounds a little like a function. However, it is the property that contains the data being dragged. That data is being passed into a class called DragSource. The DragSource class has a function called dataForFormat(). Sadly, the information for this important function is lacking detail in the ActionScript documentation. However, the dataForFormat() function handles the type of data being passed and formats it properly. If the data is being passed from a DataGrid, or any List-based control, the dataForFormat function uses an internal parameter called items. You must use this property, or the dataForFormat function will not work properly.

7. Add the following line after the instantiation of the new Object, targetRow.

```
private function testDragDrop(evt:DragEvent):void
{
    var targetRow:Object = new Object();
    targetRow = evt.dragSource.dataForFormat("items");
}
```

We haven't set up a dataProvider, of type ArrayCollection, for the List control yet. You can do that beneath the declaration for the books ArrayCollection. You should make it bindable.

8. Beneath the books declaration, instantiate a new instance of ArrayCollection and call it purchasedBooks.

```
[Bindable]
private var books:ArrayCollection;
[Bindable]
private var purchasedBooks:ArrayCollection = new ArrayCollection();
```

9. Declare purchasedBooks as the dataProvider of the List control.

```
<mx:List id="liTarget" width="225" dropEnabled="true" x="217" ➥
y="244" dragDrop="testDragDrop(event)" ➥
dataProvider="{purchasedBooks}" />
```

The code now needs to take the data inside the Object, targetRow, and add it to the ArrayCollection, purchasedBooks, for the List control. In order to accomplish this, you will use the addItem function of the ArrayCollection. You will accomplish this by passing the name to the List control. But remember, since you are only adding one item at a time, it will always be row [0] of the targetRow object.

10. Add the following third line of code to the testDragDrop() function.

```
private function testDragDrop(evt:DragEvent):void
{
    var targetRow:Object = new Object();
    targetRow = evt.dragSource.dataForFormat("items");
    liTarget.dataProvider.addItem(targetRow[0].name);
}
```

11. Remove the dragMoveEnabled property from the DataGrid control.

12. Save and run the application now; you should see that the name of the book gets transferred with some unwanted additional information, as shown in Figure 9-9. Don't worry, you will fix that in the next step.

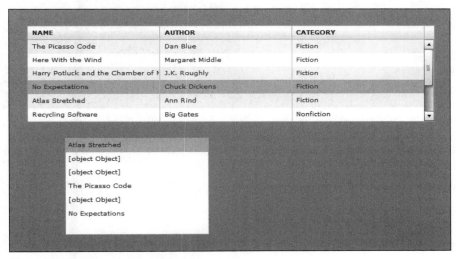

Figure 9-9. The List control populated

You are probably wondering why you are still getting the "[object Object]" message.

The "[object Object]" message is actually a default behavior of the Event class. In this case, it is a timing issue. The message is being generated before the name is being moved to the purchasedBooks ArrayCollection. Happily, it can be fixed with just one line of code. The Event class has a function, preventDefault(), that suppresses this behavior.

13. Add one additional line of code to the testDragDrop() function as follows:

```
private function testDragDrop(evt:DragEvent):void
{
    var targetRow:Object = new Object();
    targetRow = evt.dragSource.dataForFormat("items");
    liTarget.dataProvider.addItem(targetRow[0].name);
    evt.preventDefault();
}
```

14. Save and run your application. All should be well now, as shown in Figure 9-10.

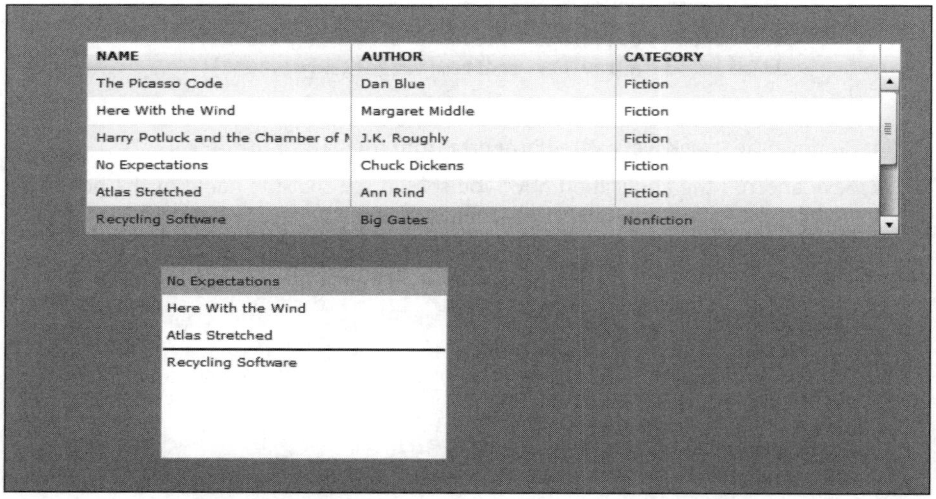

Figure 9-10. The corrected code results

So far, things have been pretty easy. But what if you wanted to add drag-and-drop capability programmatically?

Let's have a look.

Adding drag-and-drop capability programmatically

Throughout this book, I have shown you how to do equivalent jobs using just MXML and then using either just ActionScript or a combination of ActionScript and MXML. I am sure you will agree that using ActionScript gives you increased flexibility and options. That will certainly be true here.

As you progress through this section, you may find some alternative ways of doing the programming steps I am showing you here. That is fine. In any programming scenario, there are usually alternatives. I am using the steps that I am using out of a combination of style, and to show you some concepts along the way.

1. Begin by either starting a new MXML application or deleting all of the code between the opening and closing Application tags in the existing MXML application.

2. Add the following code. Notice that the layout of the Application container is set to vertical.

```
<?xml version="1.0" encoding="utf-8"?>
<mx:Application xmlns:mx="http://www.adobe.com/2006/mxml" ➥
layout="vertical">
    <mx:Script>
        <![CDATA[
            import mx.collections.ArrayCollection;

            [Bindable]
            private var targetData:ArrayCollection = ➥
new ArrayCollection();
        ]]>
    </mx:Script>

    <mx:Label id="dragLabel" text="Drag this Label"/>
    <mx:List id="liTarget" width="225" dataProvider="{targetData}"/>
</mx:Application>
```

3. Run the application. It should look like Figure 9-11.

Figure 9-11.
The example so far, with a Label and empty
List control

There are four classes associated with drag-and-drop functionality:

- **The** IUI **classes of the** mx.core **package**: These classes are the base classes for the UI components.

- **The** DragManager **class of the** mx.managers **package**: This class oversees all drag-and-drop operations.

- **The** DragSource **class, also of the** mx.core **package**: This class contains the data being dragged.

- **The** DragEvent **class of the** mx.event **package**: This class generates the event objects during a drag-and-drop operation.

4. Inside of the Script block, import the classes as follows. Since you will be using multiple classes from the mx.core package, just use the wildcard.

```
<![CDATA[
    import mx.collections.ArrayCollection;
    import mx.core.*;
    import mx.managers.DragManager;
    import mx.events.DragEvent;
```

9

In order to drag the Label control, you would need to create a mouseDown event that calls a function. However, in order for drag and drop to work, four parameters need to be passed.

The first parameter will be the ID of the Label component being dragged. The second parameter will be the data being passed. The third parameter will be the event being passed. Finally, the fourth parameter will be the format of the data being passed.

5. Create the following mouseDown event for the Label component:

```
<mx:Label id="dragLabel" text="Drag this Label" mouseDown=➡
"dragTest(dragLabel, 'This is the data', event, 'stringFormat')"/>
```

> *If you go through the ActionScript 3.0 documentation, you probably will not find a reference to the* stringFormat *property. From my experience, this is the only scenario in which you would use it. It just ensures that the data being dragged is a string.*

As you have seen in other places in this book, when you have a string within a string, you need to use single quotes. In this particular example, you are just passing a simple string as data. You will see how these four arguments come into play shortly.

We now need to create a function in the Script block to accept and process these parameters.

6. Create a dragTest function in the Script block as follows:

```
private function dragTest(initiator:Label, myData:String, ➡
event:MouseEvent, format:String):void
{

}
```

Notice that the first argument is of the type component that you are associating with it, in this case, a Label control.

7. The first line of code needs to instantiate the DragSource class, which you imported previously from the mx.core package.

```
private function dragTest(initiator:Label, myData:String, ➡
event:MouseEvent, format:String):void
{
    var ds:DragSource = new DragSource();
}
```

8. You now want to add the data and format to the DragSource object using the addData() function.

```
private function dragTest(initiator:Label, myData:String, ➡
event:MouseEvent, format:String):void
{
```

```
    var ds:DragSource = new DragSource();
    ds.addData(myData, format);
}
```

9. You finally want to add the name of the component, the DragSource object, and the event to the DragManager class using the doDrag() function. Remember, the DragManager class is serving as a central managing point and, without the information, DragManager won't know what to do. The DragManager class is static, which means it does not need to be instantiated before it can be used.

```
private function dragTest(initiator:Label, myData:String, ➥
event:MouseEvent, format:String):void
{
    var ds:DragSource = new DragSource();
    ds.addData(myData, format);
    DragManager.doDrag(initiator, ds, event);
}
```

10. Save your application and give it a try. You will see that you can drag the Label control. The only problem is that there is no place to drop it. It should look like Figure 9-12. Notice the X.

Figure 9-12.
Dragging the Label control

In order to have a functional drop target, you need to do some programming on the List side now.

11. In the List tag, create a dragEnter event, passing the event and the format to a function you will soon create.

```
<mx:List id="liTarget" width="225" dataProvider="{targetData}" ➥
dragEnter="testDragEnter(event, 'stringFormat')"/>
```

Once again, we are going to employ the DragManager class. However, we are going to pass the target property of the event object to a class that you have not come across yet in this book: IUIComponent.

Recall from earlier chapters that before you can add something to a component or container, you have to add a child container. The IUIComponent class is actually the class that is doing a lot of that work for you. In its simplest terms, it is drawing the new container. Let's say you want to add a Button to that new container now. ActionScript is actually employing a class called IButton that will tell the new container to act as a button. So the

Button is just a new container that is given the functionality you normally associate with a button.

ActionScript has number of I classes(the "I" stands for **interface**) contained within the mx.core package that handles the adding and functionality of components. Whenever you add containers and components, the I classes are invoked automatically in the background.

If you are new to OOP programming concepts, the term I just used, "interface," may be new to you. This is a pretty advanced programming concept. But in its simplest terms, an interface is a class that connects together normally unrelated classes. For the purposes of this book, you won't need to get too far into this concept.

12. Set up the testDragEnter() function in the Script block.

```
private function testDragEnter(evt:DragEvent, format:String):void
{
    DragManager.acceptDragDrop(IUIComponent(evt.target));
}
```

So, in summary, the IUIComponent will create a new container within the List component, and the evt.target will pass the data into it.

13. Go ahead and run the application. You still won't be able to drop the Label control into the List component. But notice the red X is missing (see Figure 9-13). This means that the List control is willing to accept the drop.

Figure 9-13. The List control, ready to accept the data

Before the List control will allow a drop, you need to do one last bit of programming.

14. Add a second event to the List control. A dragDrop event will call a function that, like the testDragDrop function created earlier, will pass the data into the dataProvider of the List control.

```
<mx:List id="liTarget" width="225" dataProvider="{targetData}" ➥
dragEnter="testDragEnter(event, 'stringFormat')" ➥
dragDrop="testDragDrop(event, 'stringFormat')"/>
```

15. Create the `testDragDrop` function now. Like you did earlier in this chapter, the function will create a new `Object` to accept the data, and then pass the data over to the `dataProvider` of the `List` control. Note that the `List` control uses the `addItem()` function to add the data to the `myData` object.

```
private function testDragDrop(evt:DragEvent, format:String):void
{
    var myData:Object = new Object();
    myData = evt.dragSource.dataForFormat(format);
    liTarget.dataProvider.addItem(myData);
}
```

It may not be a bad idea to review what the finished code should look like:

```
<?xml version="1.0" encoding="utf-8"?>
<mx:Application xmlns:mx="http://www.adobe.com/2006/mxml" ➡
layout="vertical">
    <mx:Script>
        <![CDATA[
            import mx.collections.ArrayCollection;
            import mx.core.*;
            import mx.managers.DragManager;
            import mx.events.DragEvent;

            [Bindable]
            private var targetData:ArrayCollection = ➡
new ArrayCollection();

            private function dragTest(initiator:Label, ➡
myData:String, event:MouseEvent, format:String):void
            {
                var ds:DragSource = new DragSource();
                ds.addData(myData, format);
                DragManager.doDrag(initiator, ds, event);
            }

            private function testDragEnter(evt:DragEvent, ➡
format:String):void
            {
                DragManager.acceptDragDrop➡
(IUIComponent(evt.target));
            }

            private function testDragDrop(evt:DragEvent, ➡
format:String):void
            {
                var myData:Object = new Object();
                myData = evt.dragSource.dataForFormat(format);
                liTarget.dataProvider.addItem(myData);
            }
```

9

```
        ]]>
    </mx:Script>

    <mx:Label id="dragLabel" text="Drag this Label" mouseDown=➥
"dragTest(dragLabel, 'This is the data', event, 'stringFormat')"/>
        <mx:List id="liTarget" width="225" dataProvider="{targetData}" ➥
dragEnter="testDragEnter(event, 'stringFormat')" ➥
dragDrop="testDragDrop(event, 'stringFormat')"/>
    </mx:Application>
```

16. Go ahead and run your application. Notice the data when you drop it on the List control. It should look like Figure 9-14.

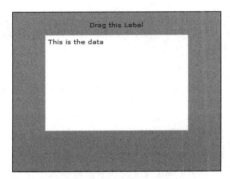

Figure 9-14. The finished drag and drop

Summary

You just encountered three potential drag-and-drop scenarios that encompass many possibilities. Much of the code you used can be reproduced verbatim for your own projects.

Now that you just finished a couple of short chapters, it is time to get back to some heavy-duty work. We will start a project that will put a lot of the concepts that you have learned together.

Grab a cup of coffee, roll up your sleeves, and let's get started on the next long chapter.

10 CASE STUDY: PART 1

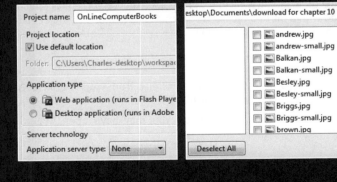

Now that you have a strong foundation in Flex basics and using MXML, and a knowledge of the fundamentals of ActionScript 3.0, this might be a good place to have a bit of a review.

Up to this point, I have shown you concepts in relatively simple and isolated environments. My hope is that you can use this information to solve problems with regard to your own applications. However, what I am hoping to do in this chapter is to put the individual pieces together and show you how to develop a Flex application from scratch. We will build a fictional online bookstore that will poke some good-natured fun at the publisher of this book. I pulled some old book covers and titles that we can use to practice using Flex.

I will not be introducing a lot of new concepts here. Instead, you will be building on the concepts you have learned already in the previous nine chapters. Along the way, I will be using the step-by-step approach I have used in the previous chapters with a little commentary between.

Just as a note, I have made every attempt to make each chapter independent and not dependent on work done on previous chapters. The same will be true of Chapter 12 onward. None of them will require that this case study be done. I do ask one thing however: in the previous chapters, because of the format, you had a lot of room to experiment. However, because things are so interconnected here, I am going to ask you to please stick with the steps outlined here. Also, please take your time with these steps and make sure you understand WHY you are using them.

We will do Part 1 of this case study in this chapter and Part 2 in the next chapter.

Keeping all of this in mind, let's get started.

The case study: a book publisher's website

For the case study, you are going to redesign the website for a well-known technical book publisher that needs a bit of a facelift (of course, the senior editor and my technical reviewer could do with a bit of a facelift also, but that is a different subject altogether, one that is well beyond the scope of this book).

Before you get going, please do two things:

1. Download the files necessary for this exercise from www.friendsofed.com. Unzip them to the directory of your choice.
2. Close or delete any previous projects you may have open. We will start from scratch.

Creating the project environment

First, we'll start by setting up our project environment.

1. Select File ➤ New ➤ Flex Project.

2. Name the project OnLineComputerBooks as shown in Figure 10-1.

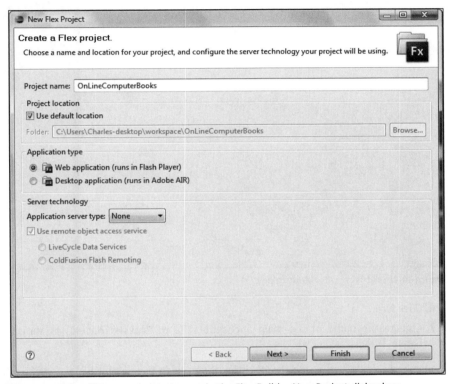

Figure 10-1. Specifying your project name in the Flex Builder New Project dialog box

3. Use the default location and set the Application type as Web application (runs in Flash Player).

4. Click Next.

5. Leave the default Output folder setting at bin-debug as shown in Figure 10-2.

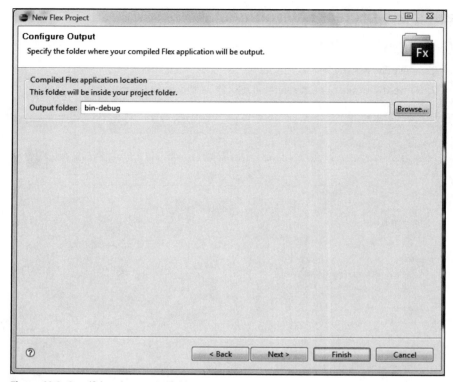

Figure 10-2. Specifying the output folder

6. Click Next.

7. Change the name of the main application file to BooksMain.mxml, as shown in Figure 10-3.

Of course, you don't have to do the last step. If you keep the default name, which is the same as the project name, things will work fine. But by putting the word "Main" into the name, you make the main application file a little easier to identify if you create a lot of components or have a lot of files.

8. Click Finish.

9. Switch to Source View.

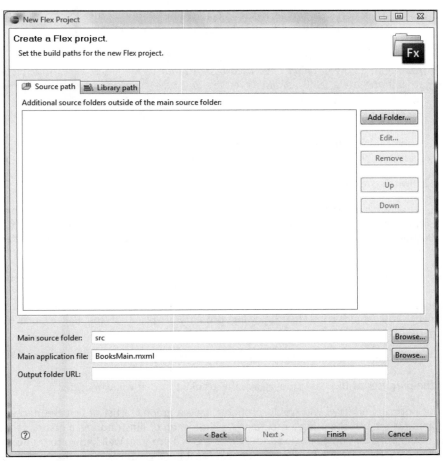

Figure 10-3. Changing the name of the main application file

Doing the initial layout

As you already know from working through the previous chapters, the code needed for Flex must be put between the opening and closing Application tags. Also, the Application tags have a property called layout. This is the layout manager, and it decides how the various containers are going to be arranged automatically. As a review, if you select a layout setting of absolute, you will need to specify the x- and y-positions of each of the components entered.

1. For the purposes of this project, you want to stack the containers vertically. If necessary, set the layout to vertical.

```
<mx:Application xmlns:mx="http://www.adobe.com/2006/mxml" ➡
layout="vertical">
```

2. The project calls for the background color to be white (because I say it is). So add a backgroundColor property and change the value to #FFFFFF.

> In traditional CSS, you could have used a shorthand technique of #FFF. That technique, unfortunately, is not available in Flex. You have to use the full hex notation shown here.

```
<mx:Application xmlns:mx="http://www.adobe.com/2006/mxml"
layout="vertical" backgroundColor="#FFFFFF">
```

3. Switch over to Design Perspective; the background should be white now.

Well, actually, it's not really white. You don't need to clean your monitor. That white background is a bit of a gradient with a bit of darkening going on toward the bottom of the application. Flex handles background colors as gradients by default. There is a bit of backward thinking here. If you want to turn off that gradient, you have to use the backgroundGradientColors property. You would then set up an array of colors or, if you didn't want the gradient, an array of one color.

As an example, let's say you wanted the background color to be pure white without the gradient. You would enter the following property in place of the backgroundColor property:

```
backgroundGradientColors="[#FFFFFF, #FFFFFF]"
```

For the purposes of this case study, leave the gradient as is. It will work fine.

In the normal workflow, you would probably have a graphic artist design the necessary graphics for the website using a program like Photoshop or Illustrator. As a matter of fact, one of the programs now bundled with Adobe CS3 is a program well known to the former Macromedia users: **Fireworks**. We will not be using it here. However, it has the unique ability to allow a graphic designer to do the layout of a Flex application and then save the layout complete with the requisite MXML code. This creates a nearly seamless workflow between designer and developer. Further, as of this writing, Adobe is introducing the beta of a new product code named **Thermo**. This promises to create an even more seamless environment.

Once the graphics are created, you import them into your Flex project. For the purposes of this project, the graphic files have been completed already.

4. To import the graphic files for the case study, select File ➤ Import. You should see the dialog box shown in Figure 10-4.

5. As you can see, you can select from a number of types of files. However, for the purposes of this case study, select File System, under the General category, and click Next to progress to the screen shown in Figure 10-5.

Figure 10-4. The Import dialog box

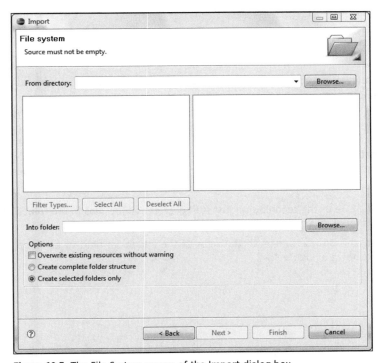

Figure 10-5. The File System screen of the Import dialog box

6. Using the Browse button, browse to the folder you unzipped the Chapter 10 files to. The folder should contain the assets for the project, as shown in Figure 10-6.

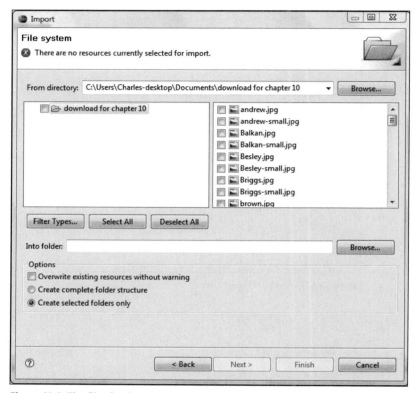

Figure 10-6. The files for download

Notice that you are receiving a warning, at the top of the dialog box, that there are no resources currently selected for import. You can do one of several things here to easily remedy that. You can click the check box to the left of the folder name in the left window, or click the Select All button to select all the files, or select the individual files you want to use.

7. Using one of the techniques I just stated, select all the files in the folder. The warning should disappear now.

8. Click the Browse button to the right of the Into folder field to bring up the dialog box shown in Figure 10-7.

Figure 10-7. The Import into Folder dialog box

9. Twirl down the OnLineComputerBooks folder and select the src folder within it.

10. Make a minor modification to the entry in the Select a folder to import into field. Add the assets folder (see Figure 10-8). Flex will create the folder when the import occurs. Note that this is a slightly different technique from what I showed you in an earlier chapter.

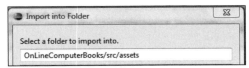

Figure 10-8. The modified field

11. Click OK.

12. Click Finish.

If you look in the Flex Navigator View, you should see that an assets folder was created with all of the assets for this project in it (see Figure 10-9). They are now officially inside of the project and can be used.

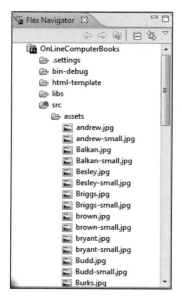

Figure 10-9.
The newly created assets folder

Starting to build the structure

Now that the environment is all set up, let's start to build the application.

1. You want to begin by adding a logo to the top of the application. In order to do this, go to the Source Perspective and, between the Application tags, insert an Image tag to place the Logo1.gif image.

This particular im<?xml version="1.0" encoding="utf-8"?>
<mx:Application xmlns:mx="http://www.adobe.com/2006/mxml" ➥
layout="vertical" backgroundColor="#FFFFFF">
    <mx:Image source="assets/Logo1.gif"/>
</mx:Application>

This particular image is called a **transparent GIF**. This means that everything except the actual lettering is transparent, and will allow any color behind the image to show through. If you want, change the background color of the application to a darker color to see how a transparent GIF works. Don't forget to change it back to #FFFFFF afterward.

2. Save and run the application. Your screen should resemble what you see in Figure 10-10.

3. Close the browser and return to Flex Builder.

We will now build the components for the project.

Figure 10-10. The application with the logo added

Creating the components

Time to divide and conquer!

As I said in Chapter 5, you want to divide your project into specialized components with the application file just serving as the controller of everything. We call this the Model-View-Controller (MVC) model. By doing this, you increase flexibility, reusability, and maintainability.

Initially, you will be building components for your home page, a gallery of book covers, a user comments page, and a shopping cart. Later on, you will be adding states to these components.

Let's begin with the BookHome component, which will serve as your home page.

BookHome component

To build the BookHome component, follow these steps:

1. In the Flex Navigator View, right-click the src folder and select New ➤ Folder.

2. Call the new folder components, as shown in Figure 10-11.

3. Click Finish.

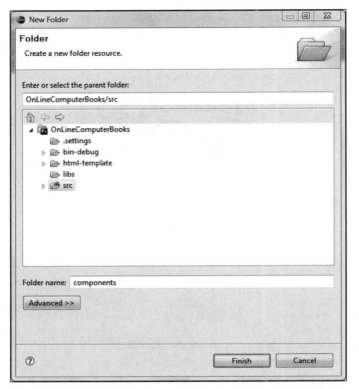

Figure 10-11. Naming the components folder in the New Folder dialog box

Look in the Flex Navigator pane, and you should now see the new folder, as shown in Figure 10-12.

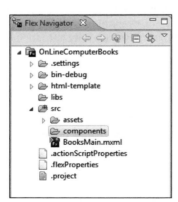

Figure 10-12.
The Flex Navigator pane with the components folder

4. Right-click the new components folder and select New ➤ MXML Component.

Recall that components have to be based on one of the container components and not on the Application tag.

5. Call the new component BookHome and base it on the VBox container, as shown in Figure 10-13. Unlike earlier examples, we will set the size of this component to a width of 400 and a height of 300.

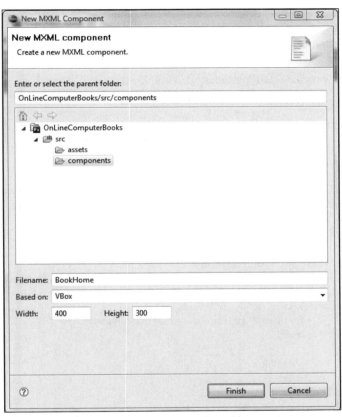

Figure 10-13. Defining the BookHome component in the New MXML Component dialog box

6. Click Finish.

The code for the new component should look as follows:

```
<?xml version="1.0" encoding="utf-8"?>
<mx:VBox xmlns:mx="http://www.adobe.com/2006/mxml" width="400" ➥
height="300">

</mx:VBox>
```

7. Within the VBox container, put an HBox container:

```
<?xml version="1.0" encoding="utf-8"?>
<mx:VBox xmlns:mx="http://www.adobe.com/2006/mxml" width="400" ➥
height="300">
    <mx:HBox>

    </mx:HBox>
</mx:VBox>
```

8. Now, within the HBox container, put an Image tag, and make the source assets/EbooksHomeAd.jpg.

```
<?xml version="1.0" encoding="utf-8"?>
<mx:VBox xmlns:mx="http://www.adobe.com/2006/mxml" width="400" ➥
height="300">
    <mx:HBox>
        <mx:Image source="assets/EbooksHomeAd.jpg"/>
    </mx:HBox>
</mx:VBox>
```

You will recall that a Flex application is built with containers within containers. The containers, in turn, handle the placement of whatever content is inside of them.

9. You now want to place some text below the image you just inserted. Put a VBox below the Image tag.

```
<?xml version="1.0" encoding="utf-8"?>
<mx:VBox xmlns:mx="http://www.adobe.com/2006/mxml" width="400" ➥
height="300">
    <mx:HBox>
        <mx:Image source="assets/EbooksHomeAd.jpg"/>
        <mx:VBox>

        </mx:VBox>
    </mx:HBox>
</mx:VBox>
```

Recall that when I talked about UI components, I talked about Text. What you need to do is create a Text container to control the font, size, color, and so forth of the text.

10. Place a Text container within the new VBox container. Give it a fontSize property of 12 and a color property of blue. Make the container 200 wide (remember, all measurements in Flex are in pixels).

```
<?xml version="1.0" encoding="utf-8"?>
<mx:VBox xmlns:mx="http://www.adobe.com/2006/mxml" width="400" ➥
height="300">
    <mx:HBox>
        <mx:Image source="assets/EbooksHomeAd.jpg"/>
        <mx:VBox>
            <mx:Text color="blue" fontSize="12" width="200">
```

```
                </mx:Text>
            </mx:VBox>
        </mx:HBox>
    </mx:VBox>
```

Notice that I didn't put the `text` property in the Text container to hold the text. I did that for a reason. Recall from the earlier discussions of states and transitions that you can take an MXML property and break it out to its own subcontainer. This is handy if the property will contain an array of objects. It is also a handy way to sometimes make blocks of text a little more readable in code.

Notice that the capital word "Text" refers to the class, while the lowercase "text" refers to the property.

11. Within the Text container, create a text container and give it the text `friends of ED eBooks are offered for sale at a discount of almost 50%`.

```
<mx:Text color="blue" fontSize="12" width="200">
    <mx:text>
        friends of ED eBooks are offered for sale at a discount ➡
of almost 50%
    </mx:text>
</mx:Text>
```

Remember, you cannot run a component as an application because it has no Application tag of its own. However, you can see it in Design View. Compare your work so far against Figure 10-14.

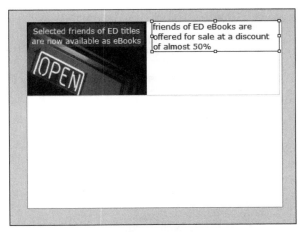

Figure 10-14. The component as of the last step

12. Return to Source Perspective so you can add some additional code.

13. To save yourself some time, copy the <mx:Text> container and paste it below the present Text container. Inside of the <mx:text> tag of the new container, replace the text with the following:

Please use our site to find the technical books you need.

14. Follow the same procedure to add one more Text container with the following text:

Keep coming back to our site to see the latest news about new ➥ books and technical information.

Your code should look as follows:

```
<?xml version="1.0" encoding="utf-8"?>
<mx:VBox xmlns:mx="http://www.adobe.com/2006/mxml" width="400" ➥
height="300">
    <mx:HBox>
        <mx:Image source="assets/ebooksHomeAd.jpg"/>
        <mx:VBox>
            <mx:Text color="blue" fontSize="12" width="200">
                <mx:text>
                    friends of ED eBooks are offered for ➥
sale at a discount of almost 50%
                </mx:text>
            </mx:Text>
            <mx:Text color="blue" fontSize="12" width="200">
                <mx:text>
                    Please use our site to find the technical ➥
books you need.
                </mx:text>
            </mx:Text>
            <mx:Text color="blue" fontSize="12" width="200">
                <mx:text>
                    Keep coming back to our site to see ➥
the latest news about new books and technical information
                </mx:text>
            </mx:Text>
        </mx:VBox>
    </mx:HBox>
</mx:VBox>
```

15. Switch to Design Perspective. Your screen should look like Figure 10-15.

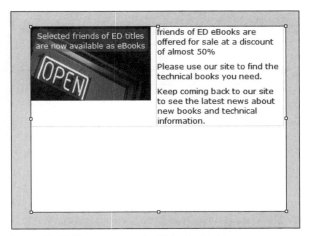

Figure 10-15. The component with text added

We will be returning to this component to make some additional changes later on. Working with components means the site will be easy to update.

When you learned how to build and attach components, you used the drag-and-drop technique to bring them into the main page. In this case, you could do that also. However, in this exercise and for the sake of review, you are going to do it manually. This will reinforce the concepts you've learned.

16. Switch back to the BooksMain.mxml file.

Recall that in the Application tag, you have to declare a namespace. For review, a namespace is simply a way of predefining a path to find an object that will be needed.

17. To define a namespace, use the xmlns property as follows:

```
<?xml version="1.0" encoding="utf-8"?>
<mx:Application xmlns:mx="http://www.adobe.com/2006/mxml"
layout="vertical" backgroundColor="#FFFFFF"
 xmlns:comp="components.*">
    <mx:Image source="assets/Logo1.gif"/>
</mx:Application>
```

The asterisk signifies all components in the directory named components. As you may recall, the name itself, comp, has absolutely no significance. However, it is a good idea to use a name that describes what is in the path. In this case, I used comp as a name to tell me that this path contains my components. Using precise terminology, the name (in this case, comp) is called a **prefix**.

18. Under the Image tag, place the component by starting the tag not with mx, as you have done with many tags up to this point, but with comp, which is the prefix of the namespace you just created.

```
<comp
```

As soon as you type the colon, after the namespace prefix, a list of components in the components directory (in this case there is only one so far) comes up, as shown in Figure 10-16.

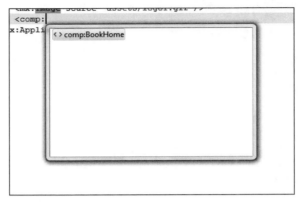

Figure 10-16. The component listing

19. Select the BookHome component.

20. For the purposes of this exercise, you want the height and width of the component to be 50% of the size the application, as shown here:

```
<?xml version="1.0" encoding="utf-8"?>
<mx:Application xmlns:mx="http://www.adobe.com/2006/mxml" ➥
layout="vertical" backgroundColor="#FFFFFF" xmlns:comp="components.*">
    <mx:Image source="assets/logo1.gif"/>
    <comp:BookHome height="50%" width="50%"/>
</mx:Application>
```

21. Save the project and run it. Your output should be as shown in Figure 10-17.

This is a good place to show you the power of components:

22. Close the browser and return to the BookHome component.

23. Under the closing HBox tag, insert a Text container with the following text. Set the fontSize to 20 and the fontWeight to bold.

```
</mx:HBox>
<mx:Text fontSize="20" fontWeight="bold">
    <mx:text>Book of the Week</mx:text>
</mx:Text>
```

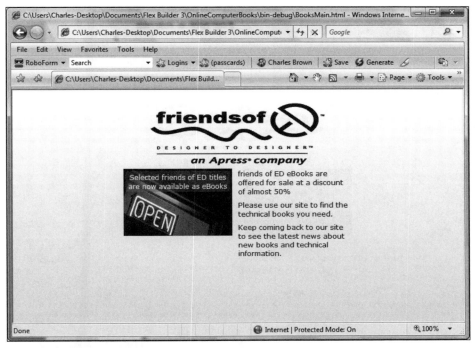

Figure 10-17. The component in the main application

24. Under the closing Text tag, place an Image tag that calls the Green.jpg file in the assets folder.

```
</mx:HBox>
<mx:Text fontSize="20" fontWeight="bold">
     <mx:text>Book of the Week</mx:text>
</mx:Text>
<mx:Image source="assets/Green.jpg"/>
```

25. Save the component.

26. Switch back to BooksMain and run the application; you should now see the updated component in the application, as shown in Figure 10-18. That is the real power of components: to be able to update easily without affecting other aspects of the application.

10

Figure 10-18. The finished home page

As you can see, once the component is updated, everything that uses that component is updated automatically as soon as the component is saved.

As you progress through this case study, you will be calling this component programmatically as well as building a navigation bar. For that reason, you need to give the call to the component an id property and a label property. In this case, we will call both home. In the label property, you must enter the name exactly the way you want it to appear in the navigation bar. So you will use a capital "H" for "home":

27. Modify the component call as follows:

```
<comp:BookHome height="50%" width="50%" label="Home" id="home"/>
```

The finished code in BooksMain.mxml should look as follows:

```
<?xml version="1.0" encoding="utf-8"?>
<mx:Application xmlns:mx="http://www.adobe.com/2006/mxml" ➥
layout="vertical" backgroundColor="#FFFFFF" xmlns:comp="components.*">
    <mx:Image source="assets/Logo1.gif"/>
    <comp:BookHome height="50%" width="50%" label="Home" id="home"/>
</mx:Application>
```

Comments component

You will now build another component that will allow readers to make comments about books sold by this publisher.

1. Once again, right-click the components folder in the Flex Navigator View.

2. Select New ➤ MXML Component.

3. Name the component Comments. Again, you will base it on the VBox container. However, in this case, change the width to 500. The dialog box should now look like Figure 10-19.

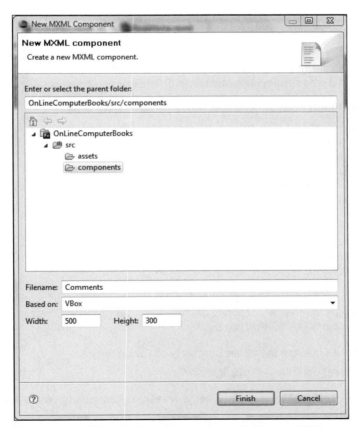

Figure 10-19. Defining the Comments component in the new MXML Component dialog box

4. Click Finish.

5. Since this is going to be a form, you will need to declare the Form container.

```
<?xml version="1.0" encoding="utf-8"?>
<mx:VBox xmlns:mx="http://www.adobe.com/2006/mxml" width="500" ➥
height="300">
    <mx:Form>

    </mx:Form>
</mx:VBox>
```

6. Next, declare a FormHeading telling the user to enter his comments, as follows:

```
<?xml version="1.0" encoding="utf-8"?>
<mx:VBox xmlns:mx="http://www.adobe.com/2006/mxml" width="500" ➥
height="300">
    <mx:Form>
        <mx:FormHeading label="Please Enter Your Rating and ➥
Comments About Our Books"/>
    </mx:Form>
</mx:VBox>
```

Recall from an earlier discussion of forms that the FormItem container helps position, as well as format, the form's various components. In Flex, it is a good practice to put each component in a separate FormItem container. The reason will be obvious in a moment.

7. Under the FormHeading control, insert a FormItem container.

```
<?xml version="1.0" encoding="utf-8"?>
<mx:VBox xmlns:mx="http://www.adobe.com/2006/mxml" width="500" ➥
height="300">
    <mx:Form>
        <mx:FormHeading label="Please Enter Your Rating and ➥
Comments About Our Books"/>
        <mx:FormItem>

        </mx:FormItem>
    </mx:Form>
</mx:VBox>
```

As you have seen before, when using the FormItem control, the label identifying the control does not get entered as a separate control with a text property. Instead, it is entered as a label property in the FormItem tag.

8. Give the FormItem tag a label property of Full Name.

```
<mx:FormItem label="Full Name">
```

9. Within the FormItem container, add a TextInput control and set the width to 250.

```
<mx:Form>
    <mx:FormHeading label="Please Enter Your Rating and Comments ➥
About Our Books"/>
```

```
<mx:FormItem label="Full Name">
    <mx:TextInput width="250"/>
</mx:FormItem>
</mx:Form>
```

Just to see what is going on, switch over to Design Perspective. Your screen should look similar to Figure 10-20.

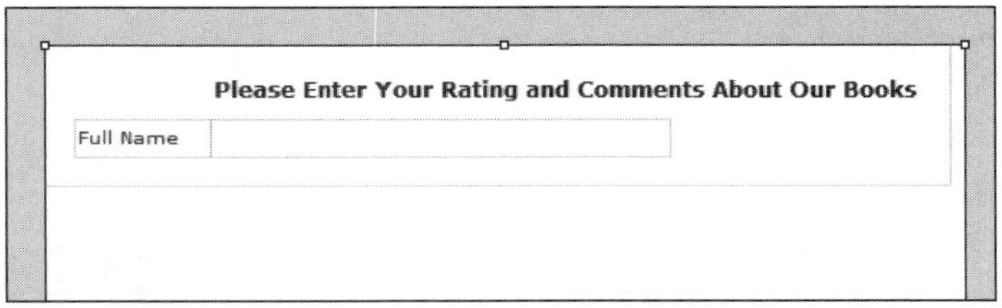

Figure 10-20. The FormHeading and FormItem controls

Notice that the Form container, coupled with the FormItem container, handles the placement of everything automatically.

10. Return to Source Perspective; you will now build a new FormItem container below the last one. Give it the label property of E-mail, and insert within it a TextInput control with a width of 250 pixels.

```
<mx:FormItem label="E-mail">
    <mx:TextInput width="250"/>
</mx:FormItem>
```

Now you will build a similar structure that will allow the user to enter the title of the book she is reviewing.

11. Put the following underneath your E-mail FormItem:

```
<mx:FormItem label="Book Title">
    <mx:TextInput width="250"/>
</mx:FormItem>
```

You now want users to enter their comments. For that, you will need to give them a larger area to work with. To accomplish that, the TextArea control works nicely.

12. Again, you need to use a FormItem container and give it the label property of Please Enter Your Comments. Set the width of the TextArea control to 250.

```
<mx:FormItem label="Please Enter Your Comments">
    <mx:TextArea width="250"/>
</mx:FormItem>
```

Switch to Design Perspective to preview the form, as shown in Figure 10-21.

10

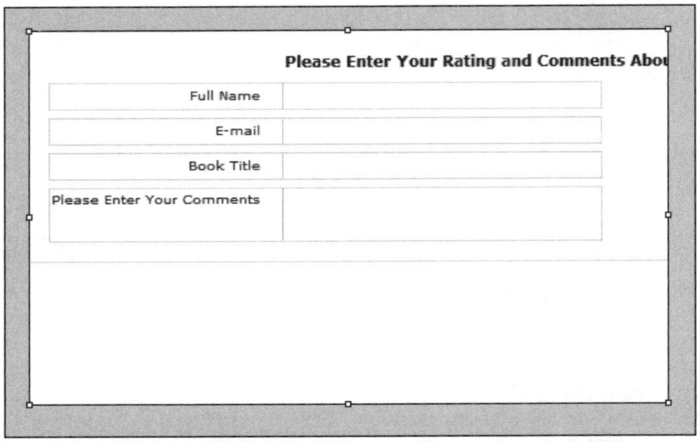

Figure 10-21. The partially completed form

Your FormHeading will appear to be cut off (as shown in Figure 10-21). Don't worry about that, it will not affect the final result when you instantiate the component in the application file. If you are bothered by it, you could change the width of the component, in the VBox container, to something like 600 pixels. But it is not really necessary.

Notice that the FormItem controls right-justify the labels for each item on the form.

You now want users to be able to rate books on a scale of 1 to 5. The NumericStepper control does that job nicely. You can give this control a minimum and maximum value. Users then just need to click the up or down arrow keys to set the value they want.

13. Switch back to Source Perspective and, underneath the Comments FormItem, set up a new FormItem with the label property of Please Rate This Book.

14. Within the container, place a NumericStepper control with the properties of minimum and maximum set to 1 and 5, respectively.

```
<mx:FormItem label="Please Rate This Book">
    <mx:NumericStepper minimum="1" maximum="5"/>
</mx:FormItem>
```

Switch again to Design View. You will see the NumericStepper control as shown in Figure 10-22. However, you cannot test it until you run the component from the application, which you will do in a moment.

Figure 10-22. The NumericStepper control

The final thing you want to do on this form is to create a Submit button and a Clear button. Initially, these buttons will not have any functionality. You will give them functionality a little further along in the process. However, initially, you have a small problem.

All of these controls are part of the larger VBox container. As you know, VBox arranges everything vertically. To compensate for this, the FormItem container has an interesting property called direction. This property allows you to override the direction of the layout container for anything within that FormItem container.

15. Under the FormItem container for the NumericStepper, set up another FormItem. There will be no label property. However, set the direction property to horizontal:

```
<mx:FormItem direction="horizontal">

</mx:FormItem>
```

16. Instead of giving the FormItem the label property, put two buttons in the container, each with its own label:

```
<mx:FormItem direction="horizontal">
    <mx:Button label="Submit Your Comment"/>
    <mx:Button label="Clear the Form"/>
</mx:FormItem>
```

In Design Perspective, the form should look like Figure 10-23.

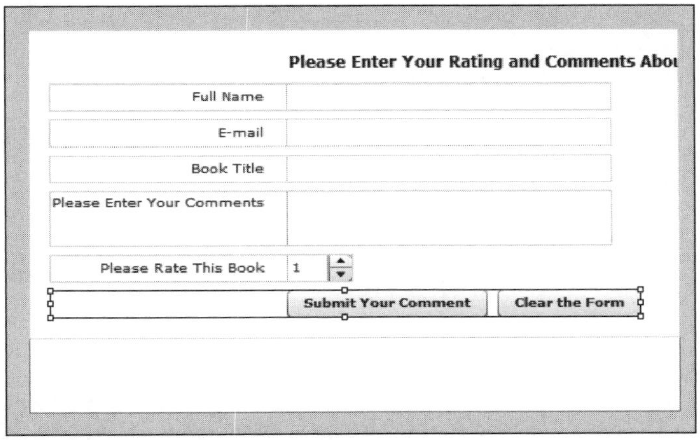

Figure 10-23. The finished Comments component

Notice that the new buttons are arranged horizontally and, by default, right-justified.

You are now finished with your forms. The next step is to build a component to display your various book covers.

BookCovers component

To build the BookCovers component, which will display, as the name says, the covers of books, follow these steps:

1. As you have done before, right-click the components folder in the Flex Navigator View and select New ➤ MXML Component.

2. Call this component BookCovers, and base it on the VBox container.

3. Set the Width property to 550 pixels. However, unlike before, delete the Height setting. By doing this, the height of the component will adjust to the content automatically. The completed dialog box should look like Figure 10-24.

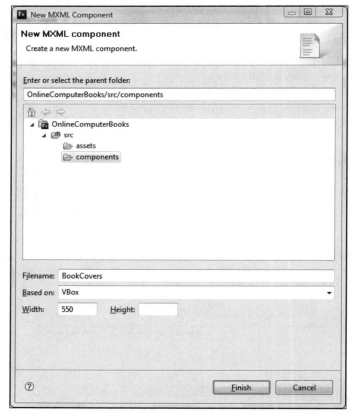

Figure 10-24. Defining the BookCovers component in the New MXML Component dialog box

4. Click Finish.

5. If necessary, switch to Source Perspective and, within the VBox container, create an HBox container.

6. Give the new HBox container a backgroundColor of #EE82EE. This is a violet. Also, set the verticalAlign attribute to middle. This will align the graphics to a middle point. Finally, set the fontSize to 12.

```xml
<?xml version="1.0" encoding="utf-8"?>
<mx:VBox xmlns:mx="http://www.adobe.com/2006/mxml" width="550">
    <mx:HBox backgroundColor="#EE82EE" verticalAlign="middle" ➥
fontSize="12">

    </mx:HBox>
</mx:VBox>
```

7. Within the HBox container, place a label control with the text property Select the Books:.

8. Below that, place a CheckBox control with the label property All Books.

```xml
<?xml version="1.0" encoding="utf-8"?>
<mx:VBox xmlns:mx="http://www.adobe.com/2006/mxml" width="550">
    <mx:HBox backgroundColor="#EE82EE" verticalAlign="middle" ➥
fontSize="12">
        <mx:Label text="Select the Books"/>
        <mx:CheckBox label="All Books"/>
    </mx:HBox>
</mx:VBox>
```

If you switch to Design Perspective, your screen should look like Figure 10-25.

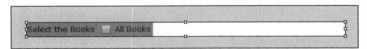

Figure 10-25. The Label and CheckBox controls

9. Under the CheckBox control, enter another Label control with the text property Select Book Category.

One of the controls that you have yet to look at is the ComboBox, which you'll be adding to this component. The ComboBox is essentially a menu within a drop box.

Normally, you would create the list in the ComboBox using an outside data source such as XML, web services, or even a database directly (using ColdFusion). Since we have not discussed server-side technology yet, you are going to manually add items to this control. This will also give you a good chance to see some of the mechanics behind this control.

10. Below the Label control you just created, create a ComboBox control with an opening and closing tag:

```xml
<?xml version="1.0" encoding="utf-8"?>
<mx:VBox xmlns:mx="http://www.adobe.com/2006/mxml" width="550">
    <mx:HBox backgroundColor="#EE82EE" verticalAlign="middle" ➥
fontSize="12">
        <mx:Label text="Select the Books"/>
```

```
                        <mx:CheckBox label="All Books"/>
                        <mx:Label text="Select Book Category"/>
                        <mx:ComboBox>

                        </mx:ComboBox>
                   </mx:HBox>
              </mx:VBox>
```

As you may recall from our discussion of XML (and the DataGrid control), many controls use a property called dataProvider. The dataProvider property links to the source of the data. Even if you are manually entering data, like we are here, the ComboBox control still needs to use this property. However, we will be using it a little differently than we have in the past. Here, we will make the dataProvider its own container.

11. Add the dataProvider property to the ComboBox control as shown here:

```
<mx:ComboBox>
     <mx:dataProvider>

     </mx:dataProvider>
</mx:ComboBox>
```

Again, referring to our past discussions of XML, ActionScript holds the data in an ArrayCollection. However, because you are manually entering data into this control, you must explicitly tell ActionScript to use the ArrayCollection class by creating an ArrayCollection container within the dataProvider container.

12. Add the ArrayCollection container as follows:

```
<mx:ComboBox>
     <mx:dataProvider>
          <mx:ArrayCollection>

          </mx:ArrayCollection>
     </mx:dataProvider>
</mx:ComboBox>
```

Once you have all these mechanics set up, you must enter the items you want contained in the control as either type Object or type String. Since you are not using any of the specific functionality of the String class, either will work. For the purposes of this exercise, we will use String. (You could have used type Object also. But since we are passing strings, I decided to use class String in this exercise.)

You are going to create five items in the ComboBox control: Dreamweaver, Flash, Graphics, Web Design, and Other. You could add more, but for this example, you may want to keep your typing down to a minimum.

13. Enter the following strings in the ComboBox:

```
<mx:ComboBox>
     <mx:dataProvider>
          <mx:ArrayCollection>
```

```
          <mx:String>Dreamweaver</mx:String>
          <mx:String>Flash</mx:String>
          <mx:String>Graphics</mx:String>
          <mx:String>Web Design</mx:String>
          <mx:String>Other</mx:String>
       </mx:ArrayCollection>
    </mx:dataProvider>
</mx:ComboBox>
```

Look at your form in Design Perspective. It should now look like what you see in Figure 10-26.

Figure 10-26. The completed search bar

Like the NumericStepper control you saw before, the ComboBox control will not work until you run it through the Application tags of the main application. All you will see is the small down arrow.

Now you will add a Tile container to your component to hold the images of the book covers. The Tile component does just as it says; it creates a grid of square boxes to display a series of similar objects. In this case, it is perfect for displaying the 20 or so book covers you need to show.

14. Under the closing HBox tag, create a Tile container.

I now have some good news and bad news for you. The good news is that manually populating the Tile container is easy. The bad news is that manually populating the Tile container requires that you type a lot of repetitious code. But have no fear—I am coming to your rescue by providing a text file so you can copy and paste the code you need.

It is easy because all you need to do is create a series of Image controls. In this exercise, you are going to use the images titled with -small. There are about 20 of them. However, you are going to go one step further. You are going to give the images a click event that will call up another state, which you will be creating, called bookDetails. You will use this later on in the project.

You are doing this so that end users can click one of the titled thumbnail book covers to bring up details about that book.

The code for each Image tag is as follows (with just the name of the image changed):

```
<mx:Image source="assets/Andrew-small.jpg" ➥
click="currentState='BookDetails'" />
    <mx:Image source="assets/Balkan-small.jpg" ➥
click="currentState='BookDetails'" />
    <mx:Image source="assets/Besley-small.jpg" ➥
```

10

```
click="currentState='BookDetails'" />
   <mx:Image source="assets/Briggs-small.jpg" ➥
click="currentState='BookDetails'" />
   <mx:Image source="assets/Brown-small.jpg" ➥
click="currentState='BookDetails'" />
```

As I mentioned, if you don't want to type all of the code necessary here, I have included a TXT file containing this code, imageLink.txt, with this chapter's download files. You can just copy and paste all of this code from there.

15. Copy and paste the code in imageLink.txt between the opening and closing Tile tags.

16. Take a quick look in Design Perspective. Your screen should look something like what appears in Figure 10-27.

Figure 10-27. The finished BookCovers component

Now that you have the basic components built, you'll start to assemble them together.

Assembling the components

Let's return to the BooksMain application file. You may recall that during the discussion of navigation containers, I said that the ViewStack container was one of the easiest and most useful to use. For that reason, you are going to use it here.

Right above the code for the home page, you will set up a ViewStack container. Because you are going to create a navigation bar from it, you will need to give it an id property. In this case, you will call it bookPages. You also want the container to automatically resize based on the content of the page called.

1. Cut the BookHome home component. Create the ViewStack container and paste the cut component within the ViewStack. Your code should look as follows:

```
<?xml version="1.0" encoding="utf-8"?>
<mx:Application xmlns:mx="http://www.adobe.com/2006/mxml" ➡
layout="vertical" backgroundColor="#FFFFFF" xmlns:comp="components.*">
    <mx:Image source="assets/Logo1.gif"/>
    <mx:ViewStack id="bookPages" resizeToContent="true">
        <comp:BookHome height="50%" width="50%" ➡
label="Home" id="home"/>
    </mx:ViewStack>
</mx:Application>
```

You will now need to put the other components you created, Comments and BookCovers, within the ViewStack container. Because you want to build a navigation bar, you will need to do what you did for the BookHome component—give each call an id and a label attribute. You will also need to make the height and width properties of each 50%.

2. Add the following code to the ViewStack container below the BookHome component:

```
<?xml version="1.0" encoding="utf-8"?>
<mx:Application xmlns:mx="http://www.adobe.com/2006/mxml" ➡
layout="vertical" backgroundColor="#FFFFFF" xmlns:comp="components.*">
    <mx:Image source="assets/Logo1.gif"/>
    <mx:ViewStack id="bookPages" resizeToContent="true">
        <comp:BookHome height="50%" width="50%" ➡
label="Home" id="home"/>
        <comp:Comments height="50%" width="50%" ➡
label="Comments" id="comments"/>
        <comp:BookCovers height="50%" width="50%" ➡
label="Our Books" id="bookCovers"/>
    </mx:ViewStack>
</mx:Application>
```

The last step in the assembly process is to add a LinkBar control right under the Image tag. In this case, the dataProvider will be the id of the ViewStack: bookPages.

10

3. Add the following LinkBar:

```xml
<?xml version="1.0" encoding="utf-8"?>
<mx:Application xmlns:mx="http://www.adobe.com/2006/mxml" ➡
layout="vertical" backgroundColor="#FFFFFF" xmlns:comp="components.*">
    <mx:Image source="assets/Logo1.gif"/>
    <mx:LinkBar dataProvider="bookPages"/>
    <mx:ViewStack id="bookPages" resizeToContent="true">
        <comp:BookHome height="50%" width="50%" ➡
label="Home" id="home"/>
        <comp:Comments height="50%" width="50%" ➡
label="Comments" id="comments"/>
        <comp:BookCovers height="50%" width="50%" ➡
label="Our Books" id="bookCovers"/>
    </mx:ViewStack>
</mx:Application>
```

4. You are now ready to give your application an initial test. Go ahead and run it. The first thing that should come up is the home page as shown in Figure 10-28.

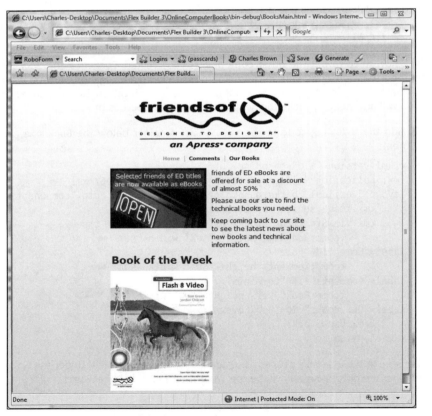

Figure 10-28. Current view of the home page

Notice that the LinkBar picked up each of the label values of the components contained within the ViewStack container.

5. Click the Comments link. Your display should resemble the screen in Figure 10-29.

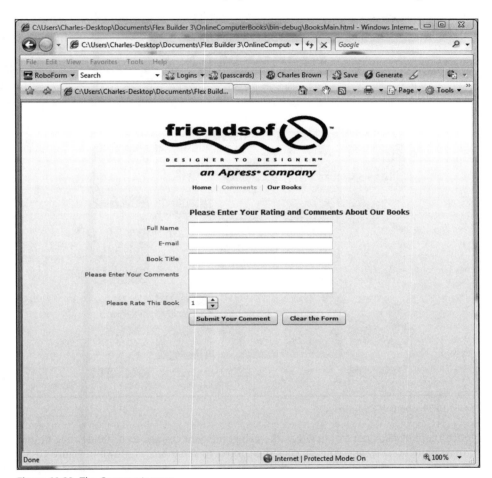

Figure 10-29. The Comments page

Notice that the NumericStepper control is now working, and you can set a number between 1 and 5 by either clicking the two arrow buttons or highlighting the field and typing the number you want. If you try to put a number in that is larger than 5, the control will just default to 5.

The two buttons will not work yet because we have not given them any functionality, or events.

6. Click the Our Books link, and you will see your tiled book covers, as shown in Figure 10-30.

Figure 10-30. The Our Books page

Notice the ComboBox control now has the categories you created in it. While they do not have any functionality yet, you can click the control to see them, as shown in Figure 10-31.

Figure 10-31.
The populated ComboBox control

If you click one of the book covers, you will receive an error. This is because we have not created the state that the images click *event is calling. Don't worry about it for now. We will fix that.*

Assume that you wanted the Our Books link to be the second selection in the navigation bar. All you need to do is go into the code and move the call to the component so that it is the second one.

7. Move the Our Books link by changing the code to match the following:

```
<mx:ViewStack id="bookPages" resizeToContent="true">
    <comp:BookHome height="50%" width="50%" label="Home" id="home"/>
    <comp:BookCovers height="50%" width="50%" ➡
label="Our Books" id="bookCovers"/>
    <comp:Comments height="50%" width="50%" ➡
label="Comments" id="comments"/>
</mx:ViewStack>
```

8. Rerun the application; you will see that the navigation has been rearranged as shown in Figure 10-32.

Figure 10-32. The rearranged LinkBar component

By now, your wow factor should be on high. However, there is one little design wrinkle we need to discuss here.

If you look at your application carefully, you will notice that it is divided into three sections: the logo image, the LinkBar control, and the ViewStack container. Their position is being automatically handled by the layout property of the Application container. At present, it is vertical and, as you can see, the three sections are arranged from top to bottom.

Using a layout such as vertical or horizontal has a few drawbacks. First of all, it limits your ability to arrange the application the way you may need to. In addition, because Flex needs to perform calculations to decide on the position of the parts each time the page is called, performance can be hurt. For that reason, there is a strong argument in favor of setting the layout property to absolute and using either Design View or setting the x and y properties in Source View to position the various parts of your page.

1. Set the layout to absolute.

If you switch to Design View, you see a not very pretty sight: everything is crunched into the upper-left corner. As we discussed toward the beginning of this book, absolute gives everything a default position of 0,0.

There are two possible approaches you can take to fix this: you can either go into your code and give each of the three parts an x and y attribute or simply drag them in Design View to manually arrange the parts.

For the purposes of this exercise, take the former approach.

2. Set the following x and y properties for the three sections of your application:

- Logo image: x: 360, y: 10
- LinkBar: x: 400, y: 130
- ViewStack: x: 290, y: 160

3. Finally, in the Application tag, set both the width and height properties to 100%. This will give you room to place your shopping cart shortly.

```
<?xml version="1.0" encoding="utf-8"?>
<mx:Application xmlns:mx="http://www.adobe.com/2006/mxml"
layout="absolute" backgroundColor="#FFFFFF"
xmlns:comp="components.*" height="100%" width="100%">
    <mx:Image source="assets/Logo1.gif" x="360" y="10"/>
    <mx:LinkBar dataProvider="bookPages" x="400" y="130"/>
    <mx:ViewStack id="bookPages" resizeToContent="true"
x="290" y="160">
        <comp:BookHome height="50%" width="50%"
label="Home" id="home"/>
        <comp:BookCovers height="50%" width="50%"
label="Our Books" id="bookCovers"/>
        <comp:Comments height="50%" width="50%"
label="Comments" id="comments"/>
    </mx:ViewStack>
</mx:Application>
```

When you run the application, the placement should be about the same as before. If there are some minor variations, don't be concerned about that.

Your next step will be to build a shopping cart in order for users to be able to purchase the books they see.

BookCart component

You are now going to build the BookCart component, which will be the shopping cart feature for your site. Again, you will not be giving it a lot of functionality until later on. However, you will be using states a bit here.

1. As you have done when building the previous components, right-click the components folder in the Flex Navigator View and select New ➤ MXML Component.

2. Call the component BookCart, base it on the Canvas container, and specify no height or width, as shown in Figure 10-33.

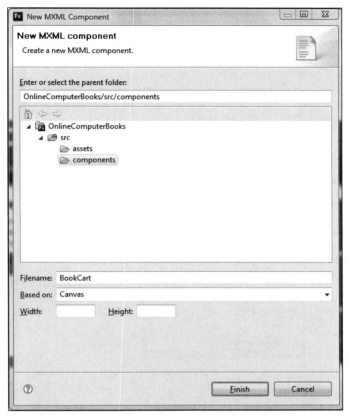

Figure 10-33. Defining the BookCart component in the New MXML Component dialog box

3. Click Finish.

4. Within the Canvas container, add a Panel container. You will give it an id property of cartContainer, a width property of 250, and a layout property of vertical.

```
<?xml version="1.0" encoding="utf-8"?>
<mx:Canvas xmlns:mx="http://www.adobe.com/2006/mxml">
    <mx:Panel id="cartContainer" width="250" layout="vertical">

    </mx:Panel>
</mx:Canvas>
```

You need to set up a temporary holding place that you can use later on to give you a count of the number of items in your cart. Later on in this case study, you will replace this Label with variables provided by ActionScript.

10

5. Add the following Label inside your Panel container:

```
<mx:Panel id="cartContainer" width="250" layout="vertical">
    <mx:Label text="There are 0 items in your cart"/>
</mx:Panel>
```

6. Add a button that will allow users to see the details of the books in their carts. You will use this button to expand the shopping cart in a bit. Add the Button control below the Label you just created:

```
<mx:Panel id="cartContainer" width="250" layout="vertical">
    <mx:Label text="There are 0 items in your cart"/>
    <mx:Button  label="See the cart details"/>
</mx:Panel>
```

7. Finally, give the Panel a title property of Shopping Cart:

```
<mx:Panel id="cartContainer" width="250" ➥
layout="vertical" title="Shopping Cart">
    <mx:Label text="There are 0 items in your cart"/>
    <mx:Button label="See the cart details"/>
</mx:Panel>
```

If you switch to Design View, your screen should look like Figure 10-34.

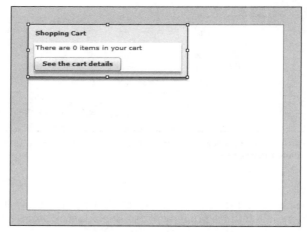

Figure 10-34. The shopping cart panel in the component

8. Save the component and return to the BooksMain file.

You need to put your BookCart component onto your BooksMain page.

9. Under the ViewStack container, place the BookCart. Give it an x property of about 890 and a y property of 200.

10. Give the application a run. It should look something like Figure 10-35. If you want, you can adjust the position of the shopping cart to suit your tastes.

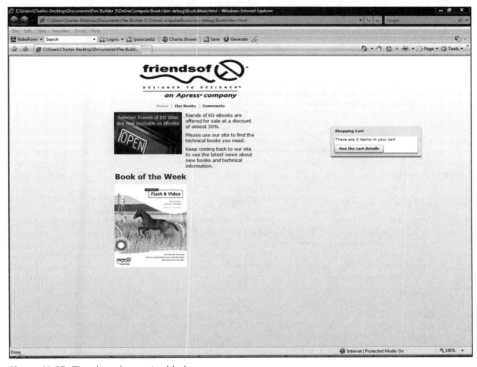

Figure 10-35. The shopping cart added

Now that you have the shopping cart in place, you want to develop a state for it so that it can expand to show details.

11. Return to BookCart.mxml.

12. Go into Source Perspective and add a click event to the Button control. Set the currentState to cartExpand. Don't forget to use single quotes around the name of the state.

```xml
<?xml version="1.0" encoding="utf-8"?>
<mx:Canvas xmlns:mx="http://www.adobe.com/2006/mxml">
    <mx:Panel id="cartContainer" width="250" ➥
layout="vertical" title="Shopping Cart">
        <mx:Label text="There are 0 items in your cart"/>
        <mx:Button label="See the cart details" ➥
click="currentState='cartExpand'"/>
    </mx:Panel>
</mx:Canvas>
```

10

13. Switch to Design Perspective and create a new state by either clicking the New State button or right-clicking in the States window.

14. As you have probably figured out already, you are going to call the state cartExpand, so specify the setting in the New State dialog box as shown in Figure 10-36.

Figure 10-36.
Defining the cartExpand state in the New State dialog box

15. Click OK.

You should see your new state in the States View, as shown in Figure 10-37.

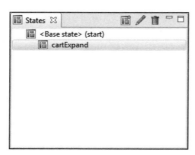

Figure 10-37.
The States panel with the new state

When working with states, while in Design Perspective, it is important that you keep an eye on the States View to know what state you are working in. For the next few steps, make sure that the cartExpand state is selected.

16. Select the Panel container and, using the Flex Properties View, change the height to 500 so that it appears as shown in Figure 10-38.

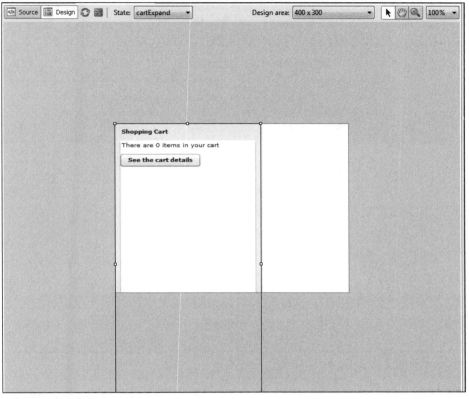

Figure 10-38. The expanded Panel container

The Panel container will look as though it is overflowing the Canvas container. Recall that earlier you didn't give the Canvas a height property value. As a result, it will expand when the Panel container expands.

17. Save the BookCart component and return to the application file. Go ahead and run the application. When you click the button in the cart, you should see it expand as shown in Figure 10-39.

10

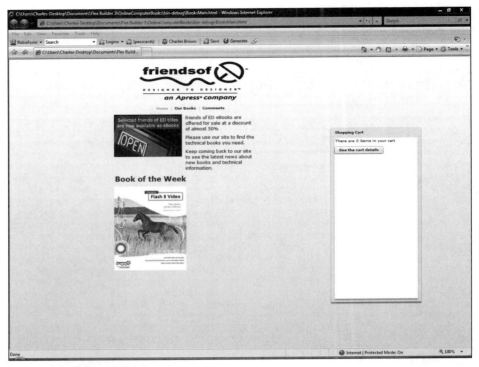

Figure 10-39. The expanded shopping cart

18. Close the browser and switch back to the BookCart component. Make sure you are in the cartExpanded state.

19. In Design Perspective, drag the DataGrid control into the expanded Panel container. Use the graphic handles to adjust the width and height so that it is within the panel and about three-quarters of the height or so. You need to leave enough room to add another button at the bottom of the panel. You may find it helpful to set the Design area control, located above the Design area, to Fit to content, as shown in Figure 10-40.

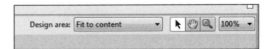

Figure 10-40. The Design area set to Fit to content

If you like to play it by the numbers, the width should be about 230, and the height about 375.

Your component should look something like the one in Figure 10-41.

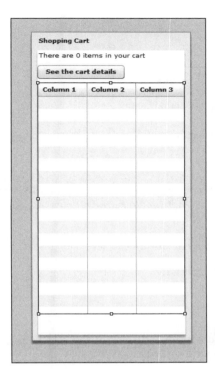

Figure 10-41.
The expanded Panel container with the
DataGrid control added

The button label See the cart details should be changed in the cartExpand state.

20. Click the button and change the `label` property to `Collapse the cart details`.

The On Click event still says currentState='expandCart'. However, you want the button to return the Panel to the collapsed, or base, state. Using empty single quotes ('') accomplishes that. It is important that you do not put a space between the single quotes. If you do, a runtime error will result.

21. Change the On Click event in the Flex Properties View to currentState=''.

22. Save the component, return to the application file, and test the application. The button should expand and contract the Panel with a corresponding change in the button's label.

You need to do one final step in this section. You will add a button at the bottom of the expanded cart with the label Click to Checkout. For the time being, the button will not have any functionality.

23. Close the browser and return to the BookCart component. Make sure you are in the cartExpand state. Add a button at the bottom of the expanded Panel container with a label property of Click to Checkout and an id property of checkout. It should look like Figure 10-42.

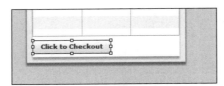

Figure 10-42. The checkout Button control

24. Save the component and test the application. You should see the button you just added when you expand the cart.

> *If the scrollbars activate when you expand the cart, just make a small adjustment to the height and width of the DataGrid control. That should fix the problem quickly.*

You are now through with the BookCart component. So you can save and close it.

We will now do a little cosmetic work to our application.

Using CSS in the project

We will add a couple of simple CSS tags to control the color of the selections in the ComboBox as well as the color of all the text in the application.

1. Right under the Application tag in BooksMain.mxml, enter a Style tag as follows:

```
<?xml version="1.0" encoding="utf-8"?>
<mx:Application xmlns:mx="http://www.adobe.com/2006/mxml" ➥
layout="absolute" backgroundColor="#FFFFFF" ➥
xmlns:comp="components.*" height="100%" width="100%">
<mx:Style>

</mx:Style>
<mx:Image source="assets/Logo1.gif" x="360" y="10"/>
```

Assume that you want the selection in the ComboBox control to be lime-green.

2. Add the following type style to the Style container:

```
<mx:Style>
     ComboBox
     {
          selectionColor: #32CD32;
     }
</mx:Style>
```

3. Save and test the application. Switch to the Our Books page and click a selection in the ComboBox control. It should come up as the color you set.

4. What about if you want to change the color of all the text to dark blue? You can define a global style to set the color. Add the following to the Style container:

```
<mx:Style>
    ComboBox
    {
        selectionColor: #32CD32;
     }

    global
    {
        color:#00008B;
    }
</mx:Style>
```

If you now run the application, all of your fonts should come up with the color specified.

Summary

This completes Part 1 of the case study. In this part, all you did was set up the basic structure. You built the components, added the graphics, assembled the components in the application file, and added some CSS. You also created a state in the BookCart component.

In the next chapter, you will do Part 2 of this case study and make the site a bit more functional by adding ActionScript code.

10

11 CASE STUDY: PART 2

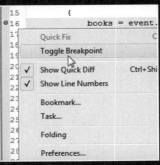

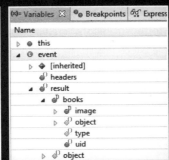

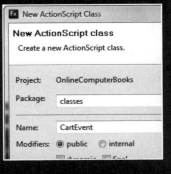

In the last chapter, we put together the structure, or graphic look and feel, of our little fictional book publisher's site. In this chapter, we are going to do some hard-wiring, or programming, to make things a bit more functional. In other words, in Chapter 10 you were a designer; in this chapter, you will be a developer.

In this chapter, I am going to renege on a small promise I made at the beginning of this book: that each chapter would be free-standing and not dependent on the work of previous chapters. However, since this is the second part of the same case study, we will be picking up where the last chapter ends. So, if you have not worked through Chapter 10, please go back and do so now.

One caveat here to readers who may be beginning programmers already:

When the first edition of this book was released, I received a great many e-mails from programmers asking me why I didn't program this way . . . or that way. In any programming scenario, there are often a number of different approaches one can take. In a book such as this, space does not permit me to explore variations. Also, doing that could end up just confusing readers who may be relatively new to programming. So, the code I use here is the code I decided to use, and if you find an alternative way of accomplishing the same tasks, please feel free to explore them.

Like Part 1, I will not be giving you a lot of room to play around, as I have in the other chapters. In a case study such as this, we need to be on the same page programmatically. So please take your time and carefully test everything each step of the way.

Connecting the data source

Let's begin by importing the XML file containing the data for your application.

1. If you have not done so already, download the resource files for this chapter from www.friendsofed.com. In the download, there is a file called books.xml. This is the file you will be importing.

2. Select File ➤ Import ➤ File System.

3. Browse to the location where you downloaded the file to.

4. Select the check box for books.xml.

5. At the Into folder field, browse to select the assets folder under the src folder. Your settings should look like Figure 11-1.

6. Click Finish.

7. Check the Flex Navigator View to make sure the file is in the assets folder, as shown in Figure 11-2.

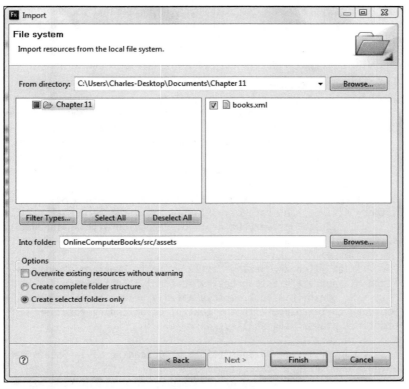

Figure 11-1. The Import dialog box with current settings

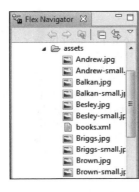

Figure 11-2.
The Flex Navigator View with the books.xml file
in the assets folder

Looking at the assets folder, notice that all of the book cover JPG images have two versions: the regular image, like Andrew.jpg, and the small image, with a -small added to the file name. The latter are thumbnail images.

When you get involved with site design, it is very important that you develop a naming convention for images and to enforce that naming system strictly. Let me show you how this could save you a ton of code and make things a lot more flexible.

8. Open the books.xml file. Let's just look at the first four records here:

```
<?xml version="1.0" encoding="UTF-8"?>
<books>
    <image filename="Andrew" title="Dreamweaver MX 2004 Design ➡
Projects" author="Rachel Andrew" category="Dreamweaver">
        <desc>Dreamweaver MX 2004 Design Projects takes you ➡
through the process of creating four real-world case studies, ➡
enabling you to take your Dreamweaver skills to a new level.</desc>
    </image>
    <image filename="Balkan" title = "Flash 3d Cheats Most Wanted" ➡
author="Aral Balkan" category="Flash">
        <desc>Improve your depth of deception with an innovative ➡
slice engine to create convincing 3D objects</desc>
    </image>
    <image filename="Besley" title = "Learn Programming with ➡
Flash MX" author="Kristian Besley" category="ActionScript">
        <desc>This book employs a truly unique classroom-based ➡
approach to learning, with the goal of establishing core, ➡
practical programming skills.</desc>
    </image>
    <image filename="Briggs" title = "Cascading Style Sheets" ➡
author="Owen Briggs" category="CSS">
        <desc>CSS is one of the trio of core client-side web ➡
professional skills: HTML for markup, JavaScript for ➡
dynamism, and CSS for style.</desc>
    </image>
```

Notice that the root node is books. But below that is a node for each book called image. The image nodes contain an attribute called filename. This attribute contains the actual name, without the extension, of each image file. Let's use the Andrew file now.

When you access these XML records, you will see that it is not that difficult to add fixed text around the name. For instance, you will add **assets/**Andrew-**small.jpg**. What is bolded is added to the original name. Because of this, you have a lot of potential programming flexibility. But, once again, in order for this to work, you must use a consistent naming convention.

Now that you understand the naming convention, the next step is to connect to the XML file from BooksMain.mxml. As you know, BooksMain.mxml is the main application file, and since everything passes through it, you only need to establish the connection once. Once the connection is made, the various components can access it easily.

9. Open the BooksMain.mxml file if it isn't opened already. If necessary, go to Source Perspective.

The placement of the HTTPService tag to connect to the XML file is not critical. For the purposes of this exercise, you will put it right below the Style tag.

10. Create an HTTPService tag below the Style tag. Give it an id property of bookDataIn, and set the url to the books.xml file located in the assets folder.

```
</mx:Style>
<mx:HTTPService id="bookDataIn" url="assets/books.xml"/>
```

In the previous chapters, you put an event called creationComplete into the Application tag, which, when the application completed loading, would instruct the HTTPService, using the send() function, to call the XML file for the data. You could do that here just as easily. However, here you'll try something a little different.

11. In the Application tag, add the creationComplete event, as you have done before. But this time, rather than make the call back to the HTTPService.send(), have it call a function, which you will write shortly, called init().

```
<mx:Application xmlns:mx="http://www.adobe.com/2006/mxml" ➥
layout="absolute" backgroundColor="#FFFFFF" ➥
xmlns:comp="components.*" height="100%" width="100%" ➥
creationComplete="init()">
```

This may seem strange to you, but in reality it is a standard programming practice and an excellent code organizing tool. You always want to keep your code as organized as possible for obvious reasons. Many programmers like to organize their setup code, such as XML calls, variable initializations, calls to other files, and so forth, inside of a single function. Traditionally, that function is called init().

Keeping that in mind, you now need to set up your Script block and create the init() function. Since this function will not return a value to the caller, it will have the return type of void. Again, placement is not critical but, for the purpose of this exercise, set it up under the Application tag and over the Style tag that was created in the last chapter.

12. Set up the following Script block and function:

```
<mx:Script>
    <![CDATA[
        private function init():void
        {

        }
    ]]>
</mx:Script>
```

Of course, as you may have guessed, you will put the HTTPService call, using the send() function, into the newly created init() function.

13. Add the HTTPService call, bookDataIn, to the init() function:

```
<mx:Script>
    <![CDATA[
        private function init():void
```

11

```
                    {
                         bookDataIn.send();
                    }
          ]]>
     </mx:Script>
```

Recall that HTTPService automatically stores the XML data as type ArrayCollection. You will now set up a property to hold that data.

14. Right above the init() function, create a private property called books of type ArrayCollection. Make the property [Bindable].

```
<mx:Script>
     <![CDATA[
          import mx.collections.ArrayCollection;
          [Bindable]
          private  var books:ArrayCollection;
          private function init():void
          {
               bookDataIn.send();
          }
     ]]>
</mx:Script>
```

Flex Builder should have added the import statement at the top of the Script block automatically.

When the HTTPService completes the loading of data, an event called result is broadcast. The resulting event object then carries the XML data to whatever function you call with it.

15. Add the following code to the HTTPService tag:

```
<mx:HTTPService  id="bookDataIn" url="assets/books.xml" ➥
result="bookHandler(event)"/>
```

Next, you will write the bookHandler() function under the init() function you created earlier. It will accept one argument, and that argument will be of the type ResultEvent.

16. Under the init() function, create the private bookHandler() function with a return type of void. When you write the function's parameter, event:ResultEvent(), the import statement should be written automatically.

```
<mx:Script>
     <![CDATA[
          import mx.rpc.events.ResultEvent;
          import mx.collections.ArrayCollection;
          [Bindable]
          private var books:ArrayCollection;
          private function init():void
          {
               bookDataIn.send();
          }
```

```
        private function bookHandler(event:ResultEvent):void
        {

        }
    ]]>
</mx:Script>
```

The ResultEvent object contains a property called result.

> *One of the quirks of ActionScript 3.0 is that sometimes properties, events, and functions could have the same name. As an example,* HTTPService *has an event called* result *that triggers when the XML file loads. In addition, the* ResultEvent *class carries the XML data in a property also called* result. *This could sometimes cause confusion. However, usage will often clarify which name is which.*

The result property contains the XML data. You will drill down to the image node, under the books node, and save that data to the books property we created earlier.

17. Set the books property in the bookHandler() function as follows:

```
private function bookHandler(event:ResultEvent):void
{
        books = event.result.books.image;
}
```

Just to recap a bit, the HTTPService creates the connection to the books.xml file. When the creationComplete event happens, the init() function is called. The init() function has code that makes the HTTPService, bookDataIn, call the XML file and get the data. Once the data is fully loaded, the result event, a ResultEvent object, is generated. The ResultEvent object is sent to the bookHandler() function, which in turn saves the image data (carried in the result property) to the property books, which is of type ArrayCollection.

Your code up to this point should look as follows:

```
<?xml version="1.0" encoding="utf-8"?>
<mx:Application xmlns:mx="http://www.adobe.com/2006/mxml" ➥
layout="absolute" backgroundColor="#FFFFFF" ➥
xmlns:comp="components.*" height="100%" width="100%" ➥
creationComplete="init()">
<mx:Script>
    <![CDATA[
        import mx.rpc.events.ResultEvent;
        import mx.collections.ArrayCollection;
        [Bindable]
        private var books:ArrayCollection;
        private function init():void
        {
```

11

```
                              bookDataIn.send();
                    }

                    private function bookHandler(event:ResultEvent):void
                    {
                              books = event.result.books.image;
                    }
              ]]>
        </mx:Script>
        <mx:Style>
              ComboBox
              {
                    selectionColor: #32CD32;
              }

              global
              {
                    color:#00008B;
              }
        </mx:Style>
        <mx:HTTPService id="bookDataIn" url="assets/books.xml" ➡
result="bookHandler(event)"/>
              <mx:Image source="assets/Logo1.gif" x="360" y="10"/>
              <mx:LinkBar dataProvider="bookPages" x="400" y="130"/>
              <mx:ViewStack id="bookPages" resizeToContent="true" ➡
x="290" y="160">
                    <comp:BookHome height="50%" width="50%" ➡
label="Home" id="home"/>
                    <comp:BookCovers height="50%" width="50%" ➡
label="Our Books" id="bookCovers"/>
                    <comp:Comments height="50%" width="50%" ➡
label="Comments" id="comments"/>
              </mx:ViewStack>
              <comp:BookCart x="890" y="200"/>
        </mx:Application>
```

It is probably a good idea to test the connection now to make sure everything is talking properly.

Testing your code

If you run the application and don't get an error, there is a reasonable chance everything is working fine. However, that is far from a reliable test. We will now tap into some of the powerful debugging features of Flex Builder.

Find the line of code, inside the bookHandler() function, that assigns the result of the XML call to the books property.

1. Right-click the line number and select Toggle Breakpoint. A small dot should appear to the left of the line number, as shown in Figure 11-3.

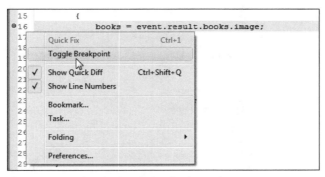

Figure 11-3. Setting the Toggle Breakpoint option

In the upper-right corner of Flex Builder, you should see a small button to the left of the Flex Developer indicator. When you click this button, you can switch between the Developer and Debugging Perspectives, as shown in Figure 11-4.

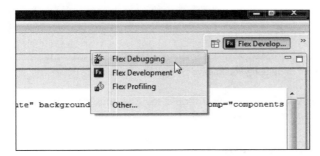

Figure 11-4. Switching to the Flex Debugging Perspective

2. Click the Flex Debugging Perspective option. Flex Builder should now look like Figure 11-5.

As mentioned previously, "Perspective" is a term Eclipse uses to define the arrangement of views that are open.

3. Click the Debug BooksMain button instead of the Run Application button. This button is just to the right of the Run Application button on the main toolbar.

Your web browser will open up. However, depending on the browser, the application may not appear. Don't worry, this is not important. The information that we want to look at is back in Flex.

4. Switch back to Flex Builder.

11

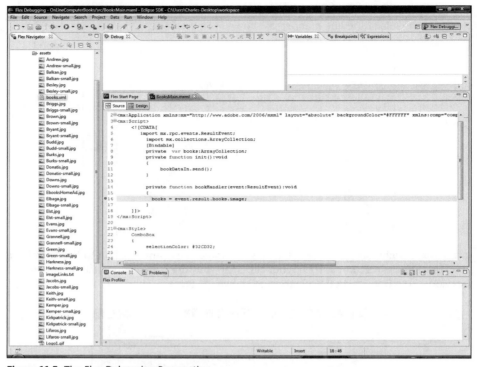

Figure 11-5. The Flex Debugging Perspective

If you look at the Variables View, you should see two lines in it. The first says this, and second says event, as shown in Figure 11-6.

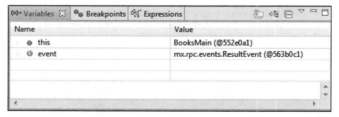

Figure 11-6. The current Variables View

5. To make things a little easier to work with, maximize the Variables View by double-clicking the tab of the View.

6. Since the XML data was carried to the bookHandler() function where you have the breakpoint set with an event, roll over the word event and twirl the arrow down (see Figure 11-7).

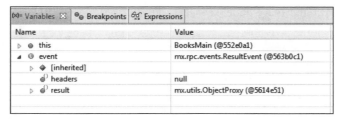

Figure 11-7. The event objects

You should see the result event that was triggered by the HTTPService, as we discussed earlier.

7. Twirl down the result event (see Figure 11-8).

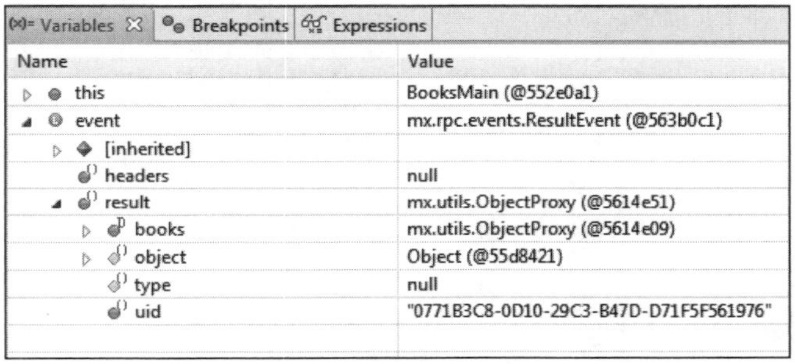

Figure 11-8. Twirling down the result event

When you twirl down the result event, you should see the books node of the XML data. From here on in we can drill down the XML file.

8. Twirl down the books node. You should now see the image node, as shown in Figure 11-9.

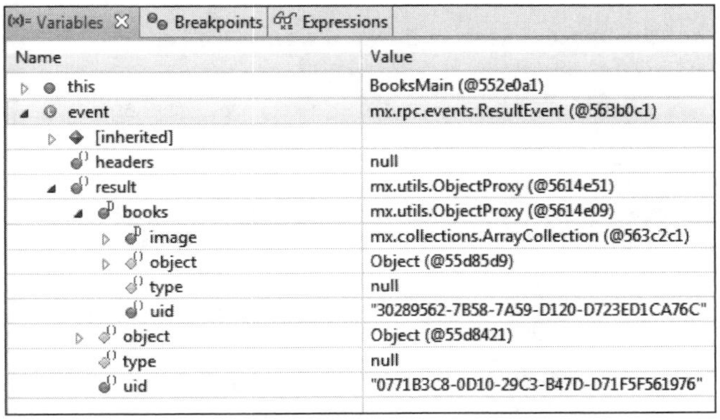

Figure 11-9. The image node

11

9. Twirl down the `image` node (see Figure 11-10).

Name	Value
(x)= Variables ⊠ ●● Breakpoints ⚷ Expressions	
headers	null
▲ result	mx.utils.ObjectProxy (@915f8b1)
▲ books	mx.utils.ObjectProxy (@916a8f9)
▲ image	mx.collections.ArrayCollection (@9201e01)
▷ ◆ [inherited]	
▷ ● [0]	mx.utils.ObjectProxy (@916aaf1)
▷ ● [1]	mx.utils.ObjectProxy (@916a8b1)
▷ ● [2]	mx.utils.ObjectProxy (@916a821)
▷ ● [3]	mx.utils.ObjectProxy (@916a7d9)
▷ ● [4]	mx.utils.ObjectProxy (@916a989)
▷ ● [5]	mx.utils.ObjectProxy (@916afb9)
▷ ● [6]	mx.utils.ObjectProxy (@916a791)
▷ ● [7]	mx.utils.ObjectProxy (@916ab81)
▷ ● [8]	mx.utils.ObjectProxy (@916aa61)
▷ ● [9]	mx.utils.ObjectProxy (@916a749)
▷ ● [10]	mx.utils.ObjectProxy (@916adc1)
▷ ● [11]	mx.utils.ObjectProxy (@916ae99)
▷ ● [12]	mx.utils.ObjectProxy (@915f701)
▷ ● [13]	mx.utils.ObjectProxy (@915f671)
▷ ● [14]	mx.utils.ObjectProxy (@915f0d1)
▷ ● [15]	mx.utils.ObjectProxy (@915f161)
▷ ● [16]	mx.utils.ObjectProxy (@915f1f1)
▷ ● [17]	mx.utils.ObjectProxy (@916a9d1)
▷ ● [18]	mx.utils.ObjectProxy (@915f749)
▷ ● [19]	mx.utils.ObjectProxy (@915f281)
▷ ● [20]	mx.utils.ObjectProxy (@915f2c9)
▷ ● [21]	mx.utils.ObjectProxy (@915f311)
▷ ● [22]	mx.utils.ObjectProxy (@915f359)
▷ ● [23]	mx.utils.ObjectProxy (@915f3a1)
▷ source	Array (@91a7511)
▷ object	Object (@91b8f61)

Figure 11-10. The image objects

Each of the 24 repeating nodes of the XML file is a separate object in an `ArrayCollection`. Like all arrays, it begins with the index of 0.

10. Pick any of the image objects and twirl it down (see Figure 11-11).

Name	Value
▲ result	mx.utils.ObjectProxy (@5614e51)
▲ books	mx.utils.ObjectProxy (@5614e09)
▲ image	mx.collections.ArrayCollection (@563c2c1)
▷ ◆ [inherited]	
▷ ● [0]	mx.utils.ObjectProxy (@5614dc1)
▲ ● [1]	mx.utils.ObjectProxy (@5614d79)
author	"Aral Balkan"
category	"Flash"
desc	"Improve your depth of deception with an i...
filename	"Balkan"
▷ object	Object (@55d8ee9)
title	"Flash 3d Cheats Most Wanted"
type	null
uid	"08AF4248-A6A8-8066-7471-D72D354CD4EC"

Figure 11-11. The details of the data

You should see the attributes and data associated with that record. As long as you are see-ing this data, you know the connection is working, and you are now ready to move forward.

11. Double-click the Variables View tab to return it to its normal size.

12. Click the red square in the Debug View to stop debugging. The browser should close. However, if it doesn't, just close it yourself.

13. Switch back to Flex Development Perspective using the same button you used earlier.

14. Right-click the toggle breakpoint and click it off.

Everything should be back to where it was before. Let's do the next step.

Handling the book cover images

If you completed the last chapter, you should have a component named BookCovers.mxml located in the components folder.

Your code, as of now, should look as follows:

```xml
<?xml version="1.0" encoding="utf-8"?>
<mx:VBox xmlns:mx="http://www.adobe.com/2006/mxml" width="550">
    <mx:HBox backgroundColor="#EE82EE" verticalAlign="middle" ➥
fontSize="12">
        <mx:Label text="Select the Books"/>
        <mx:CheckBox label="All Books"/>
        <mx:Label text="Select Book Category"/>
        <mx:ComboBox>
            <mx:dataProvider>
                <mx:ArrayCollection>
                    <mx:String>Dreamweaver</mx:String>
                    <mx:String>Flash</mx:String>
                    <mx:String>Graphics</mx:String>
                    <mx:String>Web Design</mx:String>
                    <mx:String>Other</mx:String>
                </mx:ArrayCollection>
            </mx:dataProvider>

        </mx:ComboBox>
    </mx:HBox>
    <mx:Tile>
        <mx:Image source="assets/Andrew-small.jpg" ➥
click="currentState='BookDetails'" />
        <mx:Image source="assets/Balkan-small.jpg" ➥
click="currentState='BookDetails'" />
        <mx:Image source="assets/Besley-small.jpg" ➥
click="currentState='BookDetails'" />
```

11

```
                <mx:Image source="assets/Briggs-small.jpg" ➥
        click="currentState='BookDetails'" />
                <mx:Image source="assets/Brown-small.jpg" ➥
        click="currentState='BookDetails'" />
                <mx:Image source="assets/Bryant-small.jpg" ➥
        click="currentState='BookDetails'" />
                <mx:Image source="assets/Budd-small.jpg" ➥
        click="currentState='BookDetails'" />
                <mx:Image source="assets/Burks-small.jpg" ➥
        click="currentState='BookDetails'" />
                <mx:Image source="assets/Donatis-small.jpg" ➥
        click="currentState='BookDetails'" />
                <mx:Image source="assets/Downs-small.jpg" ➥
        click="currentState='BookDetails'" />
                <mx:Image source="assets/Elbaga-small.jpg" ➥
        click="currentState='BookDetails'" />
                <mx:Image source="assets/Elst-small.jpg" ➥
        click="currentState='BookDetails'" />
                <mx:Image source="assets/Evans-small.jpg" ➥
        click="currentState='BookDetails'" />
                <mx:Image source="assets/Grannell-small.jpg" ➥
        click="currentState='BookDetails'" />
                <mx:Image source="assets/Green-small.jpg" ➥
        click="currentState='BookDetails'" />
                <mx:Image source="assets/Harkness-small.jpg" ➥
        click="currentState='BookDetails'" />
                <mx:Image source="assets/Jacobs-small.jpg" ➥
        click="currentState='BookDetails'" />
                <mx:Image source="assets/Keith-small.jpg" ➥
        click="currentState='BookDetails'" />
                <mx:Image source="assets/Kirkpatrick-small.jpg" ➥
        click="currentState='BookDetails'" />
                <mx:Image source="assets/Lifaros-small.jpg" ➥
        click="currentState='BookDetails'" />

            </mx:Tile>
        </mx:VBox>
```

1. Run the BooksMain application and click the Our Books link. You will see the results of the component, as illustrated in Figure 11-12.

As you can see, all of these book cover images are hard-wired into the component. While this certainly works, it does not allow for changes to be made easily.

What you want to do here is populate the images programmatically so that if there are changes, you don't need to go into the code and make changes. Instead, you can make the code handle changes automatically.

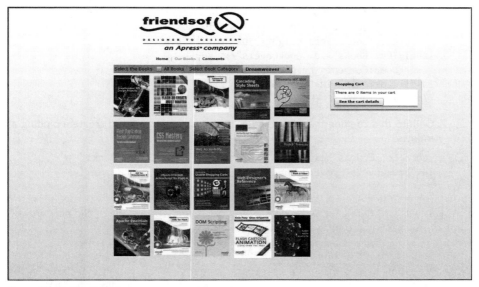

Figure 11-12. The BookCovers component

2. Close the browser and go back to the BookCovers component.

3. Delete all of the Image tags between the opening and closing Tile tags.

You are going to need to pass the ArrayCollection, books, into this component because the data contains the name of the image file (or at least part of the name as you saw earlier).

4. At the top of the BookCovers component, right underneath the opening VBox tag, create a Script block.

5. Within the block, declare a public property called coverData of type ArrayCollection. Make the property [Bindable].

```
<mx:Script>
    <![CDATA[
        import mx.collections.ArrayCollection;
        [Bindable]
        public var coverData:ArrayCollection;
    ]]>
</mx:Script>
```

Notice that Flex Builder automatically added the import statement.

You now need to get your data from the books variable in BooksMain.

6. Save the BookCovers component, switch back to BooksMain, and scroll down to the three components in the viewStack container. You should see the BookCovers component there.

```
<mx:ViewStack id="bookPages" resizeToContent="true" x="290" y="160">
    <comp:BookHome height="50%" width="50%" label="Home" id="home"/>
    <comp:BookCovers height="50%" width="50%" ➡
label="Our Books" id="bookCovers"/>
    <comp:Comments height="50%" width="50%" ➡
label="Comments" id="comments"/>
</mx:ViewStack>
```

7. Go into that the line that calls the BookCovers component and create a binding as follows:

```
<comp:BookCovers height="50%" width="50%" label="Our Books" ➡
id="bookCovers" coverData="{books}"/>
```

> As you begin to type coverData, *you should see it come up as one of the properties for the* BookCovers *component.*

What this simply says is make the coverData property, which you just declared in the BookCovers component, equal to the books property in the application file. That is why both properties are of type ArrayCollection.

You are now going to take the concept of specialized components one step further by creating a component to hold the cover image and then having the component repeat in the BookCovers component by using the Repeater component.

The CoverDetails component

To create the CoverDetails component, follow these steps:

1. Right-click the components folder in the Flex Navigator View and select New ➤ MXML Component.

2. Call the component CoverDetails and base it on the Image container, as shown in Figure 11-13.

Notice that the Image container does not have height and width properties.

3. Click Finish. Your code should look as follows:

```
<?xml version="1.0" encoding="utf-8"?>
<mx:Image xmlns:mx="http://www.adobe.com/2006/mxml">

</mx:Image>
```

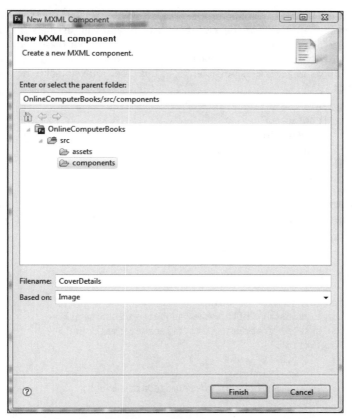

Figure 11-13. The New Component dialog box when creating the CoverDetails component

The next few steps will allow the application to populate the gallery of book covers programmatically, rather than having them hard-coded in as before. That way, it will be easily updatable. Please take it slowly and follow the steps carefully.

4. Create a Script block under the opening Image tag:

```
<?xml version="1.0" encoding="utf-8"?>
<mx:Image xmlns:mx="http://www.adobe.com/2006/mxml">
    <mx:Script>
        <![CDATA[

        ]]>
    </mx:Script>
</mx:Image>
```

11

5. Create a [Bindable] public property called coverImageData. In this case, you will not pass the data from the XML file. Instead, you will just pass it the string file name, which contains the name of the image file. For that reason, you could make this either type String or type Object. A rule of object-oriented programming is to keep things as generic as possible. So, in this case, you will make the property type Object.

```
<mx:Script>
    <![CDATA[
        [Bindable]
        public var coverImageData:Object;
    ]]>
</mx:Script>
```

6. You now need to set the source of the Image tag to call the assets folder, add the filename property of the XML file, and then add -small.jpg as follows:

```
<mx:Image xmlns:mx="http://www.adobe.com/2006/mxml" ➥
source="assets/{coverImageData.filename}-small.jpg">
```

Your finished code should look as follows:

```
<?xml version="1.0" encoding="utf-8"?>
<mx:Image xmlns:mx="http://www.adobe.com/2006/mxml" ➥
source="assets/{coverImageData.filename}-small.jpg">
    <mx:Script>
        <![CDATA[
            [Bindable]
            public var coverImageData:Object;
        ]]>
    </mx:Script>
</mx:Image>
```

7. Save this component and return to the BookCovers component.

Before you can use the CoverDetails component, you will need to define the namespace, as we have done before. Only this time, rather than put it into an Application tag, you are going to put it in the opening VBox tag. You can define a namespace within nearly any container.

8. Define the namespace as follows:

```
<mx:VBox xmlns:mx="http://www.adobe.com/2006/mxml" ➥
width="550" xmlns:comp="components.*">
```

9. Scroll down to the Tile container.

10. In between the Tile container tags, add a Repeater container. You will give it an ID of displayCovers and make the dataProvider property the coverData variable you defined in the Script block.

```
<mx:Tile>
    <mx:Repeater id="displayCovers" dataProvider="{coverData}">

    </mx:Repeater>
```

By doing this, you ensure that the Repeater component will repeat for as many items as there are in the XML file.

11. Within the Repeater component, call the CoverDetails component and pass it the currentItem of the Repeater component to display the correct image.

```
<mx:Tile>
    <mx:Repeater id="displayCovers" dataProvider="{coverData}">
        <comp:CoverDetails coverImageData=➥
"{displayCovers.currentItem}"/>
    </mx:Repeater>
</mx:Tile>
```

The code for your finished BookCovers component should look as follows:

```
<?xml version="1.0" encoding="utf-8"?>
<mx:VBox xmlns:mx="http://www.adobe.com/2006/mxml" ➥
width="550" xmlns:comp="components.*">
<mx:Script>
    <![CDATA[
        import mx.collections.ArrayCollection;
        [Bindable]
        public var coverData:ArrayCollection;
    ]]>
</mx:Script>
    <mx:HBox backgroundColor="#EE82EE" verticalAlign="middle" ➥
fontSize="12">
        <mx:Label text="Select the Books"/>
        <mx:CheckBox label="All Books"/>
        <mx:Label text="Select Book Category"/>
        <mx:ComboBox>
            <mx:dataProvider>
                <mx:ArrayCollection>
                    <mx:String>Dreamweaver</mx:String>
                    <mx:String>Flash</mx:String>
                    <mx:String>Graphics</mx:String>
                    <mx:String>Web Design</mx:String>
                    <mx:String>Other</mx:String>
                </mx:ArrayCollection>
            </mx:dataProvider>

        </mx:ComboBox>
    </mx:HBox>
    <mx:Tile>
        <mx:Repeater id="displayCovers" dataProvider="{coverData}">
```

11

```
                        <comp:CoverDetails coverImageData=➥
            "{displayCovers.currentItem}"/>
                    </mx:Repeater>
                </mx:Tile>
            </mx:VBox>
```

> There will be a state called CoverDetails later on. Don't worry, the Flex workspace will prevent any name conflicts.

12. Save everything, return to BooksMain, and click the Our Books link. You should see the book covers displayed close to how they appeared before (see Figure 11-14).

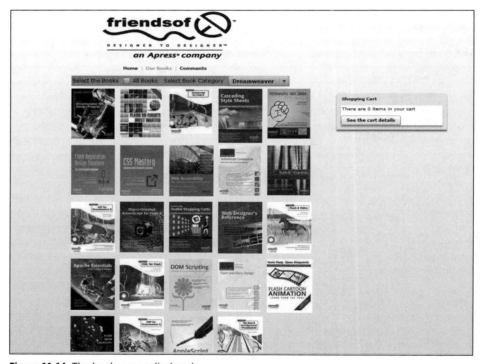

Figure 11-14. The book covers displayed

It is not a bad idea to give the Tile container a defined width. The reason for this is that as more books are added, the Tile container could readjust its width automatically to accommodate them. This could cause your book cover images to overflow into the shopping cart.

13. Close the browser, return to the BookCovers component, and change the width of the Tile container to 550.

```
<mx:Tile width="550">
    <mx:Repeater id="displayCovers" dataProvider="{coverData}">
        <comp:CoverDetails coverImageData=CCC
"{displayCovers.currentItem}"/>
    </mx:Repeater>
</mx:Tile>
```

14. Rerun the application. The width should be about the same as before (see Figure 11-15).

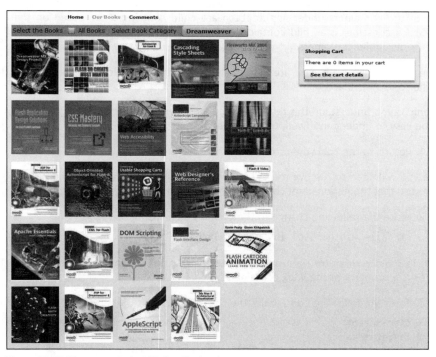

Figure 11-15. The corrected width for the book covers

You can now change your covers programmatically. As you can see, the more you break things down to individual components, the easier it will be to manage things. This will become obvious as you progress through the rest of the case study. But, for now, just understand the basic idea is to give you more flexibility. Remember, it is better to divide and conquer: break your project up into many smaller, more specialized components rather than have a few components that do a lot of work.

Hopefully, you saw the importance of having proper naming conventions for the images. If done properly, the system is almost self-running. All you need to do is place the properly named image into the assets folder and add the appropriate information to the data source.

You are now going to make it possible to click an image and see the larger version of it.

407

Changing states

As you have seen already, there are two versions of each of the cover images: the thumbnails, which you just worked with and which have the designation -small, and a larger version. What you want to do here is add the ability to click a thumbnail, close the gallery, and have the larger image appear in its place with an accompanying description. Then, once you are finished, you want to be able to return to the gallery.

As I have repeatedly said throughout this book, everything in Flex is a container held in another container. The entire application is held in one huge container called Application. Each of the containers under Application are child containers. So, based on that, the ViewStack container is a child container of Application. A child container can, in turn, have its own child containers.

When you change state, you are essentially removing one child container and putting another one in its place.

As long as you understand this relatively simple concept, the code you are about to write will be easy to understand (well, relatively easy).

1. Return to the BookCovers component.

Since you will need to remove the Tile container programmatically, you will need to give it an id so that the ActionScript code can reference it. In this case, call it coverThumbnails.

2. Make the following change to the opening Tile container:

```
<mx:Tile width="550" id="coverThumbnails">
```

Begin to build your states right under the Script block by creating an <mx:states> tag. states is a property of the VBox container.

3. Enter the following code under the Script block:

```
</mx:Script>
<mx:states>

</mx:states>
```

You must call a new State class for each state you need.

4. Enter an opening and closing State tag with the name property of coverDetails.

```
<mx:states>
    <mx:State name="coverDetails">

    </mx:State>
</mx:states>
```

The first thing you want this state to do is to remove the Tile container, which you just named coverThumbnails. To do this, you use the RemoveChild tag. The container you want to remove is the target.

5. Within the State container, remove the child coverThumbnails as follows:

```
<mx:states>
    <mx:State name="coverDetails">
        <mx:RemoveChild target="{coverThumbnails}"/>
    </mx:State>
</mx:states>
```

6. The next thing you want to do is add a new child in the same position where the Tile container was located. The lastChild position ensures that the new child is located after any other containers that may exist.

```
<mx:states>
    <mx:State name="coverDetails">
        <mx:RemoveChild target="{coverThumbnails}"/>
        <mx:AddChild position="lastChild">

        </mx:AddChild>
    </mx:State>
</mx:states>
```

You will need to make some positional adjustments later on once you have the state working and see where everything is positioned.

Next, you need to build a container to hold the image. You can use the Canvas container for this.

7. Add the Canvas container to the AddChild container as follows:

```
<mx:states>
    <mx:State name="coverDetails">
        <mx:RemoveChild target="{coverThumbnails}"/>
        <mx:AddChild position="lastChild">
            <mx:Canvas>

            </mx:Canvas>
        </mx:AddChild>
    </mx:State>
</mx:states>
```

You now need to start the coding process to make the image swapping possible. Again, please follow the steps carefully. Do not rush through this part.

8. Go down to the tag that calls the CoverDetails component.

9. Add a click event that will call a function named displayBookDetails(), to which you will pass event.currentTarget.getRepeaterItem().

```
<comp:CoverDetails coverImageData="{displayCovers.currentItem}"
click="displayBookDetails(event.currentTarget.getRepeaterItem())"/>
```

Your next step is, as you may have guessed already, to create the function displayBookDetails().

10. Return to the Script block and create the displayBookDetails() function. Have it accept the event object (of type Object). The return type is void.

```
<mx:Script>
    <![CDATA[
        import mx.collections.ArrayCollection;
        [Bindable]
        public var coverData:ArrayCollection;

        private function displayBookDetails(event:Object):void
        {

        }
    ]]>
</mx:Script>
```

11. Inside of the new function, you will use the currentState property to call the state you just created. Unlike when you used it in MXML code, earlier in this book, you can use standard double quotes here, because you are not putting it within a larger string.

```
private function displayBookDetails(event:Object):void
{
    currentState = "coverDetails";
}
```

This would be a good place to do a quick test.

12. Run the application and click the Our Books link.

13. When you get to the gallery of book covers, click one of them. If they all disappear, as shown in Figure 11-16, you are actually in good shape. It means the state is being called properly from the click event in the coverDetails component.

Figure 11-16. The empty new state

14. Close the browser and return to the function you were working on in the BookCovers component.

You now need to populate the new state with the desired cover image.

15. Return to the Canvas container, within the AddChild container, and add an Image tag. Give the Image tag an `id` property of coverState.

```
<mx:AddChild position="lastChild">
    <mx:Canvas>
        <mx:Image id="coverState"/>
    </mx:Canvas>
</mx:AddChild>
```

The Image class has a function called load(). The load() function calls the URL of a graphic you want to display, including another SWF file. In this case, you are going to use the load() function to send the correct image to the Image tag, coverState, that you just created within the state. But, at this point, you may be asking where it will get the correct image name from.

Recall from our earlier discussion that the displayBookDetails() function accepts the event object in its parameters. That event object contains all of the XML data associated with the current Repeater item. So it is just a matter of calling that event and then asking for the filename attribute, which is located in the XML file.

16. Return to the displayBookDetails() function and add the following line of code. Notice that you are using the same concatenation technique used for the gallery of book covers. This time, however, you are not going to use the thumbnails (-small). You are going to use the larger images.

```
private function displayBookDetails(event:Object):void
{
    currentState = "coverDetails";
    coverState.load("assets/" + event.filename + ".jpg");
}
```

17. Save your code and rerun the application. Like before, click the Our Books link to get the gallery of book covers. When you click one of the covers, the gallery should go away, and the larger book cover image should be displayed (see Figure 11-17).

Figure 11-17. The new state displaying the book cover

> To minimize the amount of code you need to enter for this exercise, I decided not to have you use a transition effect. However, if you are feeling brave, please feel free to apply one if you would like.

You now need a way to return to the gallery from the larger image. All you really need to do is return to the base state. Recall that the currentState property uses an empty string to return to the base state.

18. Return to the Image tag you created, within the state, and create a button below it. Give it a currentState with an empty string to return back to the base state. Remember, since you are working in MXML here, you need to use single quotes.

```
<mx:states>
    <mx:State name="coverDetails">
        <mx:RemoveChild target="{coverThumbnails}"/>
        <mx:AddChild position="lastChild">
            <mx:Canvas>
                <mx:Image id="coverState"/>
                <mx:Button label="Return to Book Covers" ➥
click="currentState=''" y="300"/>
            </mx:Canvas>
        </mx:AddChild>
    </mx:State>
</mx:states>
```

19. Run the application. You should see the new button when you go to the full cover (see Figure 11-18). When you click the button, it should return you to the gallery.

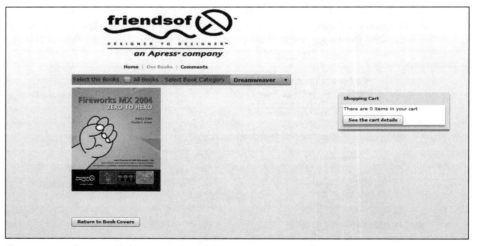

Figure 11-18. The placement of the button to return to the book covers gallery

Now that the programming work is all set up, you can easily add the additional information, such as author and description. Remember, all of the information is held inside of the event object already. Because of that, there are several ways you can code this. I am going to be a little inconsistent in my techniques here in order to illustrate the possibilities. However, all of the techniques will get you to the same place.

In the first example, you are going to add an author name to the description. As I said, my main purpose here is to illustrate technical possibilities and not necessarily ideal or consistent programming. However, this first technique will help prepare for the next section of this case study: working on the shopping cart.

20. Right above the displayBookDetails() function, create a [Bindable] public property called selectedCover of type Object.

21. Inside the displayBookDetails() function, make the selectedCover property equal to event.

```
[Bindable]
public var selectedCover:Object;

private function displayBookDetails(event:Object):void
{
    currentState = "coverDetails";
    coverState.load("assets/" + event.filename + ".jpg");
    selectedCover = event;
}
```

This has the advantage of making the event properties outside of the function accessible and a lot more. Anything that needs to access the event, like the Image tag we created before, can now access the selectedCover property. Let's see an example.

22. Return to the Canvas container. Under the Image tag, create a Text tag with the following text property binding:

```
<mx:Canvas>
    <mx:Image id="coverState"/>
    <mx:Text y="250" text="{selectedCover.author}"/>
    <mx:Button label="Return to Book Covers" ➡
click="currentState=''" y="300"/>
</mx:Canvas>
```

23. Run the application and test the Text control you just created. Your results should be similar to what you see in Figure 11-19.

11

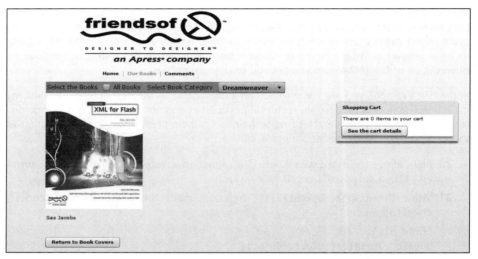

Figure 11-19. The author's name added

24. Make the author name a little more pronounced by specifying a fontSize of 18 and a fontWeight of bold. Figure 11-20 illustrates the results.

```
<mx:Text y="250" text="{selectedCover.author}" ➥
fontSize="18" fontWeight="bold"/>
```

Figure 11-20.
Changing the font size and weight

For the description, which is the attribute desc in the XML file, you can reference selectedCover exactly the same way.

25. Add another Text control in the Canvas container as follows, and also change the y property of the button to 400:

```
<mx:Canvas>
    <mx:Image id="coverState"/>
    <mx:Text y="250" text="{selectedCover.author}" ➥
fontSize="18" fontWeight="bold"/>
    <mx:Text y="300" text="{selectedCover.desc}" ➥
fontSize="14" width="400"/>
    <mx:Button label="Return to Book Covers" click=➥
"currentState=''" y="400"/>
</mx:Canvas>
```

26. Give the application a run. You should see the added book description, as shown in Figure 11-21.

Figure 11-21. The description added

> *You may notice that some of the author names appear to be cut off on top by the book cover image. This is due to a discrepancy in the sizes of the image. You can correct this a bit by returning to the* BookCovers *component, going to Design Perspective, switching to the* coverDetails *state, and making a small adjustment for the placement of the author name and description fields.*

The complete code in BookCovers.mxml should now look as follows:

```
<?xml version="1.0" encoding="utf-8"?>
<mx:VBox xmlns:mx="http://www.adobe.com/2006/mxml" width="550" ➥
xmlns:comp="components.*">
<mx:Script>
```

```
            <![CDATA[
                import mx.collections.ArrayCollection;
                [Bindable]
                public var coverData:ArrayCollection;

                [Bindable]
                public var selectedCover:Object;

                private function displayBookDetails(event:Object):void
                {
                    currentState = "coverDetails";
                    coverState.load("assets/" + event.filename + ".jpg");
                    selectedCover = event;
                }
            ]]>
        </mx:Script>
        <mx:states>
            <mx:State name="coverDetails">
                <mx:RemoveChild target="{coverThumbnails}"/>
                <mx:AddChild position="lastChild">
                    <mx:Canvas>
                        <mx:Image id="coverState"/>
                        <mx:Text y="250" text="{selectedCover.author}" ➥
fontSize="18" fontWeight="bold"/>
                        <mx:Text y="300" text="{selectedCover.desc}" ➥
fontSize="14" width="400"/>
                        <mx:Button label="Return to Book Covers" ➥
click="currentState=''" y="400"/>
                    </mx:Canvas>
                </mx:AddChild>
            </mx:State>
        </mx:states>
        <mx:HBox backgroundColor="#EE82EE" ➥
verticalAlign="middle" fontSize="12">
            <mx:Label text="Select the Books"/>
            <mx:CheckBox label="All Books"/>
            <mx:Label text="Select Book Category"/>
            <mx:ComboBox>
                <mx:dataProvider>
                    <mx:ArrayCollection>
                        <mx:String>Dreamweaver</mx:String>
                        <mx:String>Flash</mx:String>
                        <mx:String>Graphics</mx:String>
                        <mx:String>Web Design</mx:String>
                        <mx:String>Other</mx:String>
                    </mx:ArrayCollection>
                </mx:dataProvider>
            </mx:ComboBox>
        </mx:HBox>
```

```
        <mx:Tile width="550" id="coverThumbnails">
            <mx:Repeater id="displayCovers" dataProvider="{coverData}">
                <comp:CoverDetails coverImageData=➥
"{displayCovers.currentItem}" click="displayBookDetails➥
(event.currentTarget.getRepeaterItem())"/>
            </mx:Repeater>
        </mx:Tile>
    </mx:VBox>
```

By this point, your wow factor should be through the roof. However, you have a bit more to do yet. You will next get the shopping cart up and working for the most part.

Adding functionality to the shopping cart

Of course, the publisher hopes users will buy the books they see on the site you are building, and in vast quantities. You built the shopping cart component, BookCart, in the last chapter. Take a quick review of the code:

```
<?xml version="1.0" encoding="utf-8"?>
<mx:Canvas xmlns:mx="http://www.adobe.com/2006/mxml">
    <mx:states>
        <mx:State name="cartExpand">
            <mx:SetProperty target="{cartContainer}" ➥
name="height" value="500"/>
            <mx:AddChild relativeTo="{cartContainer}" ➥
position="lastChild">
                <mx:DataGrid width="230" height="375">
                    <mx:columns>
                        <mx:DataGridColumn ➥
headerText="Column 1" dataField="col1"/>
                        <mx:DataGridColumn ➥
headerText="Column 2" dataField="col2"/>
                        <mx:DataGridColumn ➥
headerText="Column 3" dataField="col3"/>
                    </mx:columns>
                </mx:DataGrid>
            </mx:AddChild>
            <mx:SetProperty target="{button1}" ➥
name="label" value="Collapse cart details"/>
            <mx:SetEventHandler target="{button1}" ➥
name="click" handler="currentState=''"/>
            <mx:AddChild relativeTo="{cartContainer}" ➥
position="lastChild">
                <mx:Button label="Click to Checkout" ➥
id="checkout"/>
            </mx:AddChild>
        </mx:State>
    </mx:states>
```

11

```
                    <mx:Panel id="cartContainer" width="250" ➥
          layout="vertical" title="Shopping Cart">
                    <mx:Label text="There are 0 items in your cart"/>
                    <mx:Button label="See the cart details" ➥
          click="currentState='cartExpand'" id="button1"/>
              </mx:Panel>
          </mx:Canvas>
```

At present, the DataGrid control has three columns. For the purpose of this exercise, you only need one column.

1. Delete the last two of the DataGridColumn controls.

2. Change the headerText property of the remaining DataGridColumn to Purchased Books and make the width 230:

```
<mx:DataGrid width="230" height="375">
    <mx:columns>
        <mx:DataGridColumn headerText="Purchased Books" ➥
dataField="col1"/>
    </mx:columns>
</mx:DataGrid>
```

Your revised DataGrid should resemble the one in Figure 11-22.

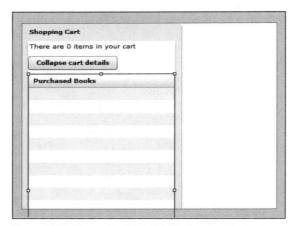

Figure 11-22. The revised DataGrid in the shopping cart

Up to this point, you have been working with classes already created in ActionScript. Classes are the basic unit of OOP. Many programmers would advocate putting nearly no code into the MXML file, instead putting it all into class files. This author is among those advocates. Demonstrations have shown that the resulting file sizes are considerably smaller and less resource intensive.

Early in this book, we discussed custom events. In order to control the shopping cart, we are going to return to that subject. Only this time, rather than use MXML, we will employ ActionScript classes.

If the term "custom event" still sounds strange to you, let me explain. In most instances, you have seen events such as click and creationComplete. The names of these events make sense to you. When either of these events happens, ActionScript knows what a click or creationComplete is due to its internal code. But what you are going to do here is create your own event. This event, which is particular to this project, will take the selected book and place it in the shopping cart.

I am going to warn you here that some of the code needed to create a custom event in ActionScript will get a little involved. I will do my best to explain each step. However, if you are new to OOP, you may have trouble with a few concepts at first. Just take your time and follow the flow.

You'll begin by putting your class file into its own directory. While this is not mandatory, it is a good idea to keep the various types of files for your projects organized into their own directories.

3. Right-click the src folder in the Flex Navigator View and select New ➤ Folder.

4. Call the new folder classes, as shown in Figure 11-23.

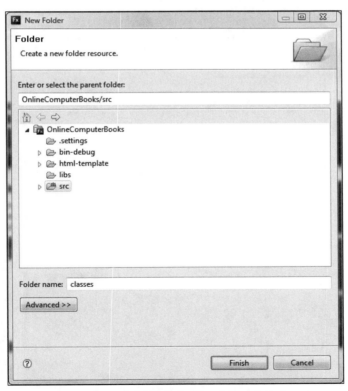

Figure 11-23. Naming your folder in the New Folder dialog box

5. Click Finish. You should see the folder in the Flex Navigator View (see Figure 11-24).

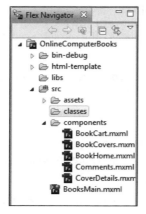

Figure 11-24.
The Flex Navigator View with the classes folder

6. Right-click the new classes folder and select New ➤ ActionScript Class to bring up the dialog box shown in Figure 11-25.

Figure 11-25. The New ActionScript Class dialog box

Much of what you will do here can be tied into this book's various previous discussions of ActionScript.

Recall that in OOP environments, the word "package" is a technical term for the folder structure the class file is located in. Notice that Flex Builder automatically enters the directory that you opened the New ActionScript Class dialog box in as the package. You will leave that as is.

> *Unlike other OOP environments, ActionScript class files require a package declaration. So, for this reason, the* Package *field must always contain information.*

Traditionally, class files begin with a capital letter.

7. Name the class file CartEvent.

8. Leave the Modifiers option set as public.

When you create a class file that will handle a custom event, that class file must be a descendent of the Event ActionScript class. That way, the new class will have access to much of the functionality of the Event class. This is called **inheritance**, and it's an important concept in OOP. If you didn't do so, you would have to define what an event is and all of the code associated with it. By using inheritance, all you have to do is add custom code for your particular needs.

Flex Builder makes inheritance easy to invoke with the Superclass field in the New ActionScript Class dialog box.

9. Click the Browse button to the right of the Superclass field. A list of available classes should come up (see Figure 11-26). Scroll down to the Event class (or type Event in the field at top). Select it and click OK.

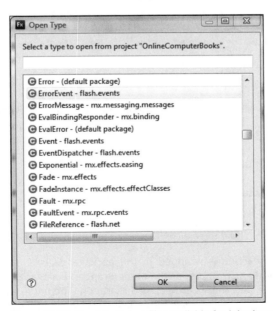

Figure 11-26. The list of class files available for inheritance

11

10. Deselect the option Generate constructor from superclass if necessary. The dialog box should look like Figure 11-27.

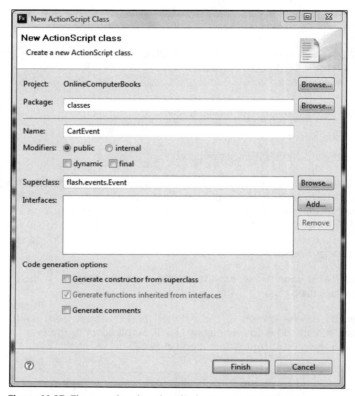

Figure 11-27. The completed settings in the New ActionScript Class dialog box

11. Click Finish.

You should see that a file, CartEvent.as, was created with the following code:

```
package classes
{
    import flash.events.Event;

    public class CartEvent extends Event
    {
    }
}
```

Notice that all of the code is wrapped in the package declaration. This is sometimes referred to as the **package wrapper**, or the **outer wrapper**. Following that are any required import statements. Finally, there is the class declaration. The name declared must be the same as the file name, minus the .as extension, or the class file will not work. The keyword extends means it is inherited from another class, which in this case is Event. This means that your new class has access to most of the functionality of the Event class.

The code necessary for the class file to run must be located between the curly braces of the class declaration.

Although it is not mandatory, most programmers traditionally declare the variables first. Here, you need to create a variable to hold the name of the book the user selected. You should make it of type String, but for this example, you will keep things as generic as possible.

12. Declare a public variable with the name selectedBook. Since you will not be using any of the specialized functionality of the String class, you can keep it generic and declare it of type Object.

```
package classes
{
        import flash.events.Event;

        public class CartEvent extends Event
        {
                public var selectedBook:Object;
        }
}
```

After declaring your variables, you need to write a special function called a **constructor**. The function runs automatically as soon as the class is called to create the object. So you would place any code inside of it that must run automatically.

The name of the constructor must be the same as the class name, and there must be no return type, not even void.

When you create the constructor for a class that is controlling a custom event, it must accept two parameters: one to accept the data being passed (which in this case is the selected book), and one for the type of event, which is of type String.

13. Create the class constructor, which accepts two parameters:

```
package classes
{
        import flash.events.Event;

        public class CartEvent extends Event
        {
                public var selectedBook:Object;

                public function CartEvent(selectedBook:Object, type:String)
                {

                }
        }
}
```

11

From here on in, the code necessary to create a custom event class is easy in practice, but tough conceptually. I say "easy in practice" because the steps for a custom class rarely change, and you can follow the sequence in a recipe-like manner. It is tough conceptually to understand why you are performing the steps that you are. I will explain each step along the way.

All the code necessary to handle the event, which is passed into the constructor with the parameter type, is located in the Event class (thus, why you extended that class when you created this class). The Event class is called the superclass. The first thing you need to do is send the type back to the Event class because it knows how to handle it. You do that with a super() call. The super() call must be the first line of the constructor. If it isn't, it will not work properly.

14. Add the following super() call, sending the type to the Event superclass:

```
public function CartEvent(selectedBook:Object, type:String)
{
     super(type);
}
```

In all OOP environments, there are two levels of variables: A variable located inside of a function is called a **local property**. A variable located outside of a function is called an **object-level property**. The keyword this, when inside of a class file, means it refers to an object-level property. The name of the book comes into the constructor through the selectedBook parameter. You want to then set the object-level property, selectedBook, to equal that parameter.

15. Add the following line after the super() call:

```
public function CartEvent(selectedBook:Object, type:String)
{
     super(type);
     this.selectedBook = selectedBook;
}
```

> Many programmers frown upon the practice of making the object-level property name the same as the name of the function parameter. I do not share that view, because the keyword this can make the distinction.

Let's look at the flow of this so far:

Inside the MXML file, there will be a call to this class file (you haven't created it yet). When the call is made, two parameters will be passed: the name of the book selected and the type of event it was. These parameters will be passed to the constructor automatically when the class is called. The constructor, in turn, will send the type back up to the super-class, Event, and let its already-created code handle it. Then the constructor will set the property selectedBook with the information passing into the parameter selectedBook.

So far, there does not seem to be anything going on that you probably couldn't have done right in the Event class itself. Here is where we start doing a little customizing.

The Event class has a method called clone(). The clone() function makes a copy of the event and data. The reason for this is important in understanding some of the functionality of Flex.

As I have stated repeatedly, everything is in a container. Let's assume the event occurs in a container contained within a container, contained within yet another container. That event must **bubble up** each level of container until it gets to the main, or Application, container. From there on in, the Application container will send that event to wherever it needs to be sent. While this was a slightly simplified explanation of the mechanics, it is the clone function that handles that bubbling up.

The Event class has a generic version of the clone() function that can handle a variety of events. In the class you are writing here, you will need to rewrite that generic function for your specific needs. In order to do that, you use the keyword override. That tells the class you are writing, CartEvent, to go up to the Event class, get the clone() function, and then add your customized code to it.

16. Override the clone() function as follows under the constructor:

```
public function CartEvent(selectedBook:Object, type:String)
{
    super(type);
    this.selectedBook = selectedBook;
}

override public function clone():Event
{

}
```

Notice that the return type of the function is Event, the same as the class.

You will now tell the clone() function to make a new copy (instance) of the CartEvent class you are creating, with the book data and the type of event, for each level of container until it gets to the Application container.

17. Add the following code to the overridden clone() function:

```
override public function clone():Event
{
    return new CartEvent(selectedBook, type);
}
```

Each time the event bubbles up to the next level of container, the CartEvent class is instantiated with the two parameters specified.

This is a good place to double-check your code.

11

```
package classes
{
    import flash.events.Event;

    public class CartEvent extends Event
    {
        public var selectedBook:Object;

        public function CartEvent(selectedBook:Object, type:String)
        {
            super(type);
            this.selectedBook = selectedBook;
        }

        override public function clone():Event
        {
            return new CartEvent(selectedBook, type);
        }
    }
}
```

That is all that is involved with building a class to handle custom events. Anytime this class is called, from anywhere, these events will run. Now it is time to put it to work.

18. Save your class file and open the BookCovers.mxml component.

19. Right below the present import statement, import mx.collections.ArrayCollection, import your new class as follows:

```
import mx.collections.ArrayCollection;
import classes.CartEvent;
```

You can define a Metadata tag to predefine an event name of your choice. The tag will be set up in such a way so that every time that event happens, the class you just defined will run.

20. Under the opening VBox tag and above the Script block, define the Metadata tag as follows:

```
<?xml version="1.0" encoding="utf-8"?>
<mx:VBox xmlns:mx="http://www.adobe.com/2006/mxml" ➥
width="550" xmlns:comp="components.*">
<mx:Metadata>

</mx:Metadata>
```

21. Within the Metadata container, define the custom event as follows:

```
<mx:Metadata>
    [Event(name="bookSelected", type="classes.CartEvent")]
</mx:Metadata>
```

Notice that there is no semicolon at the end of the definition. If you put one in, an error will occur.

22. Scroll down to the Canvas container. Below the existing button, add another Button control. Give it a `label` property of Add to Cart, an x property of 200, a y property of 400, and a `click` event that will call a function (which you will need to create) called purchaseBook().

```
<mx:Canvas>
     <mx:Image id="coverState"/>
     <mx:Text y="250" text="{selectedCover.author}" fontSize="18" ➥
fontWeight="bold"/>
     <mx:Text y="300" text="{selectedCover.desc}" fontSize="14" ➥
width="400"/>
     <mx:Button label="Return to Book Covers" ➥
click="currentState=''" y="400"/>
     <mx:Button label="Add to Cart" x="200" y="400" ➥
click="purchaseBook()"/>
</mx:Canvas>
```

If you want to test the positioning of the button, you will need to cut the click *event for now, or else an error will prevent the code from running.*

Figure 11-28 shows the new Add to Cart button.

11

Figure 11-28. The addition of the Add to Cart button

If you tested the position of the new button, make sure you reinsert the click event after you have completed the test.

23. Scroll back up to the Script block and define the private function purchaseBook(), making the return type void.

```
private function displayBookDetails(event:Object):void
    {
        currentState = "coverDetails";
        coverState.load("assets/" + event.filename + ".jpg");
        selectedCover = event;
    }

    private function purchaseBook():void
    {

    }
```

You already have a variable with all of the book information called selectedCover. This is the object you created in the previous function and saved as a [Bindable] property defined in the Script block.

You need to create a new object from the class CartEvent and then pass to its constructor the information in selectedCover and your new event: bookSelected.

24. Create a new CartEvent object and pass it the proper parameters as follows:

```
private function purchaseBook():void
{
    var eventObj:CartEvent = new CartEvent(selectedCover, ➡
"bookSelected");
}
```

Notice that the first parameter is the name of the book, and the second parameter is the custom event.

Finally, to make it all happen, you have to send the new event object, eventObj, to the class by using the function dispatchEvent().

25. Add the dispatchEvent() function under the CartEvent instantiation as follows:

```
private function purchaseBook():void
{
    var eventObj:CartEvent = new CartEvent(selectedCover, ➡
"bookSelected");
    dispatchEvent(eventObj);
}
```

I hope you are taking the time to look up all of these structures in the ActionScript 3.0 Language Reference for even more details than I am presenting here. If necessary, take a few moments and trace the flow of the code presented here.

If you save your code, there should be no errors generated. The complete code in BookCovers.mxml should now look as follows:

```
<?xml version="1.0" encoding="utf-8"?>
<mx:VBox xmlns:mx="http://www.adobe.com/2006/mxml" width="550" ➥
xmlns:comp="components.*">
<mx:Metadata>
    [Event(name="bookSelected", type="classes.CartEvent")]
</mx:Metadata>
<mx:Script>
    <![CDATA[
        import mx.collections.ArrayCollection;
        import classes.CartEvent;
        [Bindable]
        public var coverData:ArrayCollection;

        [Bindable]
        public var selectedCover:Object;

        private function displayBookDetails(event:Object):void
        {
            currentState = "coverDetails";
            coverState.load("assets/" + event.filename + ".jpg");
            selectedCover = event;
        }

        private function purchaseBook():void
        {
            var eventObj:CartEvent = new CartEvent➥
(selectedCover, "bookSelected");
            dispatchEvent(eventObj);
        }
    ]]>
</mx:Script>
<mx:states>
    <mx:State name="coverDetails">
        <mx:RemoveChild target="{coverThumbnails}"/>
        <mx:AddChild position="lastChild">
            <mx:Canvas>
                <mx:Image id="coverState"/>
                <mx:Text y="250" text="{selectedCover.author}" ➥
fontSize="18" fontWeight="bold"/>
                <mx:Text y="300" text="{selectedCover.desc}" ➥
fontSize="14" width="400"/>
                <mx:Button label="Return to Book Covers" ➥
click="currentState=''" y="400"/>
                <mx:Button label="Add to Cart" x="200" y="400" ➥
click="purchaseBook()"/>
            </mx:Canvas>
```

11

```
                    </mx:AddChild>
            </mx:State>
    </mx:states>
            <mx:HBox backgroundColor="#EE82EE" verticalAlign="middle" ➥
    fontSize="12">
                    <mx:Label text="Select the Books"/>
                    <mx:CheckBox label="All Books"/>
                    <mx:Label text="Select Book Category"/>
                    <mx:ComboBox>
                            <mx:dataProvider>
                                    <mx:ArrayCollection>
                                            <mx:String>Dreamweaver</mx:String>
                                            <mx:String>Flash</mx:String>
                                            <mx:String>Graphics</mx:String>
                                            <mx:String>Web Design</mx:String>
                                            <mx:String>Other</mx:String>
                                    </mx:ArrayCollection>
                            </mx:dataProvider>

                    </mx:ComboBox>
            </mx:HBox>
            <mx:Tile width="550" id="coverThumbnails">
                    <mx:Repeater id="displayCovers" dataProvider="{coverData}">
                            <comp:CoverDetails coverImageData=➥
    "{displayCovers.currentItem}" click="displayBookDetails➥
    (event.currentTarget.getRepeaterItem())"/>
                    </mx:Repeater>
            </mx:Tile>
    </mx:VBox>
```

Now we start to bring all the pieces together.

26. Open the BooksMain.mxml application file.

27. Import the CartEvent class into this file.

```
<![CDATA[
        import mx.rpc.events.ResultEvent;
        import mx.collections.ArrayCollection;
        import classes.CartEvent;
```

As soon as the BookCovers component is called, you want the event bookSelected to run, which will create the objects necessary for you to pass data to the shopping cart component.

28. Scroll down to where the call to the BookCovers component is located.

29. At the end of the BookCovers tag, press the spacebar. If you scroll down or start to type book, you should see the custom event you just created, bookSelected, come up on the list (see Figure 11-29).

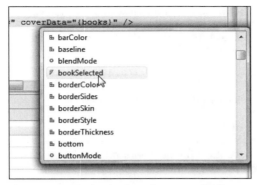

Figure 11-29. The bookSelected event availability

30. You will have it call a function, which you will write shortly, named bookSelectionHandler(). You will pass it the event object as follows:

```
<comp:BookCovers height="50%" width="50%" ➥
label="Our Books" id="bookCovers" coverData="{books}" ➥
bookSelected="bookSelectionHandler(event)"/>
```

Notice that you can use bookSelected like any other event.

The tough stuff is done now, and things will start getting familiar again.

31. Go up to the Script block and create the function bookSelectionHandler(). Pass it one parameter, event, and make it of type CartEvent because that is the class that is handling the event.

```
private function bookSelectionHandler(event:CartEvent):void
{

}
```

You will need to pass XML data, specifically the book title (title), to the shopping cart. For that reason, you will need to set up a variable of type ArrayCollection to handle it (remember, ActionScript handles XML data as type ArrayCollection).

32. In the variables declaration section of your Script block, create a [Bindable] and public variable called purchasedBooks. Make it of type ArrayCollection. However, because this ArrayCollection was not created by using HTTPService, you will need to create it as follows:

```
import mx.rpc.events.ResultEvent;
import mx.collections.ArrayCollection;
import classes.CartEvent;
[Bindable]
private var books:ArrayCollection;
[Bindable]
public var purchasedBooks:ArrayCollection = new ArrayCollection();
```

11

431

The ArrayCollection allows you to add to it with a function called addItem().

33. Inside of the bookSelectionHandler() function, add the selectedBook to purchasedBooks as follows:

```
private function bookSelectionHandler(event:CartEvent):void
{
     purchasedBooks.addItem(event.selectedBook);
}
```

The CartEvent is passed to the function with the event parameter. The selectedBook property, in CartEvent, contains the book information. Notice that as soon as you type the period after event, you see selectedBook come up.

34. Scroll down to where you called the BookCart component. Pass purchasedBooks to the BookCart as follows:

```
<comp:BookCart x="890" y="200" purchasedBooks = "{purchasedBooks}"/>
```

When you save the file, you will see an error in the Problems View. This is because you have not yet created the purchasedBooks property in the BookCart component. You will fix that shortly.

Before you leave the code in BooksMain, please check it against the following code:

```
<?xml version="1.0" encoding="utf-8"?>
<mx:Application xmlns:mx="http://www.adobe.com/2006/mxml" ➥
layout="absolute" backgroundColor="#FFFFFF" ➥
xmlns:comp="components.*" height="100%" ➥
width="100%" creationComplete="init()">
<mx:Script>
     <![CDATA[
          import mx.rpc.events.ResultEvent;
          import mx.collections.ArrayCollection;
          import classes.CartEvent;
          [Bindable]
          private var books:ArrayCollection;
          [Bindable]
          public var purchasedBooks:ArrayCollection = ➥
new ArrayCollection();
          private function init():void
          {
               bookDataIn.send();
          }

          private function bookHandler(event:ResultEvent):void
          {
               books = event.result.books.image;
          }
```

```
        private function bookSelectionHandler(event:CartEvent):void
        {
                purchasedBooks.addItem(event.selectedBook);
        }
    ]]>
</mx:Script>
<mx:Style>
    ComboBox
    {
        selectionColor: #32CD32;
    }

    global
    {
        color:#00008B;
    }
</mx:Style>
<mx:HTTPService id="bookDataIn" url="assets/books.xml" ➡
result="bookHandler(event)"/>
    <mx:Image source="assets/Logo1.gif" x="360" y="10"/>
    <mx:LinkBar dataProvider="bookPages" x="400" y="130"/>
    <mx:ViewStack id="bookPages" resizeToContent="true" x="290" ➡
y="160">
            <comp:BookHome height="50%" width="50%" label="Home" ➡
id="home"/>
            <comp:BookCovers height="50%" width="50%" ➡
label="Our Books" id="bookCovers" coverData="{books}" ➡
bookSelected="bookSelectionHandler(event)"/>
            <comp:Comments height="50%" width="50%" ➡
label="Comments" id="comments"/>
    </mx:ViewStack>
    <comp:BookCart x="890" y="200" purchasedBooks = ➡
"{purchasedBooks}"/>
</mx:Application>
```

35. Save your work and go to the BookCart.mxml component.

36. Just below the opening Canvas tag, insert a Script block, import the ArrayCollection class, and make a [Bindable], public variable of purchasedBooks of type ArrayCollection.

```
<mx:Script>
    <![CDATA[
        import mx.collections.ArrayCollection;
        [Bindable]
        public var purchasedBooks:ArrayCollection;
    ]]>
</mx:Script>
```

11

37. Since purchasedBooks contains the XML data, all you need to do is assign it as the dataProvider to the DataGrid component.

```
<mx:DataGrid width="230" height="375" dataProvider="{purchasedBooks}">
```

The only thing left to do is to tell the DataGridColumn which XML attribute to use. In this case, it will be the title attribute.

38. Modify the DataGridColumn as shown:

```
<mx:DataGridColumn headerText="Purchased Books" dataField="title"/>
```

Your finished BookCart component should look as follows:

```
<?xml version="1.0" encoding="utf-8"?>
<mx:Canvas xmlns:mx="http://www.adobe.com/2006/mxml">
<mx:Script>
    <![CDATA[
        import mx.collections.ArrayCollection;
        [Bindable]
        public var purchasedBooks:ArrayCollection;
    ]]>
</mx:Script>
    <mx:states>
        <mx:State name="cartExpand">
            <mx:SetProperty target="{cartContainer}" ➡
name="height" value="500"/>
            <mx:AddChild relativeTo="{cartContainer}" ➡
position="lastChild">
                <mx:DataGrid width="230" height="375" ➡
dataProvider="{purchasedBooks}">
                    <mx:columns>
                        <mx:DataGridColumn ➡
headerText="Purchased Books" dataField="title"/>
                    </mx:columns>
                </mx:DataGrid>
            </mx:AddChild>
            <mx:SetProperty target="{button1}" name="label" ➡
value="Collapse cart details"/>
            <mx:SetEventHandler target="{button1}" ➡
name="click" handler="currentState=''"/>
            <mx:AddChild relativeTo="{cartContainer}" ➡
position="lastChild">
                <mx:Button label="Click to Checkout" ➡
id="checkout"/>
            </mx:AddChild>
        </mx:State>
    </mx:states>
    <mx:Panel id="cartContainer" width="250" layout="vertical" ➡
title="Shopping Cart">
        <mx:Label text="There are 0 items in your cart"/>
```

```
              <mx:Button label="See the cart details" ➥
click="currentState='cartExpand'" id="button1"/>
          </mx:Panel>
</mx:Canvas>
```

39. Save and run your application.

40. Click the Our Books link.

41. Click a book cover and click the Add to Cart button.

If you expand your cart, you should see the book title in it (see Figure 11-30).

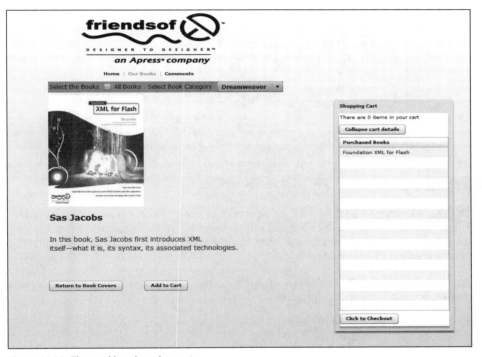

Figure 11-30. The working shopping cart

Try adding a few books to the shopping cart by returning to the gallery and selecting different books.

> *As of now, you can add a book multiple times to the shopping cart. At the end of this book, we will be returning to this case study in a new environment.*

You need to do one additional minor task: set up the counter that shows how many items are in the cart.

The ArrayCollection has a property called length. This returns how many elements are in it. You can use that to do an item count for the shopping cart.

42. Find the Label control in the BookCart.mxml component. Alter the text property as follows:

```
<mx:Label text="There are {purchasedBooks.length} items in your cart"/>
```

43. Run the application again and add items to the cart. The counter should increment as shown in Figure 11-31.

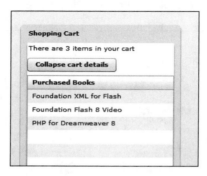

Figure 11-31.
The incrementing counter

Summary

This chapter covered a lot of intricate ActionScript code and, if you are a beginning programmer, you may have been confused with some of it. While the syntax is relatively easy, the concepts can sometimes take a while to fully grasp. You spent a lot of time learning how to create a custom event.

At the end of this book, you will be returning to this case study to do make a surprising change, so do not delete this project.

In case anything went seriously wrong, I have included the completed project file with the downloads for this chapter.

Let's now turn our attention to handling data.

12 FLEX AND DATA

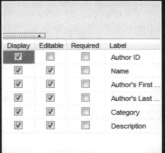

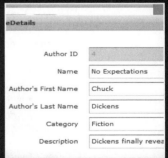

Let's begin with a premise that I have repeatedly stated throughout this book: Flex is a presentation server!

This means that it sits over middleware technology like ColdFusion, .NET, PHP, and Java. The purpose of Flex is not to replace this technology, but to present the output of this technology with all of the flexibility we have seen up to this point.

The subject of Flex and data is an immense one and could be the focus of several volumes of books. The whole subject is treated with great detail in *Foundation Flex for Developers: Data-Driven Applications with PHP, ASP.NET, ColdFusion, and LCDS* by Sas Jacobs and Koen De Weggheleire (Apress, 2007).

Happily, Flex Builder 3 simplified the ability to connect with the technologies just listed.

In the writing of this book, I decided to place the focus on Adobe's own dynamic application server: ColdFusion 8. However, in the process of discussing Flex and ColdFusion, I will be showing you how to link with the other technologies listed previously.

In this chapter, I am making two assumptions:

- You installed the ColdFusion 8 application server as shown in the Appendix.
- When you installed Flex, you installed the ColdFusion extensions as shown in Chapter 1.

Provided both of those conditions are met, you are good to go. Let's get to work.

In this chapter, we will be looking at the wizards available for linking to the dynamic data technology servers. Then, after a look at ColdFusion, we will be taking a brief look at the LiveCycle Data Services (LCDS) server.

The ColdFusion Server

Depending on the technology you are working with, you will need to install an application server to serve as the connection between Flex and a database technology. For instance, if you were working with PHP, you would need to install the Apache server, MySQL as the database server, and the PHP application server.

> *There is a great site that will allow you to download an all-in-one package:* www.apachefriends.org/en/xampp-windows.html *(XAMP stands for Windows Apache MySQL PHP server). This gives you everything you need to get started with PHP. However, as of this writing, it is only available for the Windows environment. For the Mac environment, there is a similar package located at* www.mamp.info *(MAMP stands for Macintosh Apache MySQL PHP). If you install one of these packages, it won't be difficult for you to translate many of the steps I am showing for ColdFusion to PHP.*

ColdFusion is available for a variety of platforms, with the installation and operation being nearly identical across them all.

Interestingly, ColdFusion's scripting language, CFML, is the philosophical basis for Flex's MXML language. The whole idea behind ColdFusion was to do Java programming while using HTML-like tags. This greatly simplifies the programming process. For example, if you wanted to set a variable, it would go something like this:

```
<cfset  myName = "Charles E. Brown">
```

In the end, ColdFusion translates that simple tag to Java code in the background, just like MXML translates to ActionScript code.

Assuming you have ColdFusion 8 installed, as shown in the Appendix, the first thing you are going to need to do is install your data source. For the purposes of this example, you will use a small Access database. Since it is my goal to show you how to use Flex and ColdFusion (as well as other technologies) together, and not to get into a discussion about database design or SQL, I kept this database very simple, with only a few records and a couple of tables.

You can download this database from www.friendsofed.com with the Chapter 12 downloads—do this now, as you will need it in the upcoming steps. The location of the database is not important. ColdFusion can run it from anywhere.

Installing a data source

ColdFusion makes installing a data source very simple.

> In the following example, I am demonstrating using Windows Vista. Both ColdFusion and Flex run on a variety of platforms. If you are on a different platform, the steps for accessing the ColdFusion Administrator will vary. Please check your system's documentation.

1. Select Start ➤ All Programs ➤ Adobe ➤ ColdFusion 8 ➤ Administrator. Your screen might look different from what is shown in Figure 12-1. Don't be concerned, we will all be together in a second.

Notice that the ColdFusion Administrator runs in your default browser as localhost:8500 (127.0.0.1:8500). Keep this in mind, as you will need to remember this in a few steps.

Look at the left side of the administrator. You will see a series of links, divided into categories, for accessing the various parts of the administrator.

12

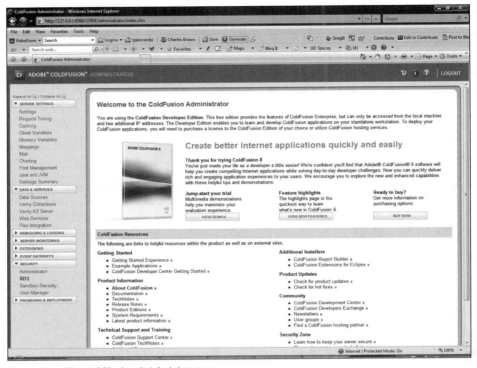

Figure 12-1. The ColdFusion 8 Administrator

2. Under the Data & Services category, click the Data Sources link. You should see the screen shown in Figure 12-2.

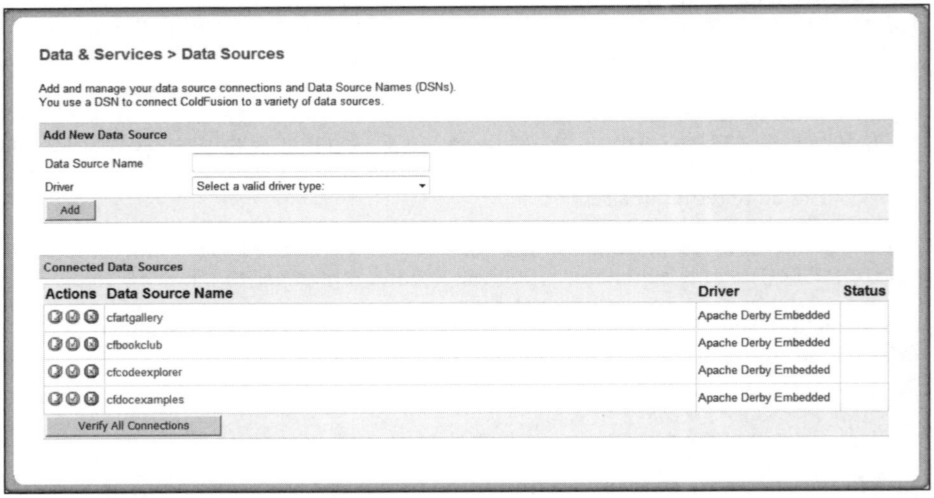

Figure 12-2. The Data Sources screen

> *When you first install ColdFusion, there are default data sources for practice purposes. Those are shown in Figure 12-2. However, if they are not there, don't worry about it.*

In the Data Source Name field, you will need to give the connection to your database a unique name. It could be a name of your choosing.

3. Give the Data Source a name of bookData as shown in Figure 12-3.

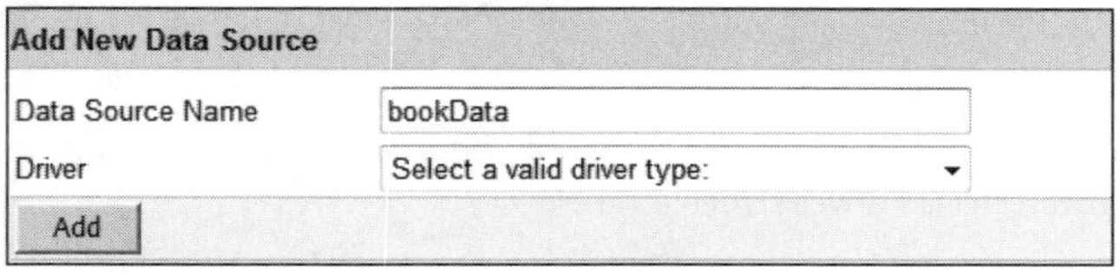

Figure 12-3. Naming the data source

Because each database system has its own requirements, drivers are needed to help ease the ability of the application server to communicate seamlessly with it. ColdFusion comes with two types of drivers: the Open Database Connectivity (ODBC) database drivers, which have been around for a long time and are very widely used in a variety of situations, and the newer Java Database Connectivity (JDBC) drivers, which are considered by many to be much more robust. A detailed discussion of the drivers, and when to use which driver, is beyond the scope of this book.

For the purpose of this exercise, we will use the JDBC driver for Microsoft Access (Microsoft Access with Unicode).

4. In the driver drop-down list, select the Microsoft Access with Unicode driver as shown in Figure 12-4.

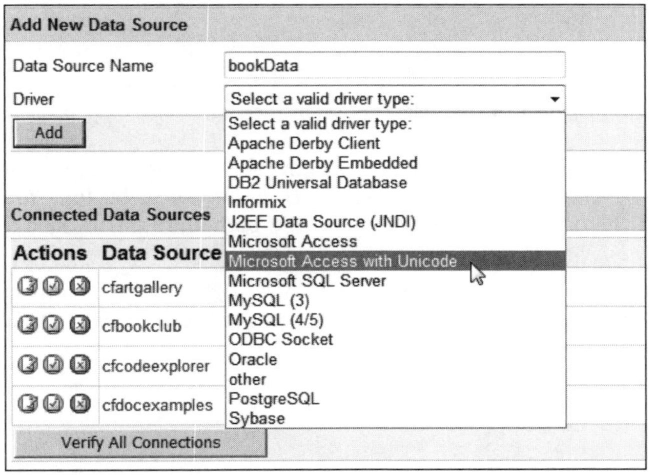

Figure 12-4. The available database drivers

12

443

5. Click the Add button. The screen should be as shown in Figure 12-5.

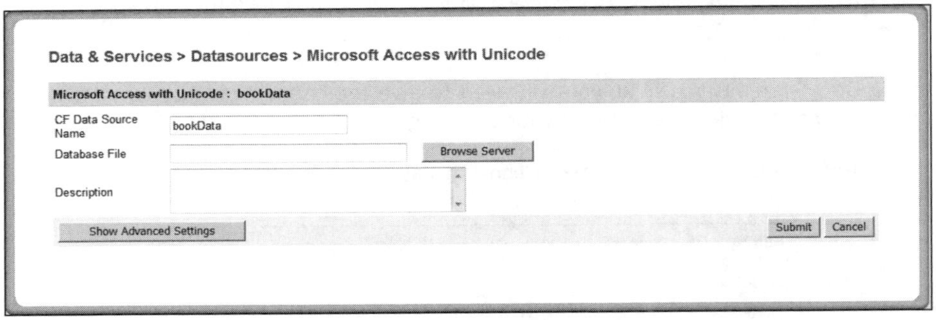

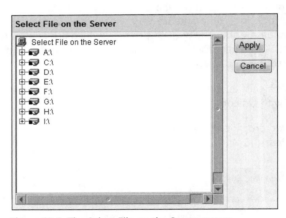

Figure 12-5. Microsoft Access driver screen

Your next step is to tell ColdFusion where the database is located.

6. Click the Browse Server button to the right of the Database File field to bring up the screen shown in Figure 12-6.

Figure 12-6. The Select File on the Server screen

7. Navigate to the folder to which you downloaded the database for this chapter, bookdata. Once you have located it, click the Apply button. You are brought back to the previous screen with all of the path information filled in, as shown in Figure 12-7.

8. Click the Submit button located in the lower-right corner of this screen. If everything was done correctly, you should see the word OK located in the status column as shown in Figure 12-8.

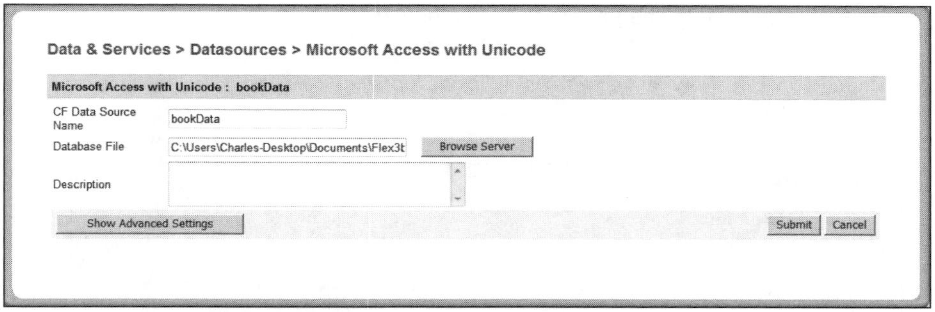

Figure 12-7. The database path information filled in

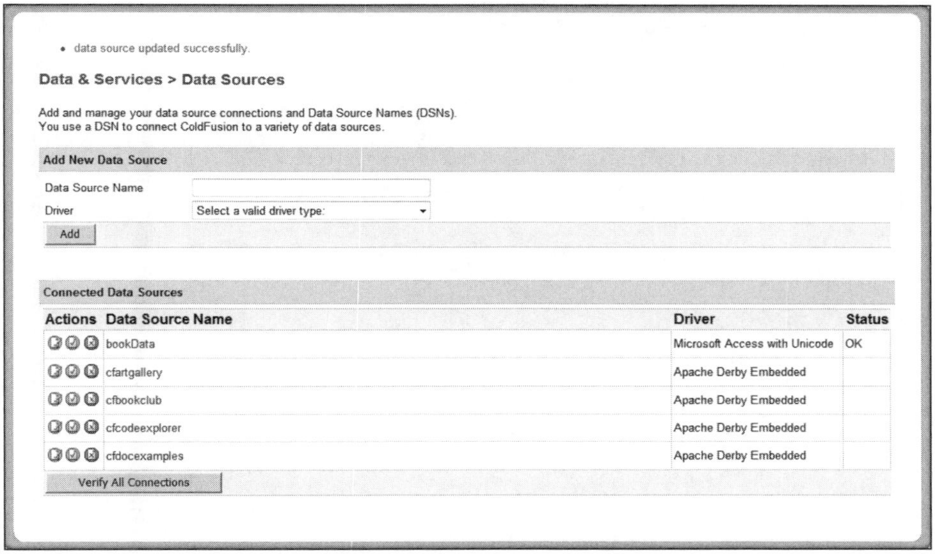

Figure 12-8. The status column is showing that the database is connected properly.

As long as you have OK in the status column, ColdFusion is ready to go. That is how easy it is to use it.

9. Go ahead and close the ColdFusion Administrator. Believe it or not, you won't need to access it again.

Connecting Flex to ColdFusion 8

If you used Flex Builder 2 and connected to ColdFusion 8 (or any of the other dynamic technologies), you are going to see some substantial differences in setting up the connection.

12

445

1. If necessary, close the project from the preceding chapter. Do not delete the files because we will be returning to them in a later chapter.

2. Select File ➤ New ➤ Flex Project to bring up the New Flex Project dialog box (see Figure 12-9).

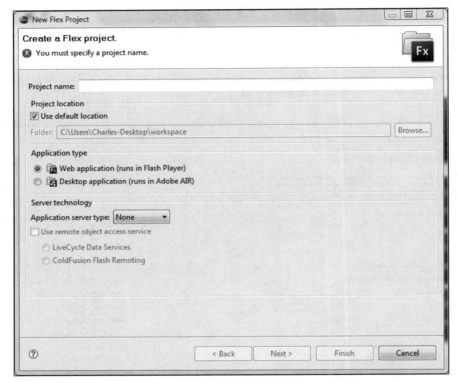

Figure 12-9. The New Flex Project dialog box

3. Enter Chapter12_project as the project name.

Here is where things are going to change a bit from the previous exercises, as well as working in Flex Builder 2.

4. Leave the Use default location option selected.

In the Application server type drop-down box, you can select which of the application servers you are working with, as shown in Figure 12-10.

Figure 12-10. Selecting the application server type

Depending on which server you select, the Project Wizard will take you to some different options. We will be focusing on ColdFusion here. However, you will be easily able to apply many of the concepts to other server technologies.

5. Select ColdFusion as the Application server type.

If you select ColdFusion or J2EE, the option of using the **LiveCycle Data Services** server will probably come on. This is Adobe's Flex server for handling advanced data functions such as remote objects, messaging, and proxy functions. We will briefly discuss this later in this chapter.

6. If it comes on, uncheck the check box for the Use remote object access service option.

7. Select Next to bring up the dialog box shown in Figure 12-11.

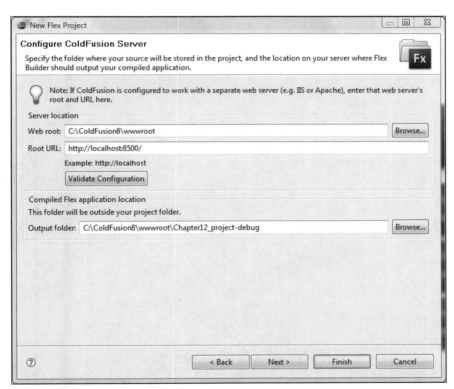

Figure 12-11. The Configure ColdFusion Server dialog box

Depending upon the server technology you select, and your platform, you may see different options and settings from those shown in Figure 12-11. In this exercise, ColdFusion is running locally on port 8500 (localhost:8500). The web root of the ColdFusion server is "wwwroot."

Flex Builder makes every attempt to detect the server settings, based on which server you selected on the previous screen, and automatically set up the proper folders. Of course, depending on your particular configuration, you may need to make some adjustments to these settings. Once the settings are properly configured to your server, you will want to click the Validate Configuration button. If everything is talking to each other properly, you should see a message confirming this in the header of the dialog box, as shown in Figure 12-12.

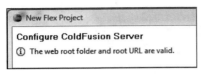

Figure 12-12. Confirming the server configuration

Notice that the Output folder field is set automatically to the server's web root. In this case, it is the wwwroot folder under the ColdFusion8 folder.

This new wizard makes hooking into a variety of application servers easier than it was in Flex Builder 2.

8. Provided everything is working, click Next.

Here you are back in familiar territory, as shown in Figure 12-13.

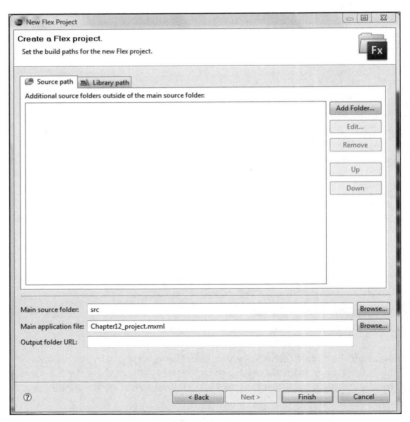

Figure 12-13. Creating a Flex project dialog box

9. Click Finish.

If you navigate to your server's web root folder (wwwroot), you should see the Chapter12_project folder set up, with a little surprise in it as shown in Figure 12-14 (which is how it's displayed in the Windows Vista environment).

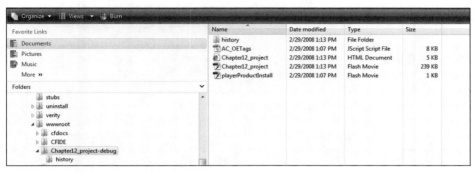

Figure 12-14. The files deployed to the server's web root

As we discussed in Chapters 1 and 2, the files that need to be deployed for your application to run properly are usually stored in the bin-debug folder. However, now they are being deployed to the proper root of the server instead.

> *You will still see the files in the* bin-debug *folder in Flex Navigator. But in reality, they are now on the server.*

Remember that Flex Builder handled most of the mechanics in the background.

Using data

Now that everything is hopefully up and operating, we are ready to start consuming data.

In the following steps, we will not be concerned with graphic issues, just hooking to data. So our outputs for these exercises will be pretty plain vanilla.

If you look along the menu for Flex Builder 3, you will see an option for Data.

1. Select Data ➤ Create Application from Database.

Figure 12-15 shows the dialog box that appears.

12

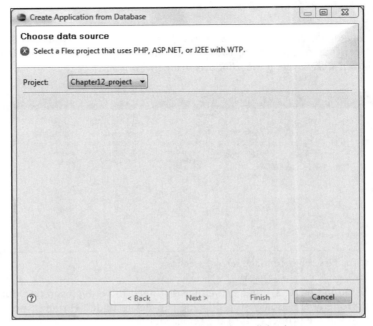

Figure 12-15. The Create Application from Database dialog box

If you are using any of the technologies other than ColdFusion, this is the wizard to help you connect to a database. However, since I am demonstrating ColdFusion in this chapter, we will not be using this dialog box.

2. Click Cancel.

> From this point on, I am going to assume that you installed the ColdFusion extensions for Flex as instructed in Chapter 1. There may be some slight variation with steps depending on whether you installed the stand-alone or plug-in version of Flex Builder. Further, there may be some slight variations depending on your platform.

While the preceding wizard is used for PHP, ASP.NET, or J2EE technologies, Flex 3 uses a different wizard when working with ColdFusion 8.

3. Select File ➤ New ➤ Other to bring up the dialog box shown in Figure 12-16.

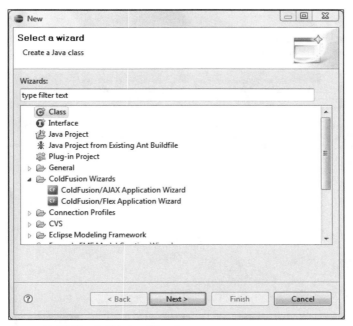

Figure 12-16. The ColdFusion Wizards

When you installed those extensions for ColdFusion, what you really installed were two wizards: the **ColdFusion/AJAX Application Wizard** and the **ColdFusion/Flex Application Wizard**. We will look at the former a bit later on in this book. For now, it is the ColdFusion/Flex Application Wizard we are interested in.

4. Select ColdFusion/Flex Application Wizard and click Next.

> *Depending on your ColdFusion 8 installation, you may be prompted for a Remote Data Service (RDS) password. If you used a password, and kept it, during the ColdFusion 8 installation, enter it here. If not, just leave it blank.*

The next screen is just an introduction to this wizard, as shown in Figure 12-17.

12

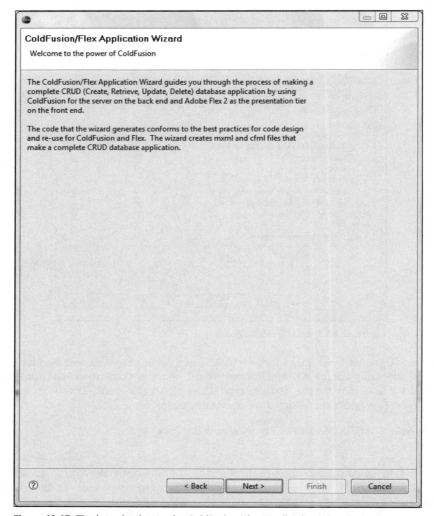

Figure 12-17. The introduction to the ColdFusion/Flex Application Wizard

At the time of this writing, with Flex 3 just released, the introduction makes a reference to Flex 2. I am sure Adobe will fix that in a future update.

5. Click Next to move on to the screen shown in Figure 12-18.

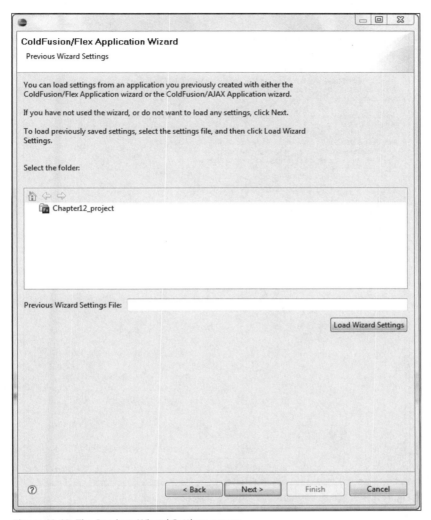

Figure 12-18. The Previous Wizard Settings screen

This screen will not apply to you for now. You use this screen to call up saved settings from previous wizard sessions. We will just ignore it for now.

6. Click Next to go to the screen shown in Figure 12-19.

12

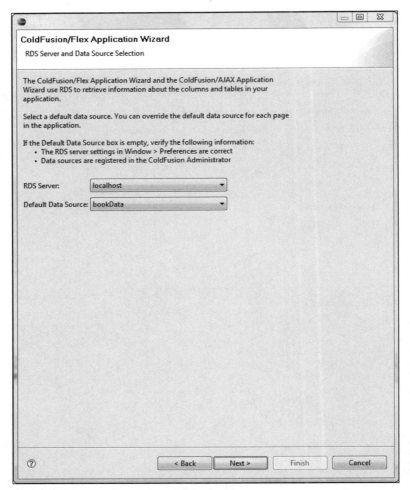

Figure 12-19. RDS Server and Data Source Selection screen

This is one of the really cool new features. **RDS**, or **Remote Data Services**, is how applications can access databases through ColdFusion. By default, the RDS Server setting is localhost. This setting will vary depending on the settings used when creating this project.

The default data source is unique in that it can see all of the data sources in the ColdFusion Administrator.

   7. Click the combo box for the Default Data Source setting (see Figure 12-20).

Notice that you see all the ColdFusion data sources on the list.

   8. Make sure that bookData is selected and click Next.

Figure 12-21 shows the next screen of the wizard.

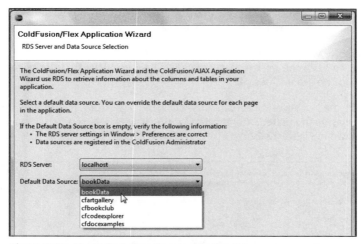

Figure 12-20. The Default Data Source selection list

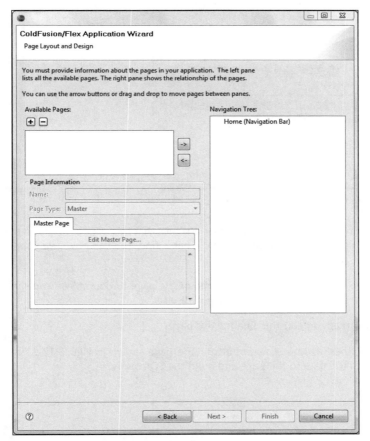

Figure 12-21. The Page Layout and Design screen

It is here that the real work will begin. This is where you will lay out what data you want to appear on your page, as well as how it will appear.

The first thing we will do is design the main page. Again, for the purposes of this exercise, we are going to keep the design pretty plain vanilla. I want the focus here to be on capturing data, not on graphic design.

9. Under the Available Pages category, click the + button. You should see the new page has been created, as indicated by the New Page listed under Available Pages, as shown in Figure 12-22.

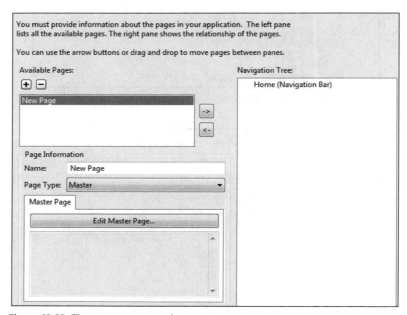

Figure 12-22. The new page created

With this being the first page, Flex Builder assumes that this will be the Home page and will have the navigation bar associated with it. That is fine. You can now give your new page a name.

10. In the Name field, change the name of the page to booksMain. You should see the name change in the Available Pages list also.

You are now ready to edit the data for this page.

11. Click the Edit Master Page button. The page shown in Figure 12-23 is where you assign the data to the page and build the SQL query.

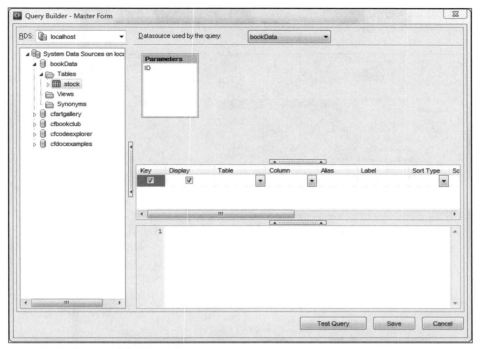

Figure 12-23. The Query Builder screen

As you can see, this screen shows you the structure of the database (as a matter of fact, all of the databases in the ColdFusion Administrator) and allows you to build a **Structured Query Language** (**SQL**) query using an Access-like interface.

The simple database used in this exercise has only one table: stock. But that will serve the purposes for this example.

If you twirl down the stock table, located on the left-side of the dialog box, you will see the columns in this table.

12. Twirl down the stock table to see its columns, as shown in Figure 12-24.

For your first simple page, you will just use the authorFName and authorLName fields. However, since you will be eventually linking this to another page, you also want to include the authorID field. We will hide it as we go along.

Figure 12-24. The structure of the stock table

> The structure of this simple database mimics the books.xml file you worked with in earlier chapters.

13. Double-click the authorID, authorFName, and authorLName fields to add them to your query (see Figure 12-25).

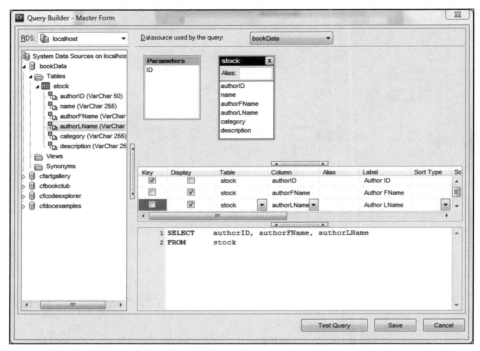

Figure 12-25. The fields added to the query

Notice a few things here:

First of all, the SQL query was built automatically for you. This means that even if your knowledge of SQL is minimal, this wizard will help you out and do most of the work for you. Also, notice that Flex Builder recognized that the authorID field was a database key field. As a result, it automatically checked the Key field and deselected the Display field. This means that it will not be displayed in the final page. In dynamic page design, this is a common scenario. The authorID field will be used to help us link to another page later on.

14. Give the query a quick test by clicking the Test Query button at the bottom of the screen. You should get the output shown in Figure 12-26.

15. Close the query test window.

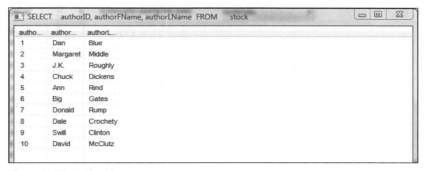

Figure 12-26. Testing the query

I think it is a safe assumption to make that you don't want field names like authorFName and authorLName to appear on the final page. You want more user-friendly names like Author's First Name or Author's Last Name. You can easily adjust that under the Label column.

16. Under the Label column, change authorFName and authorLName to Author's First Name and Author's Last Name, as shown in Figure 12-27.

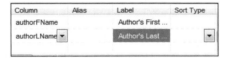

Figure 12-27. Changing field labels

Finally, you want your data sorted by the author's last name.

17. Click the Sort Type drop-down arrow in the Author's Last Name row and select Ascending. Notice that the SQL query now shows an ORDER BY statement (see Figure 12-28).

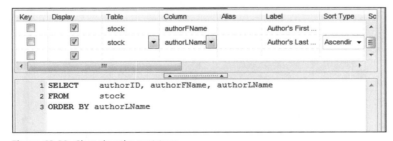

Figure 12-28. Changing the sort type

We now have our main page built.

12

18. Click the Save button located at the bottom of the screen. You should be returned to the Page Layout and Design screen. The page should display the built SQL code (see Figure 12-29).

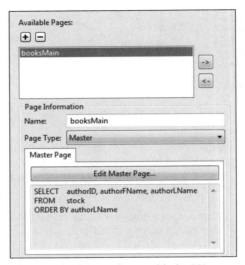

Figure 12-29. The page layout with the SQL information added

You are going to build a master-detail scenario now. This means that key data appears on the main page. But when you click the link, you are taken to the details of that particular record. You just built the master page. You will now build the detail page.

19. Under Available Pages, click the + button again. Give the page the name of pageDetails.

20. In the Page Type combo box, select Detail.

Notice that the lower window now says Edit Detail Page (see Figure 12-30).

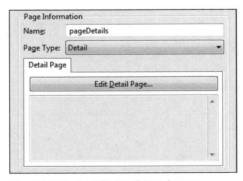

Figure 12-30. The Edit Detail Page button

21. Click the Edit Detail Page button to bring up the screen shown in Figure 12-31.

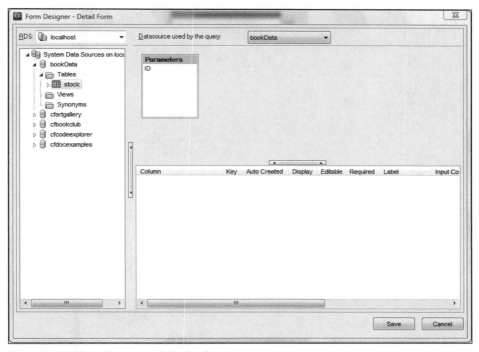

Figure 12-31. Editing the query of the detail page

For this exercise, you will include all of the fields of the table on this page. Rather than double-click each field, you can just double-click the table name.

22. Double-click the stock table name. All of the fields should appear in the query. Like you did in the last page, fix the labels so that they are user friendly.

Notice that since the authorID field is a key field, the Auto Created box is checked. This tells Flex that the database will automatically populate this field when a new record is created.

23. Check the Display check box for the authorID field. However, leave the Editable box unchecked.

Your Form Designer screen should look like Figure 12-32.

12

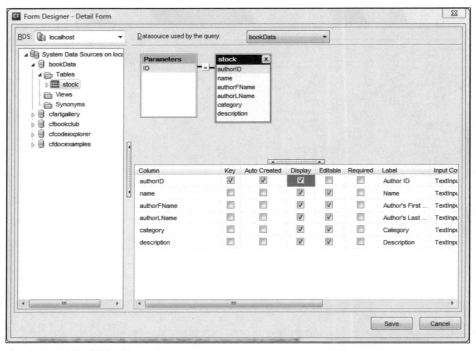

Figure 12-32. The finished Form Designer screen

24. Click Save. Again, you should see the SQL code displayed on the Page Layout and Design screen.

You have one more small step to make before you move on to finish the project.

25. On the Page Layout screen, select the booksMain page and click the right arrow. Then select pageDetails and the right arrow. You should see both pages under the Home page indented under the Navigation Tree, as shown in Figure 12-33. Notice that pageDetails is a subpage to booksMain. This relationship will become obvious when you see the application run in a few moments.

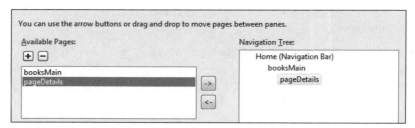

Figure 12-33. The Navigation Tree

You are now ready for the next step.

26. Click Next. You should see the screen shown in Figure 12-34.

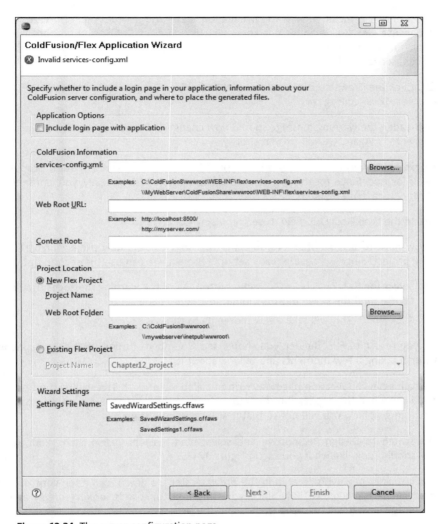

Figure 12-34. The server configuration page

We have a lot to talk about here. Let's take a few minutes and discuss this page line by line.

First of all, you may see the message Invalid services-config.xml. Don't worry about that for now. You will fix that shortly.

If you want to include a login page, you could select that option. For now, however, leave it off.

ColdFusion links to Flex through an XML file called services-config.xml. Older versions of ColdFusion would need to have this file manually installed. However, beginning with ColdFusion 8, it is included with the installation under the wwwroot\WEB-INF\flex directory. Because Flex Builder does not know which version of ColdFusion you are working with, or if that file has been moved for some reason, you need to tell it where to find the services-config.xml file.

27. Click the Browse button and navigate to C:\ColdFusion8\wwwroot\WEB-INF\flex\ services-config.xml.

In the header, the warning message should now change to Invalid web root folder (the path is not a directory). Again, we will fix that shortly.

The next field, Web Root URL, is where you tell Flex where the ColdFusion production server is located. Since for this exercise we are using ColdFusion locally, you can specify it as http://localhost:8500/.

28. In the Web Root URL field, type http://localhost:8500/.

You now have to decide whether you want this work to be a new project or part of an existing project. Since we have already set up a project, we can use the second option.

29. Select the Existing Flex Project radio button. All of the warning messages should disappear, and the Finish button should now be available.

30. Click Finish. This will take a few moments to run.

When you return to Flex Builder, you should see a number of things that have happened. It is worth taking a few moments and talking about it.

First of all, a new application page was written called main.mxml. This will be the first page that will run when the application starts up. So it is in this page that you want to put your web design graphics. You will notice that it also contains a state.

31. Switch to Design Perspective and select start mainApplication (start). Your screen should look like what you see in Figure 12-35.

For each master page you created in the previous steps, a new linkButton control is put on the ApplicationControlBar. Since you only built one, it is looking pretty anemic. However, for now, it will help you understand the process.

Look in the Flex Navigator, shown in Figure 12-36.

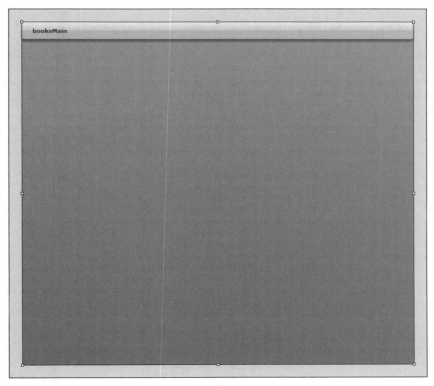

Figure 12-35. The Main.mxml page in Design View

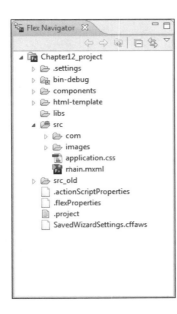

Figure 12-36.
The reconfigured Flex Navigator

You should see a new folder called src_old. This is where your original application file is backed up to. As we just saw, Main.mxml is the new application file.

Where the real action is taking place is under the src.com folder. Here, a number of MXML and ColdFusion components, as well as .as files, are located to facilitate the running of the application and the connection to the data source (see Figure 12-37). All of them were written automatically for you by the wizard. To try and go through all of this code would be a formidable task.

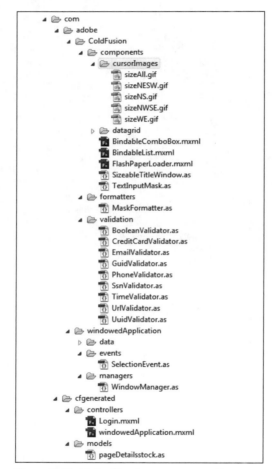

Figure 12-37. All the files that are generated by the wizard

Well, I am sure you are anxious to see the application running.

32. Run the application. Your results should resemble Figure 12-38.

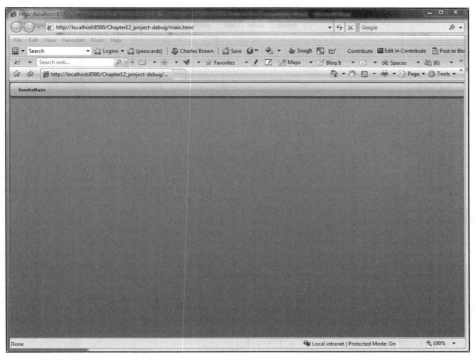

Figure 12-38. The Main application

33. Click the booksMain link to open the booksMain component (see Figure 12-39).

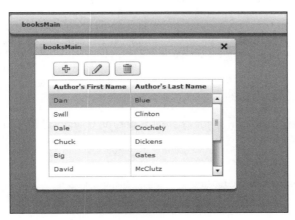

Figure 12-39. The booksMain component

Notice that the booksMain component has now opened. My wording was quite specific here: it is a component. Notice also that controls are added for adding, editing, and deleting records.

Let's see the pageDetails component.

34. Double-click one of the records. Your screen should resemble Figure 12-40.

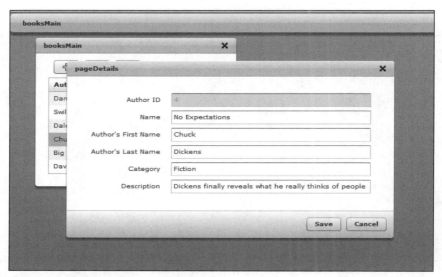

Figure 12-40. The pageDetails component

Here you see the page details. Since the Author ID field is not editable, it is grayed out. But the other fields are fully editable.

35. Close the browser and return to Flex Builder. Close any open MXML files.

As you can see, you have a fully functioning Flex application, connected to a data source with ColdFusion, without doing any programming whatsoever. There is a seamless integration. With Flex 3, you can enjoy a similar integration with .NET, JSP, and PHP also.

Variation on a theme

The layout you saw previously in the chapter is not the only possibility. Let's try something else:

1. Select File ➤ New ➤ Other.

2. Once again, select the ColdFusion/Flex Application Wizard.

3. Click the Next button twice, and you will be greeted by the screen shown in Figure 12-41.

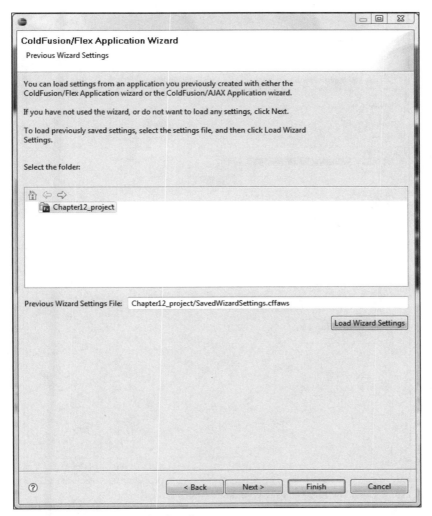

Figure 12-41. The Previous Wizard Settings screen

The previous wizard settings are held in a file, saved with the project, called Settings. cffaws. This makes editing really easy. You recall those settings with the Load Wizard Settings button.

4. Click the Load Wizard Settings button.

5. Click Next twice. You should be returned to the screen shown in Figure 12-42. This is the Page Layout and Design screen you saw earlier.

469

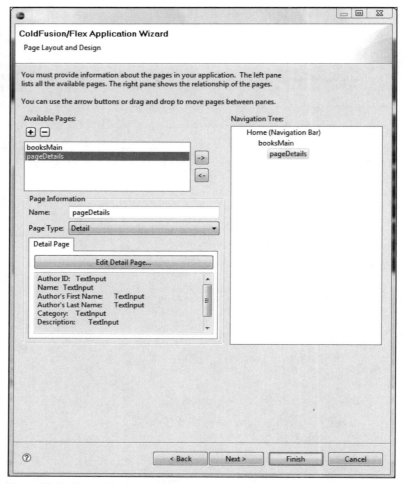

Figure 12-42. The revisited Page Layout and Design screen

The names bookMain and pageDetails are not particularly desirable on a navigation bar.

6. Click the booksMain name and change it to Find Books.

> *Since the wizard is doing internal naming, you can use friendly names here, including spaces.*

7. Change the name of pageDetails to Book Details. This will change the heading of the form.

8. Click Finish to recompile the application.

If you click the links now, you will see that the LinkButton and form headings have much more user-friendly names, as shown in Figure 12-43.

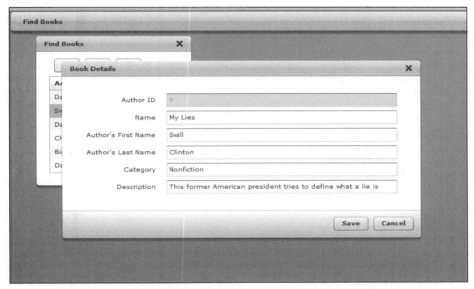

Figure 12-43. The completed ColdFusion project

Whether you are using ColdFusion, or one of the other technologies listed previously, Flex 3 has the tools necessary to help you get the job done quickly. But now we are going to turn our attention to yet another relatively new technology: LiveCycle Data Services.

LiveCycle Data Services

The latest server technology released by Adobe is **LiveCycle Data Services**, or **LCDS**. This server, which employs J2EE technology, works with Flex on three levels:

- It handles **Flex Messaging**. This means that if a Flex application is running on two or more client machines, data can be shared between them.

- Earlier in this book, we saw how to retrieve XML data using HTTPService. LCDS's **Remote Objects** bypasses the need for XML by being able to read ColdFusion or Java objects directly. We actually got a slight taste of this in the previous ColdFusion exercise in this chapter.

- Earlier in this book, we discussed the security restrictions associated with the Flash Player. LCDS helps overcome many of these restrictions by serving as a proxy server between Flash Player and the data services used.

The LiveCycle Data Services server is actually an update to the Flex Data Server. The name was changed due to a new product line Adobe is starting to release as of this writing:

12

LiveCycle. LiveCycle is a monumental series of module programs that handles the management of documents. Eventually LiveCycle, Flex, and Acrobat will be all tied together for LiveCycle.

LiveCycle Data Services server comes as part of the ColdFusion server. However, if you are using Java, you need to install LCDS as its own server (it could also be installed within any standard J2EE server). Like ColdFusion, there is a free developer's edition with limited connectivity. This free version is called the **LiveCycle Data Services ES Express** (the ES stands for Enterprise Server). For this next exercise, that is the one we will use. You can download this version by going to the www.adobe.com site and looking for the LiveCycle Data Services ES Express download area. Like ColdFusion, the developer's edition runs locally under localhost. However, it uses port 8700 (localhost:8700) instead of ColdFusion's localhost:8500.

1. Close and delete the files from the previous exercise.

2. Download LiveCycle Data Services ES Express from the Adobe site and start the install process (see Figure 12-44).

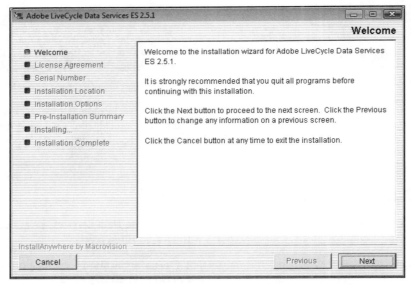

Figure 12-44. The opening screen of the LiveCycle Data Services installation

3. Click Next to bring up the license agreement (see Figure 12-45).

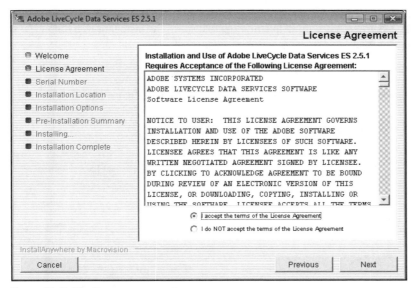

Figure 12-45. The license agreement

4. Accept the license agreement and click Next to go to the next screen (see Figure 12-46).

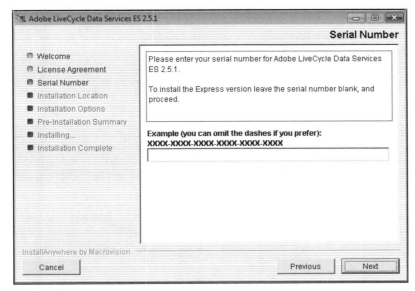

Figure 12-46. The Serial Number screen

12

Here you are asked for a serial number if you are using the full version of LiveCycle Data Services. However, not putting in a number will cause the installation to default to the free version: Express.

5. Leave the number field blank and click Next.

You are now prompted as to the installation location (see Figure 12-47).

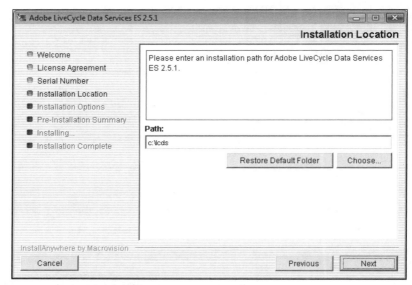

Figure 12-47. The installation location

For the purposes of this exercise, the default location (lcds) is fine.

6. Click Next to bring up the Installation Options screen (see Figure 12-48).

As I mentioned at the beginning of this section, LCDS can be installed either as part of an existing J2EE server, such as the Apache Tomcat server, or with its own J2EE server, Adobe's own product: JRun. As I mentioned earlier, it also comes as part of ColdFusion, which is also a J2EE server. For the purposes of this exercise, we will install it with the integrated JRun server.

7. Select the option LiveCycle Data Services with integrated JRun and click Next.

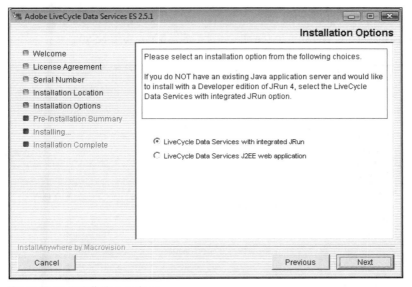

Figure 12-48. Installation options

The final screen, shown in Figure 12-49, will allow you to review the default settings. Notice that the license type is showing as Express.

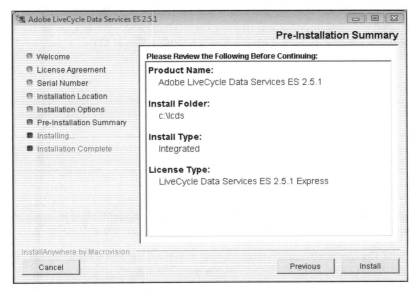

Figure 12-49. The Pre-Installation Summary

12

8. Click Install.

If all was successful, you should see the screen shown in Figure 12-50.

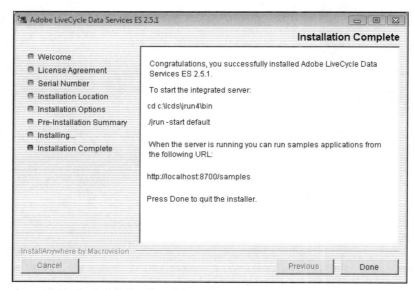

Figure 12-50. The Installation Complete screen

Notice that it is telling you that it is running on localhost:8700. We will get to try it out in a moment. As a matter of fact, it even has some sample files at http://locathost:8700/ samples.

9. Click Done.

You are probably anxious to try it out now.

10. Open a browser and type http://localhost:8700/samples.

Whoops! What happened?

This is a common mistake if you are new to LCDS. In order for it to work, you need to actually start the server. It can be started from either a system prompt or the Adobe menu. For this exercise, you will take the easier route: the Adobe menu. Depending on what platform you are on, the following step may vary slightly. I am using Windows Vista here.

11. Click the Start button and select All Programs ➤ Adobe ➤ LiveCycle Data Services ES [version number] ➤ Start Integrated LiveCycle Data Server.

Your command prompt window should open up where you can observe the startup process (see Figure 12-51). Depending on your system, the startup process should take between 15–30 seconds.

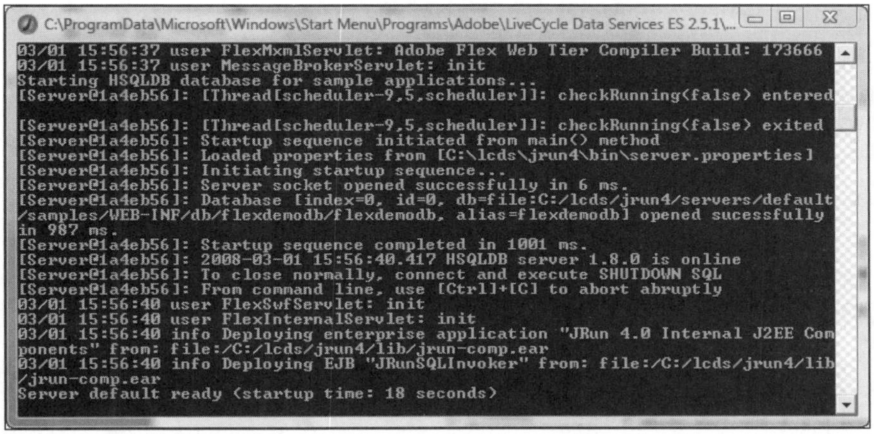

Figure 12-51. Starting the LCDS server

This window must remain open while you use LCDS. If you close it, the server will automatically stop.

12. Return to the browser and type in the URL shown in step 10 again. You should see what is shown in Figure 12-52.

Figure 12-52. The LCDS sample screen

That is much better.

The best way to learn many of the features of LCDS is to take the 30 Minutes Test Drive. This will be a guided tour through the various processes. When you are finished, close the browser window, but keep the server running. We will discuss how to connect Flex to LCDS.

See you after 30 minutes.

Connecting Flex to LCDS

As I stated at the outset, and as you saw in the 30 Minutes Test Drive, LCDS is a large subject. The following exercise will show only the most basic aspects of linking Flex to LCDS. The subject is treated with greater detail in the book *Foundation Flex for Developers: Data-Driven Applications with PHP, ASP.NET, ColdFusion, and LCDS* by Sas Jacobs and Koen De Weggheleire (Apress, 2007).

Keeping that in mind, let's get started.

1. In Flex Builder, select File ➤ New ➤ Flex Project to bring up the New Flex Project screen (see Figure 12-53).

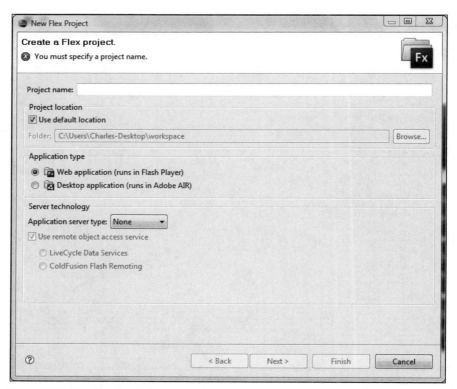

Figure 12-53. The New Flex Project screen

If your settings look a bit different from those in Figure 12-53, don't worry about that for now.

2. Name your project Chapter12_lcds.

3. Under the Application server type **select** J2EE **and make sure** LiveCycle Data Services is selected.

4. Click Next to bring up the screen in Figure 12-54.

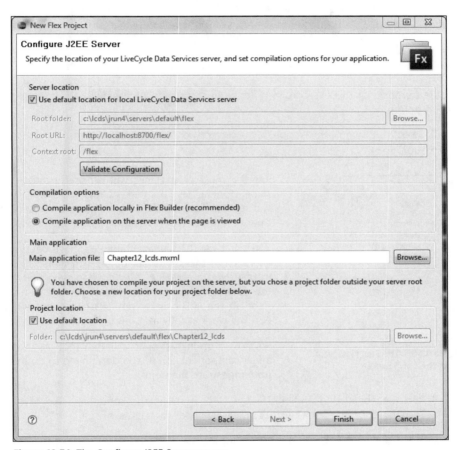

Figure 12-54. The Configure J2EE Server screen

As you saw with the previous ColdFusion exercises, Flex Builder automatically detected the default settings for the server.

5. Click the Validate Configuration **button. If the header says** The web root folder and root URL are valid, **you should be good to go. If the LCDS server is not running, you will get an error.**

The section Compilation options *is a bit of a controversy among the developer's community. The default,* Compile application locally in Flex Builder (recommended), *is the best way to use LCDS if you are new to it. However, the option* Compile application on the server when the page is viewed *is an interesting one. It will put the project MXML files right on the LCDS server (we will discuss the location shortly). If you choose that option, the SWF file will be compiled anew each time it is called. That way, the caller is always getting the latest version of the application each time it is called. However, there is a price to be paid: this option could significantly slow load time because it must first compile before it loads. As a developer, you will need to test your application both ways, and under a variety of circumstances, to see which option is best for you.*

For the purposes of this exercise, in order to demonstrate something in a bit, select the second option.

6. Select the Compile application on the server when the page is viewed **option**.

7. Click Finish.

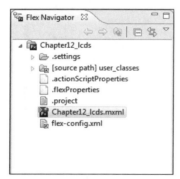

Figure 12-55. The Flex Navigator using the LCDS server

For the most part, things will be pretty much the same from a development standpoint. Where you will see a difference, because we choose the second option, is in the Flex Navigator (see Figure 12-55).

You don't see the familiar things you have been seeing, such as the src folder or the bin-debug folder. Instead, you are seeing the fully deployed files and the flex-config.xml. Remember, you are working right on the LCDS server now. Past that, everything else will work exactly as it has before.

From here on in, just build a simple application with a few components on it. You don't need to do much to demonstrate the point.

8. Run the application and notice the URL. It should be something like http://localhost:8700/flex/Chapter12_lcds/Chapter12_lcds.mxml.

You are now looking at your simple application on the LCDS server.

It is worth taking a few moments and looking behind the scenes a bit.

9. In your File Explorer, navigate to C:\lcds\jrun4\servers\default\flex.

You should see the folder with the project name Chapter12_lcds. If you look inside of that folder, you will see the Chapter12_lcds.mxml file and the corresponding SWF file. As you can see, the work is all on the LCDS server.

While this chapter only touched on the various aspects of data services with Flex, I hope I whetted your appetite sufficiently to want to explore them more.

10. Stop the LCDS server by closing the command window. If you want, you can delete the project from Flex Builder.

Flex and PHP

I want to thank my technical editor, David Powers, for providing the next section. His expertise in PHP certainly goes way beyond mine, and his book *The Essential Guide to Dreamweaver CS3 with CSS, Ajax, and PHP* (Apress, 2007) is one of the defining works on the subject.

The following is a great introduction to PHP and ASP.NET in Flex.

Using PHP or ASP.NET as the application server

Adobe recognizes that not everyone will want to use ColdFusion as their application server, so Flex Builder 3 also has options to create Flex projects that hook up to other widely used server technologies. The options for other server technologies are nowhere near as extensive as those offered by the ColdFusion/Flex Application Wizard, and the result is a much simpler application. Nevertheless, Flex Builder automatically generates the main connection scripts for you, so you might find that selecting the appropriate application server when first defining a Flex project speeds up your development process.

I assume that you have a PHP or ASP.NET testing server on your local computer or network.

Preparing the database

The database for this exercise contains a single table called stock. For PHP, you need to create a database called bookdata in MySQL, and then populate it with data from stock.sql in the download files for this chapter. You can do this with a front end for MySQL, such as phpMyAdmin or Navicat, or straight from the command line. The SQL file automatically defines the stock table before populating it with data. You also need to give a MySQL user account access to the bookdata database with SELECT, INSERT, UPDATE, and DELETE privileges.

If you are using ASP.NET, you need to migrate the Access database file, bookdata.mdb, in the download files to SQL Server.

Building the application

The following instructions use PHP and a MySQL database, but the steps for ASP.NET are almost identical (Flex Builder 3 does not provide support for classic ASP). You can close any existing project before starting.

12

1. Select File ➤ New ➤ Flex Project. Name the project Ch12_dataApp, and select the server technology you want to use from the Application server type drop-down menu, as shown in Figure 12-56. Then click Next.

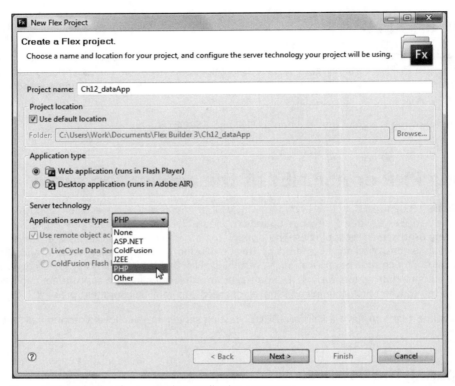

Figure 12-56. Selecting the appropriate application server type

2. The next dialog box asks you to configure the server. You can type the details directly into the Web root and Root URL fields. However, rather than work directly in your server root, it's a good idea to create a dedicated folder.

If you're using Apache as your web server, click the Browse button alongside the Web root field. Navigate to your server root (typically htdocs), and click Create new folder. I'm going to call it flex_ch12, but choose anything you like. Click OK.

If you're using IIS, create a virtual directory, and use the Browse button alongside the Web root field to navigate to the virtual directory.

3. Click OK. This brings you back to the server configuration dialog box and fills in the Web root field. You now need to fill in the Root URL field. If you used the same folder name as me, this will be http://localhost/flex_ch12.

4. Click the Validate Configuration button, as shown in Figure 12-57, to make sure that you have configured the server correctly. If everything is OK, Flex Builder will display a message confirming that the web root folder and root URL are valid. Note also that the output folder is located inside the flex_ch12 folder.

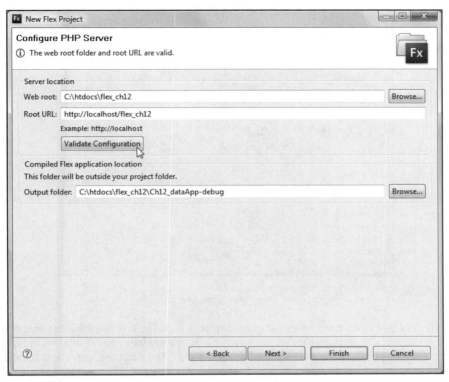

Figure 12-57. You must check that the web root folder and root URL are valid.

5. Click Finish to create the project and load Ch12_dataApp.mxml into Flex Builder.

6. You're now ready to build the connection to the database. Select Data ➤ Create Application from Database. This opens a dialog box asking you to choose a data source. If this is the first time you have connected to a database in a project, you are warned that you must add a connection. Click the New button alongside the Connection field.

7. This opens another dialog box to create a connection profile. Type books in the Name field. The Description field is optional, so you can leave that blank. Click Next.

8. Fill in the connection details for the database, as shown in Figure 12-58, and click Test Connection to make sure that Flex Builder can communicate successfully with the database. I have created a MySQL user account called flexbuilder, but you should use your own account details.

9. Assuming you connected successfully, click Next. You are then presented with a summary of your connection profile. If you want to make any changes, click Back. Otherwise, click Finish.

12

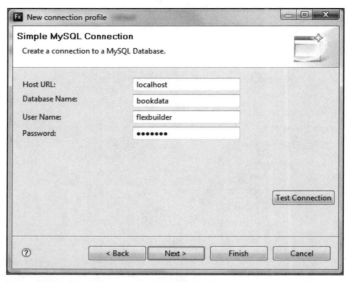

Figure 12-58. To connect to MySQL, Flex Builder needs to know the server location, database name, username, and password.

10. This takes you back to the Choose data source dialog box. Flex Builder automatically fills in all the fields. In this case, it gets the choices right, as shown in Figure 12-59; but if you are working with a more complex database, you need to select the correct values for Table and Primary key. Click Next.

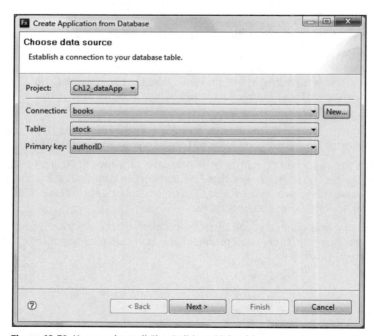

Figure 12-59. You need to tell Flex Builder which table you want to use and the name of the primary key.

11. The next dialog box tells you the name of the server-side file it's going to generate and where it will stored. You can change these settings if necessary. There's also a warning that the generated code contains no user authentication. Adobe leaves it up to you to build in the necessary security measures before deploying the application to a public server. Assuming you're happy with the file name and location, click Next.

12. The final dialog box (see Figure 12-60) gives you the opportunity to choose which columns to display. All are selected by default. To hide a column, deselect the check box alongside the column name. You can't do that with the primary key, nor can you rearrange the order of the columns.

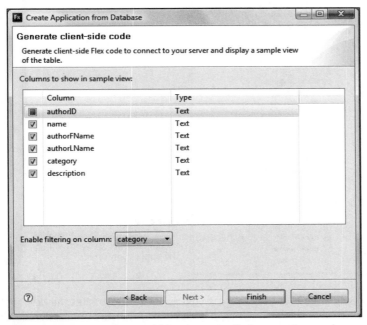

Figure 12-60. You can choose which columns to display, as well as a column to act as a search filter.

The only other changes you can make are setting the column's data type and selecting a column to use as a search filter. I have chosen the category column.

13. When you click Finish, Flex Builder generates all the necessary files to build and run the application. If you look inside the bin-debug folder in Flex Navigator, you'll see about a dozen PHP (or ASP.NET) files have been created inside the folder on your testing server (see Figure 12-61).

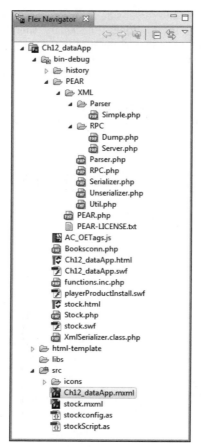

Figure 12-61.
Flex Builder creates the necessary server-side files to communicate with the application server.

14. Flex Builder ignores the Ch12_dataApp.mxml file and creates the new application in stock.mxml, named after the database table. Run the application and view it in your browser. As you can see from Figure 12-62, it's much simpler than the master/detail page set created by the ColdFusion/Flex Application Wizard. You can edit the table fields directly by clicking inside the data grid. There are also icons to add new records and delete existing ones. At the bottom right is a search form that filters the records according to the column you chose in step 12.

If you study the PHP or ASP.NET files generated by Flex Builder, you'll see that it has done a lot of coding on your behalf. However, the application created by this method is very crude, and certainly not something that you would want to deploy on a live website. Nevertheless, it gives you a head start in building an application that communicates with an application server. Since all the source files are created in the bin-debug and src folders, you can adapt them freely to suit your own needs.

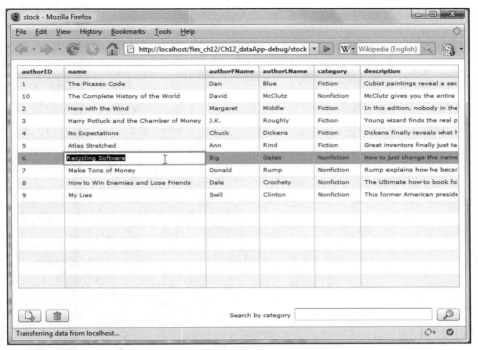

Figure 12-62. The application is much simpler than the one produced by the ColdFusion/Flex Application Wizard.

Summary

This chapter introduced you to using Flex with dynamic technologies. While the focus was on ColdFusion, the same concepts can easily apply to any of the other servers mentioned. Of course, each one of these technologies could be a book in itself.

You got to see the wizards that are available to help facilitate linking with these technologies. You also got to see how to interface Flex with the powerful new LiveCycle Data Services server.

We are now going to turn our attention to printing in Flex.

12

13 PRINTING

description	name	Author Name
Cubist paintings reveal	The Picasso Code	Dan Blue
In this edition, nobody		Margaret Middle
Young wizard finds the	Here With the Wind	J.K. Roughly
Dickens finally reveals		Chuck Dickens
Great inventors finally i	Harry Potluck and the Chamber of Mor	

Sooner or later, you will probably want to print from a Flex application. In the past, printing from web applications has posed difficult challenges: users would need to print from a browser application, and because websites and applications are often not designed with the printed page in mind, the look of the printout would be less than ideal.

Flex now addresses these problems with two new classes: FlexPrintJob and PrintDataGrid.

As you will see, the FlexPrintJob class manages the printing and serves as the interface with the printer. As a matter of fact, you will use the start() function to call the Print dialog box. What's more, you will add items to print by using the addObject() function of this class.

Along the way, you will need to make a few decisions, which we will discuss, about how you want the data to print. If you just want a page to print, the FlexPrintJob class handles that nicely. But if you want to format your data into a printable table, you will need to call the PrintDataGrid class.

An additional decision we will discuss is whether you want your printing handled by the main MXML file or by a component. You will see the implications of that in this chapter.

With Flex 3, printing is really an easy process once you understand a few general concepts. Let's get to work.

The printing process

As I stated in the introduction, odds are good that at some point you will want to print from Flex 3. For example, if you are creating an e-commerce site, you may want to give the customer a printable receipt for his purchase, or there may be cases when you need a printout of data lists of some sort. As you are about to see, Flex makes the process a lot easier than traditional XHTML environments.

As I also stated in the introduction to this chapter, the printing process revolves around two class files:

- FlexPrintJob: This class, which needs to be instantiated, serves as a container for the objects you want to print. What is great about this is you can use this class to split larger print jobs over multiple pages or scale the content to fit a specific page size.

- PrintDataGrid: You would use this class, which is a subclass of the DataGrid class, to print data that has to be in grid or table format. It also allows you to print over multiple pages.

  1. Close or delete the Chapter 12 projects and create a new project called Chapter13_project.

You will begin with a simple exercise: printing out a label.

2. Set up the following simple code example:

```
<?xml version="1.0" encoding="utf-8"?>
<mx:Application xmlns:mx="http://www.adobe.com/2006/mxml" ➡
layout="absolute">
     <mx:VBox id="printContent" backgroundColor="#FFFFFF">
          <mx:Label text="This is your first print text"/>
     </mx:VBox>
<mx:Button x="30" y="30" label="Print This"/>
</mx:Application>
```

3. Next, create a Script block that will import the FlexPrintJob class. FlexPrintJob is located in the mx.printing package.

```
<mx:Script>
     <![CDATA[
          import mx.printing.FlexPrintJob;
     ]]>
</mx:Script>
```

> As you have seen in earlier chapters, if you hadn't imported the FlexPrintJob class, then Flex Builder 3 will do it for you automatically after you create the FlexPrintJob variable.

From here on in, you will find the code very logical and easy to follow.

4. Create a function called testPrint(). The return type will be void.

```
<mx:Script>
     <![CDATA[
          import mx.printing.FlexPrintJob;

          private function testPrint():void
          {

          }
     ]]>
</mx:Script>
```

The first line of code needs to create an instantiation of the FlexPrintJob class. You have seen this syntax many times in earlier chapters.

5. Instantiate the FlexPrintJob class as follows:

```
private function testPrint():void
{
     var myPrintJob:FlexPrintJob = new FlexPrintJob();
}
```

13

The next step is to open the Print dialog box. This can be done by using the start() function of the FlexPrintJob class.

6. Use the start() function as follows:

```
private function testPrint():void
{
    var myPrintJob:FlexPrintJob = new FlexPrintJob();
    myPrintJob.start();
}
```

Once the printer is selected, the object you want to print needs to be added to the FlexPrintJob container. In this case, you want to add the contents of the printContent VBox container, which consists of the label you want to print.

In order to add your object to the FlexPrintJob container, you need to use the addObject() function of the FlexPrintJob class.

7. Add the addObject() function as follows:

```
private function testPrint():void
{
    var myPrintJob:FlexPrintJob = new FlexPrintJob();
    myPrintJob.start();
    myPrintJob.addObject(printContent);
}
```

Finally, the last step is to have the FlexPrintJob object send the object to be printed to the printer. This is accomplished with the send() function of the FlexPrintJob class.

8. Add the final line to the testPrint() function as follows:

```
private function testPrint():void
{
    var myPrintJob:FlexPrintJob = new FlexPrintJob();
    myPrintJob.start();
    myPrintJob.addObject(printContent);
    myPrintJob.send();
}
```

In its simplest form, that is all there is to the printing process. The only thing you need to do is to add a click event to the button that will call the testPrint() function.

9. Add a click event to the Button control.

```
<mx:VBox id="printContent" backgroundColor="#FFFFFF">
    <mx:Label text="This is your first print text"/>
</mx:VBox>
<mx:Button x="30" y="30"  label="Print This" click="testPrint()"/>
```

10. Go ahead and run the application. Just click the Print button, and your Print dialog box should pop up, prompting you to print the label. Try a test print.

As you can see, it is all quite simple . . . except for one slight problem (and yes, it is slight).

11. Click the Print button again. When the Print dialog box appears, click Cancel.

You will see the contents of the VBox container suddenly disappear from the application. The reason for this is a bit convoluted. Internally, Flex sends the content to be printed to another container. If you cancel the print job, the function never gets to the send() function, and the send() function controls the returning of the container back to the application after the print job is completed. Control is never being returned to the application.

If you were to look up the documentation for the FlexPrintJob class, you would see that the start() function returns a Boolean result. Because of this, it can easily be placed as the Boolean test in an if structure. In this case, you indicate that if start() isn't true (i.e., if you cancel the print job), then control must be returned to the application.

12. Add the following modification to the testPrint() function:

```
private function testPrint():void
{
    var myPrintJob:FlexPrintJob = new FlexPrintJob();
    if(myPrintJob.start() != true)
    {
        return;
    }
    myPrintJob.addObject(printContent);
    myPrintJob.send();
}
```

13. Run the application again, click the Print button, and then cancel the print job. The application should function as expected now.

Creating a separate Print container

In many cases, your data may not be in a form that is conducive for printing. If that is the case, you can create an invisible container to format your data and print the contents of that container using the same techniques you just learned.

Let's give it a try.

1. Download the books.xml file found in the Chapter 13 downloads for this book. This is the same books.xml file you used in earlier chapters. Once downloaded, import it into a created assets folder.

2. Delete all of the code between the opening and closing Application tags in the application file you used in the last exercise.

3. Create the following code. The code found here is code you have seen several times in earlier chapters.

```
<?xml version="1.0" encoding="utf-8"?>
<mx:Application xmlns:mx="http://www.adobe.com/2006/mxml" ⮕
layout="vertical" creationComplete="bookDataCall.send()">
    <mx:Script>
        <![CDATA[
            import mx.rpc.events.ResultEvent;
            import mx.collections.ArrayCollection;
            [Bindable]
            public var bookData:ArrayCollection;

            private function bookFunction(event:ResultEvent):void
            {
                bookData = event.result.books.stock;
            }
        ]]>
    </mx:Script>

    <mx:HTTPService id="bookDataCall" url="assets/books.xml" ⮕
result="bookFunction(event)"/>

    <mx:Form id="myForm">
        <mx:DataGrid id="bookInfo" dataProvider="{bookData}">
            <mx:columns>
                <mx:DataGridColumn dataField="name" ⮕
headerText="Book Name"/>
                <mx:DataGridColumn dataField="author" ⮕
headerText="Author Name"/>
                <mx:DataGridColumn dataField="category" ⮕
headerText="Book Category"/>
            </mx:columns>
        </mx:DataGrid>
        <mx:Button id="myButton" label="Print"/>
    </mx:Form>
</mx:Application>
```

4. Go ahead and run the application; your screen should look like Figure 13-1 at this point. The button isn't functioning yet.

Figure 13-1. The DataGrid layout

As you can see, this is not ideal for printing. So you are going to create a flexible version for printing.

You are now going to pull off a little sleight of hand here. You will create a VBox container, complete with an ID, background color (white), and a PrintDataGrid component. It will be created like any other component you have created. However, you are going to set its visibility property to false. It will be on the page, but not seen.

As you will see, the PrintDataGrid class has nearly the same functionality of the DataGrid class (the PrintDataGrid is a subclass of the DataGrid class). What is different is that the output is formatted more as a printed table rather than the output for a web page seen in the DataGrid control. You'll see what I mean in a minute.

5. Below the closing Form tag, create the following code:

```
<mx:VBox id="printArea" height="300" width="500" ➥
backgroundColor="#FFFFFF" visible="false">

</mx:VBox>
```

You may be asking why you set the background color to white if the container is invisible. The answer is that a white background is usually preferable for most printing scenarios.

6. Within the VBox container, create the PrintDataGrid container as follows. You will assign the dataProvider property with ActionScript shortly.

```
<mx:VBox id="printArea" height="300" width="500" ➥
backgroundColor="#FFFFFF" visible="false">
        <mx:PrintDataGrid id="myPrintDataGrid" ➥
height="100%" width="100%"/>
</mx:VBox>
```

Notice that you made the PrintDataGrid the full size of the container. That VBox itself defines the size of the print area.

7. Return to the Script block and create a new function called printJob(). Instantiate the FlexPrintJob class using a variable name of myPrintJob. Then, as discussed in the previous exercise, use the start() function within a decision structure to return control to the application. The import of the FlexPrintJob class should be created automatically.

```
<mx:Script>
    <![CDATA[
        import mx.printing.FlexPrintJob;
        import mx.rpc.events.ResultEvent;
        import mx.collections.ArrayCollection;
        [Bindable]
        public var bookData:ArrayCollection;

        private function bookFunction(event:ResultEvent):void
        {
            bookData = event.result.books.stock;
        }
```

13

```
        private function printJob():void
        {
            var myPrintJob:FlexPrintJob = new FlexPrintJob();
            if(myPrintJob.start() != true)
            {
                return;
            }
        }
    ]]>
</mx:Script>
```

The next step, after the if block, is to assign the dataProvider of the PrintDataGrid class, myPrintDataGrid, equal to the dataProvider of the actual DataGrid component, bookInfo. That way, if you change the dataProvider of the DataGrid for any reason, the PrintDataGrid will always reflect that change.

8. After the if block, set the dataProvider of the PrintDataGrid as follows:

```
private function printJob():void
{
    var myPrintJob:FlexPrintJob = new FlexPrintJob();
    if(myPrintJob.start() != true)
    {
        return;
    }
    myPrintDataGrid.dataProvider = bookInfo.dataProvider;
}
```

From here on in, this exercise works like the last one. You will use the addObject() and send() functions of the myPrintJob object.

9. Add the following code after the dataProvider assignment:

```
private function printJob():void
{
    var myPrintJob:FlexPrintJob = new FlexPrintJob();
    if(myPrintJob.start() != true)
    {
        return;
    }
    myPrintDataGrid.dataProvider = bookInfo.dataProvider;
    myPrintJob.addObject(printArea);
    myPrintJob.send();
}
```

One last thing to do.

10. Add a click event to the button and have it call the printJob() function.

```
<mx:Button id="myButton" label="Print" click="printJob()"/>
```

11. Run the application; your printed page should be similar to the table in Figure 13-2.

author	category	description	name
Dan Blue	Fiction	Cubist paintings reveal	The Picasso Code
Margaret Middle	Fiction	In this edition, nobody	Here With the Wind
J.K. Roughly	Fiction	Young wizard finds the	Harry Potluck and the (
Chuck Dickens	Fiction	Dickens finally reveals \	No Expectations
Ann Rind	Fiction	Great inventors finally j	Atlas Stretched
Big Gates	Nonfiction	How to just change the	Recycling Software
Donald Rump	Nonfiction	Rump explains how he	Make Tons of Money
Dale Crochety	Nonfiction	The Ultimate how-to bo	How to Win Enemies an
Swill Clinton	Nonfiction	This former American p	My Lies
David McClutz	Nonfiction	McClutz gives you the €	The Complete History o

Figure 13-2. The PrintDataGrid results

Notice that there seems to be a few things wrong—the application printed all of the columns, the headers could look a little nicer, and text seems to be overflowing the page. We can fix all of that.

The PrintDataGrid class has three properties, fontSize, fontFamily, and wordWrap, that can all be used to create a better looking print result. The settings I am about to show worked great on my equipment. You may need to play with your settings for optimal results.

12. Add the following to the PrintDataGrid component:

```
<mx:PrintDataGrid id="myPrintDataGrid" height="100%" width="100%" ➡
fontSize="6" fontFamily="Arial" wordWrap="true"/>
```

13. Run the application again; your printed page should look something like Figure 13-3.

author	category	description	name
Dan Blue	Fiction	Cubist paintings reveal a secret society of people who really look like that	The Picasso Code
Margaret Middle	Fiction	In this edition, nobody in the south really gives a damn	Here With the Wind
J.K. Roughly	Fiction	Young wizard finds the real pot-of-gold and retires	Harry Potluck and the Chamber of Money
Chuck Dickens	Fiction	Dickens finally reveals what he really thinks of people	No Expectations
Ann Rind	Fiction	Great inventors finally just take the money and run	Atlas Stretched
Big Gates	Nonfiction	How to just change the name and interface of the same old software and sell it as new	Recycling Software
Donald Rump	Nonfiction	Rump explains how he became a billionaire while constantly declaring bankruptcy	Make Tons of Money
Dale Crochety	Nonfiction	The Ultimate how-to book for people who want to stay loners	How to Win Enemies and Lose Friends

Figure 13-3. The adjusted PrintDataGrid result

The syntax for PrintDataGrid is nearly identical to that of the DataGrid control. So you can limit the columns in exactly the same way.

14. Change the PrintDataGrid as follows:

```
<mx:VBox id="printArea" height="300" width="500" ➥
backgroundColor="#FFFFFF" visible="false">
    <mx:PrintDataGrid id="myPrintDataGrid" height="100%" ➥
width="100%" fontSize="6" fontFamily="Arial" wordWrap="true">
        <mx:columns>
            <mx:DataGridColumn dataField="name" ➥
headerText="Book Name" />
            <mx:DataGridColumn dataField="author" ➥
headerText="Author Name"/>
            <mx:DataGridColumn dataField="category" ➥
headerText="Book Category"/>
        </mx:columns>
    </mx:PrintDataGrid>
</mx:VBox>
```

15. Rerun and reprint the page, and you will see a very different result, as shown in Figure 13-4.

Book Name	Author Name	Book Category
The Picasso Code	Dan Blue	Fiction
Here With the Wind	Margaret Middle	Fiction
Harry Potluck and the Chamber of Money	J.K. Roughly	Fiction
No Expectations	Chuck Dickens	Fiction
Atlas Stretched	Ann Rind	Fiction
Recycling Software	Big Gates	Nonfiction
Make Tons of Money	Donald Rump	Nonfiction
How to Win Enemies and Lose Friends	Dale Crochety	Nonfiction
My Lies	Swill Clinton	Nonfiction
The Complete History of the World	David McClutz	Nonfiction

Figure 13-4. The reformatted PrintDataGrid output

> You could have set the properties fontSize, fontFamily, and wordWrap in the DataGrid columns as well. In this example, either way works fine.

As you can see, there is very little difference between using the PrintDataGrid and the DataGrid. In addition, it should now be obvious why you needed to make the VBox container's visibility property false. It is not needed for the web output, only for printing.

However, what if you were to put the printing functionality into its own component?

Let's see.

Printing and components

I am sure you can easily see why it might sometimes be better to relegate printing functions to a component. For instance, placing the PrintDataGrid, and its subsequent invisible container, in a component could result in cleaner code. In addition, this could centralize many of your printing functions. Finally, that component does not need to be called until it is time to print.

You will use the existing code to create the component.

1. In the Flex Navigator, create a new folder called components under the src folder.

2. In the components folder, create a new MXML component called PrintComp. Base it on the VBox container. Make the background color white, the height 300, and the width 500. Finally, set the visibility to false.

```
<?xml version="1.0" encoding="utf-8"?>
<mx:VBox xmlns:mx="http://www.adobe.com/2006/mxml" ➡
backgroundColor="#FFFFFF" width="500" height="300" visible="false">

</mx:VBox>
```

3. Cut the PrintDataGrid component from the application file.

4. Paste the code into the VBox of the PrintComp component. Your code should look as follows:

```
<?xml version="1.0" encoding="utf-8"?>
<mx:VBox xmlns:mx="http://www.adobe.com/2006/mxml" ➡
backgroundColor="#FFFFFF" width="500" height="300" visible="false">

    <mx:PrintDataGrid id="myPrintDataGrid" height="100%" ➡
width="100%" fontSize="6" fontFamily="Arial" wordWrap="true">
        <mx:columns>
            <mx:DataGridColumn dataField="name" ➡
headerText="Book Name" />
            <mx:DataGridColumn dataField="author" ➡
headerText="Author Name"/>
            <mx:DataGridColumn dataField="category" ➡
headerText="Book Category"/>
        </mx:columns>
    </mx:PrintDataGrid>
</mx:VBox>
```

5. Save the component.

You are now finished setting up the component.

6. Return to the application file and import the new component in the Script block.

```
<mx:Script>
    <![CDATA[
        import mx.printing.FlexPrintJob;
        import mx.rpc.events.ResultEvent;
        import mx.collections.ArrayCollection;
        import components.PrintComp;
```

7. Below the if block, in the printJob() function, instantiate the component. For purposes of this exercise, call it myPrintComp.

```
private function printJob():void
{
    var myPrintJob:FlexPrintJob = new FlexPrintJob();
    if(myPrintJob.start() != true)
    {
        return;
    }
```

```
var myPrintComp:PrintComp = new PrintComp();
```

Under the instantiation, you are going to bring the component into the application file temporarily by using the addChild() function. It will not be seen, because visibility of the VBox container in the component is set to false. Since you are going to add it to the application file, you will use the keyword this on the left side of the dot.

8. Add the component to the application container as follows:

```
var myPrintComp:PrintComp = new PrintComp();
this.addChild(myPrintComp);
```

You need to make a modification to the line that links the dataProvider properties. Remember that myPrintDataGrid is now located in the myPrintComp. As such, you have to reference that location.

9. Modify the dataProvider link as follows:

```
var myPrintComp:PrintComp = new PrintComp();
this.addChild(myPrintComp);
myPrintComp.myPrintDataGrid.dataProvider = bookInfo.dataProvider;
```

10. Change the object you are adding to the FlexPrintJob to myPrintComp.

```
var myPrintComp:PrintComp = new PrintComp();
this.addChild(myPrintComp);
myPrintComp.myPrintDataGrid.dataProvider = bookInfo.dataProvider;
myPrintJob.addObject(myPrintComp);
```

Once the print job is finished, you will no longer need to use the component. You can remove it from the application file by simply using the removeChild() function.

11. Add the following after the send() function:

```
var myPrintComp:PrintComp = new PrintComp();
this.addChild(myPrintComp);
myPrintComp.myPrintDataGrid.dataProvider = bookInfo.dataProvider;
myPrintJob.addObject(myPrintComp);
myPrintJob.send();
this.removeChild(myPrintComp);
```

The completed code should look as follows:

```
<?xml version="1.0" encoding="utf-8"?>
<mx:Application xmlns:mx="http://www.adobe.com/2006/mxml" ➡
layout="vertical" creationComplete="bookDataCall.send()">
    <mx:Script>
        <![CDATA[
            import mx.printing.FlexPrintJob;
            import mx.rpc.events.ResultEvent;
            import mx.collections.ArrayCollection;
            import components.PrintComp;
            [Bindable]
            public var bookData:ArrayCollection;

            private function bookFunction(event:ResultEvent):void
            {
                bookData = event.result.books.stock;
            }

            private function printJob():void
            {
                var myPrintJob:FlexPrintJob = new FlexPrintJob();
                if(myPrintJob.start() != true)
                {
                    return;
                }

                var myPrintComp:PrintComp = new PrintComp();
                this.addChild(myPrintComp);
                myPrintComp.myPrintDataGrid.dataProvider = ➡
bookInfo.dataProvider;
                myPrintJob.addObject(myPrintComp);
                myPrintJob.send();
                this.removeChild(myPrintComp);
            }
        ]]>
    </mx:Script>

    <mx:HTTPService id="bookDataCall" url="assets/books.xml" ➡
result="bookFunction(event)"/>
```

13

```
<mx:Form id="myForm">
    <mx:DataGrid id="bookInfo" dataProvider="{bookData}">
        <mx:columns>
            <mx:DataGridColumn dataField="name" ➥
headerText="Book Name"/>
            <mx:DataGridColumn dataField="author" ➥
headerText="Author Name"/>
            <mx:DataGridColumn dataField="category" ➥
headerText="Book Category"/>
        </mx:columns>
    </mx:DataGrid>
    <mx:Button id="myButton" label="Print" click="printJob()"/>
</mx:Form>

</mx:Application>
```

If you run the application now, it works exactly the same way as before; but this time, you have added flexibility due to centralizing your print functionality in a component.

Summary

We printed a simple label, printed data in a `PrintDataGrid`, and then placed that `PrintDataGrid` in a separate component. As you can see, printing is a relatively simple process. The great part is that it uses consistent syntax in a whole variety of situations.

We will now turn our attention to the chart functions of Flex 3.

14 CHARTING

Technology represents
24.250681198910083%
of our sales

Self-h
30.517
of our

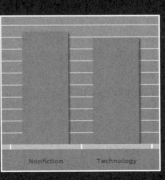

Nonfiction   Technology

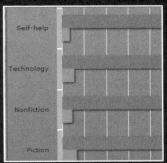

Self-help

Technology

Nonfiction

Fiction

There is an old adage that a picture is worth a thousand words. You can show someone endless tables of data, but a picture will greatly simplify the interpretation of that data.

Flex comes with easy-to-use components that allow you to create many different types of charts with, as you will see, many variations within those types.

In this chapter, you will

- Create a chart.
- Link data to a chart.
- Examine the various parts of a chart.
- Create chart events.
- Animate a chart.
- Apply styles to a chart.

The chapter assumes that you have the Professional version of Flex Builder 3. If you have the Standard version, the chart renderings will open in the browser with a watermark control. Also, the trial version of the Professional version will watermark the charts. The Professional version, with a valid serial number, has no such watermark. Past that, everything should work the same way.

Using the PieChart component

Let's start off by building a simple pie chart example. You will learn a lot of important concepts in doing that.

1. Delete or close the Chapter 13 files and start a new project called Chapter14_ project.

2. In the application file, set up a Script block, create an ArrayCollection called bookSales, and manually enter data into it as follows:

```
<?xml version="1.0" encoding="utf-8"?>
<mx:Application xmlns:mx="http://www.adobe.com/2006/mxml" ➥
layout="absolute">
    <mx:Script>
        <![CDATA[
            import mx.collections.ArrayCollection;
            [Bindable]
            private var bookSales:ArrayCollection = ➥
new ArrayCollection(
                [{bookType: "Fiction", Sales: 143},
                 {bookType: "Nonfiction", Sales: 189},
                 {bookType: "Technology", Sales: 178},
                 {bookType: "Self-help", Sales: 224}]);
        ]]>
    </mx:Script>
</mx:Application>
```

Recall from earlier discussions of the class ArrayCollection in Chapter 6 that each data element is a separate object.

You could have just as easily gotten your data from any data source, like the ones you've used in past chapters. However, though simple, this will serve our purposes nicely.

The next step, under the Script block, is to call the PieChart component. You will make the height and width properties 50%, and make the dataProvider property the ArrayCollection you just created: bookSales.

3. Add the PieChart component under the Script block.

```
<mx:PieChart width="50%" height="50%" dataProvider="{bookSales}">

</mx:PieChart>
```

If you were to run the application now, you wouldn't get any errors. You also wouldn't get any chart.

While you gave the PieChart class a dataProvider property, Flex has no way of knowing what data you want inside of the pie slices. What would happen if there were more data series than just Sales? There could be another series called Returns, and so forth. To give the PieChart the information it needs to render the pie properly, you must start off with the series container to provide the details.

4. Add the series container as follows:

```
<mx:PieChart width="50%" height="50%" dataProvider="{bookSales}">
    <mx:series>

    </mx:series>
</mx:PieChart>
```

Within the series container, since you are creating a PieChart, you need to use the PieSeries class to indicate that you want to assign the correct data series to the slices of the pie.

> As you will soon discover, you have to match the chart series with the type of chart. For instance, if you have a ColumnChart, you would use the ColumnSeries class.

You tell the PieSeries which data series to use by using the field property.

5. Add the following to series container:

```
<mx:PieChart width="50%" height="50%" dataProvider="{bookSales}">
    <mx:series>
        <mx:PieSeries field="Sales"/>
    </mx:series>
</mx:PieChart>
```

14

6. Run the application now. Your results should look like Figure 14-1.

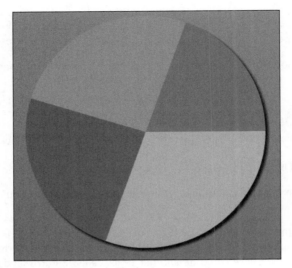

Figure 14-1. The basic PieChart component

It looks very nice. But without labels, the chart is meaningless. You want to label the pieces of the pie somehow.

7. Start by using the `labelPosition` property of the `PieSeries` class as follows. This not only turns on the label, but also decides where that label will be placed.

```
<mx:PieChart width="50%" height="50%" dataProvider="{bookSales}">
    <mx:series>
        <mx:PieSeries field="Sales" labelPosition="inside" />
    </mx:series>
</mx:PieChart>
```

This adds the labels as shown in Figure 14-2.

This is a step in the right direction. However, without labels, the numbers have little meaning.

You are probably looking for a `label` property that will add the labels from the bookType field. That is not how it is handled in Flex. Instead, when using the `PieChart` component, you need to create a function that will allow you to format the label exactly as it should appear.

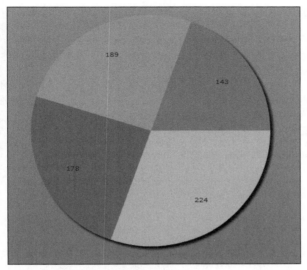

Figure 14-2. The PieChart with data added

The function you set up, using any name of your choice, will need to accept four parameters:

The first parameter is of type Object and represents the entire record being charted. The second argument is of type String and represents the name of the field being graphed. The third parameter is of type int and is the item number being charted. Finally, the fourth argument is of type Number and is the percentage of the pie this item represents.

The function must have a return type of String.

You may be thinking that you have a lot of programming ahead of you just to get a label. Don't worry, you have a few surprises coming up.

> **8.** Return to the Script block and enter the following function. For the purposes of this exercise, call the function chartLabel.
>
> ```
> private function chartLabel(dataItem:Object, field:String, ➥
> index:int, dataPercent:Number):String
> {
>        return dataItem.bookType;
> }
> ```

In this particular example, you can see that the function is only returning the bookType data: Fiction, Nonfiction, Technology, and Self-help. The names of the arguments are your choice, but the data types must be as shown.

14

509

Now here is the first surprise:

9. Return to the PieSeries tag and add the `labelFunction` property as follows:

```
<mx:PieChart width="50%" height="50%" dataProvider="{bookSales}">
    <mx:series>
        <mx:PieSeries field="Sales" labelPosition="inside" ➥
labelFunction="chartLabel" />
    </mx:series>
</mx:PieChart>
```

If you run the application, your chart should look like Figure 14-3.

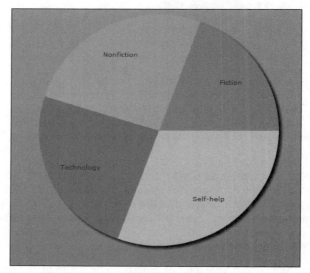

Figure 14-3. The labels added from the labelFunction property

First of all, the `labelFunction` property handled all of the complexities of the function call. You do not need to assign the arguments as you would with most function calls. Secondly, the `labelFunction` property overrides just the numbers that you saw in Figure 14-2.

This powerful feature will allow you to format the labels to look the way you want them to look, and not be the products of some predefined format. Here is an example:

10. Change the `chartLabel` function as follows:

```
private function chartLabel(dataItem:Object, field:String, ➥
index:int, dataPercent:Number):String
{
    return dataItem.bookType + " represents \n" + dataPercent + ➥
"% \n of our sales";
}
```

> Within a string, \n is used to create a new line. In programming parlance, this is called an **escape sequence**. Many programming languages, such as Java and C#, use this same symbol.

If you run your application, your chart should look like Figure 14-4.

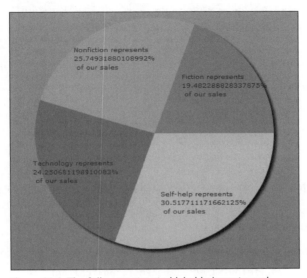

Figure 14-4. The fully concatenated label being returned

Unless you are working with the space shuttle program, that number may have a few more decimal places than you might want. There are a few ways you could approach this problem. Here, we'll use the round function of the Math class, which returns a rounded integer.

11. Make the following adjustments to the chartLabel function:

```
private function chartLabel(dataItem:Object, field:String, ➡
index:int, dataPercent:Number):String
{
    var rounded:Number = Math.round(dataPercent);
    return dataItem.bookType + " represents \n" + rounded + ➡
"% \n of our sales";
}
```

If you run the application, your chart should look like Figure 14-5.

14

511

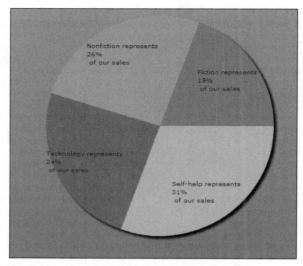

Figure 14-5. The adjusted label format in the chart

See how powerful this is? You can set up virtually any label format you might want.

It's beyond the scope of this book to discuss all of the options available in charts. However, let's look at a couple more options.

12. Inside of the PieSeries tag, change the labelPosition property to callout.

```
<mx:PieSeries field="Sales" labelPosition="callout" ➥
labelFunction="chartLabel" />
```

13. Run the application. Your chart should look like Figure 14-6.

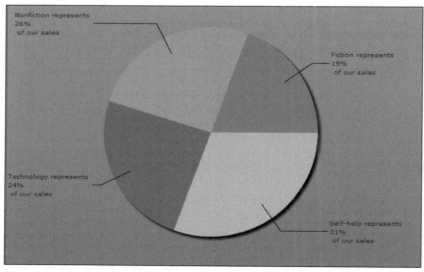

Figure 14-6. The labels placed as callouts

The chart could be made a lot more interesting visually by adding some gradient fills. This can be done easily by using the <mx:fills> container within the PieSeries container. Within that container, you place a second container called <mx:RadialGradient> (you could also insert a LinearGradient) for each slice of the pie. Within each RadialGradient container, there needs to be an <mx:entries> container. Finally, within the entries container, you place two <mx:GradientEntry> tags: one for the opening color and one for the closing color.

Don't worry if you just got confused about the order of the containers. The following code example will clarify this concept for the four slices of your pie.

14. Change the PieSeries tag's close from /> to > so that there is an opening and closing tag. Then, within the container, place the following code. As an interesting exercise, after you build each of the RadialGradient containers, run the application. You will see how these containers build the slices. After the first one, you will have one big slice. The second will give you four slices in matching pairs. The third will give you three slices, and the fourth will give you four distinct slices.

```
<mx:PieChart width="50%" height="50%" dataProvider="{bookSales}">
    <mx:series>
        <mx:PieSeries field="Sales" labelPosition="callout" ➥
labelFunction="chartLabel">
            <mx:fills>
                <mx:RadialGradient>
                    <mx:entries>
                        <mx:GradientEntry color="#E9C836"/>
                        <mx:GradientEntry color="#AA9127"/>
                    </mx:entries>
                </mx:RadialGradient>
                <mx:RadialGradient>
                    <mx:entries>
                        <mx:GradientEntry color="#A1AECF"/>
                        <mx:GradientEntry color="#47447A"/>
                    </mx:entries>
                </mx:RadialGradient>
                <mx:RadialGradient>
                    <mx:entries>
                        <mx:GradientEntry color="#339933"/>
                        <mx:GradientEntry color="#339998"/>
                    </mx:entries>
                </mx:RadialGradient>
                <mx:RadialGradient>
                    <mx:GradientEntry color="#6FB35F"/>
                    <mx:GradientEntry color="#497B54"/>
                </mx:RadialGradient>
            </mx:fills>
        </mx:PieSeries>
    </mx:series>
</mx:PieChart>
```

14

When completed, you results should resemble Figure 14-7.

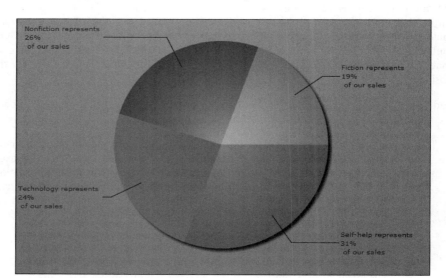

Figure 14-7. The chart with fills added

Now, using the same data, let's turn our attention to the ColumnChart component.

Using the ColumnChart component

A ColumnChart component uses a different set of class files from a PieChart component, as you'll see for yourself in the example. However, many of the concepts are exactly the same as those for the PieChart component.

1. Since you will be using the same small data model that you used in the PieChart example, just delete all of the code from the opening to the closing PieChart tag.

2. As you did with the PieChart component, call the ColumnChart component as follows. Place the code below the Script block.

   ```
   <mx:ColumnChart dataProvider="{bookSales}" width="50%" height="50%">

   </mx:ColumnChart>
   ```

3. Run the application; you will get a skeletal structure that won't be very informative, as shown in Figure 14-8.

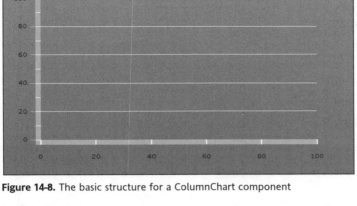

Figure 14-8. The basic structure for a ColumnChart component

Unlike the pie chart, a column chart has two axes. The horizontal, or x-axis, is called the **Category axis**; the vertical axis, the y-axis, is called the **Data axis**. The Category axis will contain the bookType data: Fiction, Nonfiction Technical, Self-help.

4. Make the following changes to your code:

```
<mx:ColumnChart dataProvider="{bookSales}" width="50%" height="50%">
    <mx:horizontalAxis>
        <mx:CategoryAxis categoryField="bookType"/>
    </mx:horizontalAxis>
</mx:ColumnChart>
```

5. Run your code; your results should be like Figure 14-9.

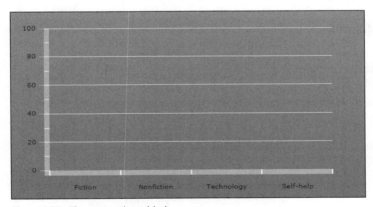

Figure 14-9. The categories added

Like you did with the pie chart, you will now create a series container that will contain a ColumnSeries class (as opposed to the PieSeries class). However, the ColumnSeries class will have two different properties: xField and yField. Here you match the data with the axis. We already established that the x-axis is bookType. The category Sales contains the actual data.

14

6. Add the following series container and the ColumnSeries class below the closing horizontalAxis tag:

```
<mx:ColumnChart dataProvider="{bookSales}" width="50%" height="50%">
    <mx:horizontalAxis>
        <mx:CategoryAxis categoryField="bookType"/>
    </mx:horizontalAxis>
    <mx:series>
        <mx:ColumnSeries xField="bookType" yField="Sales"/>
    </mx:series>
</mx:ColumnChart>
```

7. Run the application; your results should look similar to Figure 14-10.

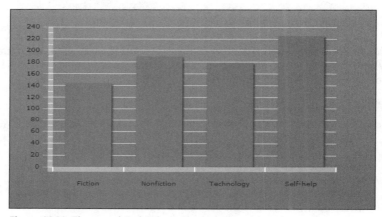

Figure 14-10. The completed ColumnChart component

One handy feature of the ColumnChart class is the showDataTips property. This will allow the user to roll over a bar on the chart and see the specific data.

8. Return to the ColumnChart opening tag and add the showDataTips property as follows:

```
<mx:ColumnChart dataProvider="{bookSales}" width="50%" ➥
height="50%" showDataTips="true">
```

9. Run the application. Watch what happens when you roll your mouse over one of the columns (see Figure 14-11).

Figure 14-11. Adding the DataTip feature

That's all well and good, but what happens when you are working with multiple sets of data? Let's add some more data to our ArrayCollection and see.

10. Begin by making a modification to your ArrayCollection as follows:

```
private var bookSales:ArrayCollection = new ArrayCollection(
    [{bookType: "Fiction", Sales: 143, returns: 13},
     {bookType: "Nonfiction", Sales: 189, returns: 9},
     {bookType: "Technology", Sales: 178, returns: 11},
        {bookType: "Self-help", Sales: 224, returns: 7}]);
```

You would add this second series by adding a second ColumnSeries class to the series container, as shown here. Do so now.

11. Add a second ColumnSeries below the existing one. This time, make the value of the yField property returns.

```
<mx:series>
    <mx:ColumnSeries xField="bookType" yField="Sales"/>
    <mx:ColumnSeries xField="bookType" yField="returns"/>
</mx:series>
```

12. Run the application, and you should get the results shown in Figure 14-12.

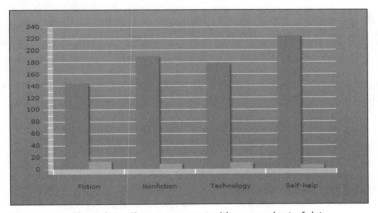

Figure 14-12. The ColumnChart component with a second set of data

You can easily see the second set of data charted, but at this point you have no idea which column shows sales and which column shows returns. In order to make the distinction, you need to add a legend to the chart. To accomplish this, you need to make a few minor adjustments to the code.

13. Give the ColumnChart an id property. For this example, name it myChart.

```
<mx:ColumnChart dataProvider="{bookSales}" width="50%" ➡
height="50%" showDataTips="true" id="myChart">
```

14

14. Under the closing ColumnChart tag, add the Legend class and bind it to myChart. Depending on where you want the legend placed, you will need to set x and y values. For the purposes of this exercise, I specified these properties as 630 and 10, respectively. However, you can use your own settings.

```
</mx:ColumnChart>
<mx:Legend dataProvider="{myChart}" x="630" y="10"/>
```

15. Run the application. You will see the beginnings of a legend. However, as shown in Figure 14-13, there is a problem.

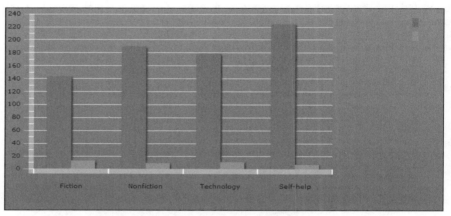

Figure 14-13. The Legend component in the upper-right corner

You see the colors associated with the columns, but no text to identify what they stand for. In order to get that, you need to add the displayName property to the two ColumnSeries tags.

16. Modify the two ColumnSeries tags as follows:

```
<mx:series>
    <mx:ColumnSeries xField="bookType" yField="Sales" ➥
displayName="Book Sales"/>
    <mx:ColumnSeries xField="bookType" yField="returns" ➥
displayName="Book Returns"/>
</mx:series>
```

17. Run the application. The legend is now successfully completed, as shown in Figure 14-14.

As you can see, you just created a nice-looking chart. You could also add the gradient effects that you used in the pie chart earlier. But, instead of that here, let's try something even more exciting: animating your charts.

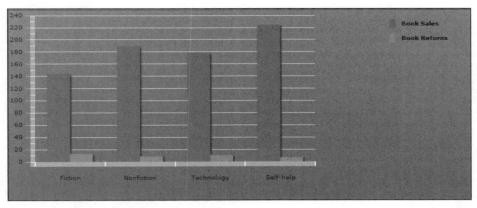

Figure 14-14. The complete chart with Legend

Animating the chart

Let's say you need to compare data from Company A to data from Company B. With Flex, You can create great-looking transitions between the data sets of the different companies. As you are about to see, the programming is not all that difficult.

You can use the ColumnChart component you created in the last exercise. However, you need to make a few adjustments to the animation concept.

1. Rename your existing ArrayCollection as bookSalesA. Then create a second ArrayCollection called bookSalesB. It should look as follows:

```
[Bindable]
private var bookSalesA:ArrayCollection = new ArrayCollection(
    [{bookType: "Fiction", Sales: 143, returns: 13},
    {bookType: "Nonfiction", Sales: 189, returns: 9},
    {bookType: "Technology", Sales: 178, returns: 11},
    {bookType: "Self-help", Sales: 224, returns: 7}]);

[Bindable]
private var bookSalesB:ArrayCollection = new ArrayCollection(
    [{bookType: "Fiction", Sales: 91, returns: 20},
    {bookType: "Nonfiction", Sales: 142, returns: 28},
    {bookType: "Technology", Sales: 182, returns: 30},
    {bookType: "Self-help", Sales: 120, returns: 10}]);
```

2. Adjust the ColumnChart's dataProvider property to look initially at bookSalesA.

```
<mx:ColumnChart dataProvider="{bookSalesA}" width="50%" ➥
height="50%" showDataTips="true" id="myChart">
```

There are three potential types of transitions:

- SeriesInterpolate
- SeriesSlide
- SeriesZoom

You will look at all three types, starting with SeriesInterpolate, which is the easiest to do.

3. Right below the Script block, set up the <SeriesInterpolate> tag. To use this, it must be given an id and duration property (recall from earlier chapters that duration is expressed in milliseconds).

```
<mx:SeriesInterpolate id="chartChange" duration="2000"/>
```

You now need to tie the ColumnSeries element to the effect, which in this case is SeriesInterpolate. You will use two instances of the showDataEffect event.

4. Add the following showDataEffect events to the ColumnSeries tags:

```
<mx:ColumnChart dataProvider="{bookSalesA}" width="50%" ➥
height="50%" showDataTips="true" id="myChart">
    <mx:horizontalAxis>
        <mx:CategoryAxis categoryField="bookType"/>
    </mx:horizontalAxis>
    <mx:series>
        <mx:ColumnSeries xField="bookType" yField="Sales" ➥
displayName="Book Sales" showDataEffect="{chartChange}"/>
        <mx:ColumnSeries xField="bookType" yField="returns" ➥
displayName="Book Returns" showDataEffect="{chartChange}"/>
    </mx:series>
</mx:ColumnChart>
```

Notice that bookSalesA is still the default dataProvider. As you will see momentarily, this will be the initial data with the chart. Without this default, the chart will not render.

The two ColumnSeries now use the property showDataEffect and reference the id of the SeriesInterpolate class.

You now need to create a means of switching between the data sets bookSalesA and bookSalesB. The best tool for doing this will probably be the RadioButton component. Since you have already learned to use this, I will not discuss the mechanics in great detail here.

For this example, use the HBox container to contain the RadioButton component.

5. Below the Legend tag, create the following code:

```
<mx:HBox x="20" y="400">
    <mx:RadioButton groupName="books" label="Book Sales A" ➥
selected="true"  click="myChart.dataProvider = bookSalesA"/>
```

```
            <mx:RadioButton groupName="books" label="Book Sales B" ➥
        click="myChart.dataProvider = bookSalesB"/>
        </mx:HBox>
```

Notice that you made the Book Sales A button the default. When a RadioButton is selected, a click event is created. The event will call the dataProvider attribute of the chart and call the desired data set.

That is all there is to it.

6. Go ahead and run the application. When you click the RadioButtons, the bars on the chart will animate, and the whole chart will rescale.

Now you'll make a few minor changes that demonstrate the SeriesSlide effect.

To accomplish this, you need to create two effects: one to "slide" the columns in and one to "slide" the columns out.

7. Replace the SeriesInterpolate tag with the two SeriesSlide tags as shown here:

```
<mx:SeriesSlide id="chartSlideIn" duration="2000" direction="up"/>
<mx:SeriesSlide id="chartSlideOut" duration="2000" direction="down"/>
```

Notice that you need to specify a direction attribute. In this case, you will specify values that make the columns rise up to slide the new data in and collapse down to take the old data out. If you can't visualize this, you will in a moment.

In the ColumnSeries tags, you will need to change the existing showDataEffect properties to tie them to chartSlideIn. However, to slide the chart out, you need to first hide it. The hideDataEffect property will do the job by tying it to the chartSlideOut SeriesSlide.

8. Make the following changes to your ColumnSeries tags:

```
<mx:series>
        <mx:ColumnSeries xField="bookType" yField="Sales" ➥
    displayName="Book Sales" showDataEffect="{chartSlideIn}" ➥
    hideDataEffect="{chartSlideOut}"/>
        <mx:ColumnSeries xField="bookType" yField="returns" ➥
    displayName="Book Returns" showDataEffect="{chartSlideIn}" ➥
    hideDataEffect="{chartSlideOut}"/>
    </mx:series>
```

There is no need to make any changes to the RadioButton components.

9. Run the application. When you click a RadioButton component, you should find the effect quite stunning. The present columns are hidden and the new ones rise up.

As a final exercise in this section, let's test the SeriesZoom effect.

14

521

10. To test out the SeriesZoom effect, substitute SeriesZoom for SeriesSlide and eliminate the direction property as follows:

```
<mx:SeriesZoom id="chartSlideIn" duration="2000" />
<mx:SeriesZoom id="chartSlideOut" duration="2000" />
```

11. Run the application. You will see the columns zoom in and out.

As you can see, you can create some really cool chart effects easily in Flex.

Using the BarChart component

As a final exercise, you can easily turn the column chart into a bar chart. As you may know already, a bar chart is a column chart turned on its side.

Use the ColumnChart component you created in the previous exercise and make a few modifications.

1. Begin by changing the opening and closing <mx:ColumnChart> tags to <mx:BarChart>. You will not need to change any other attributes.

In a ColumnChart component, the CategoryAxis is the horizontal axis. However, in a BarChart component, the CategoryAxis becomes the vertical axis.

2. Change the horizontalAxis container to verticalAxis.

```
<mx:verticalAxis>
    <mx:CategoryAxis categoryField="bookType"/>
</mx:verticalAxis>
```

Finally, you need to change the series from a ColumnSeries to a BarSeries. However, remember that the xField and yField are also reversed within the series.

3. Make the following changes:

```
<mx:series>
    <mx:BarSeries yField="bookType" xField="Sales" ➥
displayName="Book Sales" showDataEffect="{chartSlideIn}" ➥
hideDataEffect="{chartSlideOut}"/>
    <mx:BarSeries yField="bookType" xField="returns" ➥
displayName="Book Returns" showDataEffect="{chartSlideIn}" ➥
hideDataEffect="{chartSlideOut}"/>
</mx:series>
```

That is all there is to it—the complete chart code should look as follows:

```
<mx:BarChart dataProvider="{bookSalesA}" width="50%" height="50%" ➥
showDataTips="true" id="myChart">
    <mx:verticalAxis>
        <mx:CategoryAxis categoryField="bookType"/>
    </mx:verticalAxis>
```

```
    <mx:series>
        <mx:BarSeries yField="bookType" xField="Sales" ➡
displayName="Book Sales" showDataEffect="{chartSlideIn}" ➡
hideDataEffect="{chartSlideOut}"/>
        <mx:BarSeries yField="bookType" xField="returns" ➡
displayName="Book Returns" showDataEffect="{chartSlideIn}" ➡
hideDataEffect="{chartSlideOut}"/>
    </mx:series>
</mx:BarChart>
```

4. Run the application now. You should see something like Figure 14-15.

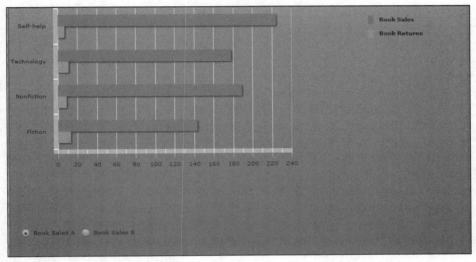

Figure 14-15. The completed BarChart

Summary

As you can see, charting is an easy-to-use and effective way of presenting your data. Or course, you can use the techniques you learned earlier in this book to import your data from an outside data source such as XML or ColdFusion.

You are near the homestretch; now let me turn your attention to a new technology just released by Adobe: the Adobe Integrated Runtime, or AIR.

14

15 ADOBE INTEGRATED RUNTIME (AIR)

Let me start off here by clearing up a very popular misconception: the purpose of Adobe Integrated Runtime (AIR) is NOT to replace existing web technologies with Flex, but to allow you to leverage your knowledge of existing web technologies to build desktop applications that can access the Web like web applications.

The new Adobe Integrated Runtime technology will take the concept of web design in a whole new direction.

This chapter will mainly focus on Flex's use of AIR. A complete treatise on AIR would be the subject of an entire book. For that, at the time of this writing, you might want to check out the following titles:

- *Creating Mashups with Adobe Flex and Air* by John Crosby, David Hassoun, and Chris Korhonen (friends of ED, 2008)
- *AdvancED AIR Applications* by Marco Casario, Koen De Weggheleire, Peter Elst, and Zach Stepek (Apress, 2008)

However, keeping that in mind, we will take a pretty extensive overview as to what this technology is and how you can harness it.

Understanding AIR

In Chapter 1 of this book, I put forth the premise that the lines of distinction between desktop and web applications are becoming blurred. We are now seeing the beginning of desktop applications that access data on the Web. One of the best examples of this can be downloaded from a major website:

http://desktop.ebay.com

*If this is the first time you are downloading an AIR application, you will be prompted to download a second piece of software: **the Adobe AIR Runtime**. While this analogy is not exact, it is the equivalent of the Flash Player plug-in for desktop AIR applications. Once installed, it does not need to be installed again.*

If you download it and sign in using your existing eBay account information, you will see a working AIR application, as shown in Figure 15-1.

Notice that it is installed as an icon on your desktop.

In this application, you can carry on the same functionality as you could on the regular website. You can search for sale items, place bids, and upload items you may want to sell. However, it has the look and feel of a desktop application and does not require the use of a web browser. Because it is not using a web browser, the overall resources used are far less than a traditional website. Further, it makes for faster and smoother connections if you access it using a portable device such as a cell phone.

Figure 15-1. The Ebay AIR application

> *While not all cell phones are Flash equipped yet, the number is growing rapidly.*

As of this writing, Adobe is releasing updates to its most popular web design tools, including Flash and Dreamweaver CS3, to facilitate the building of AIR applications. However, you do not need to use any of these tools to develop AIR applications. You could write an AIR application using a simple text editor and HTML. The reason for this is that the foundation of an AIR application is not the tool itself, but the **Adobe Integrated Runtime**: a library of class files that supports the building of desktop applications in Flex, Flash, or HTML. This runtime can be installed in a number of operating systems including any version of Windows from Windows 2000 (SP4) on and most of the Mac systems, including PowerPC, Tiger (10.4), and Leopard (10.5).

> *As of this writing, a version of AIR for Linux is in development. However, there is still no firm release date.*

Let me repeat something: with Adobe AIR, you do not need to learn new web design technologies; instead, you will need to rethink how you deploy and package them. Keeping that in mind, let's try our first AIR application.

15

Hello World

Since you have reached the last chapter in this book about Flex 3, I think I can safely assume you have Flex 3 installed. As a result, you do not need to download anything additional in order to create AIR applications. The same is true if you use Flash CS3. However, a person who does not use one of these technologies would need to begin developing AIR applications by first going to the Adobe site and downloading the free Adobe Integrated Runtime. Since we are working with Flex 3, that will not be necessary here.

1. Start a new Flex project called Chapter15_project (see Figure 15-2).

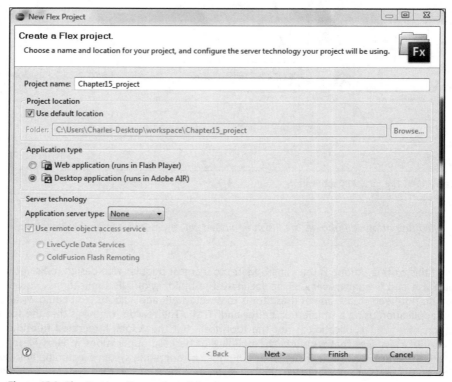

Figure 15-2. The Create a Flex project dialog box

Notice in Figure 15-2, under the category Application type, Desktop application (runs in Adobe AIR) is selected. This will automatically invoke the proper library of class files necessary to build and deploy an AIR application.

2. Click Next to bring up the dialog box shown in Figure 15-3.

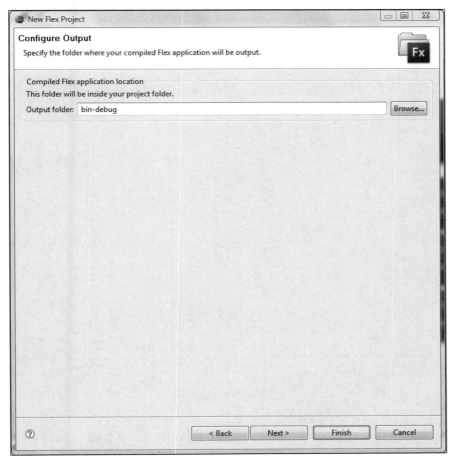

Figure 15-3. The Configure Output dialog box

Once again, the Output folder setting is the bin-debug, as it has been for all of your previous projects. There is little or no reason to change that.

3. Click Next. You'll be taken to the dialog box shown in Figure 15-4.

If you look at Figure 15-4, or at your own application, you will see the first difference between a standard Flex project and an AIR application. Notice that the source folder is still the src folder and that an MXML file is still being created. However, we see something new called the **Application ID**. This will be a unique string to identify your AIR application. This identifier must be a maximum of 212 characters in length, and can use any combination of letters, numbers, dots, and hyphens.

For the purposes of this exercise, the default Application ID of Chapter15-project (note that it uses the hyphen in place of the underscore, which is not allowed in the identifier) will be fine.

15

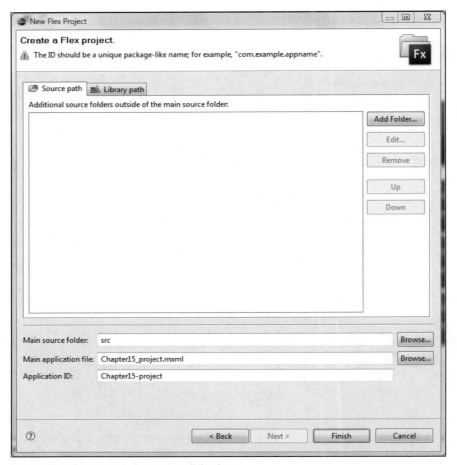

Figure 15-4. The Create a Flex project dialog box

4. Click Finish. You will now see the real differences between a Flex application and an AIR application.

Let's begin by looking at the code:

```
<?xml version="1.0" encoding="utf-8"?>
<mx:WindowedApplication xmlns:mx="http://www.adobe.com/2006/mxml" ➥
layout="absolute">

</mx:WindowedApplication>
```

Notice that in place of the opening and closing Application tags, you have a new tag called WindowedApplication. This is the class that Flex needs to access the class files necessary to compile the code into an AIR application. The properties associated with this class are identical to those used in the Application tag.

However, there is another significant difference.

Look in the Flex Navigator. You will see a second file created called Chapter15_project-app.xml (see Figure 15-5).

Figure 15-5.
The Flex Navigator with the new XML file

5. Open this file. You will see the following code:

```xml
<?xml version="1.0" encoding="UTF-8"?>
<application xmlns="http://ns.adobe.com/air/application/1.0">

<!-- Adobe AIR Application Descriptor File Template.

	Specifies parameters for identifying, installing, and ➥
launching AIR applications.
	See http://www.adobe.com/go/air_1.0_application_descriptor ➥
for complete documentation.

	xmlns - The Adobe AIR namespace: http://ns.adobe.com/air/➥
application/1.0
			The last segment of the namespace specifies the version
			of the AIR runtime required for this application to run.

	minimumPatchLevel - The minimum patch level of the AIR ➥
runtime required to run
			the application. Optional.
-->

	<!-- The application identifier string, unique to this ➥
application. Required. -->
	<id>Chapter15-project</id>

	<!-- Used as the filename for the application. Required. -->
	<filename>Chapter15_project</filename>

	<!-- The name that is displayed in the AIR application ➥
installer. Optional. -->
	<name>Chapter15_project</name>
```

15

```
      <!-- An application version designator (such as "v1", ➡
"2.5", or "Alpha 1"). Required. -->
      <version>v1</version>

      <!-- Description, displayed in the AIR application ➡
installer. Optional. -->
      <!-- <description></description> -->

      <!-- Copyright information. Optional -->
      <!-- <copyright></copyright> -->

      <!-- Settings for the application's initial window. Required. -->
      <initialWindow>
            <!-- The main SWF or HTML file of the application. ➡
Required. -->
            <!-- Note: In Flex Builder, the SWF reference is set ➡
automatically. -->
            <content>[This value will be overwritten by Flex ➡
Builder in the output app.xml]</content>

            <!-- The title of the main window. Optional. -->
            <!-- <title></title> -->

            <!-- The type of system chrome to use (either ➡
"standard" or "none"). Optional. Default standard. -->
            <!-- <systemChrome></systemChrome> -->

            <!-- Whether the window is transparent. Only applicable ➡
when systemChrome is false. Optional. Default false. -->
            <!-- <transparent></transparent> -->

            <!-- Whether the window is initially visible. Optional. ➡
Default false. -->
            <!-- <visible></visible> -->

            <!-- Whether the user can minimize the window. ➡
Optional. Default true. -->
            <!-- <minimizable></minimizable> -->

            <!-- Whether the user can maximize the window. ➡
Optional. Default true. -->
            <!-- <maximizable></maximizable> -->

            <!-- Whether the user can resize the window. ➡
Optional. Default true. -->
            <!-- <resizable></resizable> -->

            <!-- The window's initial width. Optional. -->
            <!-- <width></width> -->
```

```
        <!-- The window's initial height. Optional. -->
        <!-- <height></height> -->

        <!-- The window's initial x position. Optional. -->
        <!-- <x></x> -->

        <!-- The window's initial y position. Optional. -->
        <!-- <y></y> -->

        <!-- The window's minimum size, specified as a ➡
width/height pair, such as "400 200". Optional. -->
        <!-- <minSize></minSize> -->

        <!-- The window's initial maximum size, specified as a ➡
width/height pair, such as "1600 1200". Optional. -->
        <!-- <maxSize></maxSize> -->
    </initialWindow>

    <!-- The subpath of the standard default installation ➡
location to use. Optional. -->
    <!-- <installFolder></installFolder> -->

    <!-- The subpath of the Windows Start/Programs menu to use. ➡
Optional. -->
    <!-- <programMenuFolder></programMenuFolder> -->

    <!-- The icon the system uses for the application. For at ➡
least one resolution,
         specify the path to a PNG file included in the AIR ➡
package. Optional. -->
    <!-- <icon>
        <image16x16></image16x16>
        <image32x32></image32x32>
        <image48x48></image48x48>
        <image128x128></image128x128>
    </icon> -->

    <!-- Whether the application handles the update when a ➡
user double-clicks an update version
    of the AIR file (true), or the default AIR application ➡
installer handles the update (false).
    Optional. Default false. -->
    <!-- <customUpdateUI></customUpdateUI> -->

    <!-- Whether the application can be launched when the ➡
user clicks a link in a web browser.
    Optional. Default false. -->
    <!-- <allowBrowserInvocation></allowBrowserInvocation> -->
```

15

```
        <!-- Listing of file types for which the application ➥
can register. Optional. -->
        <!-- <fileTypes> -->

            <!-- Defines one file type. Optional. -->
            <!-- <fileType> -->

                <!-- The name that the system displays for ➥
the registered file type. Required. -->
                <!-- <name></name> -->

                <!-- The extension to register. Required. -->
                <!-- <extension></extension> -->

                <!-- The description of the file type. Optional. -->
                <!-- <description></description> -->

                <!-- The MIME type. Optional. -->
                <!-- <contentType></contentType> -->

                <!-- The icon to display for the file type. ➥
Optional. -->
                <!-- <icon>
                    <image16x16></image16x16>
                    <image32x32></image32x32>
                    <image48x48></image48x48>
                    <image128x128></image128x128>
                </icon> -->

            <!-- </fileType> -->
        <!-- </fileTypes> -->

</application>
```

This file is called the **Application Descriptor**. The purpose of this XML file is to tell the AIR compiler how the application should be built. We will be examining this in greater detail in a few moments. However, for now, return to the MXML application file.

6. Change the layout property in the opening WindowedApplication tag to vertical.

```
<?xml version="1.0" encoding="utf-8"?>
<mx:WindowedApplication xmlns:mx="http://www.adobe.com/2006/mxml" ➥
layout="vertical">

</mx:WindowedApplication>
```

7. Within the opening and closing WindowedApplication tags, put a Label tag with the text property of Hello From Adobe AIR. It Is Easy to Use. Make the fontWeight bold and the fontSize 24.

```
<?xml version="1.0" encoding="utf-8"?>
<mx:WindowedApplication xmlns:mx="http://www.adobe.com/2006/mxml" ➥
layout="vertical">
    <mx:Label text="Hello from Adobe AIR. It Is Easy to Use" ➥
fontWeight="bold" fontSize="24"/>
</mx:WindowedApplication>
```

8. Go ahead and run the application. Your results should resemble Figure 15-6.

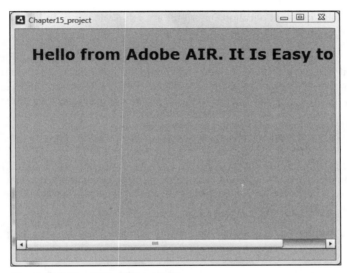

Figure 15-6. The Adobe AIR application

Notice that the traditional browser window didn't open up. Instead, in this particular case, an application window started with its own scrollbar and its own window controls. The window can even be resized, and, if you make it large enough, the scrollbar will disappear.

If you look at the bin-debug folder within the Flex Navigator View, you will see that there are only two files deployed: the Application Descriptor XML file and a SWF file (see Figure 15-7).

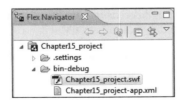

Figure 15-7.
The deployed files in the Flex
Navigator View

Now that you have a little feel as to how Adobe AIR works, this is a good time to turn your attention back to the Application Descriptor.

15

The Application Descriptor

If necessary, reopen the XML file Chapter15_project-app.xml. There is a lot here. We will be only touching on the main sections you should know about. The reason is because you are using Flex Builder, most of the values entered here will be overridden by the settings in the MXML file in Flex Builder. As a result, most of the mechanics of this file are not necessary to touch and would only be needed if you were manually creating an AIR application.

Most of the fields in the Application Descriptor are self-explanatory and accompanied with a comment describing what the field does as well as any default values.

Once again, there will be very little need for you to touch the fields in this file. As a matter of fact, if you were to enter values, your compiled application may not reflect those changes. However, it is still a good idea to at least have a working knowledge of the contents of this file. Keeping that in mind, let's do a review of the salient sections.

```
<?xml version="1.0" encoding="UTF-8"?>
<application xmlns="http://ns.adobe.com/air/application/1.0">
```

The Application Descriptor always begins with an XML declaration and an opening application tag. Within the application tag, the compiler version is declared in the XML namespace. As of this writing, that compiler version is version 1.0, which is the initial public release of the AIR compiler.

After some comments in the XML code, at approximately line 18, you should see a tag named id.

```
<!-- The application identifier string, unique to this ➡
application. Required. -->
    <id>Chapter15-project</id>
```

This is the Application ID you named earlier when creating the Flex project. If you were not working in Flex Builder, you would need to name the Application ID here. An emerging standard is to use a reverse domain for an ID. For instance, assuming we use the domain www.friendsofed.com, your id might be something like this:

```
com.friendsofed.chapter15-project
```

Each application should have its own unique identifier. For the purposes of this exercise, there is no reason to change it. Flex Builder handles it automatically.

As you move down to about lines 23–28, you should see name and version tags with corresponding comments.

```
<!-- The name that is displayed in the AIR application ➡
installer. Optional. -->
    <name>Chapter15_project</name>

    <!-- An application version designator (such as "v1", ➡
"2.5", or "Alpha 1"). Required. -->
    <version>v1</version>
```

Here Flex automatically assigns the name of the MXML file. Also, as you update your application, you can change the version number to reflect these changes. This is required.

If you come down to lines 29–33, you should see the description and copyright information.

```
<!-- Description, displayed in the AIR application installer. ➥
Optional. -->
     <!-- <description></description> -->

     <!-- Copyright information. Optional -->
     <!-- <copyright></copyright> -->
```

These tags, as most of them are for this file, are pretty self-explanatory. For instance, let's say you want to give your application a description that will be compiled with it. You can do the following as an example:

```
<!-- Description, displayed in the AIR application installer. ➥
Optional. -->
     <!-- <description>My first Adobe AIR application.➥
</description> -->
```

Up to this point, the tags you have been looking at have no real effect on the application itself. They are just descriptive in nature. However, the next group will affect the application.

Let's look at the group of files, from about line 35 to about 80, grouped together with the <initialWindow> tag<$I~<initialWindow> tag>.

```
<!-- Settings for the application's initial window. Required. -->
     <initialWindow>
          <!-- The main SWF or HTML file of the ➥
application. Required. -->
          <!-- Note: In Flex Builder, the SWF reference is set ➥
automatically. -->
          <content>[This value will be overwritten by Flex ➥
Builder in the output app.xml]</content>
```

Normally, if you were building an AIR application manually, not using one of the Adobe technologies, you would fill this information in. However, as I have mentioned several times, Flex Builder overrides any information you would enter here. As an example, notice that there is a title field. If you enter a title into that field, you would expect that the title of the AIR application window would be the title you entered. If you were not working in Flex Builder, that would certainly be true. However, since Flex Builder overrides many of the settings of this file, the compiled application will not reflect the change. Instead, you would need to change the title property of the WindowedApplication tag in the MXML file.

Once again, the rest of the tags are self-explanatory; they handle items like window size, x- and y-positions, transparency, and visibility.

15

Past the `<initialWindow>` group, most of the information in the Application Descriptor XML file has to do with the packaging and the icons involved. In most instances, the default information will work fine, and there is very little reason to change this information.

Go ahead and close this file now. We will not need to go into it further.

We will now talk about deploying an AIR application.

Deploying an AIR application

Once your application is created, and ready for prime time, you will need to deploy it. **Deploying** means compiling the application, giving it a security certificate, and packaging the application in an installer file. Of course, when you save a Flex application, everything is compiled. So let's start the deployment process.

1. Select Project ➤ Export Release Build to bring up the dialog box shown in Figure 15-8.

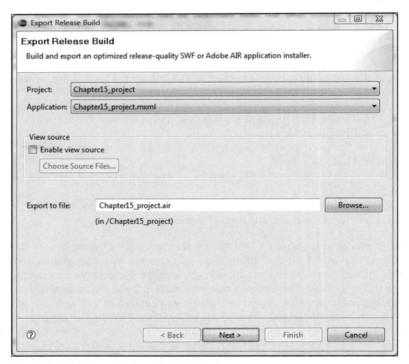

Figure 15-8. The Export Release Build dialog box

Here you can select the project and the application file that needs to be compiled.

Notice that there is a check box called Enable view source. This will enable the button Choose Source Files, which brings up the dialog box shown in Figure 15-9.

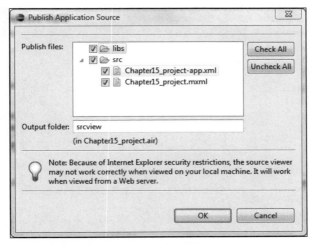

Figure 15-9. The Choose Source Files dialog box

In most instances, you will not need to use this feature. You would use it only if you had a situation in which you needed to select files (or deselect files) required or (not required) for your project. Past that, all of the files in the src and libs folders will be selected automatically. For the purposes for this example, that is fine.

The next step is to choose where you want the install file to export to. You choose this in the Export to file field. Notice that Adobe AIR applications package with the file extension of .air.

While it is not necessary, I am a strong believer in deploying applications to their own folders. You can do this by clicking the Browse button to the right of the field.

2. Click the Browse button. The Save As dialog box will appear (see Figure 15-10).

This screen will vary a bit depending on your operating system. For the purposes of this exercise, I created a folder called HelloWorld and changed the output filename to HelloWorld.air.

3. Create a new folder in your operating system and change the output file name to HelloWorld.

4. Click Save.

5. Click Next to bring up the dialog box shown in Figure 15-11.

15

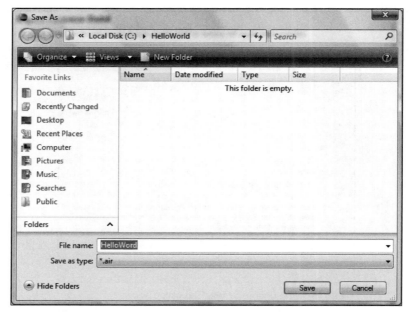

Figure 15-10. The Save As dialog box

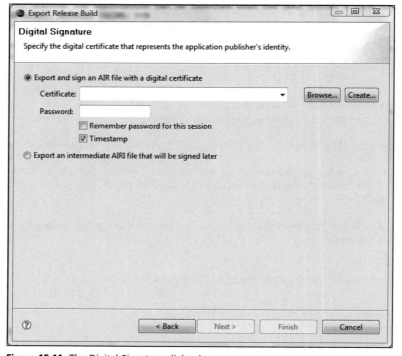

Figure 15-11. The Digital Signature dialog box

Let's talk a little about digital signatures before continuing on with this exercise.

Digital signatures

All Adobe AIR applications must have a digital security certificate, even if it is self-signed.

Self-signed security certificates are appropriate for internal or limited-distribution applications. But if you are going to distribute your application commercially, you are going to want to look at one of the security certificate vendors such as VeriSign.

The first thing you need to do is create a certificate and tell Flex Builder where you want it to be stored. In most instances, the application folder you created (in this case, HelloWorld) is fine.

1. Click the Create button to the right of the Certificate field. This will bring up the screen shown in Figure 15-12.

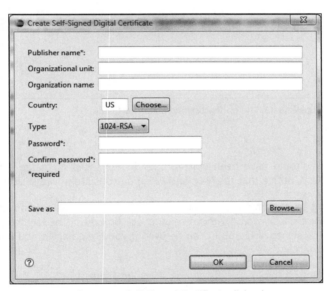

Figure 15-12. The Create Self-Signed Certificate dialog box

2. Let's give the certificate a Publisher name setting of friendsofed.com. You can leave the Organizational unit and Organizational name fields blank.

3. There are two types of certificate, 1024-RSA and 2048-RSA, depending on the desired level of encryption. For the purposes of this exercise, 1024-RSA is fine.

4. Enter a password of your choice and then confirm that password.

5. The final step is to select where you want to save the certificate. In most situations, you can save it in the same folder that you are exporting your application to: in this case, the HelloWorld folder created in the last section. Do this by clicking the Browse button.

15

6. Give the file a name of HelloWorldCertificate. Flex Builder will automatically add the .p12 file extension to it.

7. Click Save. Your finished certificate should look something like Figure 15-13.

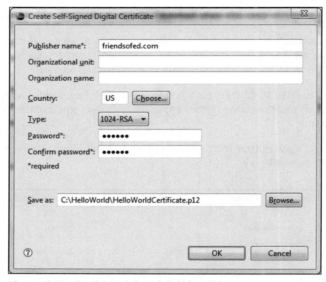

Figure 15-13. The finished signed digital certificate

8. Click OK.

The information should have been written back to the Digital Signature dialog box (see Figure 15-14). Also, notice that the Next and Finish buttons are now available.

If you are going to be compiling multiple times during this session, you might want to check the Remember password for this session check box. Also, the Export an intermediate AIRI file that will be signed later option can be used if you are going to add a signed certificate later on.

9. Click Next to bring up the dialog box shown in Figure 15-15.

The Included files dialog box will show you which files are being included in the exported application. Notice that in this case, there are only two files: the Application Descriptor XML file and the SWF file. In most instances, you will not need to change anything here.

10. Click Finish.

The application is now created.

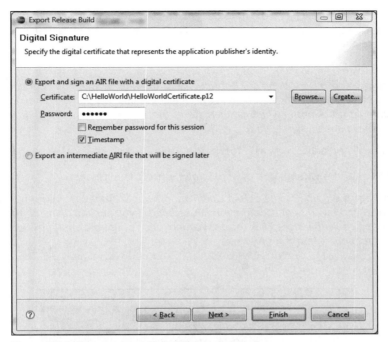

Figure 15-14. The completed Digital Signature dialog box

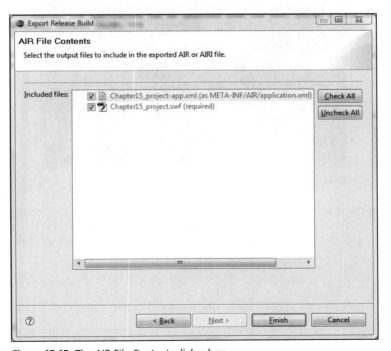

Figure 15-15. The AIR File Contents dialog box

15

11. Maneuver to the HelloWorld folder you created. You should see two files in it, the .air installer and the .p12 certificate file. Double-click the installer file to bring up the dialog box shown in Figure 15-16.

> If for some reason the Adobe AIR Runtime is not already installed on your computer, you will be prompted to download and install it. As of this writing, several people have encountered situations in which an alert states that the application is not recognized. Should that happen, simply go to
>
> http://get.adobe.com/air/?promoid=BUIGQ
>
> (the link as of this writing) and download and install the runtime.
>
> Notice that the name of the actual application being installed is the project name: Chapter15_project This contains the AIR files needed. If you need to uninstall the application, you can either right-click the application's icon or use the appropriate uninstall method for your operating system.

Figure 15-16. The Application Install dialog box

Notice that because we used a self-signed certificate, the Publisher Identity setting is classified as UNKNOWN. Also, because we have not created security restraints in this exercise (a discussion of which is beyond the scope of this book), the System Access is UNRESTRICTED.

12. Click Install. The application will install and run as a desktop application.

Congratulations, you just created your first Adobe AIR application and deployed it.

But what about if you have an existing application? Let's take a look at that now.

Converting an existing Flex application

With just a few steps, it is relatively easy to convert an existing Flex application to an AIR application.

Earlier in this book, you created a case study (in Chapters 10 and 11). If you recall, I told you not to delete the files for that case study, because we would be revisiting them. Well, that time is here. However, if you did not save your files or complete the case study, no worries; I have included them with the download for this chapter.

Let's get started.

1. Delete or close the Chapter15_project that you were just working on. It is up to you whether to delete the files or not; however, we will not be revisiting them.

2. Start a new Flex project called OnlineComputerBooksAIR, making it an AIR project using the techniques you just learned.

   If you need to import the case study, please complete the following steps:

   a. Download the files for this chapter from www.friendsofed.com.

   b. Unzip them to the directory of your choice.

   c. Select File ➤ Import to bring up the dialog box shown in Figure 15-17.

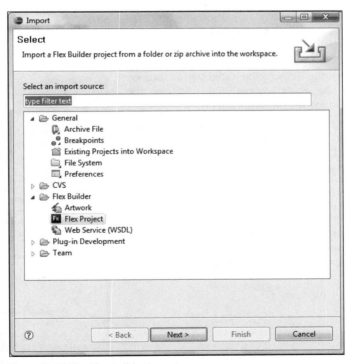

Figure 15-17. The Flex Builder Import screen

15

d. Select Flex Project and click Next. This will take you to the dialog box shown in Figure 15-18.

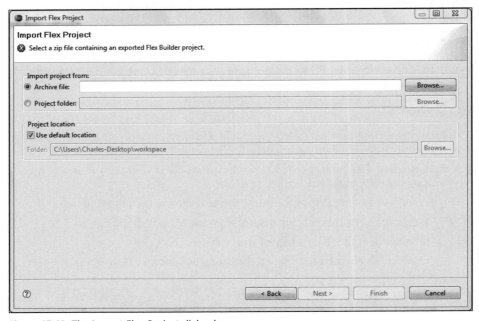

Figure 15-18. The Import Flex Project dialog box

e. Click the Project folder radio button, browse to the folder where you unzipped the downloaded file, and select it.

f. Click OK and then Finish. You should now see both projects, OnlineComputerBooks and OnlineComputerBooksAIR, in the Flex Navigator View (see Figure 15-19).

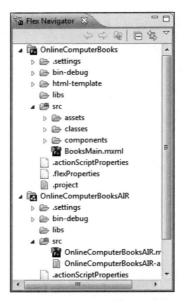

Now that you have both projects available, you are ready to convert your existing Flex application.

For the next few steps, I caution you not to get the two projects mixed up. We will be transferring the files from the original project to the new AIR project.

Figure 15-19.
The Flex Navigator View with
the two projects

3. If necessary, close the `OnlineComputerBooks.mxml` file. We will no longer be using it.

4. Switch to the original project in the Flex Navigator, `OnlineComputerBooks`, and Ctrl-click to select the assets folder, classes folder, components folder, and `BooksMain.mxml` file.

5. Right-click the highlighted area and select Copy.

6. Click the `src` folder of the new project, `OnlineComputerBooksAir`, and paste the copied folders and file into it.

7. To avoid confusion, you can close the original project now. You will not be needing it again.

8. Open `BooksMain.mxml` in the new project.

Recall that an AIR application does not use the opening and closing Application tags. Instead, it uses the tag `WindowedApplication`. This will need to be changed in the `BooksMain.mxml` file.

9. Change the opening and closing Application tag to `WindowedApplication`.

10. In the Flex Navigator View, right-click the `BooksMain.mxml` file and make it the default application file (see Figure 15-20).

Figure 15-20.
Setting the default application

The AIR application dialog box should open up to give your application an ID (see Figure 15-21).

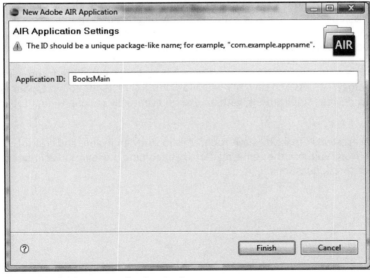

Figure 15-21. The AIR Application Settings

You can keep this ID if you want, or you can change it. For the purposes of this exercise, let's change it.

11. Change the ID of the application to read OnlineComputerBooksAIR and click Finish.

You should see the Application Descriptor in the Flex Navigator View, as shown in Figure 15-22.

Theoretically, your application is ready to roll. However, you will find the size a little small. We need to do one final step.

Figure 15-22. The new Application Descriptor XML file

12. Return to the opening WindowedApplication tag and change the width and height properties from 100% to 1200 and 680, respectively.

```
<mx:WindowedApplication xmlns:mx="http://www.adobe.com/2006/mxml"
layout="absolute" backgroundColor="#FFFFFF" xmlns:comp=
"components.*" height="680" width="1200" creationComplete="init()">
```

The application should run exactly as it did before, only not in a browser. If you want to, use the techniques I showed you in this chapter and export it for installation.

As you can see, it is very easy to convert an existing Flex application to an AIR application.

Conclusion

In all the previous chapters, this section was called "Summary." Here, I am calling it "Conclusion" because this concludes our journey together with this project. However, as much as this concludes our journey, it should only begin your own journey. A program like Flex requires constant learning and refining of skills. That is true if you learn any program. No one book will give you complete knowledge of a product.

It is appropriate that we ended our road together looking toward the future with Adobe's new technology: AIR. As you saw, AIR will allow you to create, or convert, your web applications into desktop applications, with an eye on eventually making them mobile applications.

It is my sincerest wish that you have found this journey enjoyable and fruitful. I also hope that I hear from you in either an e-mail or by becoming a friend in Facebook. Please do not hesitate to ask questions.

APPENDIX INSTALLING COLDFUSION 8

Download ColdFusion Tria

Thank you for your interest in ColdFusion. In
options for ColdFusion 8 and ColdFusion M)
Developer Edition and Trial Edition. The Dev
version of ColdFusion for the local developm
be deployed on either ColdFusion Standard
Access to applications running on a Develop
machines. ColdFusion Trial Edition is fully fu
production and evaluation purposes only. Th
Enterprise Edition features and will timeout a
product. After the timeout period, the Trial Ed

- Introduction
- License Agreement
- Configure Installer
- Configure ColdFusion 8
- Pre-Installation Summary
- Installing...
- Installation Complete

Installatio
the Follow

ADOBE SY
ADOBE C(
Software

NOTICE 7
INSTALL/
DESCRIBE
LICENSEE
WRITTEN
BY CLICI
DURING F
LICENSE.

CF
ADOBE® COLDFUSION® 8

Several server examples in this book employ the use of ColdFusion 8. Of all of the technologies, I choose this because it is the easiest (in my opinion) to install and link with Flex. I say this because the Developer Edition is actually two servers in one: a web server to handle web requests with localhost:8500 and the ColdFusion application server.

The purpose of this appendix is to walk you through the installation process step by step. I will show you a couple of installation options for making it a smooth-running test server.

As of this writing, the link for downloading ColdFusion can be found at

> www.adobe.com/products/coldfusion/

You are presented with two download options: Download the Free Trial or Download the Free Developer Edition. It doesn't make a difference which one you download. The Free Trial will give you the ability to run ColdFusion 8 as a full-fledged production server for a 30-day period. After that, it will automatically revert to the Developer Edition. The Developer Edition has all of the same functionality as the full edition, but is limited to access only by localhost and one remote IP address.

Once you click the link for either edition, you will be prompted to either sign in to your free Adobe account or, if necessary, create one. After a brief survey, you will be taken to the screen shown in Figure A-1.

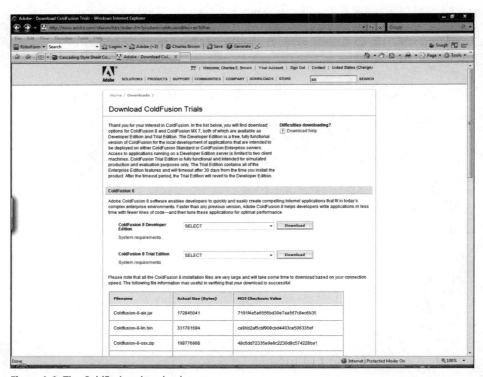

Figure A-1. The ColdFusion download screen

Here ColdFusion can be downloaded for a variety of operating systems. While the screen-shots show the installation for Windows, I will point out any important differences on Mac OS X.

Let's walk through this step by step:

1. Select the operating system you will be installing on from the ColdFusion 8 Developer Edition list. The size of the download will vary with the operating system, with a range from about 165MB to about 350MB for the Japanese Windows edition.

2. On Windows, you will be prompted to either Save or Run the installation, as shown in Figure A-2. Because of the size, I like to click Save. This way, if something goes wrong or you need to reinstall ColdFusion on another machine, you won't need to be concerned about downloading it again. The Mac OS X version is a ZIP file, so you have no choice but to download it.

Figure A-2. Prompt for saving the download file

3. If you clicked Save, you will be prompted for the folder you want to save to (see Figure A-3).

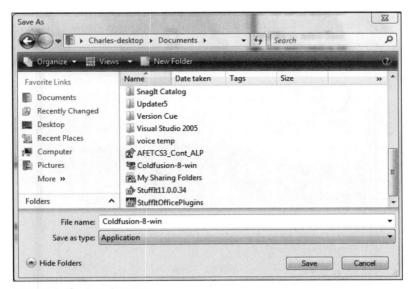

Figure A-3. The Save As screen

4. Once you select the folder and click the Save button, the download will start. Upon completion, Windows users will be prompted with a security screen as shown in Figure A-4.

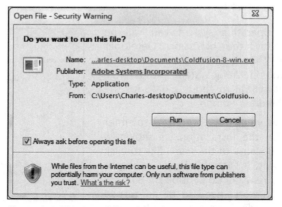

Figure A-4. The Open File – Security Warning screen

5. On Windows, click Run. Adobe's installation client, InstallAnywhere, will take a few minutes to do some initial housekeeping and prepare to install.

6. On Mac OS X, double-click Coldfusion-8-osx.zip to decompress it, and then double-click the ColdFusion 8 Installer icon on your Desktop.

You will be presented with the screen shown in Figure A-5.

Figure A-5. The opening screen

7. Click OK.

The next screen, shown in Figure A-6, is just an introduction to the ColdFusion installation process.

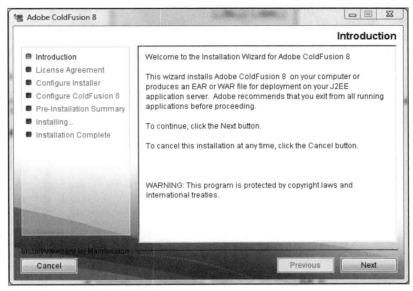

Figure A-6. The Introduction screen

8. Click Next.

As with most software programs, you have to accept the terms of the license agreement (see Figure A-7).

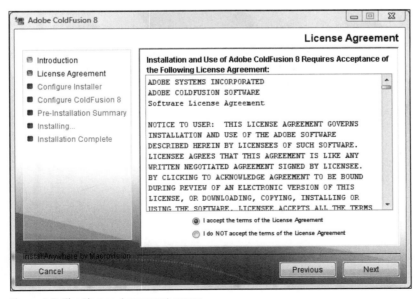

Figure A-7. The License Agreement screen

9. Unless you have a strong objection, click the I accept the terms of the License Agreement radio button and click Next.

As I said at the outset, you can either install the Free Trial version or Developer Edition of ColdFusion. Of course, if you bought the program, you would have a full serial number. For the purposes of this book, I will be using the Developer Edition, as shown in Figure A-8. This has all the functionality of the Full Edition, but with access limited to localhost and one remote IP address.

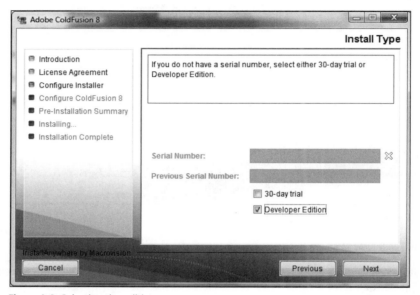

Figure A-8. Selecting the edition

10. Select the Developer Edition check box and then Next.

The next screen, shown in Figure A-9, will ask you if you want to install ColdFusion as a self-contained server or with other J2EE servers. Just as a bit of background, ColdFusion is built over the Java programming environment. If you select the first option, Server configuration, a runtime version of the Adobe Java server (J2EE), JRun, will be installed with it. In most scenarios, this will be the option of choice and the one we will use for this book.

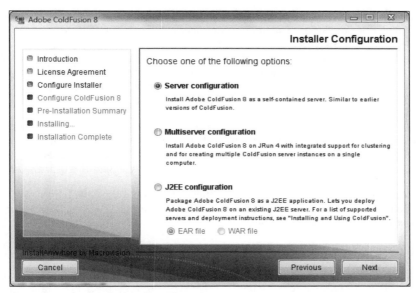

Figure A-9. Selecting the install configuration

11. Select Server configuration and click Next.

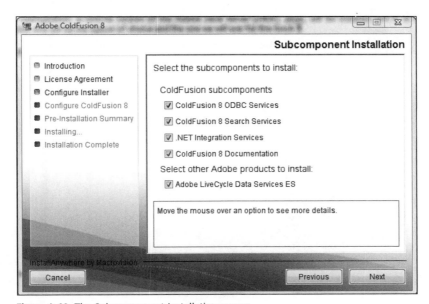

Figure A-10. The Subcomponent Installation screen

The Subcomponent Installation screen, shown in Figure A-10, allows us to select optional components for ColdFusion. The options are slightly different on Windows and Mac OS X. First, Windows . . . The ODBC services allow ColdFusion to internally connect with a database and is quite important. The Search Services sets up a small Verity database that allows you to set up a search box for the website. The .NET Integration Services does what it says: it installs components necessary for ColdFusion to integrate with .NET. The ColdFusion 8 Documentation will install some practice databases for learning purposes.

The final selection, Adobe LiveCycle Data Service ES, is important for Flex to integrate properly with dynamic data. We will not get into great detail in this book about that. Instead, I refer you to *Foundation Flex for Developers: Data-Driven Applications with PHP, ASP.NET, ColdFusion, and LCDS* by Sas Jacobs and Koen De Weggheleire (Apress, 2007).

On a Mac, you have just three options: to install ColdFusion 8 documentation, to start the ColdFusion server when your computer starts up, and to install LiveCycle Data Services ES. I suggest you leave all three selected.

12. Accept all the options and click Next.

The next screen, shown in Figure A-11, allows you to change the default installation folder. The default is c:\ColdFusion8 (/Applications/ColdFusion8 on a Mac), and I will be assuming you are using that for the purposes of this book.

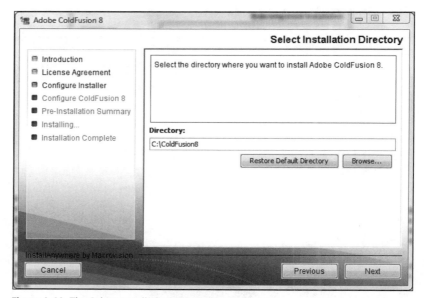

Figure A-11. The Select Installation Directory screen

13. Click Next.

You will need to accept a second license agreement for Adobe Live Cycle Data Service ES (see Figure A-12).

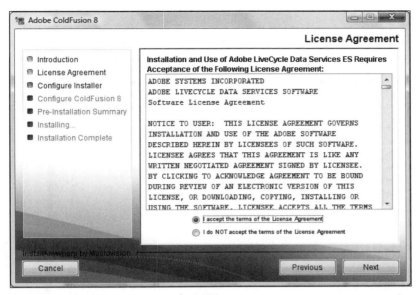

Figure A-12. The License Agreement for LCDS

14. Accept the license agreement and click Next.

Like before, if you have a serial number for LCDS, you can enter it in the next screen (see Figure A-13). If you don't, it will revert to a Developer Edition with limited IP access.

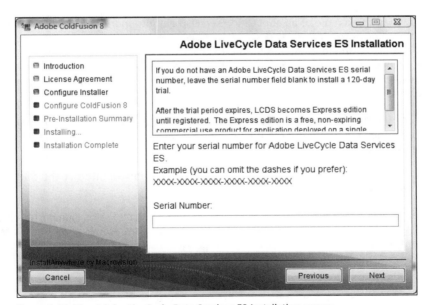

Figure A-13. The Adobe LiveCycle Data Services ES Installation screen

15. Click Next.

The next screen, which you can see in Figure A-14, is an important one in the installation process.

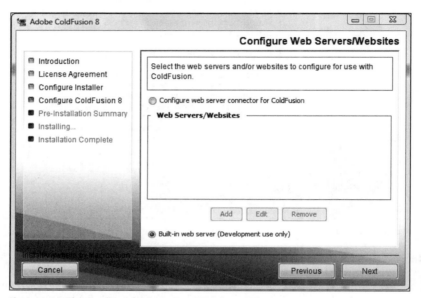

Figure A-14. The Configure Web Servers/Websites screen

ColdFusion is an example of an application server (I get into more detail about this in the book). In other words, it does a specific job. A web server, however, accepts requests for information from the Internet and then turns over the request to the proper application server. ColdFusion's Developer Edition has a unique ability to use, for test purposes only, a built-in web server that runs on localhost:8500. I find this invaluable for training and testing purposes.

In this screen, you can either link ColdFusion to an existing web server, such as Apache or IIS, or click the radio button to use the built-in web server. I will be using the latter option for the examples in this book.

16. Click the Built-in web server (Development use only) radio button at the bottom of the screen, and then click Next.

The next screen requires that you enter a password for the ColdFusion Administrator (see Figure A-15). Because it is required, you must enter a password. However, as you will see a few steps from now, we will be removing that password.

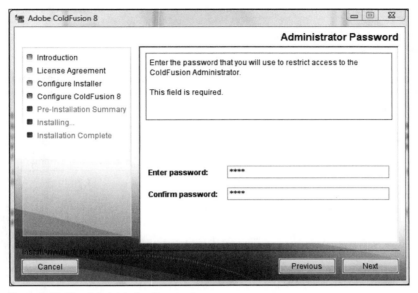

Figure A-15. The Administrator Password screen

17. Enter and confirm the password, and click Next.

The next screen, shown in Figure A-16, allows you to enable the ColdFusion Remote Development Service (RDS). ColdFusion RDS allows the developer to access ColdFusion remotely, test functionality of the web application, and run reports. It is also where most of the debugging functions are located. I cannot imagine using ColdFusion without it.

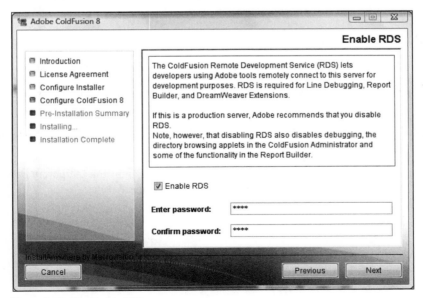

Figure A-16. The Enable RDS screen

18. Click the Enable RDS check box.

19. Enter and confirm a temporary password.

20. Click Next.

On a Mac, if you elected to start the ColdFusion server when your computer starts up, you will be prompted to enter your Mac password. The final screen will allow you to review the installation options (see Figure A-17).

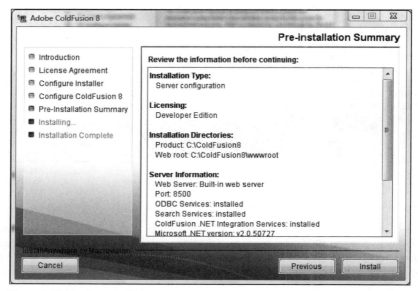

Figure A-17. The Pre-Installation Summary screen

21. Assuming everything is correct, click the Install button.

The installation process could take up to 5–10 minutes depending on your system.

Provided all went well, you are presented with a Installation Complete screen (see Figure A-18). Unfortunately, there are a few more steps.

22. Make sure the Launch the Configuration Wizard in the default browser check box is selected and click Done.

Your web browser will open, and you will be prompted to enter the temporary password for the administrator you created a few steps ago (see Figure A-19).

23. Enter the password created earlier and click the Login button.

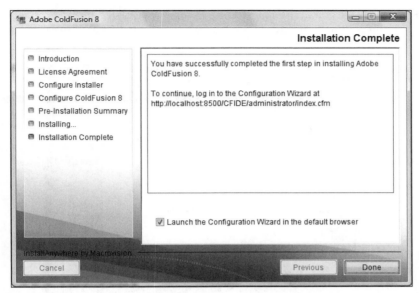

Figure A-18. The Installation Complete screen

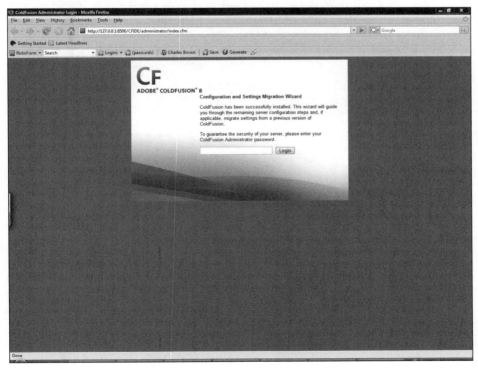

Figure A-19. The final configuration screen

ColdFusion will take another few minutes to do some additional setup and configuration. This could take up to 5 minutes or so. You will be tempted to click the Continue link. DON'T!!! It could mess up the installation. Just let ColdFusion do its job.

Once the configuration is finished, you will see the screen shown in Figure A-20.

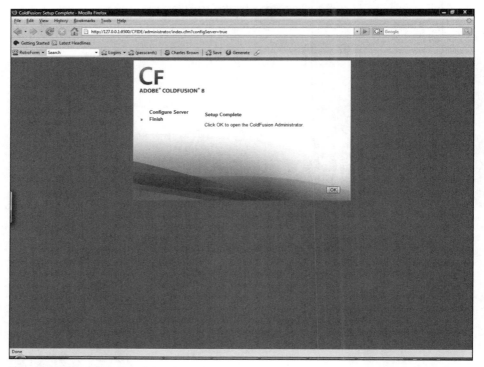

Figure A-20. The Setup Complete screen

24. Click OK.

After you click OK, you will be taken to the ColdFusion 8 Administrator in the browser (see Figure A-21). If your screen looks different from Figure A-21, don't worry about that. We will fix that shortly.

Since the focus of this book is about Flex, and not ColdFusion, we will not be getting into the various aspects about this tool here. However, it is worth noting the URL in Figure A-21, which contains 127.0.0.1:8500. The URLs containing 127.0.0.1 and localhost mean exactly the same thing (although Flash Player will make that distinction in a demonstration located in Chapter 5 of this book). The colon (:) followed by 8500 is the port it is running on. Think of localhost as an apartment building and 8500 as the apartment.

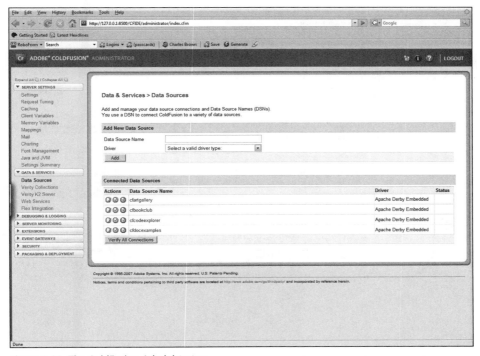

Figure A-21. The ColdFusion Administrator

As I mentioned earlier, the passwords we set were temporary. Because we are running the program locally, with just some practice files, there is little chance of outside security risks here. As a result, it would be very inconvenient if we had to enter the password each time we wanted to use the administrator. For that reason, for the purposes of this book, we will disable the passwords.

25. Along the left side of the ColdFusion 8 Administrator, click the Security drop-down list (see Figure A-22).

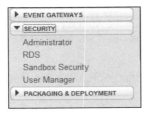

Figure A-22.
The Security drop-down list

26. Select Administrator.

This brings up the screen shown in Figure A-23.

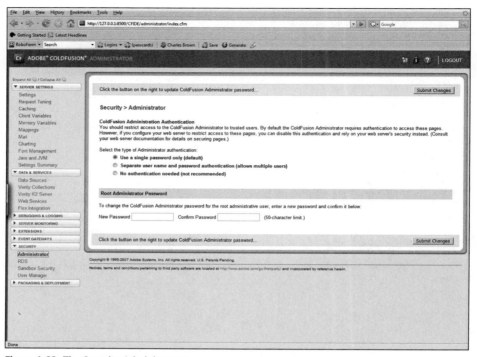

Figure A-23. The Security Administrator

27. In the middle of the screen, select the No authentication needed (not recommended) radio button.

28. Click Submit Changes.

Along the top of the screen, you should receive a message informing you that the server was successfully updated.

29. Along the left, click the RDS link, again under the Security category, and use the same technique to disable that password.

This has now disabled both passwords and will make working with the administrator a bit easier. Of course, I would not recommend doing this if you were working in a secured situation.

If you are in the administrator, odds are everything is running fine. But, if you want, you can give ColdFusion one final test.

In the URL field of the browser, type http://localhost:8500.

You should get something like Figure A-24.

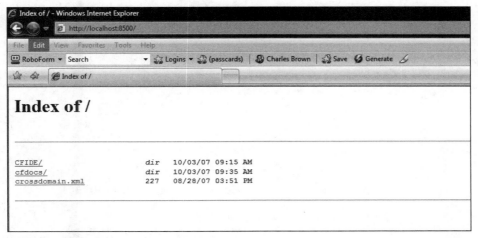

Figure A-24. The ColdFusion directory screen

If you do not get this screen, check your installation and the Services Administrator of your operating system.

> *You may not see the* `crossdomain.xml` *file shown in Figure A-24. We will discuss that in the course of this book.*

Hopefully all went well, and you are now up and running with ColdFusion 8.

INDEX

B

C